Google Cloud Certified Professional Cloud Network Engineer Guide

Design, implement, manage, and secure a network architecture in Google Cloud

Maurizio Ipsale

Mirko Gilioli

BIRMINGHAM—MUMBAI

Google Cloud Certified Professional Cloud Network Engineer Guide

Copyright © 2021 Packt Publishing

All rights reserved. No part of this book may be reproduced, stored in a retrieval system, or transmitted in any form or by any means, without the prior written permission of the publisher, except in the case of brief quotations embedded in critical articles or reviews.

Every effort has been made in the preparation of this book to ensure the accuracy of the information presented. However, the information contained in this book is sold without warranty, either express or implied. Neither the authors, nor Packt Publishing or its dealers and distributors, will be held liable for any damages caused or alleged to have been caused directly or indirectly by this book.

Packt Publishing has endeavored to provide trademark information about all of the companies and products mentioned in this book by the appropriate use of capitals. However, Packt Publishing cannot guarantee the accuracy of this information.

Group Product Manager: Vijin Boricha
Publishing Product Manager: Mohd Riyan Khan
Senior Editor: Shazeen Iqbal
Content Development Editor: Rafiaa Khan
Technical Editor: Shruthi Shetty
Copy Editor: Safis Editing
Project Coordinator: Shagun Saini
Proofreader: Safis Editing
Indexer: Manju Arasan
Production Designer: Aparna Bhagat

First published: January 2022

Production reference: 1171121

Published by Packt Publishing Ltd.
Livery Place
35 Livery Street
Birmingham
B3 2PB, UK.

ISBN 978-1-80107-269-4

www.packt.com

Writing this book was harder than I thought but more rewarding than I could have ever imagined. None of this would have been possible without the support of my wonderful children, Simone and Alessia, and my lovely wife, Liliana: I feel so grateful to have such a loving family. I would like to thank my dear parents, Pippo and Maria, and my brother, Marco, for everything I have learned from them.

Thanks to all my colleagues and co-workers in K Labs in Italy and ROI Training in the U.S.A. Everything I know about technology is also due to the ongoing cooperation with them.

Thanks to everyone in the Packt team who helped me so much in writing this book.

– Maurizio Ipsale

To my sweet daughter, Alessia, my lovely wife, Fiorenza, my dear parents, Mara and Mauro, and my sister, Elena, whose never-failing encouragement made this book possible. To all my colleagues and co-workers at K Labs (Italy) and ROI Training in the U.S.A. Thanks to everyone on the Packt team who helped me so much.

– Mirko Gilioli

Contributors

About the authors

Maurizio Ipsale was born in Messina (Italy) in 1978, where he graduated in electronic engineering at the age of 23 and obtained a PhD. Passionate about the ICT world, his professional curriculum has been enriched with many certifications, even as an instructor of official training courses, such as Cisco, Juniper, Huawei, AWS, and Google Cloud. He delivers training courses all around the world on many state-of-the-art technologies, including the cloud, machine learning, DevOps, data engineering, IoT, and Kubernetes. Maurizio currently lives in Modena (Italy) with his wife, Liliana, and two children, Simone and Alessia. He is a Training and Professional Service Engineer at K Labs, and a Google Cloud Authorized Trainer at ROI Training.

Mirko Gilioli was born in Reggio Emilia (Italy) in 1983, where he graduated with an MSc in computer science and engineering after spending 1 year in the USA as a research assistant at the IHMC in Pensacola, Florida. At the early age of 27 years old, he started his career as an ICT instructor at K Labs, an Italian company focused on ICT training services. Here, Mirko developed long training records in many technological areas, including networking and cloud technologies. He has been awarded as a Cisco Certified System Instructor (CCSI#35749) and Google Cloud Authorized Trainer.

Mirko currently lives in Sassuolo (Italy) with his wife, Fiorenza, and his daughter, Alessia. He is a passionate trainer at K Labs and a Google Cloud Authorized Trainer at ROI Training.

About the reviewer

Fady Ibrahim is a Google Cloud Authorized Trainer certified by Google Cloud as a Professional Cloud Network Engineer. He holds other certificates from Google Cloud, such as Professional Cloud Security Engineer and Professional Cloud Architect. As a cloud consultant, he helps people and the community deploy their apps to Google Cloud.

He has volunteered as a Learning Community Ambassador for the Google Africa Developer Scholarship for Google Cloud Track for 3 consecutive years.

Fady has a PhD thesis in computer engineering titled *Using Trusted Cloud Computing to Provide Trust in Multi-blockchain Ecosystems.* He has more than 12 years of experience as an instructor at Cisco Networking Academy, teaching CCNA and Linux Essentials.

I need to thank the Google Developer Group - Cairo Chapter team for their outstanding community. Especial thanks to the chapter leaders, Bassant and Mo Nagy, for all their support, encouragement, and patience.

I need to thank the team at Cloud11, a Google Cloud Partner. Special thanks to Abdel-Rahman Wahid, the CEO of Cloud 11, for his understanding and support.

Finally, to all my friends and family, all the love and gratitude.

Table of Contents

3
Implementing a GCP Virtual Private Cloud (VPC)

Section 2: Network Services and Security

4
Configuring Network Services in GCP

8

Advanced Networking in Google Cloud Platform

9

Professional Cloud Network Engineer Certification Preparation

Other Books You May Enjoy

Index

Preface

Google Cloud, the public cloud platform from Google, has a variety of networking options, which are instrumental in managing a networking architecture. This book will give you hands-on experience of implementing and securing networks in **Google Cloud Platform** (**GCP**).

You will understand the basics of Google Cloud infrastructure and learn to design, plan, and prototype a network on GCP. After implementing a **Virtual Private Cloud** (**VPC**), you will configure network services and implement hybrid connectivity. Later, the book focuses on security, which forms an important aspect of a network. You will also get to grips with network security and learn to manage and monitor network operations in GCP. Finally, you will learn to optimize network resources and delve into advanced networking.

By the end of this book, you will have gained a complete understanding of networking in Google Cloud and learned everything you need to pass the certification exam.

Who this book is for

This Google Cloud certification book is for cloud network engineers, cloud architects, cloud engineers, administrators, and anyone who is looking to design, implement, and manage network architectures in Google Cloud Platform. You can use this book as a guide for passing the Professional Cloud Network Engineer certification exam. You need to have at least a year of experience in Google Cloud, basic enterprise-level network design experience, and a fundamental understanding of Cloud Shell to get started with this book.

What this book covers

Chapter 1, Google Cloud Platform Infrastructure, provides an overview on what cloud computing is and a description of Google Cloud Platform architecture and its main components. Moreover, Chapter 1 introduces Google Compute Engine, Cloud DNS, Cloud Load Balancing, Google Kubernetes Engine, and DevOps culture.

Chapter 2, Designing, Planning, and Prototyping a GCP Network, provides guidelines on how to design, plan, and prototype a Google Cloud network. It also discusses the main disaster recovery and failover strategies as well as IP network planning in the Google Cloud Virtual Private Cloud (VPC). Chapter 2 continues by describing interconnection options between an on-premises network and VPC in Google Cloud. Finally, Chapter 2 discusses Google Kubernetes Engine network design principals for large-scale application deployments.

Chapter 3, Implementing a GCP Virtual Private Cloud (VPC), describes how to implement VPC resources in Google Cloud. The main topics covered here are VPC subnets, Cloud Router, VPC interconnection, and Cloud NAT.

Chapter 4, Configuring Network Services in GCP, deep dives into Google Cloud Load Balancing and Cloud CDN services. Indeed, the chapter describes how to implement Global and Internal Network Load Balancing services with Google Cloud Platform. Moreover, the chapter covers how to implement Cloud CDN to reduce network latency for static content stored in Google Cloud Storage.

Chapter 5, Implementing Hybrid Connectivity in GCP, focuses on hybrid connectivity between on-premises and Google Cloud networks. The chapter describes how to implement Dedicated Interconnect, Partner Interconnect, and IPsec VPN in Google Cloud Platform as well as diving into Cloud Router.

Chapter 6, Implementing Network Security, deep dives into security implementation in Google Cloud Virtual Private Cloud. The chapter shows how to configure Identity and Access Management and Google Cloud Armor. Moreover, the chapter describes how to insert a third-party next-generation firewall into the VPC with multiple network interface cards.

Chapter 7, Managing and Monitoring Network Operations, describes how to use Google Cloud Logging and Monitoring to monitor network and security operations.

Chapter 8, Advanced Networking in Google Cloud Platform, describes Google Traffic Director, Service Directory, and Network Connectivity Center. Indeed, the chapter describes what Service Mesh networks are and how they fit into Traffic Director. Then, the chapter moves on to exploring how to discover services with Service Directory and its implementation in Google Cloud Platform. Finally, the chapter shows how to build Hub and Spoke network topologies with Google Cloud Network Connectivity Center.

Chapter 9, Professional Cloud Network Engineer Certification Preparation, provides a set of questions that would work as preparation for the Google Cloud Professional Network Engineer exam.

To get the most out of this book

You should have a basic knowledge about the current IP networking technologies.

Software/Hardware covered in the book	OS Requirements
Google Cloud Platform	Windows, macOS, and Linux (any)
IP Networking	Browser (Chrome, Firefox, Edge)
Virtualization	

Download the color images

We also provide a PDF file that has color images of the screenshots/diagrams used in this book. You can download it here: `https://static.packt-cdn.com/downloads/9781801072694_ColorImages.pdf`.

Conventions used

There are a number of text conventions used throughout this book.

`Code in text`: Indicates code words in text, database table names, folder names, filenames, file extensions, pathnames, dummy URLs, user input, and Twitter handles. Here is an example: "To configure the host side of the network, you need the `tunctl` command from the User Mode Linux (UML) project."

A block of code is set as follows:

```
for ((i=0;i<10;i++)); \
do curl \
-w %{time_total}\n \
-o /dev/null \
-s http://$LB_IP_ADDRESS/cdn.png; \
done
```

Any command-line input or output is written as follows:

```
gcloud compute networks peerings list
```

Bold: Indicates a new term, an important word, or words that you see onscreen. For example, words in menus or dialog boxes appear in the text like this. Here is an example: "Click **Flash** from Etcher to write the image."

> **Tips or important notes**
> Appear like this.

Get in touch

Feedback from our readers is always welcome.

General feedback: If you have questions about any aspect of this book, mention the book title in the subject of your message and email us at customercare@packtpub.com.

Errata: Although we have taken every care to ensure the accuracy of our content, mistakes do happen. If you have found a mistake in this book, we would be grateful if you would report this to us. Please visit www.packtpub.com/support/errata, selecting your book, clicking on the Errata Submission Form link, and entering the details.

Piracy: If you come across any illegal copies of our works in any form on the Internet, we would be grateful if you would provide us with the location address or website name. Please contact us at copyright@packt.com with a link to the material.

If you are interested in becoming an author: If there is a topic that you have expertise in and you are interested in either writing or contributing to a book, please visit authors.packtpub.com.

Share Your Thoughts

Once you've read *Google Cloud Certified Professional Cloud Network Engineer Guide,* we'd love to hear your thoughts! Scan the QR code below to go straight to the Amazon review page for this book and share your feedback.

https://packt.link/r/1801072698

Your review is important to us and the tech community and will help us make sure we're delivering excellent quality content.

Section 1: Network Infrastructure

In the first part of the book, you will learn how to design, plan, and implement a Google VPC network starting from Google Cloud infrastructure fundamentals.

This part of the book comprises the following chapters:

1
Google Cloud Platform Infrastructure

To learn about **Google Cloud Platform's infrastructure**, you must have a good understanding of what *cloud computing* is and the cloud service models that are available, such as **Infrastructure as a Service (IaaS)**, **Platform as a Service (PaaS)**, and **Software as a Service (SaaS)**. Moreover, since Google Cloud Platform is a public cloud provider, we will provide a brief explanation of the differences between *public*, *private*, and *hybrid* cloud services.

Google Cloud Platform's *physical architecture* will be described. We will also specify the regions and zones, as well as the logical architecture that specifies the organizations, folders, projects, and resources.

A deep explanation of what a **Google Compute Engine** instance is, and how you can use one for your workload, will be provided in the second part of this chapter.

After introducing a few of the **Google Cloud Platform (GCP)** services, such as Cloud DNS, Cloud CDN, and Cloud Load Balancer, we will provide an overview of the **DevOps** culture, as applied to Kubernetes and the Google Cloud implementation of *Kubernetes –* **Google Kubernetes Engine (GKE)**.

In this chapter, we are going to cover the following main topics:

- Introducing cloud computing and virtualization
- Introducing GCP
- Getting started with GCP
- Understanding virtual machines in the cloud
- Exploring containers in the cloud

Introducing cloud computing and virtualization

This section introduces the concepts of **cloud computing** and **virtualization**, which are fundamental to understanding how GCP works. We will go through the basic elements of cloud computing and virtualization that are required to dive into the chapter.

What is cloud computing?

Whether you are a fresh entry to the cloud or not, we can consider **cloud computing** a model that enables ubiquitous, on-demand network access to a shared pool of configurable computing resources. These resources can be servers, storage, networks, applications, and services. A great advantage that cloud computing brings to users is that you can rapidly provision and de-provision computing resources with minimal management effort.

Cloud computing models can be oriented to private customers like you or to enterprises or public organizations. Many popular internet services have been introduced over the years. Think about Dropbox, Google Photos, Apple iCloud, and so on, which let you store your files or images in a private space that can be accessed anywhere, anytime. Additionally, Amazon Web Services, Microsoft Azure, and Google Cloud brought services to the market cloud to help enterprises and organizations scale their IT infrastructures and applications globally.

The cloud computing model is based on several important pillars:

- **Data center**: This refers to a large building with independent power and cooling systems that hosts a large number of servers, storage, and networking devices.
- **Virtualization**: This is an enabling technology that allows physical resources to be shared across multiple users privately.

- **Programmability**: Every cloud resource (compute, storage, network, and so on) is software-driven. This means that there is no human interaction to request, deploy, or release a resource-enabling self-service model.

- **Global network**: This refers to the global private physical network that interconnects all the data centers around the world.

Consumers can rent these services from cloud providers on-demand in a self-service manner. This model allows cloud users to pay only for the resources they reserve and consume, thus reducing **Capital Expenditure (CAPEX)** and **time-to-market**.

More specifically, cloud computing is built on five fundamental attributes:

- **On-demand self-service**: Cloud users can request cloud computing services with a self-service model when they need them. This can be achieved with automated processes without any human interaction.

- **Broadband network access**: Cloud users can access their resources anytime, anywhere, through a broadband connection. This lets cloud users interact with remote resources as if they were on-premises.

- **Resource pooling**: Cloud users can access a wide, almost infinite pool of resources without worrying about its size and location.

- **Rapid elasticity**: Cloud users can rapidly scale their resources elastically based on their actual workload needs. This allows cloud users to increase resource utilization and reduce costs.

- **PAYG (Pay As You Go) model**: Cloud users only pay for what they reserve or use. This allows them to greatly reduce CAPEX, increase agility, and reduce time-to-market.

There are three distinct kinds of cloud services that a user can choose from:

- **Infrastructure as a Service (IaaS)**: Cloud users can rent the entire IT infrastructure, including virtual machines, storage, network, and the operating system. With this type of service, the user has full access to and control over the virtual infrastructure and is responsible for it. The cloud provider is responsible for the physical architecture and virtualization infrastructure.

- **Platform as a Service (PaaS)**: This type of service is ideal for developers who want an on-demand environment for developing, testing, and delivering applications. Here, developers can quickly deploy their applications without worrying about the underlying infrastructure. There is no need to manage servers, storage, and networking (which is the responsibility of the cloud provider) since the focus is on the application.

- **Software as a Service (SaaS)**: Cloud providers can lease applications to users, who can use them without worrying about managing any software or hardware platforms.

The following diagram shows a comparison between these three cloud services:

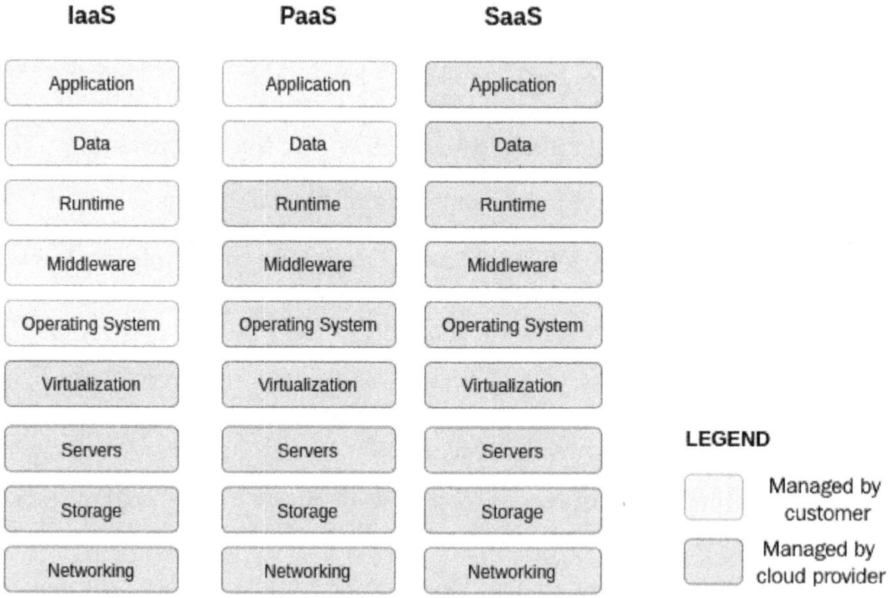

IaaS	PaaS	SaaS
Application	Application	Application
Data	Data	Data
Runtime	Runtime	Runtime
Middleware	Middleware	Middleware
Operating System	Operating System	Operating System
Virtualization	Virtualization	Virtualization
Servers	Servers	Servers
Storage	Storage	Storage
Networking	Networking	Networking

LEGEND

Managed by customer

Managed by cloud provider

Figure 1.1 – A comparison of the IaaS, PaaS, and SaaS services

Your cloud infrastructure can be deployed in two ways:

- **On-premises**: This deployment refers to resources that are deployed on a private data center that belong to a single organization.

- **On a public cloud**: This deployment refers to resources that are deployed in third-party data centers owned by the cloud provider. These resources will be running in a virtual private space in a multi-tenant scenario or sole-tenant scenario (https://cloud.google.com/compute/docs/nodes/sole-tenant-nodes) with dedicated hardware.

It is quite common that cloud users need to interconnect services that are running *on-premises* and services that have been deployed on the public cloud. Thus, it is particularly important to create **hybrid cloud services** that span both private and public cloud infrastructure. GCP offers many services to build public cloud infrastructure and interconnect them to those running on-premises.

Now that you have learned what cloud computing is, let's introduce virtualization.

What is virtualization?

Sometimes, in the **Information Technology** (**IT**) industry, there is the need to abstract hardware components into software components. **Virtualization** is the technology that does this. Today, virtualization is used on servers to abstract hardware components (CPU, RAM, and disk) to virtual systems that require them to run. These virtual systems are commonly referred to as **virtual machines** and the software that abstracts the hardware components is called a **hypervisor**. By using virtualization, IT administrators can consolidate their physical assets in multiple virtual machines running on one or few physical servers. Hypervisors lets you have multiple virtual machines with different requirements in terms of the hardware and operating system. Moreover, the hypervisor isolates operating systems and their running applications from the underlying physical hardware. They run independently of each other.

The following diagram shows the architecture for virtualization:

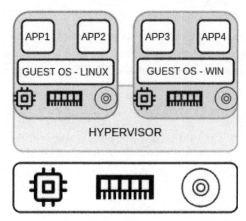

Figure 1.2 – Virtualization architecture

As we can see, the hypervisor virtualizes the hardware and provides each operating system with an abstraction of it. The operating systems can only see the virtualized hardware that has been provisioned in the hypervisor. This allows you to maximize the hardware resource utilization and permits you to have different operating systems and their applications on the same physical server.

Virtualization brings several benefits compared to physical devices:

- **Partitioning**: Virtualization allows you to partition virtual resources (vCPU, vRAM, and vDISK) to give to the virtual machine. This improves physical resource utilization.

- **Isolation**: Virtual machines are isolated from each other, thus improving security. Moreover, they can run operating systems and applications that can't exist on the same physical server.

- **Encapsulation**: Virtual machines can be backed up, duplicated, and migrated to other virtualized servers.

Now that we have introduced cloud computing and virtualization, let's introduce GCP.

Introducing GCP

This section will provide an overview of GCP and its services. Additionally, we will look at the Google Cloud global network infrastructure, which includes regions and zones. Finally, we will describe the concepts of **projects**, **billing**, and **quotas** in GCP.

GCP's global infrastructure – regions and zones

Over the years, Google has invested billions of dollars to build its private network and today can carry 40% of the world's internet traffic every day. The customers who decide to deploy their cloud services on GCP will benefit from the highest throughput and the lowest latency. Google offers connection to their cloud services from over 140 network edge locations (`https://cloud.google.com/vpc/docs/edge-locations`), as well as via private and public internet exchange locations (`https://peeringdb.com/api/net/433`). Thanks to Google's edge caching network sites, which are distributed all around the globe (`https://cloud.google.com/cdn/docs/locations`), latency can be reduced, allowing customers to interact with their cloud services in near real time. In the following diagram, you can see where Google's network has its presence in terms of regions and PoP:

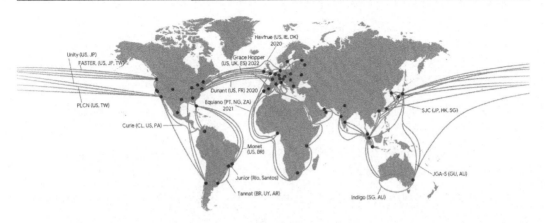

Figure 1.3 – GCP regions and global network

As you can see, GCP data centers are organized into **regions** and **zones** around the globe and are interconnected with Google's physical private network. Regions are independent geographic areas that include three or more zones. For example, the `us-central1` region includes the `us-central1-a`, `us-central1-b`, and `us-central1-c` zones. In GCP projects, there are global resources such as **static external IP addresses**:

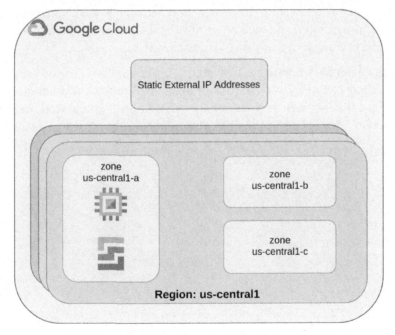

Figure 1.4 – GCP regions, zones, and global resources

To design a robust and failure-tolerant cloud infrastructure, it is important to deploy resources across zones or even regions. This prevents you from having an infrastructure outage that affects all resources simultaneously. Thus, it is particularly important to know which of the following categories your resources belong to, as follows:

- **Zonal resource**: This is a resource that is specific to a zone, such as a virtual machine instance.

- **Regional resource**: This is a resource that is specific to a region and spans over multiple zones, such as a static IP address.

- **Global resource**: This is a location-independent resource, such as a virtual machine instance image.

Choosing a region and a zone where your resources should be deployed, as well as where data should be stored, is an especially important design task. There are several reasons you should consider this:

- **High availability**: Distributing your resources across multiple zones and regions will help mitigate outages. Google has designed zones to minimize the risk of correlated failures caused by power, cooling, or networking outages. In the case of a zone outage, it is very easy to migrate to another zone to keep your service running. Similarly, you can mitigate the impact of a region outage by running backup services in another region, as well as using load balancing services.

- **Decreased network latency**: When latency is a crucial topic in your application, it is very important to choose the zone or region closest to your point of service. For example, if the end users of a service are located mostly in the west part of Europe, your service should be placed in that region or zone.

At the time of writing, there are 24 available regions and 73 zones. Recently, Google announced that five new regions will be available soon in Warsaw (Poland), Melbourne (Australia), Toronto (Canada), Delhi (India), and Doha (Qatar). The full list of available regions can be queried from Cloud Shell, as shown in the following screenshot. Cloud Shell is a ready-to-use command-line interface that's available in GCP that allows the user to interact with all GCP products:

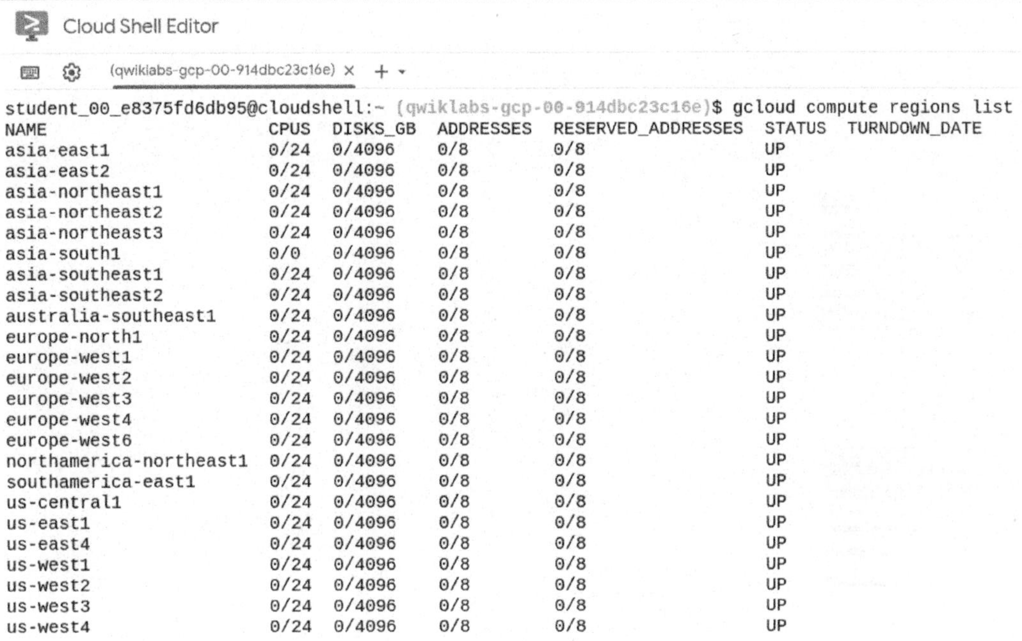

Figure 1.5 – GCP region list from Cloud Shell

The full list of available zones can also be queried from Cloud Shell, which is available in GCP, as shown in the following screenshot:

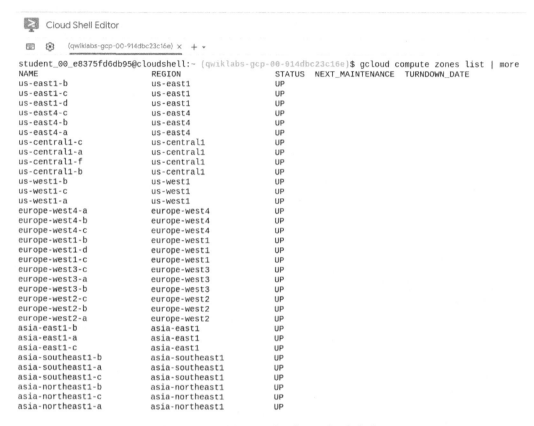

Figure 1.6 – GCP zone list from Cloud Shell

Each zone supports several types of CPU platforms between Ivy Bridge, Sandy Bridge, Haswell, Broadwell, Skylake, or Cascade Lake. This is an important aspect to know when you decide to deploy your virtual machine instance in one particular zone. You need to make sure that the zone you choose supports the instance that you are willing to deploy. To find out what CPU platform one zone supports, you can use Cloud Shell, as shown in the following screenshot:

Figure 1.7 – GCP CPU platform list from Cloud Shell

When selecting zones, keep the following tips in mind:

- **Communication within and across regions will have different costs**:
  Generally, communication within regions will always be cheaper and faster than
  communication across different regions.

- **Apply multi-zone redundancy to critical systems**: To mitigate the effects of
  unexpected failure on your instances, you should duplicate critical assets in multiple
  zones and regions.

Now, let's look at projects, billing, and quotas.

Projects, billing, and quotas

When cloud users request a resource or service in GCP, they need to have a project to
track resources and quota usage. GCP projects are the basis for enabling and using GCP
services. Inside a GCP project, users must enable billing to monitor, maintain, and address
the costs of the GCP services running on the project itself.

Moreover, projects are separate compartments, and they are isolated from each other.
GCP resources belong to exactly one project and they cannot be shared across projects,
except for shared VPC networks, which can be shared with other projects. In addition,
GCP projects can have different owners and users with several rights, such as project
editor or project viewer. They are managed hierarchically using the Google Cloud
resource manager, which will be described shortly.

GCP projects have three identifying attributes that uniquely distinguish them globally. These are as follows:

- **Project ID**: This is a permanent, unchangeable identifier that is unique across GCP globally. GCP generates one at project creation time but you can choose your unique ID if needed. The project ID is a human-readable string that can be used as a seed for uniquely naming other GCP resources, such as Google Cloud Storage bucket names.

- **Project name**: This is a nickname that you can assign to your project for your convenience. It does not need to be unique, and it can be changed over time.

- **Project number**: This is a permanent, unchangeable number that is unique across GCP globally. This number is generated by GCP and it cannot be chosen.

Projects can belong to a GCP **organization** for business scenarios, or they can exist without an organization. This happens when we have an individual private project. However, you can always migrate to a private project inside a GCP organization.

Projects must belong to a **billing account**, which is used as a reference for paying for Google Cloud resources. This billing account is linked to a **payment profile**, which contains payments methods that costs are charged for. As shown in the following diagram, one billing account can have multiple projects assigned:

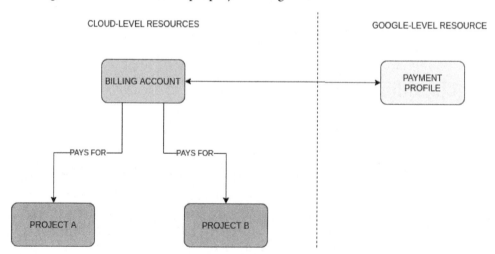

Figure 1.8 – GCP billing and payment profile relation

The cloud billing account is responsible for tracking all the costs that are incurred using the GCP resources for all the projects attached to it. In practice, cloud billing has the following key features:

- **Cost reporting**: This can monitor, share, and print monthly costs and keep track of the cost trends of your resource spending, as shown in the following screenshot:

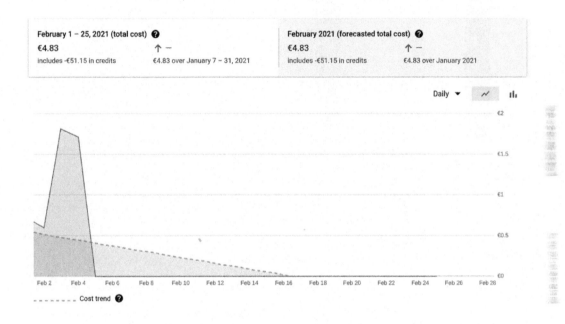

Figure 1.9 – Cost reporting in GCP

- **Cost breakdown**: This shows how many discounts your base usage cost will benefit from in a month. This is shown as a waterfall chart, starting from the base cost and subtracting discounts progressively until you see the final costs, as shown here:

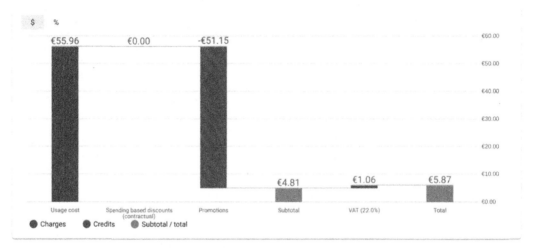

Item	Cost breakdown	Effective rate	Amount
Usage cost ❓	View report ↗	100%	€55.96
Spending based discounts (contractual) ❓		0%	€0.00
Promotions ❓		-91.4%	-€51.15
Cost	View report ↗		€55.96
Total credits (discounts, promotional & other credits)		-91.4%	-€51.15

Figure 1.10 – Cost breakdown in GCP

- **Budget and alerts**: This is very important for setting budgets for your projects to avoid surprises at the end of the month. Here, you can decide the upper limit for a monthly expense and generate alerts for billing administrators to control costs once the trigger is reached. The following screenshot shows an example of a budget of 100 euros with the actual monthly expenses and three thresholds that trigger emails:

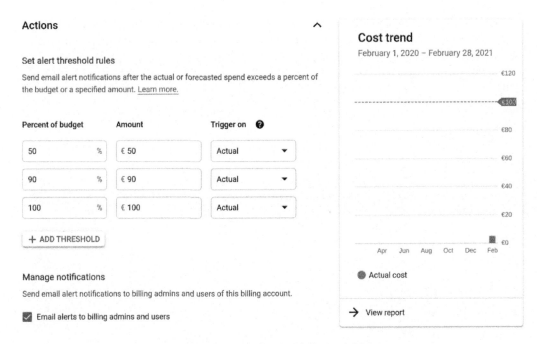

Figure 1.11 – Budgets and alerts in GCP

Resources in projects can be limited with **quotas**. Google Cloud uses two categories of quotas:

- **Rate quotas**: This limits a certain number of API requests to a GCP resource within a time interval, such as a minute or a day, after which the resource is not available.

- **Allocation quotas**: This limits the number of GCP resources that are available to the project at any given time. If this limit is reached, the resource must be released so that you can request a new one.

Projects can have different quotas for the same services. This may depend on various aspects; for example, the quota administrator may reduce the quota for certain resources to equalize the number of services among all projects in one organization.

To find out what the quota is for the service you want to use in GCP, you can search for it on the **Cloud IAM Quotas** page. Here are all the quotas assigned to your project and you can request different quota sizes if needed. As shown in the following screenshot, you can display the actual usage of CPU quotas in all project regions:

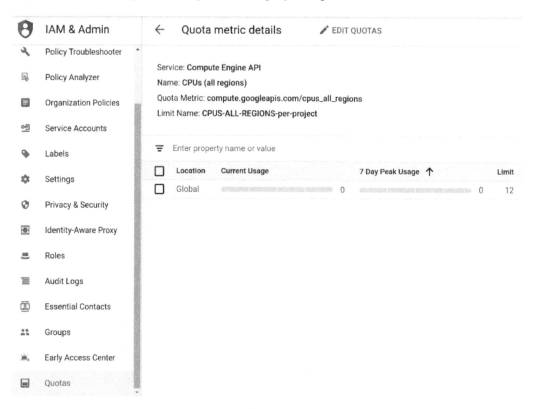

Figure 1.12 – CPU quotas in the GCP project

In this section, you learned about the physical architecture of GCP. However, to start using it, you must understand how Google architects the resources that are available to users. This will be described in the next section.

Getting started with GCP

In this section, we are going to describe how resources are organized inside GCP and how to interact with them. This is important, especially when the projects and their resources belong to large enterprises. Moreover, this section describes what tools users can use to interact with GCP.

GCP resource hierarchy

The cloud resource hierarchy has two main functions inside GCP:

- To manage a GCP project life cycle hierarchically inside one organization.

- Organization and **Identity and Access Management (IAM)** policies can be applied for project and resource access control.

The best way to understand the GCP resource hierarchy is to look at it from the bottom up. Resources are grouped into projects, which may belong to a single folder or organization node. Thus, the resource hierarchy consists of four elements, as shown in the following diagram:

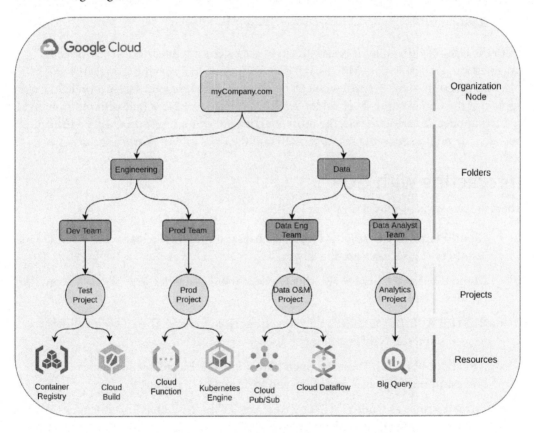

Figure 1.13 – Resource hierarchy in GCP

Let's understand what each of the four elements is, as follows:

- **Organization node**: This is the root node for your organization and it centralizes the project's management in a single structure. The organization node is associated with a Google workspace or cloud identity account, which is mandatory.

- **Folders**: This is an additional grouping method that wraps projects and other folders hierarchically to improve separation and policy administration. You can apply an access control policy to the folder or even delegate rights to all the sub-folders and projects that are included.

- **Projects**: This is the fundamental grouping method for containing GCP resources and enabling billing. They are isolated from each other.

- **Resources**: These are GCP services that users can deploy.

With the resource hierarchy, it is easy to apply access control at various levels of your organization. Google uses IAM to assign granular access to a specific Google resource. IAM administrators can control who can do what on which resources. IAM policies can be applied at the organization level, folder level, or project level. Note that with multiple IAM policies applied at various levels, the most effective policy for a resource will be the union between the policy set on the resource itself and the ones inherited from the ancestors.

Interacting with GCP

There are five ways of interacting with GCP:

- **Cloud Platform Console**: This is a web user interface that allows you to use all GCP resources and services graphically.

- **Cloud Shell and Cloud SDK**: This is a command-line interface that allows you to use all GCP resources.

- **RESTful API**: This is an API that can be accessed via RESTful calls and allows you to access and use GCP resources and services.

- **API client libraries**: These are open libraries that are available in various programming languages and allow you to access GCP resources.

- **Infrastructure as Code (IaC)**: Open source IaC tools such as Terraform or Google Deployment Manager can be used to deploy and manage IaaS and PaaS resources on GCP (`https://cloud.google.com/docs/terraform`).

The first two operating modes are more appropriate for cloud architects and administrators who prefer to have direct interaction with GCP. The other two are chosen by programmers and developers who build applications that use GCP services. In this book, we will focus more on the **Console** and **Cloud Shell** to explain GCP features.

The following screenshot shows the main components of the Console:

Figure 1.14 – Main components of the GCP Console

Let's explore what's labeled in the preceding screenshot:

- The navigation menu lets you access all the GCP services and resources (**1**).
- The combo menu lets you select the project you want to work with (**2**).
- The search bar lets you search for resources and more within the project (**3**).
- The Cloud Shell button lets you start the Cloud Shell (**4**).
- The **Project Info** card lets you control the project settings (**5**).
- The **Resources** card lets you monitor the active resources (**6**).
- The **Billing** card lets you monitor the cost and its estimation (**7**).

Cloud Shell is the preferred interaction method for administrators who want to use the command-line interface. Cloud Shell also has a graphical editor that you can use to develop and debug code. The following screenshot shows Cloud Shell:

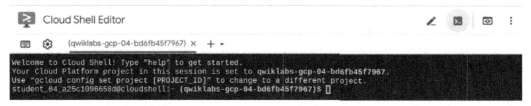

Figure 1.15 – Cloud Shell

Cloud Shell Editor is shown in the following screenshot:

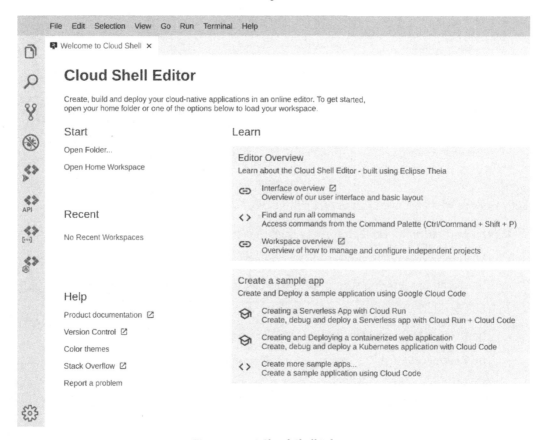

Figure 1.16 – Cloud Shell Editor

Cloud Shell comes with the Cloud SDK preinstalled, which allows administrators to interact with all GCP resources. `gcloud`, `gsutil`, and `bq` are the most important SDK tools that you will use to, for instance, manage Compute Engine instances, Cloud Storage, and BigQuery, respectively.

In this section, you learned about the logical architecture of GCP. In the next section, you will understand how virtual machines work in Google Cloud.

Understanding virtual machines in the cloud

In this section, you will learn about **Compute Engine** in GCP and its major features. This includes the virtual machine types that are available in GCP, disk options, and encryption solutions. Moreover, this section will introduce **Virtual Private Cloud** and its main characteristics. Finally, we will look at **Load Balancing**, **DNS**, and **CDN** in GCP.

Google Compute Engine

IaaS in GCP is implemented with Compute Engine. Compute Engine allows users to run virtual machines in the cloud. The use cases for Compute Engine are as follows:

- Websites
- Legacy monolithic applications
- Custom databases
- Microsoft Windows applications

Compute Engine is a regional service where, when you deploy it, you must specify the instance name, the region, and the zone that the instance will run in. Note that the instance must be unique within the zone. GCP allows administrators to deploy Compute Engine VMs with the same name, so long as they stay in different zones. We will discuss this in more detail when we look at internal DNS.

There are four virtual machine family types that you can choose from:

- **General-purpose**: This category is for running generic workloads such as websites or customized databases.
- **Compute-optimized**: This category is for running specific heavy CPU workloads such as **high-performance computing** (**HPC**) or **single-threaded applications**.
- **Memory-optimized**: This category is for running specific heavy in-memory workloads such as large **in-memory databases** or **in-memory analytics applications**.
- **GPU**: This category is for running intensive workloads such as machine learning, graphics applications, or blockchain.

In the general-purpose category, you can choose between four different machine types, as illustrated in the following diagram:

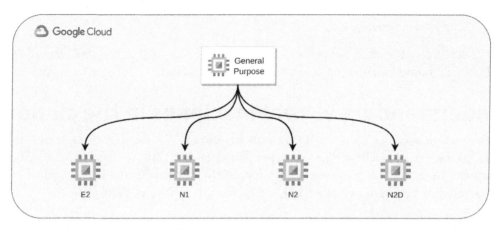

Figure 1.17 – General-purpose Compute Engine machine types in GCP

To choose the appropriate machine type for your workload, let's have a look at the following table:

Machine Type	vCPUs	Memory (per vCPU) GB	Maximum Memory (GB)
E2	2 - 32	0.5 - 8	128
N1	1 - 96	0.95 - 6.5	624
N2	2 - 80	0.5 - 8	640
N2D	2 - 224	0.5 - 8	896

Each of the previous machine types can have different configurations in terms of vCPUs and memory. Here, you can select between predefined and custom machine types. Predefined machine types let you choose a Compute Engine instance that has a predefined amount of vCPUs and RAM. On the other hand, the custom machine type allows you to select the vCPUs and RAM that are required for your workload. You can have additional options for your predefined Compute Engine instance. You can run a virtual machine that shares a core with other users to save money, or you can choose an instance that has a different balance of vCPUs and memory.

We can summarize all the machine type configurations with the following diagram:

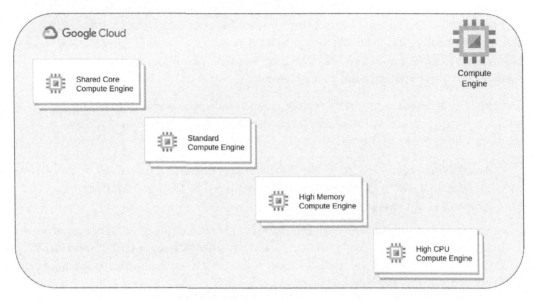

Figure 1.18 – Machine type configurations in GCP

Another important aspect of Compute Engine is its **boot disk**. Each virtual machine instance requires a boot disk to run properly. In the boot disk, the operating system is installed, as well as the main partition. The boot disk is a permanent storage disk and it can be built from several types of images. GCP offers pre-built public images for both Linux and Windows operating systems. Some of them are license free such as **CentOS, Ubuntu, and Debian**. Others are premium images, and they incur license fees.

Boot disks can be divided into three types:

- **Standard persistent disk**: This is a magnetic **hard disk drive (HDD)** that can have up to 7,500 IOPS in reading and 15,000 IOPS in writing operations.

- **Balanced persistent disk**: This is the entry-level **solid-state drive (SSD)** and can have up to 80,000 IOPS in both reading and writing operations

- **SSD persistent disk**: This is the second-level SSD and can have up to 100,000 IOPS in both reading and writing operations.

Boot disks are the primary disks for a Compute Engine instance. Additionally, you can attach more disks to your virtual machine if you need extra space or for extremely high performance. For the latter, you can add a local SSD as a secondary block storage disk. They are physically attached to the server that hosts your Compute Engine instance and can have up to 0.9/2.4 million IOPS in reading and 0.8/1.2 million IOPS in writing (with SCSI and NVMe technology, respectively).

Security is a particularly important feature when you design your Compute Engine instance. For this reason, Google lets you choose from three different encryption solutions that apply to all the persistent disks of your virtual machine, as follows:

- **Google-managed key**: This is the default encryption and it is enabled by default on all persistent disks. The encryption key is managed by Google and users do not have to worry about anything.

- **Customer-managed key**: With this encryption method, the data is encrypted with a user key that is periodically rotated via Google's **Key Management System** (**KMS**). This GCP-managed service allows users to have their encryption keys and manage them inside the user's project.

- **Customer-supply key**: With this encryption method, the data is encrypted with a user-supply key, which is stored and managed outside the GCP user's project.

In this section, you learned what options you have when you decide to run virtual machines on GCP. In the next section, you will be introduced to Virtual Private Cloud in GCP.

VPC overview

Virtual Private Cloud (**VPC**) is a virtualized private network and data center. Compute resources, storage, and load balancers live within VPC inside the Google Cloud production network that belongs to a specific project. VPC is powered by Andromeda (`https://www.usenix.org/system/files/conference/nsdi18/nsdi18-dalton.pdf`), the GCP network virtualization stack, which is fully distributed to avoid having a single point of failure. A VPC network provides the following:

- Connectivity services for interconnected Compute Engine, **Google Kubernetes Engine** (**GKE**) clusters, and an App Engine flexible environment

- Connectivity services to private on-premises networks using cloud VPN tunnels or cloud interconnect services

- Traffic distribution from Google Cloud load balancers and the backends running inside GCP

GCP projects can have multiple VPC networks that can contain several subnets for each region they cover, as shown in the following diagram:

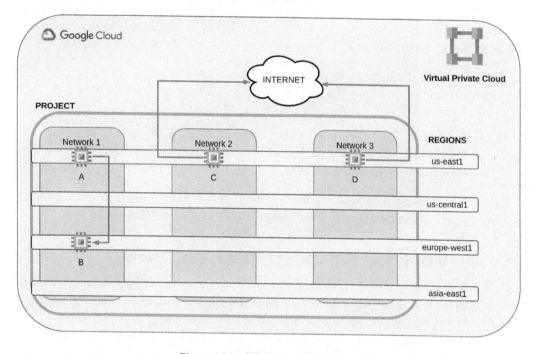

Figure 1.19 – VPC network overview

VPC networks logically separate resources, even though they are in the same project. As shown in *Figure 1.17*, Compute Engine instances that stay in the same network can communicate with each other, even though they are in different regions without using public internet. On the contrary, instances in the same regions but different networks cannot communicate with each other unless they pass through the public internet or over VPC peering between the different VPC networks.

VPC networks have the following properties:

- Networks are global resources and do not belong to any region or zone. They are contained in one specific project and may span across all the available GCP regions.

- Networks use subnets to logically group GCP resources in one region. Therefore, subnets are regional resources, and they span across zones.

- Networks do not have any IP addresses assigned, while subnets do and they belong to private IPv4 ranges.

- Routes and firewall rules are global resources, and they are associated with one network.

- Firewall rules control the traffic to and from a virtual machine.

- Networks only support IPv4 unicast traffic. Multicast, broadcast, or IPv6 traffic within the network are not supported.

There are two ways to create a VPC network within a GCP project:

- **Auto mode**: The network has one subnet for each available region and default predefined firewall rules. The IP address range has a fixed /20 for each subnet that's created.

- **Custom mode**: The network has no default preconfigured subnets and the user has full control over defining all the network resources, such as subnet IP ranges, firewalls, and routing configuration.

In this section, you learned about the basics of VPC and its main components. In the next section, you will get an overview of Load Balancing, DNS, and CDN in GCP.

Overview of Load Balancing, DNS, and CDN

In GCP, load balancers can help distribute traffic across multiple Compute Engine instances. This reduces the risk of having performance issues on the backend application and improves reliability. Moreover, Google Cloud Load Balancing services are engineered on fully distributed and scalable infrastructure that uses software-defined networking to direct traffic to VPC networks. This helps avoid a single point of failure and allows traffic at scale.

The **Google Cloud Load Balancer** architecture can be represented as follows:

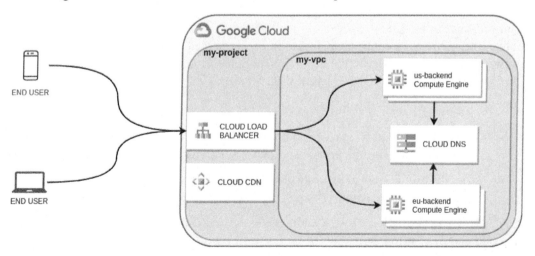

Figure 1.20 – Cloud Load Balancer architecture in GCP

External Google Cloud load balancers provide the following features:

- A single external IP address as the frontend
- Global or regional load balancing to reach your application from the internet
- Internal load balancing
- Layer 4 to Layer 7 load balancing

When it comes to DNS, it is important to clarify which Google Cloud products are needed and when. Google offers three services that deal with DNS:

- **Internal DNS**
- **Cloud DNS**
- **Cloud Domain**

Internal DNS allows Compute Engine instances in the same VPC network to communicate via internal DNS names. Internal records for the virtual machine are created in the DNS zone for `.internal` domains. These records are automatically created, updated, and removed by GCP, depending on the virtual machine's life cycle. Moreover, internal DNS is for the virtual machine's primary internal IP address resolution and it cannot be used to resolve its public IP address, nor its private secondary IP address. Additionally, Google recommends using *zonal DNS* to improve reliability. The **fully qualified domain name (FQDN)** for a Compute Engine instance has the following format:

```
instanceName.zone.c.projectId.internal
```

Note that to avoid conflict with FQDNs, two Compute Engine instances running in the same zone must have unique instance names.

Cloud DNS is a Google-managed service that allows us to publish domain names to the global DNS in a reliable, cost-effective, and scalable way. Cloud DNS provides both public and private zones and lets the user publish DNS records without worrying about managing its DNS server. Public zones are visible globally, while private zones are visible to one or more specified VPC networks.

Cloud Domain allows users to register and configure domains in Google Cloud. Through Cloud Domain, users can purchase domains and attach them to their applications. The domain is associated with a specific project and its price will be charged to the same Cloud Billing account of the user's project. Therefore, Cloud Domain can be used to search for available domains, buy them, and manage their registration.

Google Cloud offers a managed service to implement a **content delivery network** to serve content closer to users. The name of this service is **Cloud CDN**. Through Google's global edge network, Cloud CDN can accelerate websites and applications and improve the user experience. Cloud CDN requires an HTTP(S) load balancer that provides the frontend IP address that receives users' requests and forwards them to the backends. In GCP, there are distinct types of backends that can work with Cloud CDN:

- **Managed instance groups**: Groups of Compute Engine instances running on a region with autoscaling

- **Zonal Network Endpoint Groups** (**NEGs**): A group of IP addresses of running virtual machines or containers in one specific zone or a group of IP addresses and ports of running services

- **Serverless NEGs**: A group of serverless services such as Cloud Run, Cloud Functions, or App Engine sharing the same URL

- **Internet NEGs**: A group of IP addresses running outside GCP

- **Cloud storage bucket**: GCP object storage that's used to store any type of file at scale

All these backend types are called origin servers when we consider the Cloud CDN architecture. The following diagram shows how responses from origin servers flow through an HTTP(S) load balancer and are delivered to the final users via Cloud CDN:

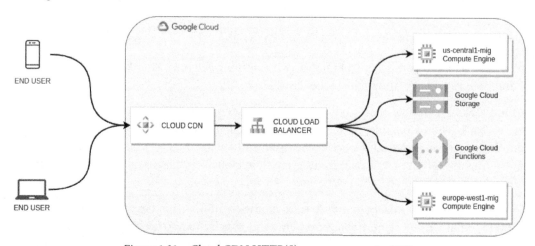

Figure 1.21 – Cloud CDN HTTP(S) user responses in GCP

In this section, you learned about the basics of global load balancer services, DNS, and CDN in GCP. In the next section, you will explore DevOps, containers, and Kubernetes.

Exploring containers in the cloud

In recent years, digital transformation has changed the way business is done. *Mobility, Internet of Things*, and *cloud computing* require agility, simplicity, and speed to meet market demands. However, traditional businesses and enterprises maintain separation between departments, especially those that are responsible for developing new features and those responsible for maintaining application stability. **DevOps** methodologies break down this dogma and create a circular environment between development and operational processes. The DevOps goal is to deliver services faster and on-demand, and this can be achieved when development and operation teams work together without any barriers.

DevOps concepts and microservice architectures

The DevOps culture introduces important guidelines, also called *CALMS*, that should be adopted at every level:

1. **Culture**: Trust, collaboration, respect, and common goals are the main pillars of DevOps culture.

2. **Automation**: Everything should be automated, from building to application delivery.

3. **Lean**: Always optimize processes and reduce waste as much as possible.

4. **Measurement**: Measure everything for continuous improvement.

5. **Sharing**: Share everything, from ideas to common problems.

DevOps culture starts with increasing velocity in software development and deployment. This Agile approach allows us to reduce the time between the application's design and deployment. Thus, DevOps culture promotes the **continuous integration**, **continuous delivery**, and **continuous deployment** model (often referred to as **CI/CD**) against the traditional waterfall model, as shown in the following diagram:

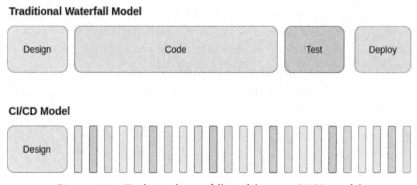

Figure 1.22 – Traditional waterfall model versus CI/CD model

Continuous integration is the process of constantly merging new code into the code base. This allows software engineers and developers to increase velocity in new feature integrations. Also, automated testing can be inserted early in the process so that it is easier to catch problems and bugs. **Continuous delivery** is the process of staging code for review and inspection before release. Here, there is manual control over the deployment phase of a new feature. On the other hand **continuous deployment** leverages automation to deploy new features in production when code has been committed and tested.

To support the CI/CD model and adopt DevOps methodology, software engineers have moved from *monolith* to *microservices* application design. A microservice is a small piece of software that is independently developed, tested, and deployed as part of a larger application. Moreover, a microservice is stateless and loosely coupled with independent technology and programming languages from other microservices. Large applications built as collections of microservices that work together have the following benefits:

- **High horizontal scalability**: Microservices can be created as workload increases.

- **High modularity**: Microservices can be reused to build modular applications.

- **High fault tolerance**: Microservices can be restarted quickly in case of crashes. Workloads can also be distributed across multiple identical microservices to improve reliability.

- **High integration with the CI/CD model**: Microservices can fit the CI/CD model because they can be quickly and easily tested and deployed in production.

The best way to follow the microservices approach is to leverage virtualization technology, or better, the containerization methodology. In the next section, we will show how containers are like virtual machines and the main differences that make them ideal for microservices implementation.

Containerization versus virtualization

Since we introduced virtual machines at the beginning of this chapter, it is time to understand what a **container** is and how it differs from virtual machines. Containers are portable software packages that are independent of the infrastructure that they run in. They wrap one application and all its dependencies that are needed for execution.

Containers fit very well into the microservice architecture because they are modular and they are easy to change and scale.

The main differences between containers and virtual machines are shown in the following diagram:

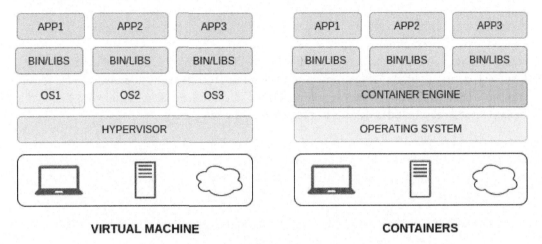

Figure 1.23 – Virtual machines versus containers

The major features of containers, compared to virtual machines, are as follows:

- **Faster deployment**: Deploying a container requires seconds rather than minutes.

- **Less overhead**: Containers do not include the operating systems. Virtual machines do.

- **Faster migration**: Migrating one container from one host to another takes seconds instead of minutes.

- **Faster restart**: Restarting one container takes seconds rather than minutes.

Usually, containers apply when users want to run multiple instances of the same application. Containers share a single operating system kernel, and they are logically separated in terms of the runtime environment, filesystem, and others. Virtual machines are logically separated operating systems running on the same general-purpose hardware. Both virtual machines and containers need to run on software that allows for virtualization. For virtual machines, the *hypervisor* is responsible for virtualizing the hardware to let multiple operating systems run on the same machine. For containers, **Container Engine** is responsible for virtualizing the operating system (binaries, libraries, filesystem, and so on) to let multiple applications run on the same OS.

It is clear from *Figure 1.21* that containers have less overhead than virtual machines. They do not need to load the operating system when the workload requires new applications. Applications can be started in seconds and their isolation is maintained as it would be with virtual machines. In addition, *application agility* is improved as applications can be created or destroyed dynamically when the workload requires it. Moreover, containers reduce the number of resources that would be needed to deploy a new application. It has been well demonstrated that running a new containerized application consumes far fewer resources than one running on a virtual machine. This is because containers do not need to load an OS that includes dozens of processes in the idle state.

One of the most popular platforms for developing, packaging, and deploying containers is **Docker**. It also includes Docker Engine, which is supported on several operating systems. With Docker, users can build container images and manage their distribution. Docker has several key concepts:

- **Portability**: Docker applications can be packaged in images. These can be built on a user's laptop and shift unchanged to production.

- **Version control**: Each image is versioned with a tag that is assigned during the building process.

- **Immutable**: When Docker containers are created, they cannot be changed. If restarted, the container is different from the previous one.

- **Distribution**: Docker images can be maintained in repositories called registries. Images can be pushed to the registry when new images are available. They can be pulled to deploy new containers in production.

Using Docker, applications can be packed into containers using `Dockerfiles`, which describe how to build application images from source code. This process is consistent across different platforms and environments, thus greatly increasing portability. The main instructions contained in a `Dockerfile` are represented in the following diagram:

DOCKERFILE EXAMPLE

```
FROM ubuntu
COPY . /app
RUN apt-get install python
WORKDIR /app
EXPOSE 8585/tcp
ENTRYPOINT python myApp.py
```

Figure 1.24 – Dockerfile example

The FROM instruction tells Docker Engine which base image this containerized application will start from. It is the first statement of every Dockerfile, and it allows users to build images from the previous one. The COPY instruction copies the code and its library files into the container image. The RUN clause instruction runs commands when the container will be built. The WORKDIR instruction works as a change directory inside the container. The EXPOSE instruction tells us which port the container will use to provide services. Finally, ENTRYPOINT starts the application when the container is launched.

> **Important Note**
>
> The EXPOSE instruction does not publish the port. It works as a type of documentation. To publish the port when running the container, the user who runs the container should use the -p flag on docker run to publish and map one or more ports.

Once the Dockerfile is ready, you can build the container image using the docker build command. It is mandatory to also include the code and the library requirement files during the building process. Additionally, it is good practice to tag images that have been built to identify the application version.

Container orchestration with Google Kubernetes Engine

So far, we have learned that containerization helps adopt DevOps culture and minimize the gap between application development and deployment. However, when large and complex applications are composed of dozens of microservices, it becomes extremely difficult to coordinate and orchestrate them. It is important to know where containers are running, whether they are healthy, and how to scale when the workload increases. All these functions cannot be done manually; they need a dedicated system that automatically orchestrates all the tasks. Here is where **Kubernetes** comes in.

Kubernetes (**K8s** for short) is an open source orchestration tool (formerly an internal Google tool) that can automatically deploy, scale, and failover containerized applications. It supports declarative configurations, so administrators describe the state of the infrastructure. K8s will do everything it can to reach the desired state. So, Kubernetes maintains the state of the infrastructure that is written in configuration files (also known as *manifest* files).

The main Kubernetes features can be listed as follows:

- **Supports both stateless and stateful applications**: On K8s, you can run applications that do not save user sessions such as web servers or some others that do store persistently.

- **Auto-scaling**: K8s can scale containerized applications in and out based on resource utilization. This happens automatically and is controlled by the cluster itself. The administrators can declare autoscaling thresholds in the deployment manifest files.

- **Portable**: Administrators are free to move their workloads between on-premises clusters and public cloud providers with minimal effort.

K8s is composed of a cluster of several nodes. The node that's responsible for controlling the entire cluster is called the master node. At least one of these is needed to run the cluster. Here, Kubernetes stores the information regarding the objects and their desired states. The most common Kubernetes objects are as follows:

- **Pod**: This object is a logical structure that the container will run in.

- **Deployment**: This object describes how one application should be deployed into the K8s cluster. Here, the administrator can decide what container image to use for its application, the desired number of Pods running, and how to auto-scale.

- **Service**: This object describes how the application that's been deployed can be reached from other applications.

In Kubernetes, worker nodes are responsible for running containers. Containers cannot run on the Kubernetes cluster in their native format. They need to be wrapped into a logical structure known as a Pod. Kubernetes manages Pods, not containers. These Pods provide storage and networking functions for containers running within the Pod. They have one IP address that is used by containers to expose their services. It is good practice to have one container running in a Pod. Additionally, Pods can specify a set of **volumes**, which can be used as a storage system for containers. Pods can be grouped into **namespaces**. This provides environment isolation and increases cluster utilization.

The Kubernetes architecture is shown in the following diagram:

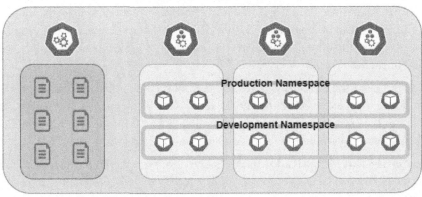

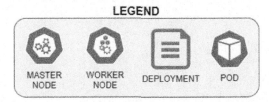

Figure 1.25 – Kubernetes architecture – clusters and namespaces

In GCP, administrators can run managed Kubernetes clusters with **Google Kubernetes Engine (GKE)**. GKE allows users to deploy Kubernetes **clusters** in minutes without worrying about installation problems. It has the following features:

- **Node autoscaling**: GKE can auto-scale worker nodes to support variable workloads.

- **Load balancing**: GKE can benefit from Google Load Balancing solutions for its workloads.

- **Node pools**: GKE can have one or more worker node pools with different Compute Engine instances.

- **Automatic repair and upgrades**: GKE can monitor and maintain healthy Compute Engine worker nodes and apply automatic updates.

- **Cluster logging and monitoring**: Google Cloud Operations lets administrators have full control over the state of the Kubernetes cluster and its running workloads.

- **Regional cluster**: GKE can run K8s clusters across multiple zones of one region. This allows you to have highly available K8s clusters with redundant masters, and multiple worker nodes spread between zones.

When it comes to networking with Kubernetes and GKE, it is important to remember the following definitions:

1. **Node IP**: This is the IP address that a worker node gets when it starts. In GKE, this IP address is assigned based on the VPC subnet that the cluster is running in. This address is used to allow communication between the master node and the worker node of the K8s cluster.

2. **Pod IP**: This is the IP address that's assigned to the Pod. This address is ephemeral and lives for as long as the Pod runs. By default, GKE allocates a /14 secondary network block for the entire set of Pods running in the cluster. More specifically, GKE allocates a /24 secondary IP address range for each worker node the cluster has.

3. **Cluster IP**: This is the IP address that's given to a service. This address is stable for as long as the service is present on the cluster. By default, GKE allocates a secondary block of IP addresses to run all the services in the cluster.

The following diagram provides a better understanding of GKE IP addressing:

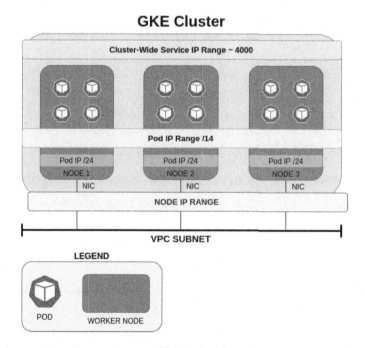

Figure 1.26 – IP addressing in the GKE cluster

Since Pods maintain a separate IP address space from worker nodes, they can communicate with each other in the same cluster without using any kind of **network address translation**. This is because GKE automatically configures the VPC subnet with an *alias IP*, which is an authorized secondary subnet in the region where the cluster is deployed.

In Kubernetes, Pods are ephemeral, and they might have a short life. K8s may create new Pods in case of a change in the deployment or may restart Pods in case of crashes or errors. Moreover, when load balancing is needed across multiple Pods, it is crucial to have load balancing services to direct traffic to Pods. Here, the Kubernetes Service comes in handy because it allocates a static IP address that refers to a collection of Pods. The link between the Service and Pods is based on Pod labels and the **Service selector**. This last parameter allows Service objects to bind one static IP address to a group of Pods.

When Services are created, the *ClusterIP* is allocated statically, and it can be reached from any other application running within the cluster. However, most of the time, traffic comes from outside the cluster, so this cannot reach Services running inside it. GKE provides four types of load balancers that address this problem, as follows:

1. **External TCP/UDP load balancer**: This is a layer 4 load balancer that manages traffic coming from both outside the cluster and outside the VPC.

2. **External HTTP(S) load balancer**: This is a layer 7 load balancer that uses a dedicated URL forwarding rule to route the traffic to the application. This is also called **Ingress**.

3. **Internal TCP/UDP load balancer**: This is a layer 4 load balancer that manages traffic coming from outside the cluster but internally to the VPC.

4. **Internal HTTP(S) load balancer**: This is a layer 7 load balancer that uses a dedicated URL forwarding rule to route the intra-VPC traffic to the application. This is also called Ingress and it is applied to internal traffic.

In this section, you learned about the basics of Kubernetes and its implementation in GCP, Google Kubernetes Engine. Since GKE is based on clusters of Compute Instance VMs, networking is a crucial part to make your Pods and Services run as you need them to.

Summary

In this chapter, you learned what cloud computing and virtualization are. You also learned what cloud service models are available for your business and their advantages. Moreover, since GCP is a public cloud provider, you have been given a brief explanation of the differences between public, private, and hybrid cloud services.

GCP's physical architecture was described, as well as its regions and zones. We also looked at its logical architecture and specified the various organizations, folders, projects, and resources.

A deep explanation of what a Google Compute Engine instance is, and how you can use one for your workload, was provided in the second part of this chapter.

After introducing a few of the GCP services, such as Cloud DNS, Cloud CDN, and Cloud Load Balancing, we looked at the DevOps culture and its implementation with Kubernetes and **Google Kubernetes Engine (GKE)**.

In the next chapter, you will learn how to design, plan, and prototype a GCP network.

Further reading

- GCP locations and services:

  https://cloud.google.com/about/locations

- GCP landscape and concepts:

  https://cloud.google.com/docs/overview

- GCP IaaS and PaaS services:

  https://cloud.google.com/docs/overview/cloud-platform-services

- GCP networking products overview:

  https://cloud.google.com/products/networking

- Resources for the certification:

  - Network Engineer learning path:

    https://cloud.google.com/training/networking-security#network-engineer-learning-path

  - Network Engineer sample questions:

    https://cloud.google.com/certification/sample-questions/cloud-network-engineer

  - Network Engineer labs:

    https://www.qwiklabs.com/

2
Designing, Planning, and Prototyping a GCP Network

In this chapter, you will learn how to design, plan, and prototype a **Google Cloud Platform** (**GCP**) network. The chapter is divided into four parts.

First, we will describe the main strategies for failover and **disaster recovery** (**DR**) that you should use when designing your network in GCP. Next, we will focus on how you should design your **virtual private cloud** (**VPC**) in terms of **Internet Protocol** (**IP**) ranges for subnets, routing, and interconnections with other VPCs. Moreover, this section will describe how to design security in your VPC.

We will also describe how you should design the interconnection between your on-premises and VPC networks. You will discover all the GCP interconnection options, and you will learn how to prototype highly available interconnection solutions.

The last section describes how to design, plan, and secure the **Google Kubernetes Engine** (**GKE**) network to support Kubernetes Pods and Services for large-scale scenarios.

In this chapter, we will cover the following main topics:

- Designing the overall network architecture
- Designing a VPC
- Designing a hybrid network
- Designing a container IP addressing plan for GKE

Technical requirements

To fully understand the topics covered in this chapter you should have basic knowledge of IP networking technologies.

Designing the overall network architecture

In this section, you will learn what the main strategies are for failover and DR. You will learn what kinds of designing options for **high availability** (**HA**) in GCP networking you can adopt and what the recommended **Domain Name System** (**DNS**) strategies in a hybrid cloud environment are that you can use in **Google Cloud**. Moreover, you will learn what the most appropriate **load-balancing** options are that you can use in your design. Then, you will go through the optimization design of latency in GCP. Finally, you will learn about Google Cloud's network security strategy.

Failover and DR strategy

When you design new cloud architecture to support your services, it is especially important to have a well-tested DR plan in case something goes wrong. Indeed, DR strategies begin by analyzing two important key metrics that characterize the business impact. These are outlined here:

1. **Recovery Time Objective** (**RTO**): This metric is the maximum acceptable time that your service can be offline. It refers to the maximum allowed downtime for a service and how quickly the service should be restored.

2. **Recovery Point Objective** (**RPO**): This metric is the maximum acceptable time that data might be lost due to a major incident. In other words, it tells you how much data your service can lose from the last backup. It also defines how frequently the data is backed up.

Typically, smaller RTOs and RPOs determine higher costs as the complexity of infrastructure and services increases. For this reason, many companies are moving their services to the cloud to take advantage of reduced costs for capacity, scalability, network infrastructure, support, and facilities.

DR scenarios really depend on your business recovery goals and thus determine the RTO and RPO. Three DR patterns indicate how readily the system can recover when something goes wrong, as described next:

1. **Cold**: This pattern applies when your business has a high RTO and RPO. Service architecture does not include spare resources to overcome issues. Here, the service is stopped until your resources are created, started, and ready to receive user traffic.

2. **Warm**: This pattern applies when your business has a medium RTO and RPO. Service architecture does have spare resources to overcome issues, but they need to be started or configured to be ready to receive user traffic.

3. **Hot**: This pattern applies when your business is mission-critical and requires a low RTO and RPO. Service architecture does have spare resources, and they are running and processing user traffic even when faults have not occurred yet.

Now that you have learned about DR strategies, let's move on to understand the options you have in networking for **HA**.

Options for HA

In Google Cloud, many services can be used as building blocks to achieve your DR scenarios. When it comes to networking, the GCP products to consider are these ones:

1. **External Cloud Load Balancing**: This provides HA for **Google Compute Engine (GCE)** by distributing user requests among groups of **virtual machines (VMs)** running in different GCP regions. It features a *health check* system to determine whether a GCE instance can receive and process user traffic. Moreover, it publishes a *single global anycast IP address* to let user traffic reach the closest group of VMs, thus reducing user latency.

2. **Cloud DNS**: This provides tools to automate the maintenance of DNS entries when recovery happens. It also leverages Google's global Anycast Domain Name Servers network to serve DNS requests. This can be done with HA and low latency. If your DNS is on premises, Cloud DNS can forward DNS requests from VMs that are running in GCP.

3. **Cloud Connectivity**: This provides several ways to interconnect your on-premises network and the VPC in Google Cloud. Among others, *Dedicated Interconnect* and *Direct Peering* are the two interconnect solutions with the highest availability.

When you start moving assets to the cloud and you want to implement one of the preceding HA options, you will come up with a hybrid solution. In GCP, you can design your **hot DR** pattern for a three-tier application, as illustrated in the following diagram:

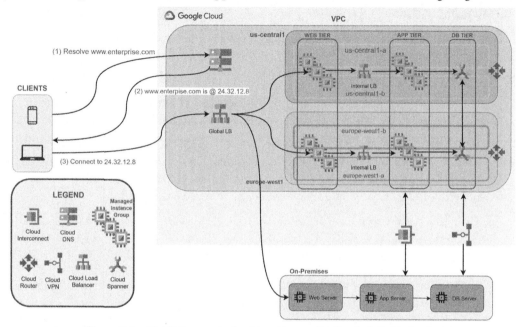

Figure 2.1 – Hot DR scenario for three-tier application in hybrid cloud

Your first move should be to migrate your on-premises DNS to Google Cloud. As shown in *Figure 2.1*, users connect to Cloud DNS to resolve the `https://www.enterprise.com` domain. Cloud DNS returns the A record of the anycast IP address of the global Cloud Load Balancing service. With Cloud Load Balancing, you can achieve hot DR, distributing traffic to different backends that can be either GCP instance groups or an on-premises web server public IP. In this manner, user traffic is served in both environments, and in the case of disaster, the entire solution keeps running, thus resulting in a hot DR solution. Additionally, on the load balancer, we can control the weighting of traffic distribution between the cloud and on-prem.

Continuing with *Figure 2.1*, you will notice that the three-tier application is composed of three different layers in both environments:

- **Web tier**: At this level, the solution includes servers that are responsible for serving the user requests and provides the web page of the web application.

- **App tier**: At this level, the solution includes the servers that are responsible for running the application.

- **Database tier**: At this level, the solution includes the servers that are responsible for running the database.

Hot DR patterns require cloning of the on-premises infrastructure in the cloud. In GCP, you can deploy clones of your infrastructure in multiple regions and load balance the traffic with a global load balancer. As depicted in *Figure 2.1*, when user traffic enters the VPC, it can be load-balanced across multiple regions with the Cloud Load Balancing service. This improves reliability since we are redistributing the risk of catastrophic events across areas that are geographically spread. Moreover, within each region, we can deploy the application tiers across multiple zones, thus improving reliability even further since the risk of having major incidents is reduced.

Additionally, within GCP, we can improve the reliability and scalability of the web and application tiers by deploying groups of **GCE** instances with the **Autoscaling** feature. These groups are called **managed instance groups** (**MIGs**). With MIGs, the architecture will be adapted to the actual workload, thus improving the resiliency of the entire system.

As shown in *Figure 2.1*, the MIGs serve the traffic that is routed from a cloud load balancer. Here, you can leverage the **Health Check** feature that allows you to automatically reroute the traffic to other GCE instances or MIGs in case something is not working as expected. Automatically rerouting traffic is an important feature you should use to improve reliability.

For the last part of your three-tier architectures, the database tier should include reliability as well. In GCP, this can be achieved with **Cloud Spanner**, which is a regional managed relational database service. Because your design includes a hybrid cloud solution, Cloud Spanner and your on-premises database must be synchronized. This must be maintained until data is completely moved from on-premises to the cloud, which is the best practice in such situations. To achieve database synchronization, the application tier must be modified to write consistently to both databases. Therefore, it is required to have highly available connectivity between the on-premises network and the VPC. This can be obtained using dual interconnection options in GCP, which are named **Dedicated Interconnect** and **Cloud VPN**. These two solutions should work in **Active Backup** mode since Dedicated Interconnect is much more reliable than Cloud VPN and offers the lowest latency possible and the highest available bandwidth. However, in case of problems, Cloud VPN could be used as a backup to provide a flexible low-cost solution to improve business continuity. To adopt active-backup internetworking, dynamic routing must be configured between on-premises routers and GCP **Cloud Router service**. In scenarios where there are workloads in multiple GCP regions, the cloud architect should include one Cloud Router per region in order to reduce latency.

When your cloud infrastructure takes most of the workload, then it is recommended to progressively turn off the tiers on-premises. This operation should be done gradually on Cloud DNS in order to reduce the workload to on-premises. When you are ready for the switch-off, this operation should be done on the maintenance windows in order to reduce possible service failure.

Now that you have learned what the possible options are to design an HA solution in Google Cloud networking, we can move on to see the strategy for DNS.

DNS strategy in a hybrid cloud environment

In the previous section, we discussed the design of HA options in a hybrid cloud scenario. Here, we have proposed a solution that included a complete migration of the on-premises authoritative DNS to Cloud DNS to resolve the enterprise public records. Sometimes, it is necessary to maintain some DNS services on-premises to resolve private names that some on-premises applications still use. For this reason, it is not always possible to completely migrate the DNS to the cloud, and DNS hybrid solutions must still be in place, especially for private scenarios. In this section, we will explore how to design a DNS management system that includes both Cloud DNS and on-premises authoritative DNS.

First, you should choose a name pattern for your corporate resources. The following options are available, depending on how many private resources you have spread between on-premises and Google Cloud:

- **Complete domain separation**: This pattern uses a separate domain for your on-premises and cloud environment, such as `corp.enterprise.com` and `gcp.enterprise.com`. This pattern is the best one to choose because it makes it extremely easy to forward DNS requests between environments.

- **Google Cloud domain as subdomain**: This pattern uses a subdomain for all GCP resources, and they are subordinate to the on-premises domain. For instance, you could use `corp.enterprise.com` for on-premises resources and `gcp.corp.enterprise.com` for Google Cloud resources. This pattern applies when the resources on-premises are far greater than ones in GCP.

- **On-prem domain as subdomain**: This pattern uses a subdomain for all on-premises resources, and they are subordinate to the Google Cloud domain. For example, you could use `corp.enterprise.com` for Google Cloud resources and `dc.corp.enterprise.com` for on-premises resources. This pattern is not common, and it applies to companies that have a small number of services on-premises.

For hybrid environments, the recommendation for private DNS resolution is to use two separate authoritative DNS systems. In this manner, Cloud DNS can be used as an authoritative DNS server for the Google Cloud environment, while the existing DNS servers on-premises can still be used as an authoritative DNS server for the on-premises resources. The following diagram shows a private DNS design with two authoritative DNS systems:

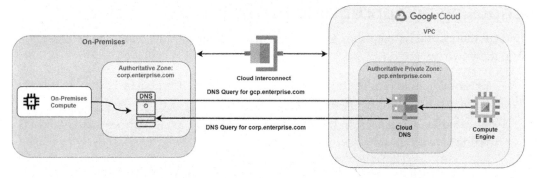

Figure 2.2 – Hybrid architecture with two authoritative DNS systems

With a two-authoritative-DNS-systems hybrid architecture, it is required to configure **forwarding zones** and **server policies**. Cloud DNS provides these two features to allow DNS name lookup between your on-premises and GCP environments.

> **Important Note**
>
> To forward DNS requests between different Google VPCs, you need to use DNS peering regardless of the type of interconnection.

Forwarding zones can be used to query DNS records in your on-premises environment for your corporate resources. Thus, if you need to query resources in `corp.enterprise.com`, you need to set up a forwarding zone. This approach is preferred because it preserves access to GCE instances and public IP addresses are still resolved without passing through the on-premises DNS server.

> **Important Note**
>
> Cloud DNS does not sync or cache on-premises requests. Therefore, it is critical to maintain the on-premises DNS server so that this is as highly available as possible.
>
> Also, Cloud DNS uses the IP address range of `35.199.192.0/19` to send queries to your on-premises environment. Make sure that your inbound firewall policies of your DNS server accept this source range.

DNS **server policies** allow on-premises hosts to query DNS records in a GCP private DNS environment. Anytime an on-premises host sends a request to resolve some GCE instance name in `gcp.enterprise.com`, you need to create an inbound DNS forwarding rule in the DNS server policy.

In this section, you have learned how to choose your DNS strategy when it comes to hybrid scenarios. In the next section, you will learn how to choose the most appropriate load-balancing option in GCP.

Choosing an appropriate load-balancing option

In GCP, there are several options for load balancing the user traffic. They can be divided into these two categories:

- **External load balancer**: In this category, GCP offers a load balancer that distributes traffic from the internet to the VPC.
- **Internal load balancer**: In this category, GCP offers a load balancer that distributes traffic between instances inside the VPC.

Moreover, GCP load balancers can be divided into **global** and **regional** categories. **Global load balancers** can be used when backends are distributed across multiple regions and you want to provide a single anycast IP address for your application. On the other hand, **regional load balancers** can be used when backends are in one region.

The following diagram shows the GCP load-balancing products for each category:

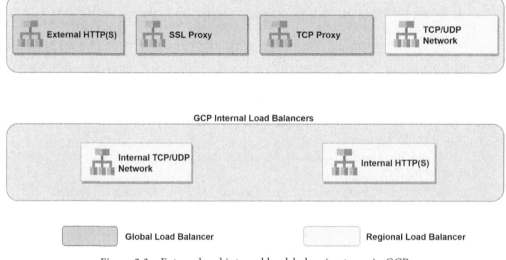

Figure 2.3 – External and internal load-balancing types in GCP

The choice of load balancer really depends on the type of traffic you need to balance. In general, you can work on the following basis:

- For **HyperText Transfer Protocol (Secure) (HTTP(S))** traffic, you can use either the **External HTTP(S)** load balancer or the **Internal HTTP(S)** load balancer, depending on the origin of the traffic.
- For **Secure Sockets Layer (SSL)** traffic except for HTTPS, you can use the **SSL Proxy** load balancer. This option can be used when you need to offload the SSL traffic to your backend running in the cloud.

- For **Transmission Control Protocol** (**TCP**) traffic, you can use the **TCP Proxy** load balancer in the case of external traffic or if a proxy service is needed. With **TCP Proxy**, you can still get the client address through the PROXY_PROTOCOL feature that can be enabled on the TCP proxy. The backend can extract the client IP from the PROXY_PROTOCOL header.

- For internal TCP traffic, you can use the **Internal TCP/UDP** load balancer when you need a Layer 4 load balancer.

- For **User Datagram Protocol** (**UDP**) traffic, you can use the **TCP/UDP Network** load balancer in case the traffic comes from outside of the VPC. For internal UDP traffic, you can use **Internal TCP/UDP** load balancer.

The flow chart shown here will help you to determine your external load-balancer solution in GCP:

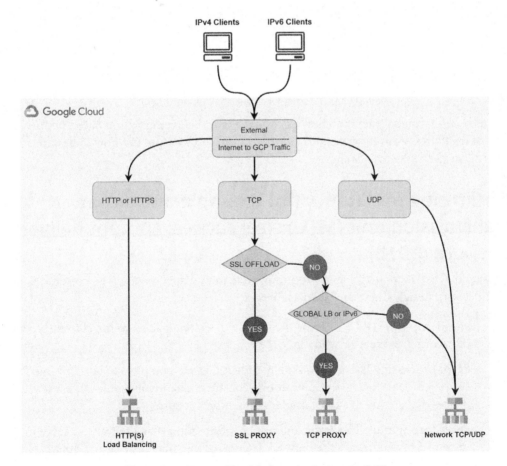

Figure 2.4 – External load-balancer solutions in GCP

And the flow chart shown here will help you to decide your internal load balancer solution in GCP:

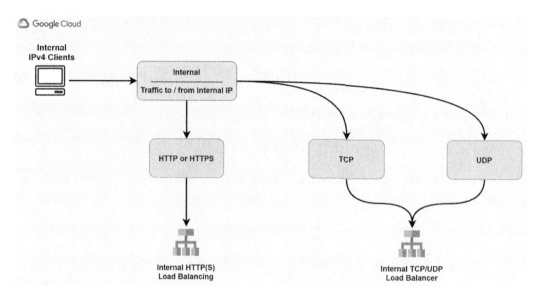

Figure 2.5 – Internal load-balancer solutions in GCP

In this section, you have learned how to choose a load-balancing option based on the type of traffic you want to serve. In the next section, you will find out how to design your network to optimize latency.

Optimizing for latency (for example, maximum transmission unit (MTU) size; caches; content delivery network (CDN))

In general, when it comes to latency optimization, many aspects should be considered in your network design. These are listed as follows:

- **Round-trip time (RTT)**: This is the time it takes for a packet to travel to the service and return it to the user who made the request.

- **Server processing latency**: This is the time it takes to complete the processing of a user request. For multi-tier applications, this time may involve multiple servers or services that are involved in completing the user request.

- **Server throughput**: This is the amount of information that a server can serve in 1 second. This influences the network latency, as the higher the throughput is, the lower the time needed to transmit the data.

In Google Cloud, there are some best practices to reduce latency and thus improve the **user experience** (**UX**). These are listed as follows:

- Deploy backends in each GCP region where your users are. Route user requests to the nearest backends using a GCP global load balancer depending on your application. An **HTTP(S)** or **SSL/TCP Proxy** load balancer can do this automatically.

- If you are deploying global services, **HTTP(S)** or **SSL/TCP Proxy** load balancers should be used to minimize both latency and **time to first byte** (**TTFB**). Because these load-balancer services proxy the user traffic, this helps to reduce the effects of TCP slow start, reduces **Transport Layer Security** (**TLS**) handshakes for every SSL offloading session, and automatically upgrades user sessions to HTTP/2, reducing the number of packets transmitted.

- If your application used multiple tiers (that is, web frontend, application, and database), they should be deployed in the same GCP region. Avoid inter-regional traffic between application tiers. Google **Cloud Trace** can help you to find out applications' interactions and allow you to decrease application latency.

- Integrate GCP **Cloud CDN** any time the user traffic is cacheable. This greatly reduces user latency because the content is served directly at the Google frontend.

- For static content, you should use Google Cloud Storage in combination with HTTP(S) load balancing and Cloud CDN to serve the content directly. This brings two benefits: it reduces the workload to the web server and reduces latency.

If you decide to use Google Cloud CDN to serve your static content, there are some best practices to follow in your network design, as follows:

- Enable automatic static content caching in Cloud CDN. Any content such as JavaScript code, images, or video should be cached automatically to reduce latency.

- Set the expiration time carefully based on how often you update the content you serve with Cloud CDN. You should identify content categories that share updating time—for example, you can define three categories, such as near-real-time updates, frequent updates, and infrequent updates.

- Use a custom cache key to improve the cache hit ratio. By default, Google Cloud CDN uses the entire **Uniform Resource Locator** (**URL**) to generate a key that is used for content searching in the CDN. Sometimes, if the static content must be available independently from the protocol (HTTP or HTTPS), you can configure a custom cache key that includes both scenarios. Thus, you can improve the cache hit ratio and reduce latency.

Now that you have learned how to optimize latency in Google Cloud VPC, let's have a look at how to design network security in GCP.

Network security design strategy

Google takes information security very seriously. When it comes to designing a secure cloud network infrastructure, Google Cloud has a clear way of how you should achieve this. The best practices recommended by the Google Cloud security team can be listed as follows:

- **Manage traffic with firewall rules**: All the traffic to and from cloud assets should be controlled using firewall rules. GCE instances and GKE clusters should receive only the traffic they need to serve. Google recommends applying firewall rules to groups of VMs with service accounts or **tags**. This helps in better administering which traffic should be received by groups of VMs. For example, you can create a firewall rule that allows HTTPS traffic to all GCE instances that stay in a MIG by using a dedicated tag such as `webserver`.

- **Limit external access**: Avoid as much as possible exposing your GCE instances to the internet. If they need to connect to public services such as operating system updates, you should deploy **Cloud NAT** to let all the VMs in one region go out to reach external services. In cases where they just have to connect to GCP **application programming interfaces (APIs)** and services such as Google Cloud Storage, you can enable **Google Private Access** on the subnet and still maintain private IP addresses to the VMs.

- **Centralize network control**: In large GCP organizations, where resources need to communicate with each other privately and they are part of different projects, it is recommended to use one **shared VPC** under one network administration. This should be an **Identity and Access Management (IAM) role** with the least number of permissions that allow network administrators to configure subnets, routes, firewall rules, and so on for all the projects in the organization.

- **Interconnect privately to your on-premises network**: Based on your network bandwidth, latency, and **service-level agreement** (SLA) requirements, you should consider either **Cloud Interconnect** options (Dedicated or Partner) or Cloud VPN in order to avoid traversing the internet to connect your on-premises network. You should choose Cloud Interconnect when you require low-latency, highly scalable, and reliable connectivity for transferring sensitive data. On the other hand, you can use Cloud VPN to transfer data using **IP Security (IPsec)**.

- **Secure your application and data**: Remember that securing your application and data in the cloud is a shared responsibility between Google Cloud and you. However, Google Cloud offers additional tools to help secure your application and data. Indeed, you can adopt **VPC Service Controls** to define a security perimeter to constrain data in a VPC and avoid data exfiltration. Additionally, you can add **Google Cloud Armor** to your HTTP(S) load balancer to defend your application from **distributed denial-of-service (DDoS)** attacks and untrusted IP addresses. Moreover, you can control who can access your application with Google Cloud **Identity-Aware Proxy (IAP)**.

- **Control access to resources**: Prevent unwanted access to GCP resources by assigning IAM roles with the least privileged approach. Only the necessary access should be granted to your resources running in Google Cloud projects. The recommendation is to assign IAM roles to groups of accounts that share the same responsibilities instead of assigning them to individuals' accounts. In cases where we have services that need access to other GCP services (a GCE instance connects to Google Cloud Storage), it is recommended to assign IAM roles to a service account.

In this section, you have learned what the failover strategies and the options for HA are. Then, you went through the best practices for DNS in a hybrid environment, and you learned what are the recommendations for load balancing. Finally, you learned strategies for minimizing latency and improving security. In the next section, you will learn how to design your VPC in GCP.

Designing a VPC

Imagine being a **network engineer**. You oversee the design and implementation of a physical network. To do that, you will need some network equipment—such as switches and routers, and cables that will connect the devices to each other—and you must choose and configure an IP addressing plan.

The same thing happens when your network is not a physical one to be implemented in a real environment, but you face a virtual environment within GCP, whose goal is to allow communication among the various Google Cloud services.

The technology that allows you to do that is called **software-defined networking** (**SDN**) and there are a lot of implementations of that. The VPC in GCP is implemented inside of Google's production network, and the network virtualization stack is called Andromeda, which is defined in the paper *Andromeda: Performance, Isolation, and Velocity at Scale in Cloud Network Virtualization*.

A VPC is a virtual network that provides connectivity for your GCE VM instances, including other Google Cloud products built on GCE VMs, such as **Google App Engine** (**GAE**) flexible environments and GKE clusters.

By default, in every new project, a default VPC is present whose name is `default`, as you can see in *Figure 2.6*. The default VPC is an auto-mode VPC network that has one subnetwork in each region.

While a VPC network is a global resource that is not associated with any region, subnets are regionally bound resources, and they define a range of IP addresses.

In every project, you can have more than one VPC. This is useful whenever you need to create virtually isolated environments in your project. This does not mean that you cannot make VMs communicate between different VPCs. Later in this chapter, we will explain how to allow interconnection between different VPCs.

You can see an overview of the default VPC in the following screenshot:

Name ↑	Region	Subnets	MTU ❓	Mode	IP address ranges	Gateways
▼ default		28	1460	Auto		
	us-central1	default			10.128.0.0/20	10.128.0.1
	europe-west1	default			10.132.0.0/20	10.132.0.1
	us-west1	default			10.138.0.0/20	10.138.0.1
	asia-east1	default			10.140.0.0/20	10.140.0.1
	us-east1	default			10.142.0.0/20	10.142.0.1
	asia-northeast1	default			10.146.0.0/20	10.146.0.1
	asia-southeast1	default			10.148.0.0/20	10.148.0.1
	us-east4	default			10.150.0.0/20	10.150.0.1
	australia-southeast1	default			10.152.0.0/20	10.152.0.1
	europe-west2	default			10.154.0.0/20	10.154.0.1
	europe-west3	default			10.156.0.0/20	10.156.0.1
	southamerica-east1	default			10.158.0.0/20	10.158.0.1
	asia-south1	default			10.160.0.0/20	10.160.0.1
	northamerica-northeast1	default			10.162.0.0/20	10.162.0.1
	europe-west4	default			10.164.0.0/20	10.164.0.1
	europe-north1	default			10.166.0.0/20	10.166.0.1
	us-west2	default			10.168.0.0/20	10.168.0.1
	asia-east2	default			10.170.0.0/20	10.170.0.1
	europe-west6	default			10.172.0.0/20	10.172.0.1
	asia-northeast2	default			10.174.0.0/20	10.174.0.1
	asia-northeast3	default			10.178.0.0/20	10.178.0.1
	us-west3	default			10.180.0.0/20	10.180.0.1
	us-west4	default			10.182.0.0/20	10.182.0.1
	asia-southeast2	default			10.184.0.0/20	10.184.0.1
	europe-central2	default			10.186.0.0/20	10.186.0.1
	northamerica-northeast2	default			10.188.0.0/20	10.188.0.1
	asia-south2	default			10.190.0.0/20	10.190.0.1

Figure 2.6 – Default VPC overview

In the next section, you will go through how to design your subnets and their IP ranges.

CIDR range for subnets

You cannot use your VPC network without adding at least one subnet, either in **Automatic mode** or in **Custom mode**.

Indeed, there are two ways to define IP address ranges in a VPC network: **Custom mode** and **Automatic mode**. More detail on these two modes is provided here:

- In **Automatic mode**, Google will assign for you a "default" IP address range for each subnet (one subnet per region), the same as the default VPC.

- **Custom mode** allows you to manually define regions and subnets (IP address ranges) that you want to assign to the resources that you will use in the VPC. Please note that no overlapping IP addresses are allowed in the same VPC.

In **Automatic mode**, when you create a VPC, Google Cloud will create one subnet in each Google Cloud region automatically. The IP address ranges for these subnets come from a predefined set of ranges that fit inside the `10.128.0.0/9` **classless inter-domain routing (CIDR)** block, as shown in the following table:

Region	IP range (CIDR)	Default gateway	Usable addresses (inclusive)
asia-east1	10.140.0.0/20	10.140.0.1	`10.140.0.2 to 10.140.15.253`
asia-east2	10.170.0.0/20	10.170.0.1	`10.170.0.2 to 10.170.15.253`
asia-northeast1	10.146.0.0/20	10.146.0.1	`10.146.0.2 to 10.146.15.253`
asia-northeast2	10.174.0.0/20	10.174.0.1	`10.174.0.2 to 10.174.15.253`
asia-northeast3	10.178.0.0/20	10.178.0.1	`10.178.0.2 to 10.178.15.253`
asia-south1	10.160.0.0/20	10.160.0.1	`10.160.0.2 to 10.160.15.253`
asia-southeast1	10.148.0.0/20	10.148.0.1	`10.148.0.2 to 10.148.15.253`
asia-southeast2	10.184.0.0/20	10.184.0.1	`10.184.0.2 to 10.184.15.253`
australia-southeast1	10.152.0.0/20	10.152.0.1	`10.152.0.2 to 10.152.15.253`
europe-north1	10.166.0.0/20	10.166.0.1	`10.166.0.2 to 10.166.15.253`

Region	IP range (CIDR)	Default gateway	Usable addresses (inclusive)
europe-west1	10.132.0.0/20	10.132.0.1	`10.132.0.2 to 10.132.15.253`
europe-west2	10.154.0.0/20	10.154.0.1	`10.154.0.2 to 10.154.15.253`
europe-west3	10.156.0.0/20	10.156.0.1	`10.156.0.2 to 10.156.15.253`
europe-west4	10.164.0.0/20	10.164.0.1	`10.164.0.2 to 10.164.15.253`
europe-west6	10.172.0.0/20	10.172.0.1	`10.172.0.2 to 10.172.15.253`
northamerica-northeast1	10.162.0.0/20	10.162.0.1	`10.162.0.2 to 10.162.15.253`
southamerica-east1	10.158.0.0/20	10.158.0.1	`10.158.0.2 to 10.158.15.253`
us-central1	10.128.0.0/20	10.128.0.1	`10.128.0.2 to 10.128.15.253`
us-east1	10.142.0.0/20	10.142.0.1	`10.142.0.2 to 10.142.15.253`
us-east4	10.150.0.0/20	10.150.0.1	`10.150.0.2 to 10.150.15.253`
us-west1	10.138.0.0/20	10.138.0.1	`10.138.0.2 to 10.138.15.253`
us-west2	10.168.0.0/20	10.168.0.1	`10.168.0.2 to 10.168.15.253`
us-west3	10.180.0.0/20	10.180.0.1	`10.180.0.2 to 10.180.15.253`
us-west4	10.182.0.0/20	10.182.0.1	`10.182.0.2 to 10.182.15.253`

Table 2.1 – Classless InterDomain Routing blocks in the VPC regions present at the time of the publication of this book; you should expect more regions in the future with additional IP subnet ranges for those new regions

In **Custom mode**, Google Cloud does not automatically create any subnet in your VPC. Remember, you must create at least one subnet to make your VPC usable with your VMs. In **Custom mode**, you must select a primary IP address range. VM instances, internal load balancers, and internal protocol forwarding addresses come from this range.

The following table lists possible valid ranges for custom subnet IP addresses:

Range	Description
10.0.0.0/8 172.16.0.0/12 192.168.0.0/16	Private IP addresses (**Request for Comments (RFC)** *1918*)
100.64.0.0/10	Shared address space (*RFC 6598*)
192.0.0.0/24	**Internet Engineering Task Force (IETF)** protocol assignments (*RFC 6890*)
192.0.2.0/24 (TEST-NET-1) 198.51.100.0/24 (TEST-NET-2) 203.0.113.0/24 (TEST-NET-3)	Documentation (*RFC 5737*)
192.88.99.0/24	**IP version 6 (IPv6)** to **IP version 4 (IPv4)** relay—deprecated (*RFC 7526*)
198.18.0.0/15	Benchmark testing (*RFC 2544*)
240.0.0.0/4	Reserved for future use—Class E (*RFC 5735* and *RFC 1112*)
Privately used public IP addresses	You can use any IP address that is not part of the RFC ranges listed in this table and not part of a restricted set, but please note that Google Cloud does not announce these routes to the internet and does not route traffic from the internet to them.

Table 2.2 – IP ranges for custom subnets in VPC

Some commonly reserved RFC ranges are not allowed in Google Cloud custom subnets, as outlined in the following table:

Range	Description
Some public IP addresses for Google APIs and services, including Google Cloud netblocks	Please find them at `https://gstatic.com/ipranges/goog.txt`
`199.36.153.4/30` and `199.36.153.8/30`	Private Google access-specific virtual IP addresses
`0.0.0.0/8`	Current (local) network (*RFC 1122*)
`127.0.0.0/8`	Localhost (*RFC 1122*)
`169.254.0.0/16`	Link-local (*RFC 3927*)
`224.0.0.0/4`	Multicast—Class D (*RFC 5771*)
`255.255.255.255/32`	Limited broadcast destination address (*RFC 8190* and *RFC 919*)

Table 2.3 – Reserved IP ranges in VPC subnets

> **Tip**
> You could also select a secondary IP address for your subnet. This secondary IP address could be used by your VMs to expose different services as well as Pods in GKE.

What is the preferrable choice between **Automatic mode** and **Custom mode**? Auto mode is a useful "quick and dirty" way to have your VPC working in every region. On the other hand, please use custom mode whenever you are in a situation such as this:

- You want to avoid overlapping IP addresses between your VPC and other VPCs.

- You plan to interconnect your VPC with other VPCs or with on-premises resources (we will see how to do that in a later section).

> **Important Note**
> You can convert a VPC subnet only once and only from auto mode to custom mode, preserving the IP addresses. The reverse conversion is not allowed.

Please remember that in every subnet, four IP addresses from the primary range are reserved, as shown in the following table:

Reserved IP address	Description	Example
Network	First address in the primary IP range for the subnet	`172.16.10.0` in `172.16.10.0/24`
Default gateway	Second address in the primary IP range for the subnet	`172.16.10.1` in `172.16.10.0/24`
Second-to-last address	Second-to-last address in the primary IP range for the subnet that is reserved by Google Cloud for potential future use	`172.16.10.254` in `172.16.10.0/24`
Broadcast	Last address in the primary IP range for the subnet	`172.16.10.255` in `172.16.10.0/24`

Table 2.4 – Reserved IP addresses in VPC subnets

Important Note

At the time of writing this book, Google Cloud VPC networks only support IPv4 unicast traffic. Neither multicast nor broadcast IPv4 traffic is supported, nor IPv6 traffic within the VPC. Despite that, you could create an IPv6 address for a global load balancer.

Your subnet can have primary and secondary CIDR ranges. This is useful if you want to maintain network separation between the VMs and the services running on them. One common use case is GKE. Indeed, worker Nodes get the IP address from the primary CIDR, while Pods have a separate CIDR range in the same subnet. This scenario is referred to as **alias IPs** in Google Cloud. Indeed, with alias IPs, you can configure multiple internal IP addresses in different CIDR ranges without having to define a separate network interface on the VM.

IP addressing

The IP address ranges that we talked about in the previous section are *internal addresses*—that is, addresses that are not advertised on the public internet.

> **Important Note**
>
> Please do not be confused with internal, external, private, and public addresses. When we speak about public and private addresses, we refer to *RFC 1918* (*Address Allocation for Private Internets*), in which the **Internet Assigned Numbers Authority** (**IANA**) has reserved the following three blocks of the IP address space for private internets: `10.0.0.0 - 10.255.255.255` (10/8 prefix); `172.16.0.0 - 172.31.255.255` (172.16/12 prefix); `192.168.0.0 -192.168.255.255` (192.168/16 prefix). All the other addresses are potentially public addresses.
>
> With internal and external addresses, on the other hand, we refer to addresses assigned to Google Cloud resources that can be publicly accessible via the internet (external addresses), or not (internal addresses).

In Google Cloud, internal addresses can be private addresses (from *RFC 1918*) or public addresses that are reserved for internal use only. External IPs, on the other hand, must be publicly routable; otherwise, it would not be possible to reach them through the internet.

When you use VM instances (including GKE Nodes, Pods, and services), internal load balancing (either **TCP/UDP load balancing or HTTP(S) Load Balancing**), and internal protocol forwarding, the assigned IP addresses are internal and labeled as *regional*.

For private services' access, your resource will be assigned *global* internal IP addresses.

Static IP and ephemeral IP addresses

Whatever IP address you are using, be it an internal or an external one, it can be static or ephemeral.

By default, the IP addresses that are assigned to your resource have a lifetime that is related to the life of the resource itself; so, that IP address will be released when your resource is deleted (or stopped), and the next time you create a new resource, a new IP address will be assigned to it.

On the other hand, if you plan to assign a static IP address to your resource so that the IP address lifetime is beyond the lifetime of your resource, you must reserve that IP (and you could incur additional charges if you reserve an external IP address, even when you are not using it).

The following diagram shows how static IP address reservation will happen in the VPC:

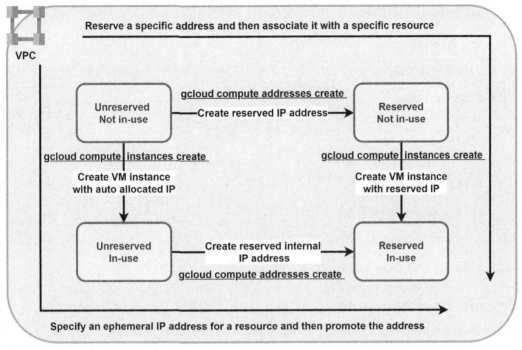

Figure 2.7 – Static IP address reservation

You can see in *Figure 2.7* the two ways to reserve a static IP address (either internal or external), as described in more detail here:

- You can start a new resource with an ephemeral address and then promote it to a static IP address.
- You can reserve a static IP address and only after that create an associated resource.

Routes

In every GCP VPC, you can find a **routing table** that defines the path (physical or virtual) that your IP packet follows whenever it starts from a VM and tries to reach some other destination, be it internal or external to your VPC. The routing table is defined at the VPC level and it is composed of many routes whose order of applicability is defined depending on some predefined rules.

Each route is composed of a single destination prefix and a unique next hop.

There are three types of routes, as outlined here:

1. **System-generated routes**

    • Default route

    • Subnet routes

2. **Custom routes**

    • Static routes

    • Dynamic routes

3. **Peering routes**

    • Peering subnet routes

    • Peering custom routes

Let's look at each of these in the next sections.

System-generated routes

System-generated routes are spawned automatically whenever you create a VPC network.

Default route

The system-generated default route (`0.0.0.0/0`) is the *gateway of last resort* used by your packet to leave your VPC whenever a more specific route is not present in the routing table. It is the default path toward every out-of-VPC destination, including the public internet and private Google access (more on that later). If you want to control your outward traffic, you could delete this route. The default route priority is `1,000`.

Subnet routes

Every created subnet in your VPC implies an automatic route added by Google Cloud pointing to the subnet's primary IP address range (and another route pointing to the secondary IP address range if it is defined). The subnet route priority is 0 (the highest priority).

Custom routes

To have customized routes in the VPC routing table, you can add them statically or dynamically.

Static routes

You can create a static route manually inside your VPC (defining the destination prefix, the priority, the next hop, and an optional tag), by means of the Google Cloud console (`gcloud compute routes create`) or the `routes.insert` API.

Dynamic routes

If you want to leverage dynamic routes, you must us Cloud Router (more on that later). A dynamic route is a route that your Cloud Router service learns by means of the **Border Gateway Protocol (BGP)**.

Peering routes

As we will see in the next section, we can interconnect with more than one VPC, and so we need to exchange routing information among them. That is the reason we can have peering routes.

Peering subnet routes

Peering subnet routes represent the necessary information to reach any resource located in any other VPC that we created some peering with.

Peering custom routes

We have peering custom routes when we configure peer networks to export or import user-defined static or dynamic routes.

Note on BGP

BGP is the most important (and only) routing protocol used nowadays on the internet to make every network aware of the direction to follow to reach any other network in the world. It is considered an **exterior gateway protocol (EGP)** because it is used mainly to exchange routing information among different **autonomous systems (ASes)**, which are networks under the control of a single administrative entity. When we establish BGP sessions between routers belonging to different ASes, we refer to them as **external BGP (EBGP)** sessions.

BGP can also be used to exchange IP prefixes between routers belonging to the same AS. In such a case, we refer to them as **internal BGP (IBGP)** sessions.

EGPs are the opposite of **interior gateway protocols (IGPs)**, which, on the contrary, are used only internally in any AS, to get full IP reachability for all the prefixes that belong to them. Some examples of IGPs are **Open Shortest Path First (OSPF)**, **Intermediate System to Intermediate System (IS-IS)**, and **Enhanced Interior Gateway Routing Protocol (EIGRP)**. In GCP, we take care of BGP only.

Routes order

The route selection process makes a lookup on the routing table adhering to the following criteria:

1. Longest prefix match

2. Route priority

3. Route type and next hop

Longest prefix match

As per *RFC 1812* (*Requirements for IP Version 4 Routers*), the main criterion to select the best route for any destination is the "longest prefix match", which means selecting the route with the longest prefix among all the routes whose destination prefix matches the IP packet destination address. Here is an extract from *RFC 1812*, *Section 5.2.4.3 (2)*:

"*For example, if a packet's IP Destination Address is 10.144.2.5 and there are network prefixes 10.144.2.0/24, 10.144.0.0/16, and 10.0.0.0/8, then this rule would keep only the first (10.144.2.0/24) because its prefix length is longest.*"

Following the preceding rule, in GCP the subnet routes come first as you are not allowed to define any custom route that has an equal or more specific destination than any subnet route or any peering subnet route.

Route priority

If more than one route has the same most specific destination, Google Cloud prefers the route with the highest set priority (please note that the highest priority corresponds to the lowest number, so a route priority 100 is higher than a route priority 200).

Route type and next hop

If, after the previous criteria, we still have more than one route with the same prefix length and the same priority, the preference criteria are as follows:

1. Custom static routes are the first choice if the next hop is one of the following:

    *   Next-hop instance

    *   Next-hop IP

    *   Next-hop **virtual private network** (**VPN**) tunnel

2. Custom dynamic routes are selected if no custom static routes are present.

3. Custom static routes whose next hop is an internal TCP/UDP load balancer.

4. Custom static routes whose next hop is the default internet gateway.

Now that you have learned how Google Cloud builds a VPC routing table, let's go on to learn how to design interconnections between two or more VPCs.

Shared VPC versus VPC Network Peering

When it comes to designing interconnections between two or more VPCs in Google Cloud, you have two options, as outlined here:

- **Shared VPC**: This option allows multiple projects within the same organization to share one VPC.

- **VPC Network Peering**: This option allows two or more VPCs to be interconnected even if they belong to different projects or organizations.

In the following sections, we will understand what these features are and when we should choose them.

Shared VPC

Sometimes within your organization, you might have projects that have resources that need to be interconnected. They can be GCE instances, GCE services, or just Cloud Function instances. Because these services are in different projects, you are required to configure and manage a VPC for each project you have, and—more importantly—you must handle VPC interconnections. This is clearly not what you want. Indeed, you can leverage Google Shared VPC, which allows you to configure one VPC that can be shared across different projects. Therefore, projects do not need a VPC to deploy their services, and these services can communicate securely in the same VPC. Moreover, Shared VPC is under the responsibility of one unique administrator that has the IAM role of **Shared VPC Admin**. Project administrators can use Shared VPC, but they cannot make any changes to it. This improves security and stability, making it easier to deploy GCP services within the organization.

Shared VPC has the following components in its architecture:

- **Host project**: This is a project that contains one or more Shared VPC networks. It is created by the Shared VPC Admin and can have one or more service projects attached to it.

- **Service project**: This is any project that is attached to a host project. This can be done by the Shared VPC Admin. The service project belongs to only one host project.

When you create a Shared VPC network, you need to decide whether to use automatic or custom mode. The recommendation is to use custom mode in order to have full control of the subnet addresses. Moreover, you need to decide how to share subnets with service projects. Here, you have the following two options:

- **Share all subnets**: This option allows you to share all subnets created in the host project VPC with all service projects.

- **Share some subnets**: This option allows you to control which subnet can be shared with service projects.

The following diagram shows a basic example of a Shared VPC scenario:

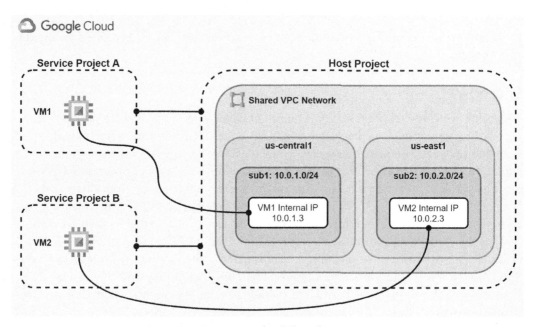

Figure 2.8 – Basic example of Shared VPC scenario

As you can see from *Figure 2.8*, the host project has the VPC network that contains one subnet for each GCP region. Additionally, the host project has two **service projects** attached. You will note that service projects do not have any VPC network. However, they can deploy GCE instances that get private IP addresses from the region in which they run.

> **Important Note**
>
> The communication between resources in service projects depends on the sharing policy adopted in the Shared VPC and on the firewall rules applied.

If you need to interconnect Shared VPC with your on-premises network, this must be done through the host project. For example, if you are using Cloud VPN as an interconnection solution, this service must be deployed in the Shared VPC that is contained within the host project. The following diagram shows an example of hybrid connectivity with Shared VPC:

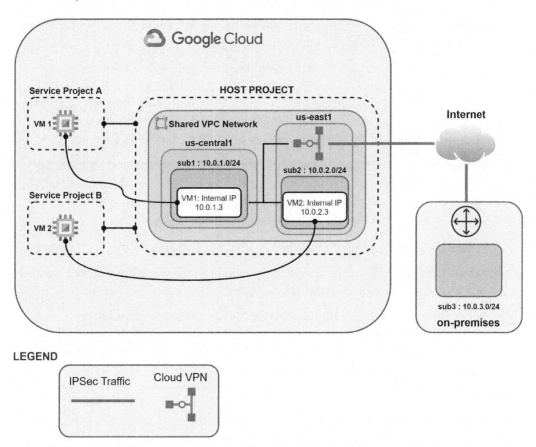

Figure 2.9 – Hybrid connectivity with Cloud VPN and Shared VPC

Now that you have learned how to use Shared VPC to interconnect different projects within your organization, let's move to the next section with VPC Network Peering.

VPC Network Peering

A clever design for your cloud solution is always based on a **separation of duties (SoD)**. The same idea is true for your **cloud networking** design.

From a networking point of view, this means that it is always a promising idea to use more than one VPC network—one for every network administrative domain in your organization. This way, every VPC network maintains its own administration—for routes, firewalls, VPNs, and other traffic management tools.

So, with that said, even with many VPC, most of the time you want to keep the IP reachability of every resource in your organization, be they in the same VPC or not. That is the main reason Google Cloud provides us with a way to exchange routing information among different VPCs and allow us to reach any resource in our organization, even though it could be attached to a different VPC network: **VPC Network Peering**.

First, let's specify that VPC Network Peering is a way to exchange internal IP addresses among different VPCs (meaning that it is not possible to exchange external reachability information with that). Indeed, this is done on purpose, with the goal of granting advantages of avoiding external IP addresses, including the following:

- **Network security**: The services do not need to be exposed to the public internet.

- **Network latency**: All the traffic remains confined to the Google worldwide network, which is engineered for low-latency transport.

- **Network cost**: As a rule of thumb, Google Cloud charges you an additional cost (as an egress bandwidth price) for whichever traffic uses external IPs, even if your traffic is within the same zone; using VPC Network Peering, you only pay for the regular network pricing.

As described in the previous section, through VPC Network Peering you can exchange IP routes, subnet routes, or custom routes.

Subnet routes are automatically exchanged between VPCs if they do not use privately used public IP addresses. However, you can export them explicitly. You must explicitly export custom routes, these being static or dynamic.

Note that you must avoid IP overlaps between VPCs to allow VPC Network Peering to be established.

VPC Network Peering is not transitive, so (for example), if you have three VPCs—VPC A, VPC B, and VPC C—and you have one VPC Network Peering between VPC A and VPC B and another VPC Network Peering between VPC B and VPC C, then the following traffic is allowed:

- VPC A can communicate with VPC B and vice versa.

- VPC B can communicate with VPC C and vice versa.

Transit traffic is not allowed, as outlined here:

- VPC A cannot communicate with VPC C. If you want them to communicate with each other, you should configure a new VPC Network Peering, between VPC A and VPC C explicitly.

Now that you have learned what VPC Network Peering is and how you can design inter-VPC communication, let's move on to the next topic: firewall rules.

Firewall rules

So far, we have focused on how to allow communication (at IP level) among the resources that are in your VPCs. Having IP reachability is not enough to ensure the information exchange between them. Indeed, you need to deploy firewall rules in your VPC in order to let GCE instances and other GCP resources (such as GKE, Cloud SQL, or GAE) send or receive traffic. Firewall rules are applied at the VPC network level and they work as a distributed firewall. Therefore, they do not reside on a physical device that may cause a bottleneck, but they are instead distributed into the VPC and applied at the GCE instance level.

Firewall rules have the following specifications:

- They are applied to one VPC network.

- They are **stateful**. There is no need to write a rule for returning traffic.

- They can control inbound traffic (**ingress** rule) and outbound traffic (**egress** rule).

- The direction of the traffic is always evaluated from the GCP resource (that is, GCE instance) perspective.

- They have a *target* that indicates to whom the firewall rule is applied. It can be all GCE instances or a subgroup of them (referenced by a tag). It can refer to an IAM service account as well.

- They are sorted by *priority* and they are evaluated from the lowest to the highest.

- They have a *condition* to match. This includes the source or destination of the traffic (depending on the direction of the traffic), and the protocol used by the application.

- They include one *action* to take if the condition is met. It can be either **Allow** or **Deny**.

> **Important Note**
>
> There are two implied rules to always consider. A VPC network has an egress rule to allow traffic to any destination IP address (to `0.0.0.0/0`). On the other hand, it also has an ingress rule to deny any traffic coming from any network (from `0.0.0.0/0`).

In GCP, you can enforce security even further by applying **hierarchical firewall policies**. These policies can work together with VPC firewall policies in order to provide different levels of security within the GCP organization. Indeed, you can configure firewall policies at the organization or at the folder level. They can contain rules that allow or deny connections, as VPC firewall rules do. Additionally, hierarchical firewall rules can delegate evaluation rules to lower-level policies by using a `goto_next` action.

Hierarchical firewall policies are like VPC network policies. They differ from them on the following points:

- Every rule within a policy must have a different priority that decides the evaluation order.

- In addition to **Allow/Deny** actions, rules can evaluate lower-level policies with the `goto_next` action.

- Using a tag in a target is not supported. Only networks and service accounts can be used.

In this section, you have learned how to design your VPC in terms of IP address ranges for your subnet, how routing is implemented in GCP, and how to design VPC interconnection. In the following section, you will go through designing **hybrid networks**.

Designing a hybrid network

In this section, you will learn how to design the hybrid networking between your on-premises subnets and your Google Cloud VPC subnets. You will understand which solutions Google Cloud offers you in terms of interconnections and when these should be used. **Dedicated Interconnect**, **Partner Interconnect**, **Direct** and **Partner Peering**, and **Cloud VPN** will be explained in order to give you a broad view of all possible interconnection solutions. Additionally, you will learn what Cloud Router is and how you can use it to build failover and DR strategies for your hybrid networking.

Cloud Interconnect design (for example, Dedicated versus Partner)

When it comes to designing interconnections between your on-premises network and Google Cloud VPC, the first thing you must consider is the location of your on-premises edge network. Indeed, if your network meets the Google Cloud network in a supported colocation facility, then a **virtual local-area network (VLAN) attachment** can be configured between your on-premises network and Google Edge device in a **point of presence (PoP)**. You can find an up-to-date list of Google PoPs at the following link: `https://cloud.google.com/network-connectivity/docs/interconnect/concepts/choosing-colocation-facilities#locations-table`.

In this list, you can find the **facility provider** based on the region closer to your on-premises network that will host your routers and will help to build the circuit to Google Cloud Routers. If you can bring your own devices to the facility provider, you are eligible for the Dedicated Interconnect solution. Actually, you are also eligible for Dedicated Interconnect by connecting your device from a remote location to the facility provider's location via a Layer 1 circuit such as dark fiber or 10Gbps optical wave circuits. This will be the best Cloud Interconnect option you can have in terms of reliability, throughput, and latency. Indeed, with Dedicated Interconnect, you can have a dedicated physical link on which you can build a dedicated VLAN attachment with a **Google peering edge**. However, your router must have some technical requirements in order to get attached to a Google peering edge. These are listed here:

- 10/100Gbps circuits with single-mode fiber: **The Institute of Electrical and Electronics Engineers (IEEE)** 10GBASE-LR (1310) and IEEE 100GBASE-LR4 optics
- IPv4 link-local addressing
- **Link Aggregation Control Protocol (LACP)** even with one single circuit
- EBGP-4 with multi-hop
- IEEE 802.1Q VLANs

If the technical requirements can be met, you can build dedicated interconnection to your VPC that includes multiple Ethernet links (up to 8 for 10 gigabits per second and 2 for 100 gigabits per second), each one carrying 10 or 100 gigabits per second of maximum throughput.

The following diagram shows a single Dedicated Interconnect connection between your on-premises network and Google Cloud VPC:

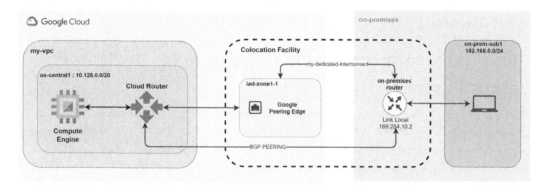

Figure 2.10 – Single Dedicated Interconnect connection

As you will have noticed in *Figure 2.10*, when creating a Dedicated Interconnect connection to connect your on-premises network with your Google Cloud VPC, you are required to build a BGP peering with Cloud Router. Cloud Router could be deployed in the same region in which you have the Google peering edge, but this is not mandatory. Google has backbone connectivity and SDN between all interconnect edge POPs and every region within a continent. So—for example—in Europe, if your physical Interconnect is in a facility provider in London, you can build a VLAN attachment and BGP session to Cloud Router, not only in the London region but to all other regions in Europe. There is no restriction between Interconnect POP and region. This is a great advantage that Google has over other cloud providers.

Since it establishes a BGP session to Google public **AS number** (**ASN**) 15169, Direct Peering forces you to have a public routable ASN assigned to your company. Moreover, your BGP peering must be negotiated with link-local addresses. In Dedicated Interconnect and Partner Interconnect, a private ASN is used on GCP and on-premises.

> **Important Note**
>
> With Direct Peering, Google Cloud requires you to have 24/7 **network operations center** (**NOC**) contact and up-to-date maintainer, ASN, AS-SET, and router objects in the **Internet Routing Registry** (**IRR**).
>
> Also, note that if your workload requires super-low latency (< 5 **milliseconds** (**ms**)) between your on-premises VMs and GCE instances, you must refer to the following list of colocation facilities: `https://cloud.google.com/network-connectivity/docs/interconnect/concepts/choosing-colocation-facilities-low-latency#locations-table`.

In the unlucky event that you are far from one of the colocation facilities, you can always rely on a Google Cloud-supported **service provider** (**SP**). An up-to-date list of all available partner SPs can be found at the following link: `https://cloud.google.com/network-connectivity/docs/interconnect/concepts/service-providers#by-provider`.

Other than being far from a colocation facility, there are more reasons to choose Partner Interconnect over Dedicated Interconnect. The main reason to use Partner Interconnect is when you require flexible bandwidth from 50 megabits per second to 50 gigabits per second (Dedicated Interconnect only gives multiple of 10 gigabits per second and 100 gigabits per second). Another reason is for customers that do not meet the device hardware requirement.

When your Cloud Interconnect design requires an SP to reach the Google Cloud network, you are configuring a Partner Interconnect solution. It comes with two connectivity options, as outlined here:

- **Layer 2 connectivity**: This emulates an Ethernet circuit across the SP network and thus allows your on-premises router to be virtually interconnected with the Google peering edge. With this solution, you are required to configure BGP peering between your on-premises router and Cloud Router in your VPC.

- **Layer 3 connectivity**: This provides IP connectivity between your on-premises router and Cloud Router in your VPC. With this option, you do not configure BGP peering with Cloud Router. Instead, the GCP partner SP establishes BGP peering with Cloud Router and extends the IP connectivity to your on-premises router. Since Cloud Router only supports BGP dynamic routing, you cannot use a static route in VPC pointing to the interconnect. Of course, the customer can configure static or dynamic routing in their on-premises router.

The following diagram shows one of the options that you can have in your Partner Interconnect design:

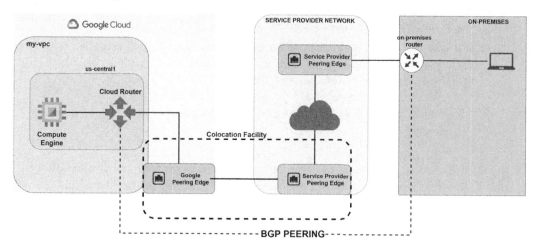

Figure 2.11 – Layer 2 Partner Interconnect

The following diagram shows another option that you can have in your Partner Interconnect design:

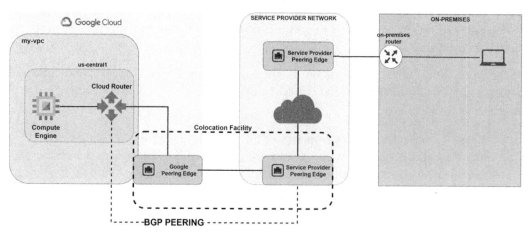

Figure 2.12 – Layer 3 Partner Interconnect

With Partner Interconnect, you can design a Cloud interconnect service between your on-premises network and the VPC that includes multiple virtual circuits that range from 50 megabits per second to 50 gigabits per second each. The throughput of each virtual circuit depends on the supported SP.

With both Dedicated Interconnect and Partner Interconnect, you can design a Cloud interconnect solution to exchange private IP addresses (that is, *RFC 1918*) between your on-premises network and your VPC in Google Cloud. These interconnection solutions are considered private, and they do not traverse over the internet. Additionally, they offer an SLA and thus they should be considered when your Cloud interconnect runs business-critical traffic.

In terms of pricing, both Cloud Interconnect solutions have costs to be considered in your network design. They are listed in the tables shown next, starting with Dedicated Interconnect:

Dedicated Interconnect pricing table	
Resource	Price
Interconnect Connection	US Dollar (USD) $2.328 per hour per 10-Gbps circuit $18.05 per hour per 100-Gbps circuit
50-, 100-, 200-, 300-, 400-, or 500-Mbps VLAN attachment	$0.10 per hour per VLAN attachment
1-, 2-, 5-, or 10-Gbps VLAN attachment	$0.10 per hour per VLAN attachment
20-Gbps VLAN attachment	$0.20 per hour per VLAN attachment
50-Gbps VLAN attachment	$0.50 per hour per VLAN attachment

Table 2.5 – Pricing table of Dedicated Interconnect options

> **Note**
>
> Up-to-date pricing information can be found at `https://cloud.google.com/network-connectivity/docs/interconnect/pricing#dedicated-interconnect-pricing`.

You may notice that there is a fixed price for the interconnection in the Dedicated Interconnect pricing table, depending on which Ethernet circuit you choose. This is different in Partner Interconnect since you are not attached directly to a GCP device. You can see this in the following table, which shows the prices of Partner Interconnect:

Partner Interconnect pricing table	
VLAN attachment capacity	Price
50 Mbps	$0.05417 per hour per VLAN attachment
100 Mbps	$0.0625 per hour per VLAN attachment
200 Mbps	$0.08333 per hour per VLAN attachment
300 Mbps	$0.1111 per hour per VLAN attachment
400 Mbps	$0.1389 per hour per VLAN attachment
500 Mbps	$0.1736 per hour per VLAN attachment
1 Gbps	$0.2778 per hour per VLAN attachment
2 Gbps	$0.5694 per hour per VLAN attachment
5 Gbps	$1.25 per hour per VLAN attachment
10 Gbps	$2.36 per hour per VLAN attachment
20 Gbps	$3.61 per hour per VLAN attachment
50 Gbps	$9.02 per hour per VLAN attachment

Table 2.6 – Pricing table of Partner Interconnect options

For both Cloud Interconnect solutions, there is an egress traffic charge, which depends on the amount of data (measured in **gigabytes (GB)**) and the region your traffic is exiting. The good news is that ingress traffic is never charged in Google Cloud interconnection. The following table shows the pricing for egress traffic:

Egress traffic pricing table	
Region	Price
Asia (asia-east1, asia-east2, asia-northeast1, asia-northeast2, asia-northeast3, asia-south1, asia-southeast1, asia-southeast2)	$0.042 per GB
Europe (europe-north1, europe-west1, europe-west2, europe-west3, europe-west4, europe-west6)	$0.02 per GB
North America (northamerica-northeast1, us-central1, us-east1, us-east4, us-west1, us-west2, us-west3, us-west4)	$0.02 per GB
South America (southamerica-east1)	$0.06 per GB
Australia (australia-southeast1)	$0.042 per GB

Table 2.7 – Pricing Table for VPC egress traffic

> **Important Note**
> With a Partner Interconnect solution, you must consider the SP additional cost in the total amount.

Now that you have learned how to design Dedicated and Partner Interconnect, let's go on to see which peering options you can choose from GCP.

Peering options (Direct versus Carrier)

The main reason to consider peering options in your design is when you want to publicly access Google Cloud services and APIs from your on-premises network. Indeed, Google allows you to exchange BGP public routes with your on-premises network by establishing BGP peering.

You can establish BGP peering with Google Cloud with two peering options, as follows:

- **Direct Peering**: This is a co-located option that requires you to have your physical device attached to a Google edge device available at a private co-location facility. Here, you can exchange BGP public routes directly with Google AS (ASN 15169). Direct Peering allows you to connect directly to public IP addresses of Google services and Google Cloud products. Note: if customers connect to a public exchange, this is not direct peering. Direct peering is when customers have a physical link connecting a port on their device directly to a Google edge device. The Google edge device is located in a colocation facility where Google is present.

- **Carrier Peering**: This option allows you to establish BGP peering with Google even though you are not co-located in one of the Google PoPs. You can achieve this through a supported SP that provides IP connectivity to the Google network.

> **Important Note**
> With both Direct Peering and Carrier Peering, Google cannot offer SLAs. If your applications require guaranteed interconnection services, the recommendation is to choose Dedicated or Partner Interconnect solutions.

In terms of pricing, Direct Peering and Carrier Peering are cheaper than Cloud Interconnect solutions. Indeed, Direct Peering offers free connections at no cost per port and per hour charges. For Carrier Peering, you instead need to consider the transport costs charged by the SP. In both solutions, the only cost billed by Google is the price for Egress traffic, as reported in the following table:

Peering Egress traffic pricing table	
Continental location	Price
North America	$0.04/GB
European Union (EU)	$0.05/GB
Asia-Pacific (APAC)	$0.06/GB

Table 2.8 – Pricing table for peering egress traffic

Now that you have learned how to choose your BGP peering option to interconnect your on-premises network with Google, let's see how to use Google Cloud VPN to build secure tunnels between your VPC and your on-premises network across the internet.

IPsec VPN

When Cloud Interconnect solutions are not at your disposal, you can interconnect your on-premises network and your VPC with Cloud VPN. Indeed, Cloud VPN allows you to establish a secure tunnel across the internet to interconnect the VPC network and your on-premises network privately. This solution can be considered an alternative Cloud Interconnect option when neither Direct Interconnect nor Partner Interconnect is available or when they are too expensive for your budget. Moreover, Cloud VPN can be used to interconnect from other VPC networks built into other cloud providers (such as **Amazon Web Services** (**AWS**) and Azure). Additionally, Cloud VPN encrypts your traffic using IPsec technology and it can be easily set up if you have a dedicated device (that is, a router or a firewall).

There are two types of Cloud VPN options you can use in your design, as outlined here:

- **Classic VPN**: This is a single IPsec VPN gateway that uses one external IP address as an endpoint to terminate a single encrypted tunnel. With Classic VPN, you can route traffic into the tunnel using both static and dynamic routing. Classic VPN will eventually be discontinued, so the new recommendation is to use HA VPN at all times. Customers on Classic VPN will eventually have to migrate to HA VPN.

- **HA VPN**: This is an HA VPN gateway that uses two external IP addresses as an endpoint to terminate two encrypted tunnels. Dynamic routing must be adopted in order to choose between active/passive and active/active IPsec solutions.

Whether you choose Classic VPN or HA VPN, you should keep in mind the following best practices:

- Use dynamic routing (that is, BGP) with Cloud Router (more detail on this in the next section) for routing failover.

- Use HA VPN and active/passive tunnel configuration when deploying a single gateway.

- If you decide to deploy multiple HA VPN gateways in multiple regions, make sure you apply active/active tunnel configuration to avoid traffic loss.

- Apply firewall rules to control traffic that travels over Cloud VPN tunnels.

- Choose a strong pre-shared key for Cloud VPN tunnels.

> **Important Note**
> Cloud VPN can carry up to 3 Gbps traffic per IPsec tunnel for both ingress and egress traffic.

When you design your Cloud VPN solution, some important specifications should be considered, as outlined here:

- **The tunnel MTU is 1,460 bytes**: To avoid packet fragmentation and improve the quality of service of your application that runs on top of the IPsec tunnel, make sure that the **maximum segment size (MSS)** is respected. This is for both TCP and UDP traffic.

- **Cloud VPN IPsec specification** For this, the following applies:

  - **Internet Key Exchange (IKE)** v1 and IKEv2 are both supported.

  - IKE pre-shared keys are only supported. **Rivest-Shamir-Adleman (RSA)** authentication is not supported.

  - **Extensible Service Proxy (ESP)** in tunnel mode is only supported. ESP in transport mode is not supported.

  - **Network Address Translation Traversal (NAT-T)** is supported.

To summarize the differences between Classic VPN and HA VPN, you can refer to the following table:

Feature	HA VPN	Classic VPN
SLA (from GCP perspective)	With two interfaces and two IP addresses reaches 99.99%.	One interface and one IP address reaches 99.9%.
Creation of external IP addresses and forwarding rules	External IP addresses are created automatically from a pool; no forwarding rules are required.	External IP addresses and forwarding rules must be created manually.
Routing options	BGP only.	Static and BGP.
Two tunnels from one Cloud VPN gateway to the same peer gateway	Supported.	Not supported.

Table 2.9 – HA VPN versus Classic VPN in GCP

Now that you have learned all the possible solutions for interconnecting your Google Cloud VPC and your on-premises network, you can learn how to design routing with Google Cloud Router.

Cloud Router

When it comes to designing your Cloud Interconnect or Cloud VPN solution, there is always one constant that shows up. This is **Google Cloud Router**. Cloud Router is neither a physical device nor a connectivity option, but it is a fully distributed and managed Google Cloud service that exchanges dynamic routes at scale. It supports static and dynamic routing (BGP only). It is a fundamental component in the following networking products:

- Cloud NAT
- Cloud Interconnect solutions (that is, Dedicated and Partner Interconnect)
- Cloud HA VPN
- Classic VPN

Indeed, when you interconnect your on-premises network to Google Cloud VPC, Cloud Router lets you exchange BGP routes dynamically between on-premises and cloud.

Cloud Router is a regional service, and therefore when created, it is deployed in one region in your VPC. You can have two different types of dynamic routing mode in your VPC that influences Cloud Router advertising behavior, outlined as follows:

- **Regional dynamic routing**: Cloud Router knows only the subnets attached to the region in which it is deployed. In this mode, by default Cloud Router advertises only the subnets that reside within its region. The routes learned by Cloud Router only apply to the subnets in the same region as the Cloud Router.

- **Global dynamic routing**: Cloud Router knows all the subnets that belong to the VPC in which it is deployed. Therefore, by default Cloud Router advertises all the subnets of the VPC. Routes learned by the Cloud Router apply to all subnets in all regions in the VPC.

In both cases, Cloud Router advertises all the routes it knows. This is the default behavior when BGP is used as a routing protocol. If you need to control which routes should be advertised to the Cloud Router peers, you need to configure **custom route advertisements**. Indeed, you can create filters that apply to which prefixes should be advertised via BGP to the Cloud Router peers. More specifically, custom route advertisements are a route policy that is applied to all BGP sessions or per individual BGP peer that Cloud Router has.

When your design includes global dynamic routing (that is, BGP) and multiple Cloud Router services in various regions, you must decide how to handle inbound and outbound routing within your VPC. In Google Cloud, this can be achieved using two methods, as outlined next:

- `AS_PATH` **prepend**: This method changes the length of the BGP `PATH` attribute to prefer one way over another. The `AS_PATH` prepend applies only within a single Cloud Router with multiple BGP sessions. With two or more Cloud Router instances, the `AS_PATH` prepend is not used for evaluating routes between the Cloud Router instances. Also, there is currently no means to change `AS_PATH` when advertising from GCP to on-premises. Only a **multi-exit discriminator** (**MED**) is used in both ingress and egress directions.

- **MED**: This method changes the cost of a given subnet prefix to prefer one way over another.

> **Important Note**
>
> In BGP, order matters when it comes to choosing the best route among many for a given destination. MED can be used when the AS_PATH prepend is the same for all routes.
>
> Cloud Router does not support other BGP attributes apart from AS_PATH and MED. For example, you cannot configure Local Preference or Community. AS_PATH only works with one Cloud Router that has multiple BGP sessions—for example, AS_PATH will not be used across two Cloud Router instances in a scenario where we have two Dedicated or Partner Interconnect connections where their VLAN attachments are attached to separate Cloud Router instances.

Now that we have introduced Cloud Router and its design recommendations, let's move on to see how to design failover and DR strategies with Cloud Routers, HA VPN gateways, and Cloud Interconnect.

Failover and DR strategy (for example, building HA with BGP using Cloud Router)

In this section, you will learn how to design failover and DR solutions using Cloud Router, Dedicated Interconnect, Partner Interconnect, and an **HA VPN gateway**.

Designing failover and DR solution with Cloud Router and a multi-regional HA VPN

Let's suppose that you want to design a multi-regional highly available Cloud VPN solution between your VPC and your on-premises network. You can see an example of this in the following diagram:

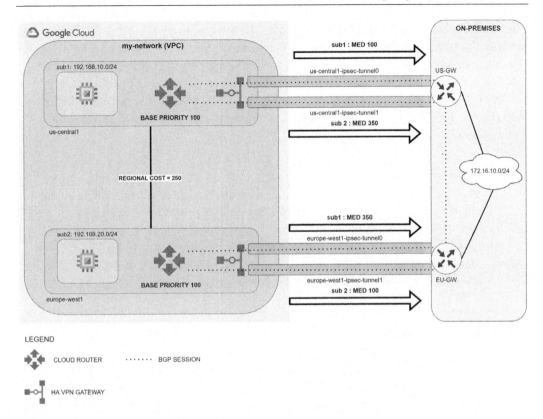

Figure 2.13 – Multi-regional HA VPN solution

As *Figure 2.13* shows, to design a multi-regional HA VPN solution, you must have two Cloud Routers and HA VPN gateways in your VPC. In addition, global routing mode should be enabled in your VPC. An HA VPN gateway allows you to have two external IP addresses on which you can build two IPsec tunnels. Moreover, Cloud Routers allow you to design active/active solutions in which both routers serve regional traffic and can be a backup for the other one in case of regional traffic loss. You can achieve this using a BGP MED attribute. As shown in the preceding diagram, each Cloud Router instance advertises VPC subnets with different MED values in order to communicate how the traffic from the on-premises network should enter the VPC. More specifically, you will notice that each Cloud Router instance announces VPC subnets with different MED values. This is because Cloud Router takes the **base priority** and adds the **regional cost** to the MED value. This happens when Cloud Router advertises subnet prefixes from other regions.

For local subnets, Cloud Router only advertises the **base priority** as BGP MED. In this manner, the traffic from your on-premises network will always use the appropriate regional gateway to reach your VPC subnets and will maintain a backup solution. In the example shown in the preceding diagram, traffic from the 172.16.10.0/24 network will use US-GW to reach sub1 because US-GW's best BGP route is the one with the lowest MED (that is, 100). On the contrary, traffic designated to sub2 will use EU-GW for the same reason.

> **Important Note**
>
> **Regional Cost** is a system-defined parameter set by Google Cloud and it is out of your control. It depends on latency, the distance measured between two regions, and it ranges from 201 to 9999.
>
> Base Priority is a parameter that you choose to provide priority on your routes. Make sure it ranges from 0 to 200 in order to guarantee that it will always be lower than regional costs. This will avoid having a strange routing within your VPC.

In order to maintain symmetric routing in your design, you must advertise your on-premises subnets using MED. Google Cloud Router accepts AS_PATH PREPEND when there are multiple BGP sessions terminated on the same Cloud Router. When you have different Cloud Routers, only MED is used in evaluating routing decisions. The recommendation is to maintain the same approach you choose with Cloud Router to have a simpler design.

Designing failover and DR with Cloud Router and Dedicated Interconnect

When you are designing hybrid Cloud interconnects for production and mission-critical applications that have a low tolerance to downtime, you should build an HA architecture that includes the following:

- At least four Dedicated Interconnection connections, two for each metropolitan area. In each metro area, you should use separate Google edge availability domains that are connected to the VPC via separate VLAN attachments.

- At least four Cloud Routers, two in each GCP rregion. Do this even if you have a GCE instance running on one single region.

- Global dynamic routing mode must be set within the VPC.

- Use two gateways in your on-premises network per each GCP region you are connecting with.

The following diagram shows one example failover DR design for your hybrid Cloud interconnect solution:

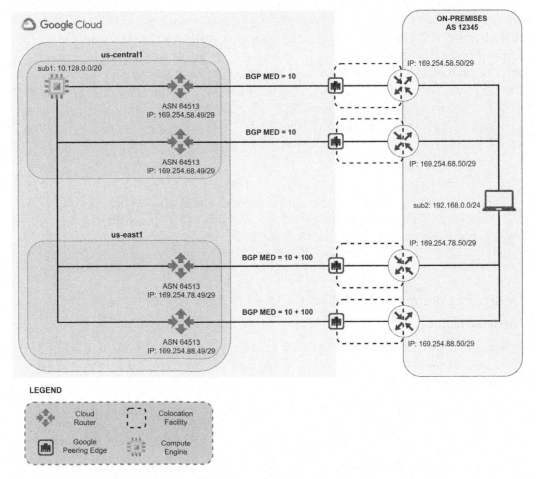

Figure 2.14 – Failover and DR design with Cloud Router and Dedicated Interconnect

As shown in *Figure 2.14*, cloud routers exchange subnet prefixes with the on-premises routers using BGP. Indeed, in the DR design, you must use four BGP sessions, one for each VLAN attachment that you have in your co-location facility. Using BGP, you can exchange prefixes with different metrics (that is, MED). In this way, you can design an active/backup connectivity between sub1 (10.128.0.0/20) in your VPC and sub2 (192.168.0.0/24) in your on-premises network. Indeed, setting a base priority of 100 to sub1 in all your Cloud Routers allows you to have us-central1 Cloud Routers advertise two routes with lower MED values. On the contrary, us-east1 Cloud Routers will advertise two routes with higher MED values because they add to the base priority the regional cost between us-central1 and us-east1. In this manner, the on-premises routers will have two active routes toward the us-central1 Cloud Routers and two backup routes toward the us-east1 Cloud Routers. In case both Dedicated Interconnect links fail in the us-central1 region, BGP will reroute the traffic activating the path via us-east1. In this manner, you can design 99.99% availability interconnection between your VPC and on-premises network.

> **Important Note**
>
> In order to maintain symmetric traffic between your VPC network and your on-premises network, you must advertise different BGP MED values from your on-premises routers. This will ensure that the incoming traffic to sub2 (192.168.0.0/24) will use the appropriate Dedicated Interconnect links.

Designing failover and DR with Cloud Router and Partner Interconnect

When your applications require high levels of availability, but you are not physically co-located in one of the Google PoPs, then you need to select one of the supported SPs that will let you interconnect with Google Cloud infrastructure.

The Partner Interconnect failover and DR solution requires the following:

- At least four VLAN attachments, each one connected to the SP peering edge.
- At least four Cloud Routers, one for each VLAN attachment.
- Global dynamic routing mode must be enabled on your VPC.
- One on-premises router for each SP peering edge.

As discussed previously, you can design a **Level 2 (L2)** or **Level 3 (L3)** Partner Interconnect connection to reach your VPC in Google Cloud. Google recommends building an L2 interconnection when you want to have full control of your BGP routing. Instead, you can build an L3 interconnection when you want to delegate BGP routing to your SP. In this last case, you need to configure routing only between your on-premises routers and the SP routers. Here you can use any routing protocol that your SP supports (that is, BGP, OSPF, EIGRP, IS-IS).

The following diagram shows an example of **failover and DR in L2 Partner Interconnect**:

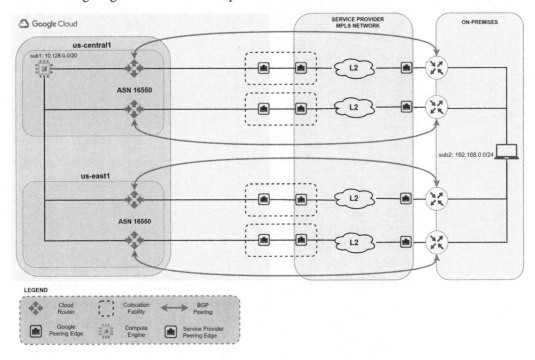

Figure 2.15 – Failover and DR in L2 Partner Interconnect

As you can see from *Figure 2.15*, the design of failover and DR in L2 Partner Interconnect is similar to what you have seen for Dedicated Interconnect except that now, the SP connects your on-premises routers to the GCP Cloud Router via the **multi-protocol label switching (MPLS)** L2 network. In this manner, you have a virtual Ethernet circuit between your on-premises routers and your Cloud Router. You can establish BGP peering between your Cloud Routers and on-premises routers directly and control the traffic as you would have done in a Dedicated Interconnect environment. Therefore, the recommendation is to use BGP MED to build active/backup connectivity between your subnets.

If you cannot have an L2 Partner Interconnect connection, or you just prefer **L3 Partner Interconnect**, you can design a failover and DR interconnection. See the following diagram for an example of this:

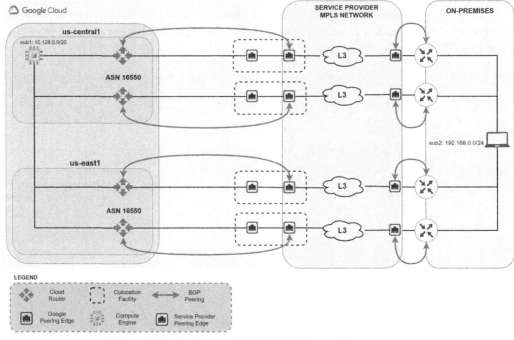

Figure 2.16 – Failover and DR with L3 Partner Interconnect

If you decide to use L3 Partner Interconnect for your failover design, you are required to establish BGP peering between your Cloud Routers/on-premises routers and the SP Edge routers. We recommend using BGP as a routing protocol to handle MED values and to easily achieve active/backup failover scenarios as well as in Dedicated Interconnect.

Now that you have been through the best practices for hybrid connectivity designs, it's time to learn how to design and plan **container IP** addressing for GKE.

Designing a container IP addressing plan for GKE

In this section, you will learn how to design a scalable GKE cluster to handle large workloads. Moreover, you will learn how to plan IP addressing for the Pods and Services running on your GKE cluster. Finally, you will learn about some recommendations for security in GKE.

Creating scalable GKE clusters

When it comes to achieving high availability in your GKE cluster, the best fit is to go for a **regional cluster**. Indeed, regional GKE clusters can have multiple Kubernetes control planes across multiple zones, and this improves greatly the resilience of the entire system. A Kubernetes control plane consists of many components, described as follows:

- `kube-apiserver`: This component is the frontend of a Kubernetes cluster and allows managers to control the entire cluster via the APIs exposed. Indeed, using the `kubectl` command-line tool, Kubernetes administrators can talk to the API server directly.

- `etcd`: This component stores all the Kubernetes cluster data in the form of key-value pairs.

- `kube-scheduler`: This component is responsible for assigning worker Nodes to the newly created Pods. The scheduler assigns Nodes based on different policies or requirements.

- `kube-dns`: This component is responsible for resolving names for Pod IPs and services.

The previous components are running on the master of a Kubernetes cluster. There are also other components that implement the control plane but reside on every worker Node. These are listed here:

- `kubelet`: This is an agent that makes sure that containers are running in Pods.

- `kube-proxy`: This component is a network proxy and implements the Kubernetes service. Therefore, it is responsible for Pod communication inside and outside the cluster.

For example, when upgrading clusters, two out of three controllers are always running and the Kubernetes API server is always reachable and responsive.

Therefore, a GKE regional cluster should be chosen when HA is needed. However, if your priority is to have a GKE cluster that upgrades rapidly, you should go for a zonal GKE cluster. Moreover, in order to increase reliability on your GKE workload, you should consider **multi-zonal Node pools** that allow you to distribute your workload uniformly across multiple compute zones within a region. Additionally, you can enable a **cluster autoscaler** within a Node pool to elastically increase or decrease the number of worker Nodes.

> **Important Note**
> With a cluster autoscaler, there is no guarantee that workers will equally distribute among zones.

When you deal with large workloads, Google Cloud recommends **regional GKE clusters** with the `VPC-native` networking mode. This allows VPC subnets to have a secondary range of IP addresses for all Pods running in the cluster. With VPC-native mode, routing traffic to Pods is automatically achieved without adding any custom routes to the VPC.

Designing scalable clusters sometimes requires security as well. In regular GKE clusters, all worker Nodes have a private and a public IP address assigned. Unless you have a specific reason to publish your worker Nodes on the internet, Google Cloud recommends using a **private cluster** instead. Here, worker Nodes only have private IP addresses and thus are isolated from the internet.

Workload scalability impacts load balancing as well. **GKE Ingress** and Cloud Load Balancing allow your service running in your GKE cluster to be reachable from outside. They include many objects such as forwarding rules, **URL maps**, **backend services**, and more (see *Chapter 4, Configuring Network Services in GCP* for more details). Any of these services has a quota, and if the limits are reached, services and Ingress cannot be deployed. Therefore, to design a scalable GKE cluster, you should be aware of the load-balancer limits. The following table shows the scaling limits:

Load balancer	Node limit per cluster
Internal TCP/UDP load balancer	<ul><li>250 nodes</li><li>No node limit for services on clusters with internal TCP/UDP load-balancer subsetting enabled</li></ul>
External HTTP(S) load balancer	<ul><li>1,000 nodes per zone</li><li>No node limit when using container-native load balancing</li></ul>
Internal HTTP(S) load balancer	No node limits

Table 2.10 – GKE Load Balancer scaling limits

Additional thoughts should also be put into DNS when it comes to cluster scalability. Indeed, service discovery in GKE is provided by `kube-dns`, which is the principal component of DNS resolution of running Pods. When the workload increases, GKE automatically scales this component. However, for very large clusters, this is not enough. Therefore, Google Cloud's recommendation for high DNS scalability is to distribute DNS queries to each local Node. This can be implemented by enabling `NodeLocal DNSCache`. This caching mechanism allows any worker Nodes to answer queries locally and thus provide faster response times.

In general, when you design a scalable GKE cluster in order to support your applications, you should be aware of the limitations of Kubernetes. Even if the limitations may seem very high, it is crucial to know all of them in order to avoid performance degradation. Therefore, a clever design approach for a scalable GKE cluster should consider the following:

- **Maximum Pods per Node are 100**: GKE has a hard limit of 100 Pods per Node. Google Cloud recommends not having more than two containers per Pod.

- **The total number of services should stay below 10,000**: The performance of `IPtables` will be impacted if there are too many services.

- **The total number of Pods behind a single service should stay below 250**: This is considered a safe threshold to maintain stability on `kube-proxy` and `etcd`, which are important components of Kubernetes.

- **The total number of services per namespace should not exceed 5,000**: Pods may experience crashes on startup if this limit is exceeded.

Now that you have learned how to design a scalable cluster in Google Cloud, let's have a look at how to plan for IP addresses with GKE.

IP address planning in GKE

GKE requires accurate IP address planning design to avoid Node, Pod, and service scalability issues. We assume that you follow the GCP recommendations in choosing **VPC-native** networking and private clusters.

Planning the IP address should follow these recommendations:

- The Kubernetes control-plane IP address range should be a private range (*RFC 1918*) and should not overlap with any other subnets within the VPC.

- The Node subnet should accommodate the maximum number of Nodes expected in the cluster. A **cluster autoscaler** can be used to limit the maximum number of Nodes in the cluster pool.

Pods and service IPs should be implemented as secondary ranges of your Node subnet, using alias IP addresses in VPC-native clusters. You should follow these recommendations:

- When creating GKE subnets, it is recommended to use custom subnet mode to allow flexibility in CIDR design.

- The subnet Pod should be dimensioned on the maximum number of Pods per Node. By default, GKE allocates a /24 range per Node, which allows 110 maximum Pods per Node. If you are planning to have fewer Pods than this, resize the CIDR accordingly.

- Avoid IP addresses overlapping between GKE subnets and on-premises subnets. Google recommends using the 100.64.0.0/10 (*RFC 6598*) range, which avoids interoperability issues.

- If you are exposing GKE services within your VPC, Google Cloud recommends using a separate subnet for internal TCP/UDP load balancing. This also allows you to improve security on the traffic to and from your GKE services.

> **Important Note**
> If you decide to use an **Autopilot** cluster (that is, GKE in auto mode) remember that the maximum number of Pods per Node is 32, with a /26 range for each Node subnet. These settings cannot be changed.

Now that you have learned how to plan IP addressing for your GKE cluster, let's explore the recommendations on how you can secure your Kubernetes cluster.

Network security design in GKE

When designing network security in GKE, the recommendation is to choose a private cluster and control access to it with **authorized networks**. Indeed, you can choose which IP addresses (both private and public) can manage your cluster, and this improves security for your GKE cluster. With a private cluster, all the IP ranges are private, but you can access the API server via the public IP. Moreover, you are recommended to use **Cloud NAT** to let the worker Nodes access the internet and to enable **Private Google Access** to let worker Nodes privately reach Google services. This is illustrated in the following diagram:

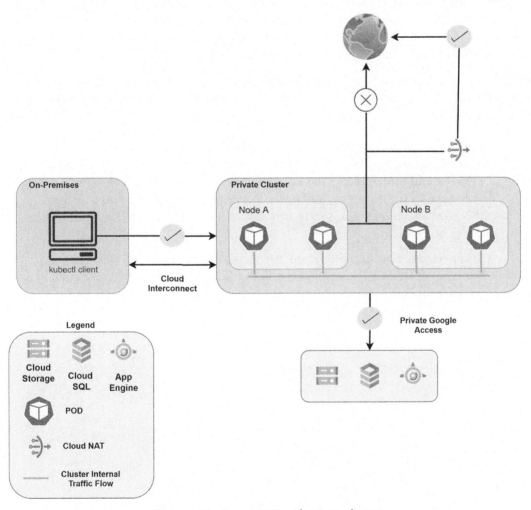

Figure 2.17 – Secure GKE with private cluster

Figure 2.17 shows a private cluster with two working Nodes and four running Pods. You will notice that in a private cluster, Pods communicate internally through the dedicated secondary subnet. Moreover, in a private cluster, worker Nodes have private IP addresses only. Therefore, if they need to reach the internet to download upgrades or system patches, they must use Cloud NAT. In the same manner, if the worker Nodes need to access GCP services such as **Google Cloud Storage** or **Google Cloud SQL**, **Private Google Access** must be enabled on the GKE cluster subnet. Additionally, you can manage your private cluster from your on-premises `kubectl` client as long as your on-premises network is interconnected with the VPC network in which the cluster is running. Here, you must have configured one of the Cloud Interconnect solutions or the HA VPN that GCP provides you with. Alternatively, you can always manage your private cluster from a Google Cloud shell that has a built-in `kubectl` client.

With a private cluster, you learn how to isolate your worker Nodes from external access. Additionally, you can minimize the exposure of your cluster control plane in two modes, outlined as follows:

- `-enable-private-endpoint`: This option can be specified during cluster creation and allows a GKE cluster to be managed using private IP only (this is called a **private endpoint**). Hence, the Kubernetes API server will get a private IP address within the VPC that can be used for processing requests from `kubectl` clients. The private IP address can also be used to communicate with other cluster worker Nodes privately.

- **Authorized networks**: This option can be used to control which IP subnet is able to access the GKE control-plane Nodes. This applies to both public and private endpoints.

The following diagram illustrates how to secure a GKE control plane through a private endpoint and authorized networks:

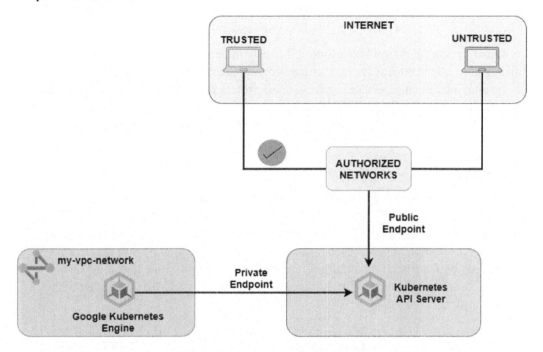

Figure 2.18 – Securing a GKE control plane

The security design of your GKE cluster can include additional layers of enforcement. Indeed, you can deploy **VPC firewall rules** to control traffic to worker Nodes and **GKE network policies** to control the traffic directed to Pods and services.

> **Important Note**
>
> Configuring VPC firewall rules override previous default firewall rules that were automatically generated during cluster creation. You need to do so in order to make sure the control-plane traffic will pass.

GKE network policies administer traffic that flows to Pods and services. If your security requirements are very high, you might consider using this option to have full control of traffic to and from your Pods and services. To enable GKE network policies, you can use the -enable-network-policy option during cluster creation.

As a final recommendation for designing security in your GKE cluster, Google Cloud offers you its Cloud Armor service, which protects against DDoS attacks and web application attacks. This service can be used to protect your web applications running in your cluster from web attacks. Cloud Armor is fully integrated with GKE Ingress and HTTP(S) Load Balancer and can include several security policies.

Summary

In this chapter, you learned how to design a GCP network. You have learned the principal strategies for failover and DR to apply to your VPC design. Then, you have been through the best practices of VPC design, understanding how IP ranges, routing, and VPC interconnection should be designed. Moreover, you learned how to design hybrid networking between your on-premises and VPC networks and how to build a network topology that is resilient to faults. Additionally, you went through the design strategies and best practices for a GKE network.

Now that you have solid knowledge about designing VPC networks in GCP, it is time to go on to implementation. Indeed, in the next chapter, you will learn how to implement a VPC in GCP.

3
Implementing a GCP Virtual Private Cloud (VPC)

In this chapter, you will start implementing **Virtual Private Cloud** (**VPC**) resources through case studies and practical exercises. You will learn how to configure VPC subnets, and static and dynamic routing using **Cloud Router**. Moreover, you will configure VPC intercommunication through **VPC peering**, and you will understand how to share VPC networks across multiple projects using services such as **Shared VPC**. Additionally, you will configure **network address translation** (**NAT**) for your **Google Compute Engine** (**GCE**) instances with **Cloud NAT**. Finally, you will discover how to implement security in your VPC by configuring firewall rules.

Therefore, the chapter will comprise two main sections, as follows:

- Configuring VPC **networks**
- Configuring and managing firewall rules

Technical requirements

To fully understand the content of the present chapter the reader, having basic networking knowledge, should have studied the previous two chapters.

Configuring VPC networks

In this section, you will learn how to configure the main **VPC** resources in **Google Cloud Platform** (**GCP**), including VPC networks, subnets, and firewall rules. Then, you will go through the routing implementation with both *static* and *dynamic* approaches. Once you have covered this, you will learn how to configure **VPC network peering** to interconnect two VPC networks either inside a project or even across different projects. Additionally, you will implement Shared VPC to interconnect resources in different projects in the same organization using one common Shared VPC network. Finally, this section will show you how to implement Cloud NAT to let private GCE instances (instances without any public **Internet Protocol** (**IP**) address) have access to public services.

Configuring VPC resources in GCP

Before starting to configure your VPC, you should be aware of the default settings that have been provisioned by **Google Cloud**. Indeed, as described in the previous chapter, GCP creates a default VPC and deploys a subnet for each region it covers. Moreover, four default firewall policies are created to facilitate communication with the GCE instances you will deploy in the VPC (either inbound or outbound), for specific protocols such as **Secure Shell** (**SSH**), **Remote Desktop Protocol** (**RDP**), or **Internet Control Message Protocol** (**ICMP**). Let's explore the default settings starting with the VPC network and subnets, as shown in the following screenshot:

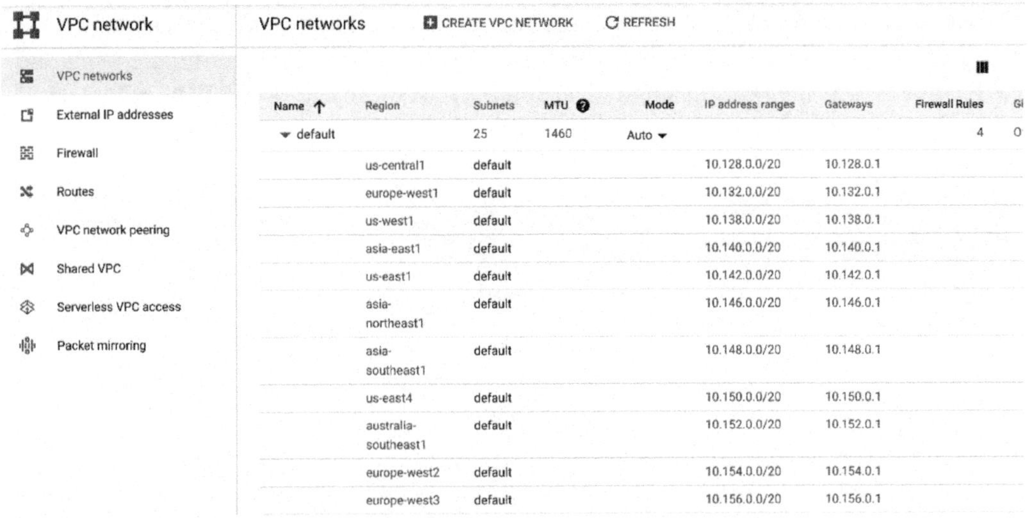

VPC network		**VPC networks** ➕ CREATE VPC NETWORK ↻ REFRESH							

Name ↑	Region	Subnets	MTU ❓	Mode	IP address ranges	Gateways	Firewall Rules	Gl
▼ default		25	1460	Auto ▼			4	0
	us-central1	default			10.128.0.0/20	10.128.0.1		
	europe-west1	default			10.132.0.0/20	10.132.0.1		
	us-west1	default			10.138.0.0/20	10.138.0.1		
	asia-east1	default			10.140.0.0/20	10.140.0.1		
	us-east1	default			10.142.0.0/20	10.142.0.1		
	asia-northeast1	default			10.146.0.0/20	10.146.0.1		
	asia-southeast1	default			10.148.0.0/20	10.148.0.1		
	us-east4	default			10.150.0.0/20	10.150.0.1		
	australia-southeast1	default			10.152.0.0/20	10.152.0.1		
	europe-west2	default			10.154.0.0/20	10.154.0.1		
	europe-west3	default			10.156.0.0/20	10.156.0.1		

VPC network sidebar items: VPC networks, External IP addresses, Firewall, Routes, VPC network peering, Shared VPC, Serverless VPC access, Packet mirroring

Figure 3.1 – Default VPC network and its subnets

Figure 3.1 shows the default VPC network that GCP preconfigures when you create a new project. It contains 25 subnets (not all are displayed), one for each GCP region (Google will increase the number of subnets for each new region that enters the service). Indeed, the VPC network was created in **Automatic** mode. Later, you will practice with **Custom** mode, which lets you personalize your VPC.

The VPC has four default firewall rules, as shown in the following screenshot:

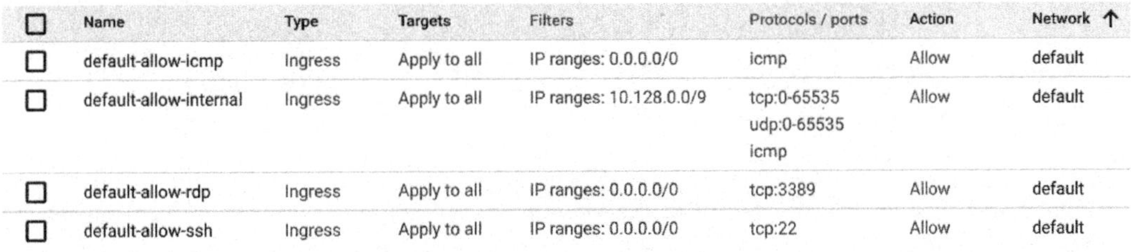

	Name	Type	Targets	Filters	Protocols / ports	Action	Network ↑
☐	default-allow-icmp	Ingress	Apply to all	IP ranges: 0.0.0.0/0	icmp	Allow	default
☐	default-allow-internal	Ingress	Apply to all	IP ranges: 10.128.0.0/9	tcp:0-65535 udp:0-65535 icmp	Allow	default
☐	default-allow-rdp	Ingress	Apply to all	IP ranges: 0.0.0.0/0	tcp:3389	Allow	default
☐	default-allow-ssh	Ingress	Apply to all	IP ranges: 0.0.0.0/0	tcp:22	Allow	default

Figure 3.2 – Default firewall rules

As *Figure 3.2* shows, the firewall rules allow incoming traffic to all GCE instances, as follows:

- ICMP, RDP, and SSH traffic is always permitted from both internal and external IP prefixes.

- Any traffic generated internally from any subnet of the VPC network is permitted.

More details about firewall rules will come later in this section. So, now, let's configure our first custom VPC network. As a first method of creating a VPC, we recommend using the GCP console, which gives you a graphical approach. You can access the **VPC networks** menu from the search box, as shown in the following screenshot (type VPC Networks in the search box and choose **VPC networks** from the result):

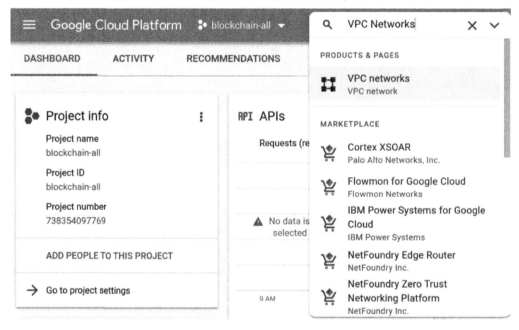

Figure 3.3 – Searching for VPC networks in the search box

Next, create a new VPC network with the **CREATE VPC NETWORK** button, as illustrated in the following screenshot:

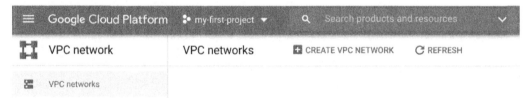

Figure 3.4 – VPC network creation on GCP console

When creating a new VPC network, you must provide a unique name within the project and you must select whether to create an **Automatic** or **Custom** mode for your VPC subnets. Let's choose **Custom** mode, as illustrated in the following screenshot, and let's add one subnet with a custom network address range of 192.168.10.0/24:

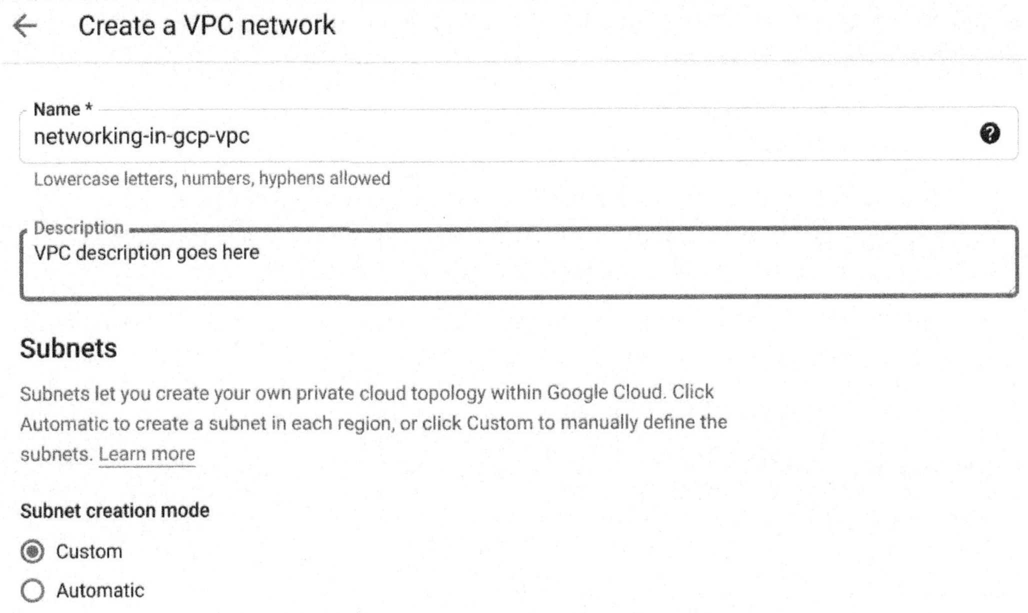

←   Create a VPC network

Name *

networking-in-gcp-vpc   ❓

Lowercase letters, numbers, hyphens allowed

Description

VPC description goes here

Subnets

Subnets let you create your own private cloud topology within Google Cloud. Click Automatic to create a subnet in each region, or click Custom to manually define the subnets. Learn more

Subnet creation mode

◉ Custom

○ Automatic

Figure 3.5 – VPC network creation in Custom mode

The following screenshot shows how to add one subnet to the VPC. Subnets must have a unique name, a GCP region, and an IP address range:

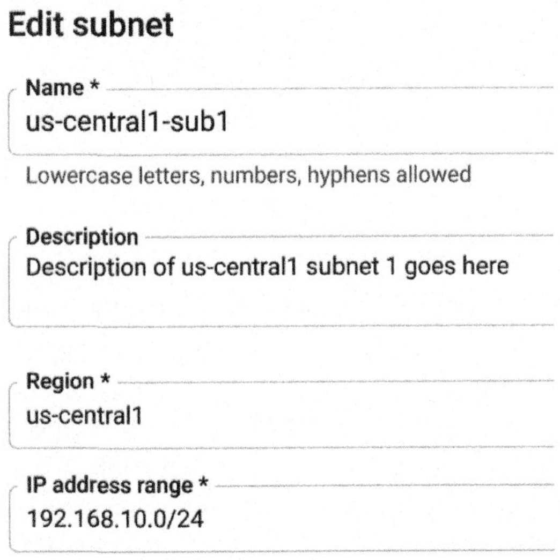

Edit subnet

Name *

us-central1-sub1

Lowercase letters, numbers, hyphens allowed

Description

Description of us-central1 subnet 1 goes here

Region *

us-central1

IP address range *

192.168.10.0/24

Figure 3.6 – Subnet creation in VPC Custom mode

Additionally, you can specify two important options when creating a custom subnet, as follows:

- **Private Google access**: This option allows private GCE instances to access Google Cloud services such as Cloud Storage.

- **Flow logs**: This option enables subnet logging, which can be used for troubleshooting and monitoring on GCP. After choosing **On** for **Flow logs**, you need to click on **Configure logs** to see these options.

- **Additional fields**: Here, you can configure the aggregation interval and sample rate of the flow logs, as well as whether to include metadata in the flow logs or not.

This option can be implemented as shown in the following screenshot:

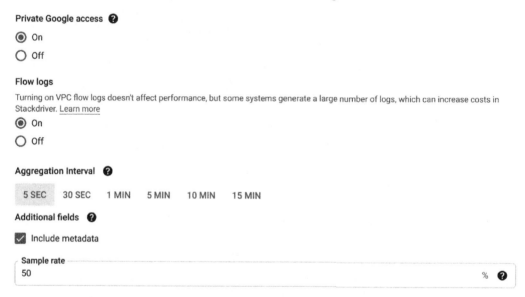

Figure 3.7 – Private Google access and VPC flow logs implementation

As you can see from *Figure 3.7*, **Private Google access** is on, and therefore GCE instances in this subnet will be able to reach Google Cloud services even if they have a private IP only. Also, you can see how to implement VPC flow logs in a VPC subnet. GCP lets you aggregate flow logs at certain intervals and sample them before sending them to GCP operations for monitoring. In the example, every 5 seconds, flow logs are aggregated and one of two are sent to GCP operations (sample rate of 50%). This helps to save some money with GCP operations. You can also include **metadata** in logging, which is additional information included in logs. More details will be covered in *Chapter 7, Managing and Monitoring Network Operations*.

Moreover, when you are creating a VPC, you must choose what kind of **dynamic routing mode** will be used. Here, you have two options, as outlined here:

- **Regional**: This option restricts **Cloud Router** (a service that we will see in more depth in the next chapter to learn only the regional routes (that are learned prefixes in their local region).

- **Global**: This option allows **Cloud Router** to learn all the routes of the VPC.

The following screenshot shows the configuration of these options:

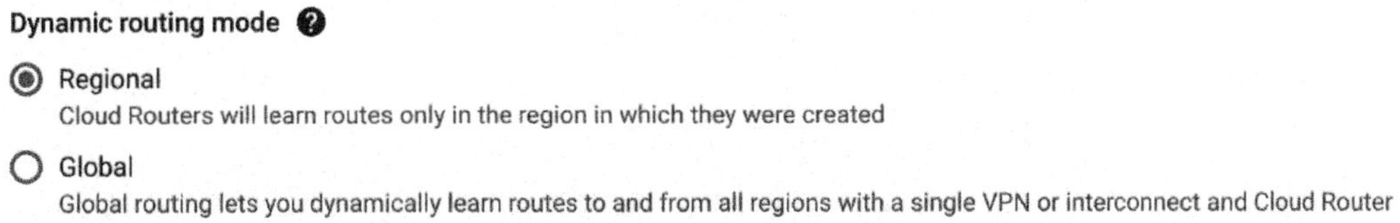

Dynamic routing mode ❓

⦿ Regional
  Cloud Routers will learn routes only in the region in which they were created

○ Global
  Global routing lets you dynamically learn routes to and from all regions with a single VPN or interconnect and Cloud Router

Figure 3.8 – Dynamic routing mode

You can also create VPC networks and subnets using **Google Cloud Shell**. The following code will create a new VPC network, and one subnet attached to it:

```
gcloud compute networks create my-vpc-network \
--subnet-mode=custom \
--bgp-routing-mode=global \

--description="This is my vpc network"
```

The command creates a VPC network called my-vpc-network that supports the **Global** dynamic routing mode and custom subnets. The command also specifies a description for the VPC network. Then, you need to create a subnet attached to the my-vpc-network network with the following command (the mandatory part of the command is just the first line; all the parameters are optional):

```
gcloud compute networks subnets create us-central-sub1 \
--network=my-vpc-network \
--range=192.168.10.0/24 --region=us-central1 \
--enable-private-ip-google-access
```

The resulting VPCs can be viewed in the following screenshot:

VPC network	VPC networks	CREATE VPC NETWORK	C REFRESH				

Name ↑	Region	Subnets	Mode	IP address ranges	Gateways	Global dynamic routing
▼ my-vpc-network		1	Custom			On
	us-central1	us-central1-sub1		192.168.10.0/24	192.168.10.1	
▼ networking-in-gcp-vpc		2	Custom			Off
	us-central1	us-central1-sub1		192.168.10.0/24	192.168.10.1	
	europe-west1	eu-west1-sub1		172.16.10.0/24	172.16.10.1	

VPC networks · External IP addresses · Firewall · Routes · VPC network peering · Shared VPC · Serverless VPC access · Packet mirroring

Figure 3.9 – VPC networks created with both the GCP console and Cloud Shell

Now that you have created VPC networks and subnets, you must configure firewall rules to govern the traffic to and from the GCE instances that will be deployed in the subnets. Indeed, with no firewall rules, you cannot have communication between instances, even though they run on the same server.

You can create a firewall rule by typing `firewall` in the search bar or finding the firewall from the left menu (**Menu | VPC network | Firewall**), as shown in the following screenshot:

Figure 3.10 – Selecting Firewall in the VPC network navigation menu

The parameters you need to enter when creating a firewall rule are provided here:

- **Name**: This is the name of the rule, and it must be unique within the project.
- **Logs**: This option generates logs when the rule is matched.
- **Network**: This is the VPC network to which the firewall rule will be applied.
- **Priority**: Rules are evaluated by priority. Lower-priority rules are evaluated before others—that is, a firewall rule with priority 1000 will be evaluated before a firewall rule with priority 2000.

- **Direction of traffic**: This determines the direction of traffic to apply control. **Ingress** controls inbound traffic to a VPC network. **Egress** controls outbound traffic from a VPC network. We can add a destination filter composed of IP ranges.

- **Action on match**: This either allows or denies traffic that matches the rule conditions.

- **Targets**: This determines to which entities the rule applies. It can be all instances in the VPC network, or some instances that have a tag or service account.

- **Source filter**: This determines the source of the traffic. It can be IP range addresses, tags, or a service account.

- **Protocols and ports**: This determines which protocol and ports (thus applications) the traffic should match in the rule.

The following screenshot shows the first set of parameters that you are required to select from when configuring a firewall rule:

Figure 3.11 – Firewall rule: first part

The following screenshot shows the second set of parameters:

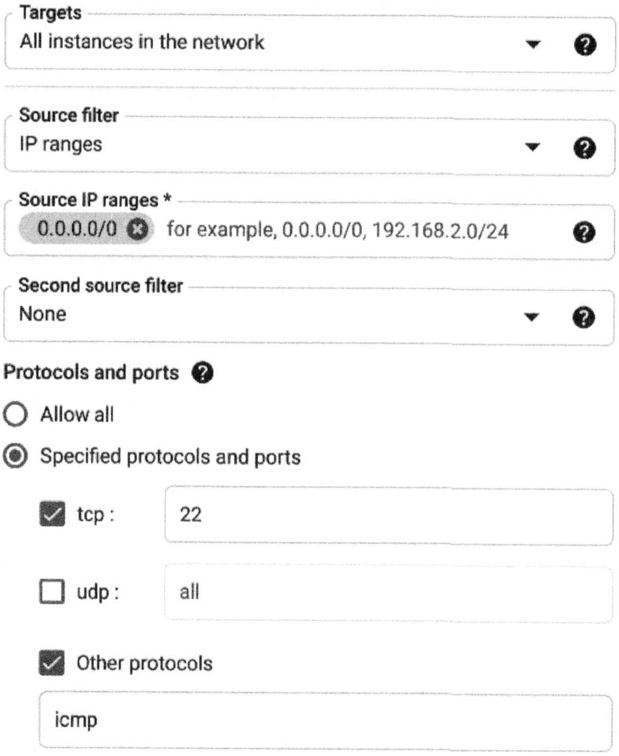

Targets
All instances in the network ▼ ❷

Source filter
IP ranges ▼ ❷

Source IP ranges *
0.0.0.0/0 ✖   for example, 0.0.0.0/0, 192.168.2.0/24 ❷

Second source filter
None ▼ ❷

Protocols and ports ❷

○ Allow all

◉ Specified protocols and ports

☑ tcp :   22

☐ udp :   all

☑ Other protocols

icmp

Figure 3.12 – Firewall rule: second part

As you can observe from the previous screenshots, the firewall rule allows *SSH* and *ICMP* incoming traffic to all GCE instances that are running on the `networking-in-gcp-vpc` VPC network. The firewall rule is valid for all traffic coming from any network range.

SSH and ICMP protocols

SSH is the secure protocol used to access a **virtual machine** (**VM**) as a remote terminal (it replaced the old *Telnet* protocol), while ICMP is the protocol used by the `ping` application that every network engineer uses as the first approach to network troubleshooting, to check the IP reachability of a VM. If you prefer to use Google Cloud Shell to configure the same firewall rule, run the following code (the `--source-ranges` parameter is an optional part of the command):

```
gcloud compute firewall-rules create my-first-rule \
 --network=networking-in-gcp-vpc \
 --allow tcp:22,icmp \
 --source-ranges=0.0.0.0/0
```

You can also disable the firewall rules singularly, keeping their configuration. By the way, you will discover more details about firewall rules in the next section.

Now that you have a basic understanding of VPC resources, let's see an example of a VPC configuration that will include two subnets in two different GCP regions and firewall rules to enable communication between two GCE instances. You can see a diagram of the VPC here:

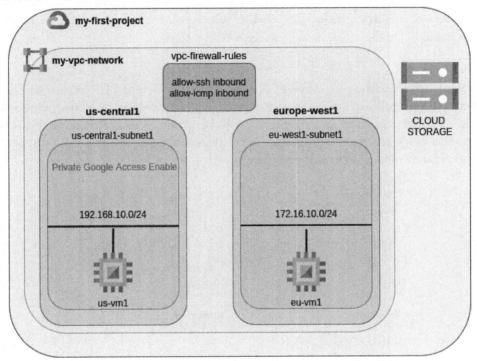

Figure 3.13 – Private Google access enabled

The first operation we will do is to create a new VPC network called `my-vpc-network` containing two subnets. `us-central1-subnet1` will have **private Google access** enabled while `eu-west1-subnet1` will not. The following screenshot shows the result:

VPC networks   ➕ CREATE VPC NETWORK   ↻ REFRESH

Name ↑	Region	Subnets	Mode	IP address ranges	Gateways
▼ my-vpc-network		2	Custom		
	us-central1	us-central1-subnet1		192.168.10.0/24	192.168.10.1
	europe-west1	eu-west1-subnet1		172.16.10.0/24	172.16.10.1

Figure 3.14 – Example of VPC network and the creation of its subnets

Next, we will create two firewall rules to permit SSH and ICMP incoming traffic to all GCE instances that we will deploy later in our VPC network. These rules (`allow-ssh` and `allow-icmp`) will both be applied to the `my-vpc-network` network. The following screenshot shows the result:

Filter   Enter property name or value

	Name	Type	Targets	Filters	Protocols / ports	Action	Network ↑
☐	allow-icmp	Ingress	Apply to all	IP ranges: 0.0.0.0/0	icmp	Allow	my-vpc-network
☐	allow-ssh	Ingress	Apply to all	IP ranges: 0.0.0.0/0	tcp:22	Allow	my-vpc-network

Figure 3.15 – Example of created firewall rules

As a third step, we will deploy two GCE instances in two different GCP regions where we have created our subnets. Both VMs will have a private IP only and they will not be able to reach any public service on the internet. We will also create a Cloud Storage bucket inside our project to test reachability from our GCE instances. An example of GCE instance creation is shown in the following screenshot:

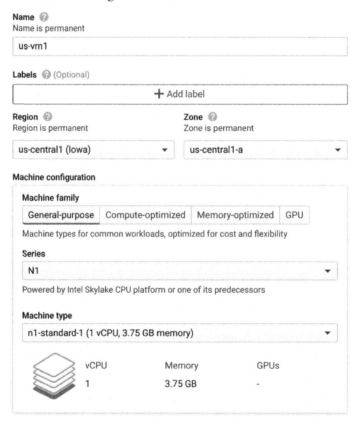

Figure 3.16 – Example of GCE instance creation

Select the **Networking** tab (to select the **Networking** tab, you have to click on **Management** -> **Security** -> **Disks** -> **Networking** -> **Sole tenancy** beforehand), then go to **Network interface**, and from there, edit the machine-network interface by clicking on the pencil icon beside the network interface (that is connected to the `my-vpc-network` network). In the **External IP** combo box, select `None` to disable IP public address assignments, as illustrated in the following screenshot:

Figure 3.17 – Example of GCE network interface

Once concluded, we should see two GCE instances in the list of VMs that you can find when in the GCE section, as shown in the following screenshot:

		Name ↑	Zone	Internal IP	Network	Connect	
☐	✓	eu-vm1	europe-west1-b	172.16.10.2 (nic0)	my-vpc-network	SSH ▾	⋮
☐	✓	us-vm1	us-central1-a	192.168.10.2 (nic0)	my-vpc-network	SSH ▾	⋮

Figure 3.18 – Example of GCE instances running in two different regions

You should notice that VMs get only an internal IP address within the address range you have defined in the VPC subnets.

Next, you will create a **Google Cloud Storage** bucket to understand how VMs can access GCP resources in your project. For learning reasons, we use the project **identifier** (**ID**) here to uniquely identify your bucket globally, as the following screenshot shows, even though this is not a good practice in a real production project (from a security perspective):

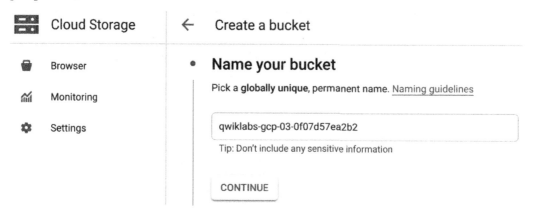

Figure 3.19 – Example of Cloud Storage bucket creation

After naming the bucket, for the purposes of this scenario, you can just click on the **Create Bucket** button, keeping the default settings. Once the bucket is created, return to the GCE **Virtual machines instances** page. Then, click on the **SSH** button for the first instance and execute the `gsutil ls` command. After that, click on the **SSH** button for the second instance, execute the same command, and access it using the **SSH** button. You can list the content of your Cloud Storage bucket by using the `gsutil ls <BUCKET_NAME>` command, where you need to replace `<BUCKET_NAME>` with the actual name of your bucket, as the following screenshot shows:

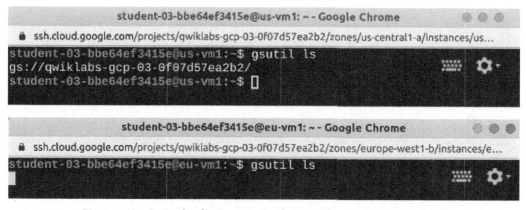

Figure 3.20 – Example of accessing Cloud Storage bucket with a private IP

You should notice that only `us-vm1` is able to run the command successfully while `eu-vm1` gets stuck. Can you guess why? This is because of **Private Google access**, which was enabled only on the `us-central1-subnet1` network. Indeed, even if `us-vm1` has a private IP address, Google private access makes it possible to reach project-wide GCP services. Therefore, we recommend enabling this feature on the subnet any time you have private VMs that need to access Google Cloud services and remain protected, thus improving security in your cloud infrastructure.

Now, let's discover more about firewall rules and communication between `us-vm1` and `eu-vm1`. Referring to *Figure 3.15*, two rules have been applied to the `my-vpc-network` VPC network. They permit inbound traffic to all VM instances deployed in the VPC network that is generated from any host's IP address. Let's try to ping between VMs, as illustrated in the following screenshot:

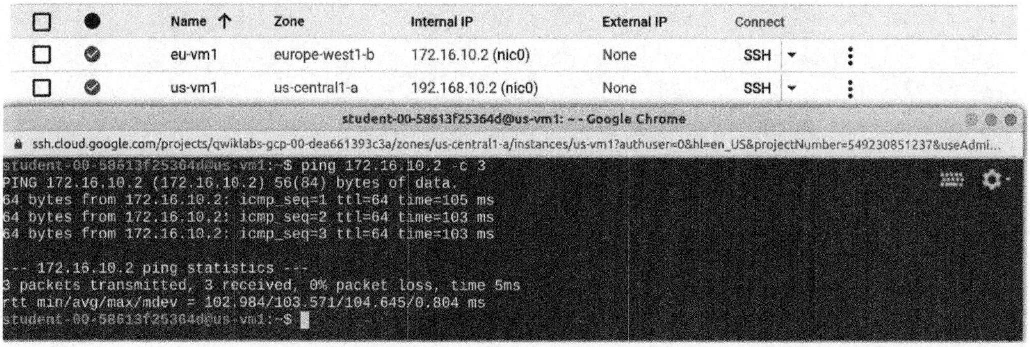

Figure 3.21 – Example of IP communication between VMs

As *Figure 3.21* shows, `us-vm1` can reach `eu-vm1` even if they are in two separate GCP regions. You should also notice these important points:

- **Egress traffic is implicitly allowed**: No firewall rules are needed to let the traffic flow out of a VM.

- **Firewall rules are stateful**: There is no need to configure rules for the returning traffic.

Now that we have explored firewall rules, let's find out a bit more about the internal **Domain Name System (DNS)** in Google Cloud. Let's create a us-vm2 VM in the same zone of us-vm1, us-central1-a. After deploying the VM, let's try to ping us-vm2 and eu-vm1 from us-vm1 using the names of VMs, as illustrated in the following screenshot:

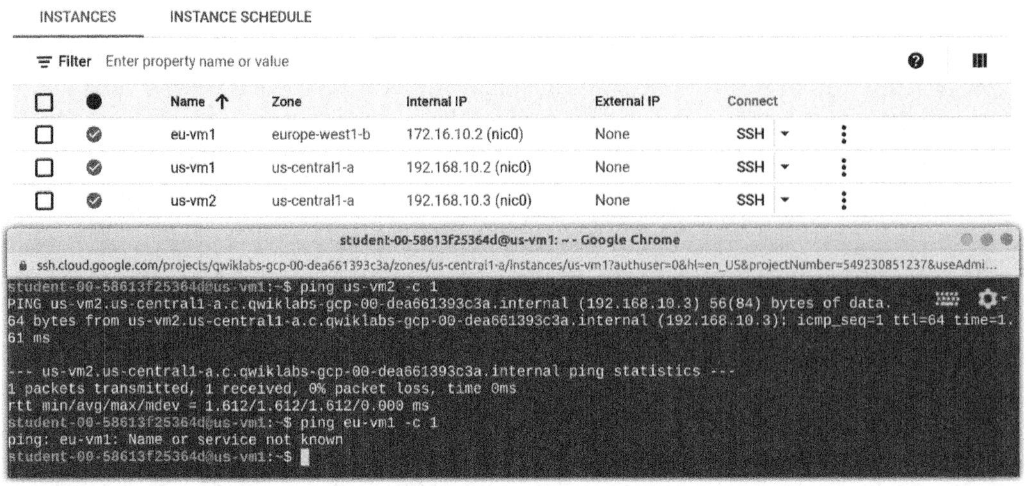

Figure 3.22 – Example of communication using VM names

As you can observe in *Figure 3.22*, pinging with VM names works only with one in the same GCP zone, us-central1-a. It fails on the eu-vm1 VM. This is because DNS internal resolution happens on the zone only. Indeed, each VM gets one unique name (us-vm2.us-central1-a.c.qwiklabs-gcp-00-dea661393c3a.internal in the preceding example) within the zone in which it runs. The name format is vm_name. zone.c.project_id.internal. This means that every VM running on the same zone must have a unique name, and you could reuse the same VM name in another zone. This behavior is called **zonal DNS**, and it happens for the DNS internal resolution of the **fully qualified domain names (FQDNs)** of the VM. From Wikipedia: "*A fully qualified domain name (FQDN), sometimes also referred to as an absolute domain name, is a domain name that specifies its exact location in the tree hierarchy of the Domain Name System (DNS). It specifies all domain levels, including the top-level domain and the root zone.*"

Zonal DNS is the default for all organizations or standalone projects that have enabled the GCE **application programming interface (API)** after September 6, 2018.

Now that you have learned the fundamentals of VPC resources, we can go through **static and dynamic routing** implementation with **Cloud Router**.

Configuring static and dynamic routing with Cloud Router

In general, you need to configure static or dynamic routing when you interconnect your VPC with an on-premises network. In this section, we will describe how to manage routing in your VPC when it is interconnected with your on-premises network. To also demonstrate dynamic and static routing, we assume Cloud VPN will be set up, but this will be covered in *Chapter 5, Implementing Hybrid Connectivity in GCP*. However, static and dynamic routing can be applied also to other Cloud Interconnect solutions, such as Dedicated Interconnect, Partner Interconnect, and so on. In the following table, you can see a comparison between the different solutions:

Connection	Provides	Capacity	Requirements	Access Type
IP Security (IPsec) VPN tunnel	Encrypted tunnel to VPC network through the public internet	1.5-3 gigabits per second (Gbps) per tunnel	On-premises VPN gateway	Internal IP addresses
Dedicated Interconnect	Dedicated, direct connection to VPC networks	10 Gbps per link 100 Gbps	Connection in colocation facility	
Partner Interconnect	Dedicated bandwidth; connection to VPC network through a service provider (SP)	50 (Mbps) – 10 Gbps per connection	SP	
Direct Peering	Dedicated, direct connection to Google's network 10 Gbps per link	Connection in GCP Points of Presence (PoPs)	Public IP addresses	
Carrier Peering	Peering through SP to Google's public network	Varies based on partner offering	SP	

Let's start introducing **static routing** into VPC. The following diagram shows the hybrid interconnection we will use as an example:

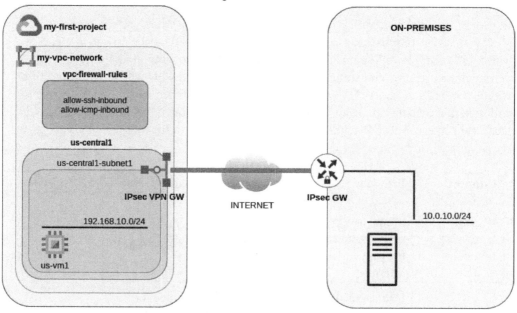

Figure 3.23 – Example of static routing configuration in IPsec VPN

Each VPC network has an assigned routing table by default, filled with some system-generated routes at the creation time. Before configuring the static routing, the default routing table contains only the routes attached to your VPC subnets and a default route pointing to the internet. Therefore, to send traffic to your on-premises networks, a static route is necessary. You can get to the wizard from **Menu** -> **VPC network** -> **Routes** -> **Create a route**, as illustrated in the following screenshot:

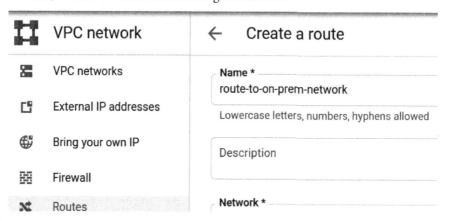

Figure 3.24 – Creating a route in a VPC network

Finally, you can easily add a new static route, as the following screenshot shows:

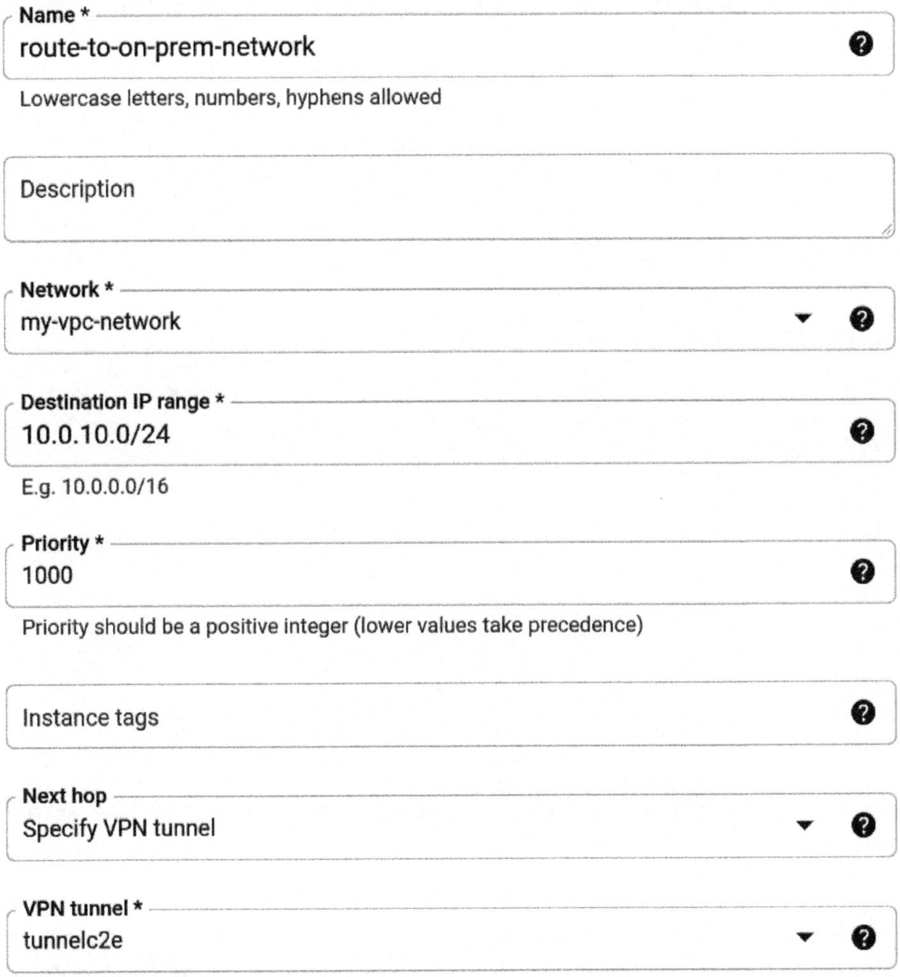

Name *

route-to-on-prem-network   ❓

Lowercase letters, numbers, hyphens allowed

Description

Network *

my-vpc-network   ▼   ❓

Destination IP range *

10.0.10.0/24   ❓

E.g. 10.0.0.0/16

Priority *

1000   ❓

Priority should be a positive integer (lower values take precedence)

Instance tags   ❓

Next hop

Specify VPN tunnel   ▼   ❓

VPN tunnel *

tunnelc2e   ▼   ❓

Figure 3.25 – Example of static routing for Cloud VPN scenario

Indeed, a static route requires to specify a unique name, a network in which the route will be applied, a destination IP address range of matching traffic, and a next hop to redirect the traffic to. In *Figure 3.25*, the route will forward traffic within my-vpc-network to the 10.0.10.0/24 on-premises network through the tunnelc2e Cloud VPN tunnel. The route will apply to all GCE instances within my-vpc-network unless you specify an **instance tag**, which lets you apply the route to only the VMs that have the tag.

> **Note**
>
> Traffic can be sent to the VPN tunnel if the IPsec VPN has been already configured and active.

Once the route is applied to your VPC network, you will see it listed in the VPC routes, as shown at the bottom of the following screenshot:

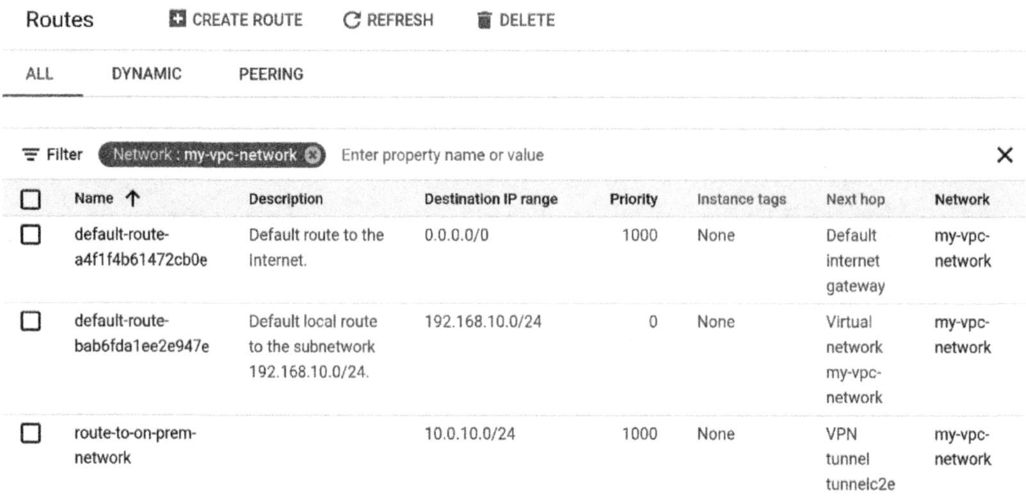
Routes
CREATE ROUTE
REFRESH
DELETE
ALL
DYNAMIC
PEERING
Filter
Network : my-vpc-network
Enter property name or value
Name
Description
Destination IP range
Priority
Instance tags
Next hop
Network
default-route-a4f1f4b61472cb0e
Default route to the Internet.
0.0.0.0/0
1000
None
Default internet gateway
my-vpc-network
default-route-bab6fda1ee2e947e
Default local route to the subnetwork 192.168.10.0/24.
192.168.10.0/24
0
None
Virtual network my-vpc-network
my-vpc-network
route-to-on-prem-network
10.0.10.0/24
1000
None
VPN tunnel tunnelc2e
my-vpc-network

Figure 3.26 – Example of static route applied in VPC routes

Static routing is great if you need to handle few routes between your VPC and on-premises networks. However, if you have a dynamic environment and you want to automatically react when the network topology changes, you should consider dynamic routing with Cloud Router.

Let's consider another example that's slightly different from the previous one. Here, we will introduce Cloud Router to build a **Border Gateway Protocol** (**BGP**) session with the on-premises router. The **BGP peering** will be built on top of the IPsec tunnel (shown in red) between the **Cloud VPN** service and the **on-premises** gateway, so there is no need to use public addresses for the BGP peering establishment. We will have more than one tunnel in the case of **high availability VPN** (**HA VPN**). The network diagram is shown here:

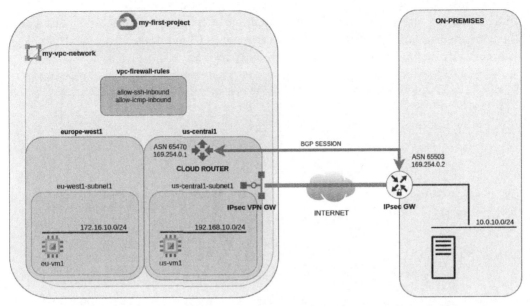

Figure 3.27 – Example of dynamic routing with Cloud Router and Cloud VPN

Please note that we still need the public IP address (from both sides) to establish the VPN connection. You may notice that in the preceding diagram, we introduced a Cloud Router in the us-central1 zone that will use AS65470 as an **autonomous system number (ASN)** and 169.254.0.1 as the IP address for setting up the BGP session. On the other side, the IPsec Gateway terminates the IPsec tunnel and establishes the BGP peering using AS65503 and the IP of 169.254.0.2. These parameters are private, and they can be used only over private interconnection such as Cloud VPN. Indeed, the 169.254/16 address range belongs to a **link-local IP version 4 (IPv4) address**, and these addresses are used to avoid any network overlapping issues. In Google Cloud, you must use a link-local address to establish BGP peering. Moreover, ASNs must belong to a private ASN range, thus between 64512-65534, or 4200000000-4294967294.

ASNs

An ASN is a **globally unique ID (GUID)** that defines a group of one or more IP prefixes run by one or more network operators that maintain a single, clearly defined routing policy. These groups of IP prefixes are known as **autonomous systems (ASes)**.

Additionally, we are using the eu-west1-subnet1 subnet in the europe-west1 region with the address of 172.16.10.0/24. This network will be advertising dynamically to the on-premises router through BGP. In general, any new subnets that will be added or removed in your hybrid environment are handled dynamically through BGP.

In the following screenshot, you can see an example of creating a Cloud Router based on the network diagram from *Figure 3.27*. You can create a Cloud Router from the **Hybrid Connectivity** menu in the **Networking** section, as you can see here:

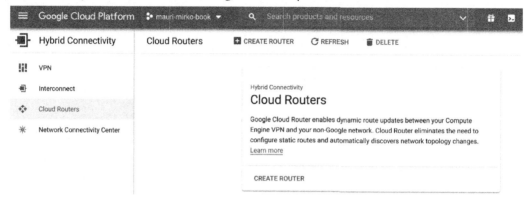

Figure 3.28 – Creating a Cloud Router from Hybrid Connectivity menu

As we introduced before, the following screenshot shows how to create a Cloud Router:

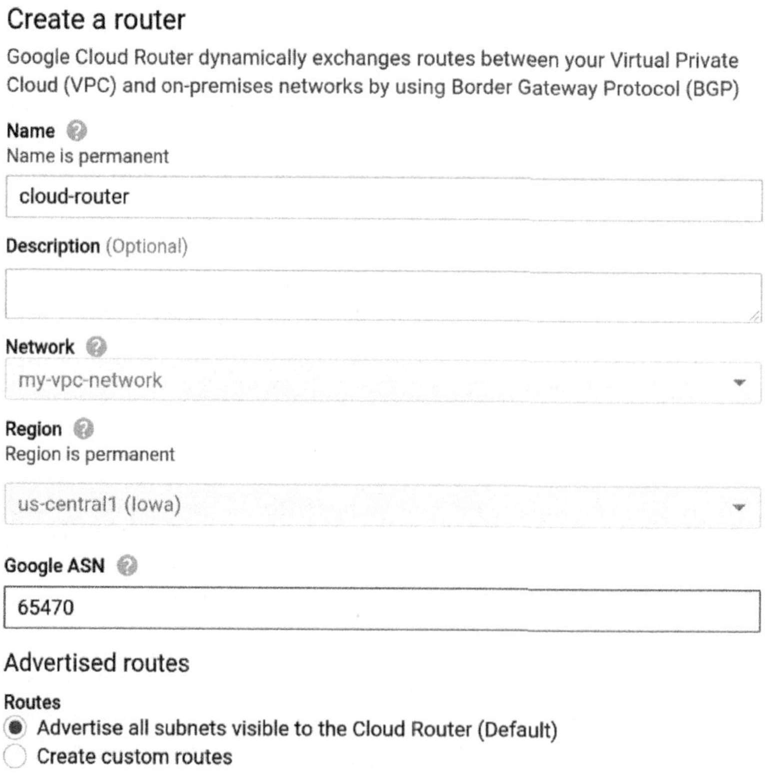

Create a router

Google Cloud Router dynamically exchanges routes between your Virtual Private Cloud (VPC) and on-premises networks by using Border Gateway Protocol (BGP)

Name ❓
Name is permanent

cloud-router

Description (Optional)

Network ❓

my-vpc-network ▼

Region ❓
Region is permanent

us-central1 (Iowa) ▼

Google ASN ❓

65470

Advertised routes

Routes
🔘 Advertise all subnets visible to the Cloud Router (Default)
⚪ Create custom routes

Figure 3.29 – Example of Cloud Router configuration

As you can see from *Figure 3.29*, Cloud Router configuration requires a unique name that is permanent, a VPC network, and a GCP region. Also, you must specify the ASN, which is a requirement for establishing BGP sessions with other BGP routers. Additionally, you can choose whether to announce all subnets visible to the Cloud Router or a subset of them. With this last option, you need to create a custom routes policy, which will be described in more detail in *Chapter 5, Implementing Hybrid Connectivity in GCP*.

> **Important Note**
> Cloud Router announces by default all visible subnets, depending on whether you choose **Regional** or **Global** dynamic routing mode (see *Figure 3.8*). In **Regional** mode, only the subnets within the Cloud Router region will be advertised. In **Global** mode, all the VPC subnets will be advertised.

Once your Cloud Router is created, you need to configure a BGP peering with the other BGP router. In the following screenshot, you can see an example of BGP peering configuration during Cloud VPN creation:

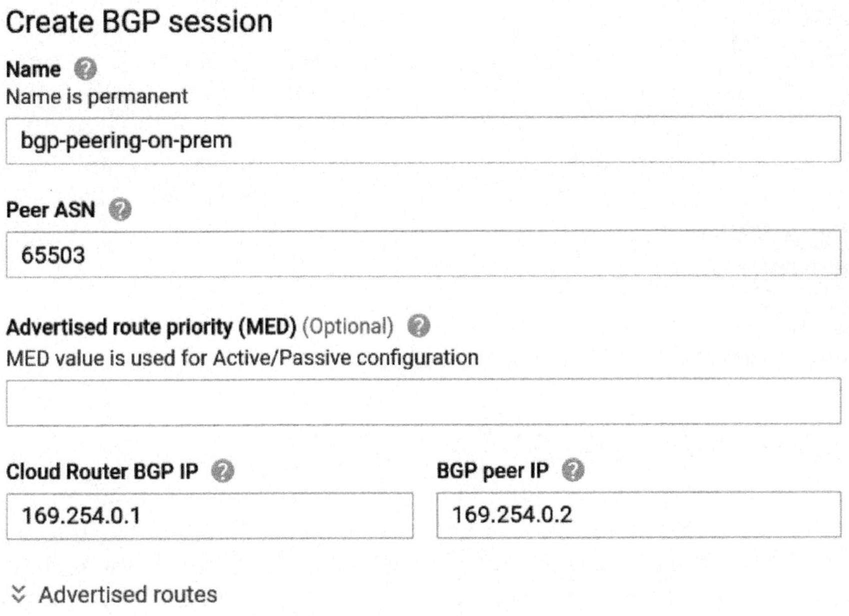

Create BGP session

Name @
Name is permanent

    bgp-peering-on-prem

Peer ASN @

    65503

Advertised route priority (MED) (Optional) @
MED value is used for Active/Passive configuration

Cloud Router BGP IP @   **BGP peer IP** @

    169.254.0.1   169.254.0.2

⌄ Advertised routes

Figure 3.30 – Example of BGP peering configuration with on-premises router

As you can see from *Figure 3.30*, BGP peering requires the following:

- A name
- The ASN of the peer you are connecting to
- The IP addresses for the local Cloud Router
- The remote on-premises router IP address

All of these are needed for a BGP session to be established. Once the BGP peering is on, you will see the dynamic on-premises network appearing in the VPC routes, as the following screenshot illustrates:

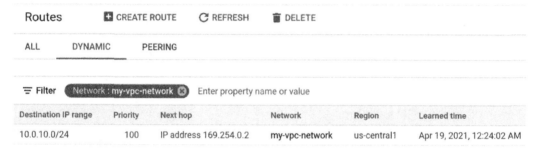

Figure 3.31 – Dynamic routes from on-premises router

As *Figure 3.31* shows, the on-premises network appears in the list of dynamic routes. You may notice that the next hop of the route is the BGP peer (with IP address 169.254.0.2). This means that traffic destined for 10.0.10.0/24 will be forwarded to the next-hop router.

Now that you have learned how to configure static and dynamic routing in your VPC in GCP, let's go through the VPC peering configuration.

Configuring VPC peering

Whenever you need to make communication possible between two or more VPC networks together, either in the same project or in two different projects, the only choice you have is **VPC peering**. VPC peering can be configured between no more than two VPC networks, but you can configure more than one peering (that is, VPC A <-> VPC B, VPC B <-> VPC C). Please note that **transitive VPC Network Peering** is not supported (so if you want to peer VPC A and VPC C, you need to configure a third VPC Peering, VPC A <-> VPC C). VPC peering can also work for two projects of two different organizations.

Indeed, you will learn how to configure it throughout a case study, as shown in the following diagram. Let's have a look at it:

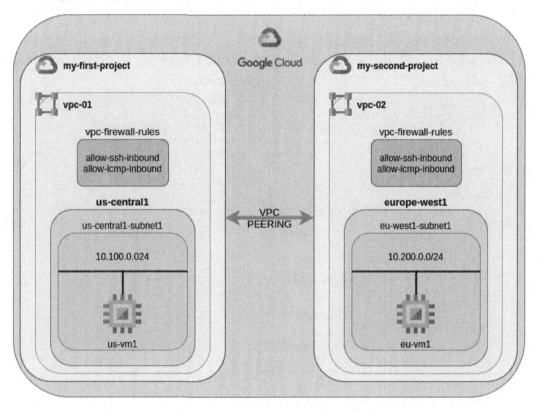

Figure 3.32 – VPC peering case study

The case study will show you how to interconnect two different VPCs in two different projects. We will deploy two VMs in two subnets. The us-vm1 VM will be deployed in us-central1-subnet1 with an IP address of 10.100.00.2/24, and the eu-vm1 VM will be run on eu-west1-subnet1 with an IP address of 10.200.0.2/24.

> **Important Note**
> VPC peering will only work when you have non-overlapping IP addresses between VPC subnets.

In addition, firewall rules are in place to let VMs communicate with each other. Indeed, allow-ssh and allow-icmp firewall rules will allow incoming traffic to both instances for SSH and ICMP traffic.

When configuring VPC peering, you need to establish a bidirectional connection. Therefore, you need to set up a VPC peering from `vpc-01` to `vpc-02` and vice versa. The VPC peering requires some parameters, as shown in the following screenshot:

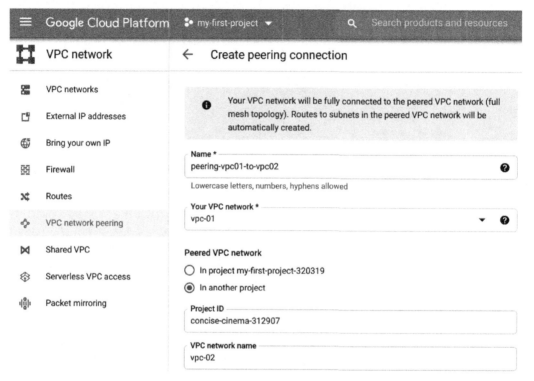

Figure 3.33 – VPC peering configuration example from vpc-01 to vpc-02

Indeed, when configuring VPC peering, you need to fulfill these parameters:

- **Name**: In the preceding example, we use `peering-vpc1-to-vpc2` as a name to refer to the VPC peering from `vpc-01` to `vpc-02`.

- **Your VPC network**: In the preceding example, we use `vpc-01`, which is the name of the starting VPC network.

- **Project ID**: In the preceding example, we use `concise-cinema-312907`, which is the project ID related to `my-second-project`. You may notice that the **Peered VPC network** option is set to **In another project** because the destination VPC belongs to a different project.

- **VPC network name**: In the preceding example, we use `vpc-02`, which is the name of the destination VPC network to whom we want to peer.

When you have configured the VPC peering from `vpc-01` to `vpc-02`, you need to configure the opposite direction, thus `peering-vpc2-to-vpc1`. For convenience, we are not going to show the VPC peering configuration as it is very similar to the previous one. Once you have configured both VPC peering directions, you will see the status of VPC peering as **Active** and a green checkmark next to it, as shown in *Figure 3.35*.

In the same manner, you also need to configure the other way around, as illustrated in the following screenshot:

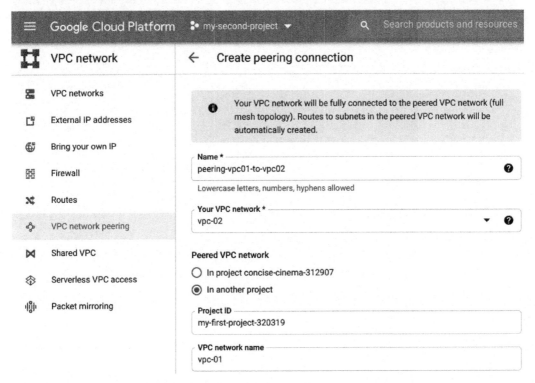

Figure 3.34 – VPC configuration example from vpc-02 to vpc-01

The result of such an operation will be an active VPC peering, as shown in the following screenshot:

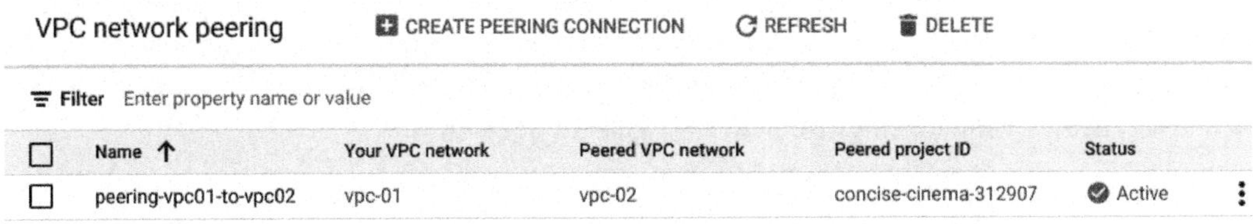

Figure 3.35 – Active VPC peering from vpc-01 to vpc-02

Now, if we check the state of the routing table, we will see that each VPC has got a new route in the table that comes from the VPC peering we have just created. Indeed, the 10.200.0.0/24 network appears on vpc-01 in my-first-project as **Auto generated route via peering [peering-vpc1-to-vpc2]**. You may also notice that the route has the highest priority; likewise, the other vpc-01 attached subnets. This is shown in the following screenshot:

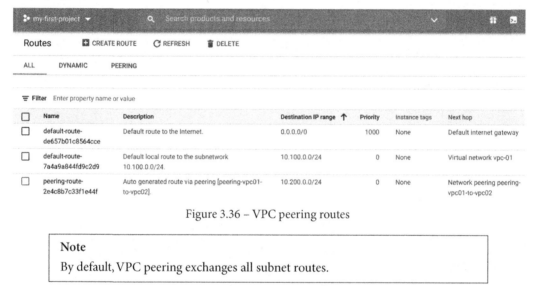

Figure 3.36 – VPC peering routes

> **Note**
>
> By default, VPC peering exchanges all subnet routes.

You can also check the **PEERING** tab to see all routes that have been learned through VPC peering, as shown in the following screenshot:

Figure 3.37 – VPC peering route from the PEERING tab

When VPC peering is **Active** and VPC routes have been exchanged, you can test connectivity between VMs. As the following screenshot shows, us-vm1 can reach eu-vm1, thus demonstrating the VPC's successful operation:

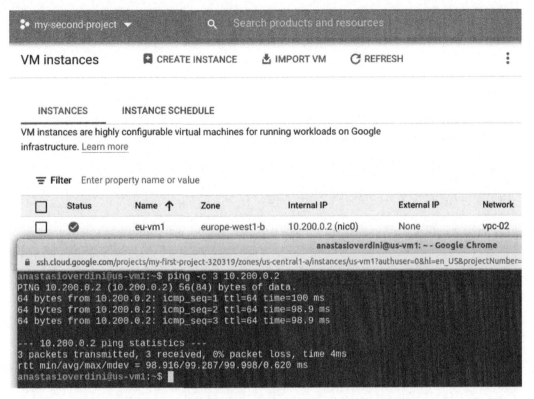

Figure 3.38 – VM communication after successful VPC peering

You have learned how to establish VPC peering using the GCP console. Additionally, you can use Cloud Shell to build VPC peering with the following equivalent commands:

```
gcloud compute networks peerings create peering-vpc1-vpc2 \
--network=vpc-01 \
--peer-network=vpc-02 \
--peer-project= concise-cinema-312907
```

The previous command creates peering from vpc1 to vpc2. Now, you need to do the opposite with the following command:

```
gcloud compute networks peerings create peering-vpc2-vpc1 \
--network=vpc-02 \
--peer-network=vpc-01 \
--peer-project=my-first-project-320319
```

As we did with the GCP console, you need to specify the name of the VPC peering and three parameters with the following options:

- `--network`: This refers to the source VPC network name.

- `--peer-network`: This refers to the destination VPC network name.

- `--peer-project`: This refers to the destination project ID in which the destination VPC network is.

To check the VPC peering, you can use the following command:

```
gcloud compute networks peerings list
```

Now that you have learned how to configure VPC peering, let's go through the Shared VPC configuration.

Configuring Shared VPC

In the previous section, you have learned that VPC peering is a powerful way to enable communication between VPC networks across different projects, and even across two projects from two different organizations. This enables VMs to communicate with each other privately without passing via public networks. So, when you have resources that are needed to communicate across different projects, VPC peering is a valid solution. However, VPC peering requires that the organization that has peered the VPC network should configure its own side. Indeed, you are required to create subnets, assign **classless inter-domain routing (CIDR)** ranges, provide firewall rules, and so on.

Here's a summary of what we've learned thus far:

- When we need to connect two VPC networks in the same project, we have to choose VPC peering.

- When we need to connect two VPC networks in two projects from two different organizations, we have to choose VPC peering.

- When we need to connect two VPC networks in two projects from the same organization, we have to choose from VPC peering and Shared VPC.

- One of the important criteria to choose is that the network administration in Shared VPC is centralized, while in VPC Network Peering it is decentralized.

- Furthermore, VPC peering does not support *transitive peering*.

This sometimes might be too much work for some users that just want to have some GCE instances in different projects to talk with each other. Here comes Shared VPC. Indeed, Shared VPC allows a complex organization with several independent projects to centralize the administration of the VPC network and lets it share the one network for multiple projects.

The Shared VPC architecture is composed of one **host project** and several **service projects**. The host project contains the shared VPC network, while the service projects rely on the host project for networking operations. The following diagram depicts the Shared VPC architecture:

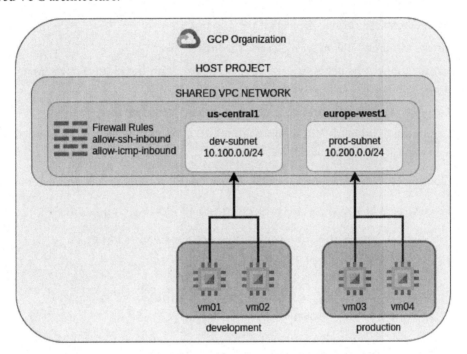

Figure 3.39 – Shared VPC architecture

From *Figure 3.39*, you may notice that there are two different service projects (**development** and **production**) containing two GCE instances. The projects do not have any network, and therefore they rely on the shared VPC configured in the **host project** to get IP addresses from the two subnets, dev-subnet (IP address range of 10.100.0.0/24) and prod-subnet (IP address range of 10.200.0.0/24). The host project has firewall rules that apply to the whole shared VPC. Indeed, allow-ssh-inbound and allow-icmp-inbound will permit incoming SSH and ICMP traffic to all the VMs that rely on the shared VPC network.

The configuration of a shared VPC requires a few steps, as follows:

1. Create host and service projects if they do not exist yet.

2. Create a shared VPC network inside the host project.

3. Create subnets inside the shared VPC network, assuming that we have created a **Custom** mode VPC network.

4. Create an appropriate firewall rule in the shared VPC network.

5. Configure the shared VPC, defining the host project along with its subnets, and select the service projects.

With Cloud Shell, you can configure such steps with the commands shown next:

- To configure host and service projects, run the following commands:

```
gcloud projects create host-project-34341212 \
  --name="host-project"


gcloud projects create serviceproject1-247521 \
  --name="development"


gcloud projects create serviceproject2-247521 \
  --name="production"
```

- To configure the shared VPC and subnets for development and production, run the following commands:

```
gcloud compute networks create shared-vpc \
  --subnet-mode=custom


gcloud compute networks subnets create dev-subnet\
  --network=shared-vpc \

  --region=us-central1 \
  --range=10.100.0.0/24


gcloud compute networks subnets create prod-subnet \
  --network=shared-vpc \

  --region=europe-west1 \
  --range=10.200.0.0/24
```

- To configure the firewall rules for Shared VPC, run the following commands:

```
gcloud compute firewall-rules create allow-icmp-inbound \
  --network=shared-vpc \
  --allow icmp \
  --source-ranges=0.0.0.0/0


gcloud compute firewall-rules create allow-ssh-inbound \
  --network=shared-vpc \
  --allow tcp:22 \
  -source-ranges=0.0.0.0/0
```

- To configure Shared VPC by enabling the host project, select the subnets (`dev-subnet` and `prod-subnet`), select users by role, and provide permissions by attaching service projects (`development` and `production`). This is illustrated in the following screenshot. To reach this page, you have to go to **Menu -> VPC Network -> Shared VPC**:

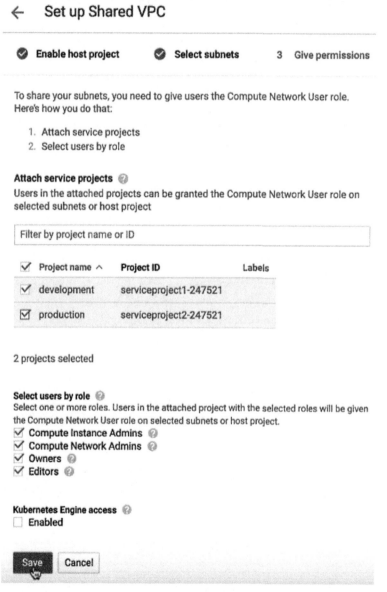

Figure 3.40 – Shared VPC configuration

After configuring Shared VPC, VMs in the development and production projects will be able to communicate with each other. Now that you have learned how to configure Shared VPC, let's move on to NAT configuration in Google Cloud.

Configuring NAT in Google Cloud

Whenever you need to supply public access to your GCE instances and they do not have a public IP address, you can use **Cloud NAT**, which is a managed service provided by Google Cloud (and obviously, firewall rules must allow this communication). Indeed, Google Cloud recommends using Cloud NAT when you have many private VMs that need to access public services such as public repositories or upgrades. Cloud NAT can also be used even for one private VM. Therefore, Cloud NAT works as a gateway for your VMs that perform **source NAT (SNAT)**.

> **SNAT and Destination NAT (DNAT)**
>
> Whenever a Cloud Router performs a NAT operation that is translating the private IP address into a public one and vice versa, the entire process is composed of two different stages.
>
> For the outbound traffic, the translation is performed on the source IP address (private to public), and we call it SNAT. For the return packets, it is the destination IP address that is translated (public to private), and that is what we call DNAT.

Cloud NAT embeds Cloud Router to route outbound traffic out of one GCP region. It is a regional service and works in a fully distributed manner as it is a **software-defined network (SDN)** component. According to *Benzekki, Kamal; El Fergougui, Abdeslam; Elbelrhiti Elalaoui, Abdelbaki (2016), "Software-defined networking (SDN): A survey", Security and Communication Networks. 9 (18): 5803–5833: Software-defined networking (SDN) technology is an approach to network management that enables dynamic, programmatically efficient network configuration in order to improve network performance and monitoring, making it more like cloud computing than traditional network management.*

The following diagram shows a case study of Cloud NAT configuration:

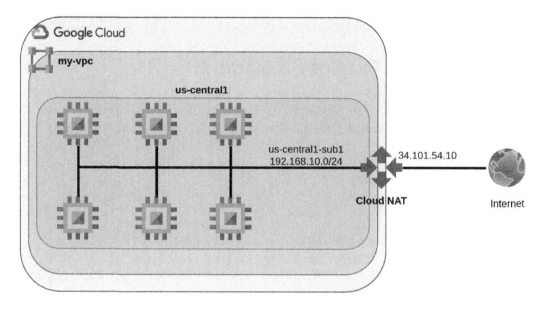

Figure 3.41 – Cloud NAT case study

As *Figure 3.41* shows, imagine having many GCE instances running as private VMs in one GCP region (for example, us-central1) inside a VPC network (my-vpc). Perhaps they belong to a **managed instance group** (**MIG**) and they regularly need access to the internet from inside the VPC. Deploying a Cloud NAT that embeds Cloud Router will allow your VMs to get to the internet without having a public IP assigned.

Assuming we have already configured the `my-vpc` VPC, the `us-central1-sub` subnet, and one `us-vm1` GCE instance as a private VM, let's see how to configure the Cloud NAT gateway for all instances in the `us-central1` region. This is what we can see in the following screenshot:

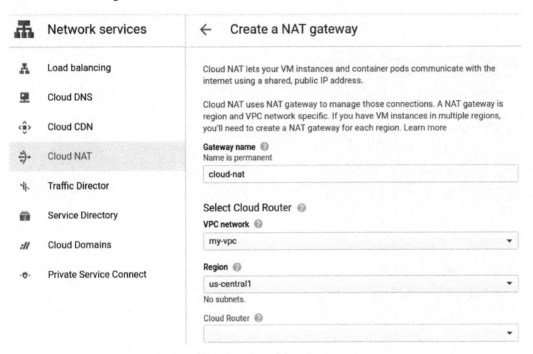

Figure 3.42 – Getting started with the Cloud NAT configuration

As *Figure 3.42* illustrates, to configure a Cloud NAT instance, you need to begin with a unique name (cloud-nat) of the Cloud NAT instance, then specify the embedded Cloud Router, which needs to be created in one GCP region (us-central1), in one VPC network (my-vpc). The following screenshot shows how to create a Cloud Router during the process of creating a Cloud NAT instance. To reach this page, you have to click on the combo box below **Cloud Router** and then click on **Create Router**:

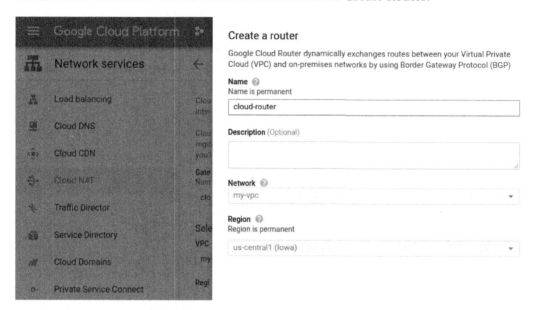

Figure 3.43 – Cloud Router creation template

Indeed, to create a Cloud Router, only the name must be specified. When you are done, you can optionally configure advanced options in the NAT gateway, as the following screenshot shows:

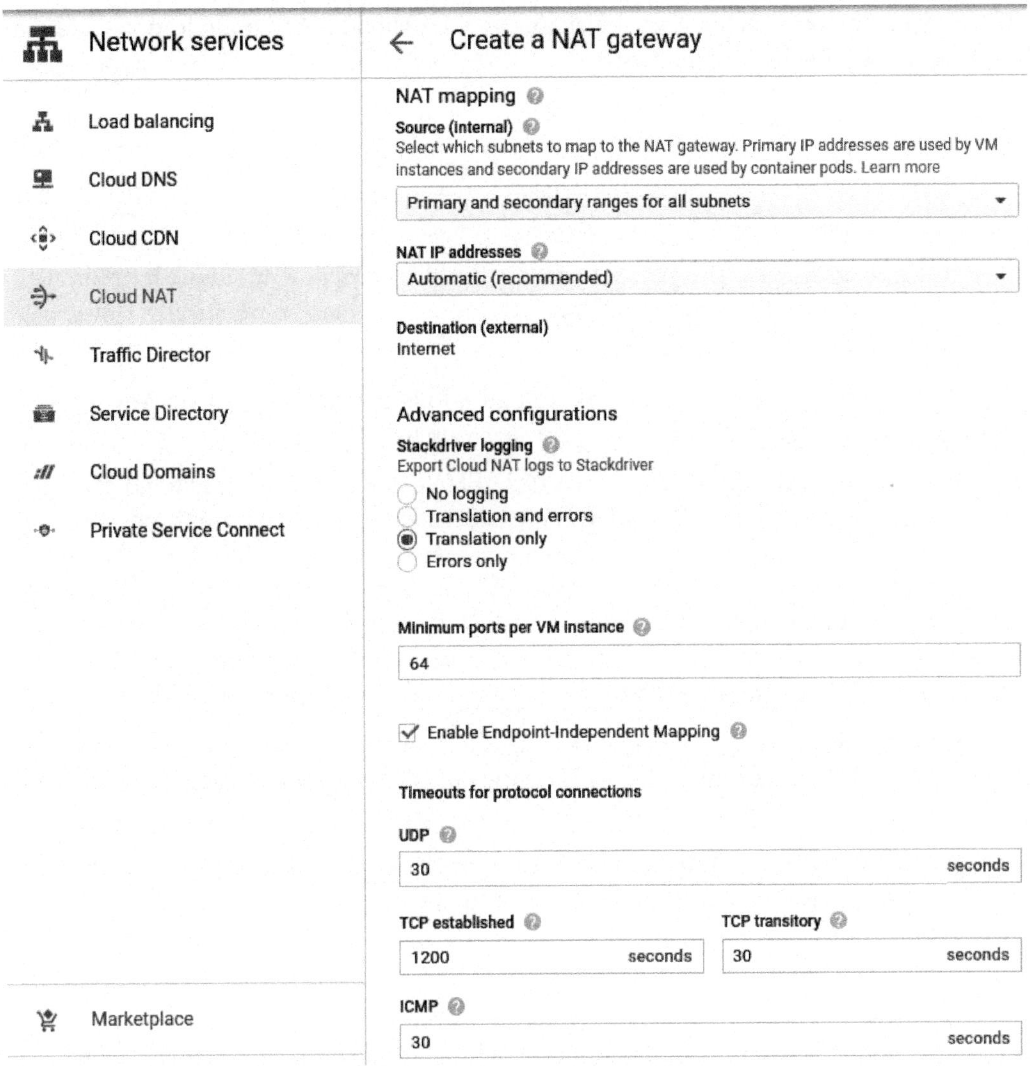

Network services

- Load balancing
- Cloud DNS
- Cloud CDN
- Cloud NAT
- Traffic Director
- Service Directory
- Cloud Domains
- Private Service Connect

- Marketplace

← **Create a NAT gateway**

NAT mapping ⓘ

Source (internal) ⓘ
Select which subnets to map to the NAT gateway. Primary IP addresses are used by VM instances and secondary IP addresses are used by container pods. Learn more

Primary and secondary ranges for all subnets   ▼

NAT IP addresses ⓘ

Automatic (recommended)   ▼

Destination (external)
Internet

Advanced configurations

Stackdriver logging ⓘ
Export Cloud NAT logs to Stackdriver
- ◯ No logging
- ◯ Translation and errors
- ◉ Translation only
- ◯ Errors only

Minimum ports per VM instance ⓘ

64

☑ Enable Endpoint-Independent Mapping ⓘ

Timeouts for protocol connections

UDP ⓘ

30	seconds

TCP established ⓘ

1200	seconds

TCP transitory ⓘ

30	seconds

ICMP ⓘ

30	seconds

Figure 3.44 – Advanced options in Cloud NAT

There are several options that you can change in your Cloud NAT configuration. Let's see the most important ones, as follows:

- **Source (Internal)**: This is the source subnets you want to translate with NAT. By default, the primary and secondary CIDR range of all region subnets will be NAT. Here, you can choose to use NAT only the primary CIDR of all subnets or a custom CIDR range.

- **NAT IP addresses**: This decides how to allocate external IP addresses to translate (NAT) your traffic. By default, Cloud NAT allocates them automatically. However, you can manually assign a fixed number of external IPs.

  From now on, these are advanced configurations. You have to click on **Advanced configurations** to make them appear. They are listed here:

  - **Stackdriver logging**: This enables Cloud NAT to export NAT logs to **GCP operations** (formerly **Stackdriver**) in order to keep track of translations. By default, this option is disabled but in this case study, we decide to log only the translation by choosing **Translation only**, as shown in *Figure 3.44*. You could also choose **Errors only** to see them in the logs. *Error* refers to a VM instance that attempts to connect to the internet by sending a packet over the connection, but the NAT gateway can't allocate a NAT IP and port due to port exhaustion.

  - **Minimum ports per VM instance**: This is the reserved number of ports that Cloud NAT holds for each VM. 64 is the default value and normally, you do not touch it.

  - **Enable Endpoint-Independent Mapping**: This option means that every packet from a given internal IP and port pair is mapped to the same public IP and port regardless of the destination of the traffic. Its purpose is to improve port utilization.

  - **Timeouts for protocol connections**: This option is related to timeouts (in seconds) for each common protocol such as **User Datagram Protocol (UDP)**, **Transmission Control Protocol (TCP)**, and ICMP. Normally, you use the default, as shown in *Figure 3.44*.

When Cloud NAT is configured correctly, it will look like this:

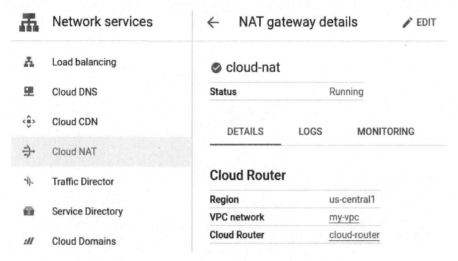

Figure 3.45 – Cloud NAT gateway fully operational

You can then test public connectivity from your private GCE instance (us-vm1), as shown in the following screenshot:

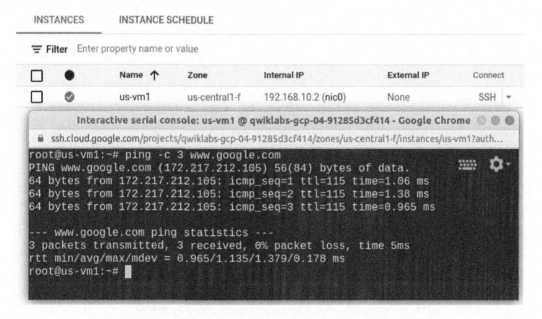

Figure 3.46 – Public connectivity check after using Cloud NAT

Since we enabled logging, after a while and after some traffic (try to upgrade the operating system of the VM) being generated, you can access Cloud NAT logs. To do so, go back to Cloud NAT, click on the instance, and choose the link from the second tab. The result will be as shown here:

Figure 3.47 – GCP operations logging for Cloud NAT

You might see that after some traffic, logs will show up and display many parameters, including public IPs and ports being used to perform NAT and **port address translation (PAT)**, private IPs and ports from which traffic was generated, and Cloud Routers and Cloud NAT gateways involved in the traffic translation. *Figure 3.47* highlights all the important information about Cloud NAT.

Now that you have learned how to configure VPC common resources, routing, VPC peering, Shared VPC, and Cloud NAT, let's move on to the next section to look at how to configure and manage firewall rules.

Configuring and managing firewall rules

In this section, we investigate how to configure and manage firewall rules in a VPC network. Firewall rules are an important element of the VPC network because they implement security in your infrastructure. Let's begin by taking the following steps:

1. First, we create a new `mynetwork` VPC with the **Automatic** subnet mode, as shown in the following screenshot:

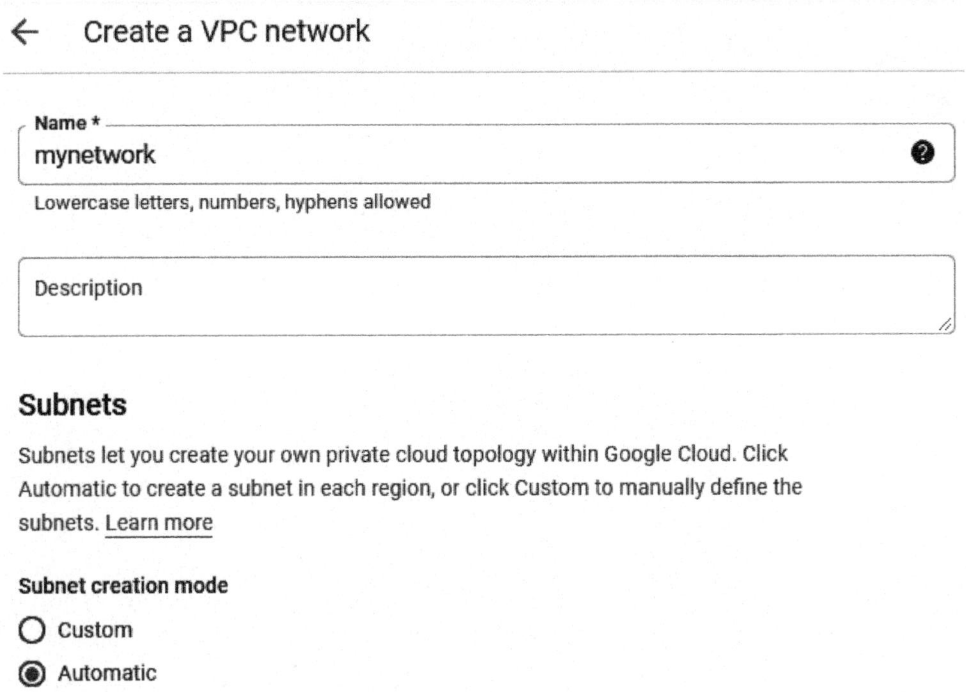

←   **Create a VPC network**

Name *

mynetwork   ❓

Lowercase letters, numbers, hyphens allowed

Description

Subnets

Subnets let you create your own private cloud topology within Google Cloud. Click Automatic to create a subnet in each region, or click Custom to manually define the subnets. Learn more

Subnet creation mode

○ Custom

◉ Automatic

Figure 3.48 – Creating a VPC with Automatic subnet mode

2. Then, we create a `privatenetwork` VPC with the **Custom** subnet mode, as shown in the following screenshot:

←   Create a VPC network

Name *
```
privatenetwork
```
Lowercase letters, numbers, hyphens allowed

Description

Subnets

Subnets let you create your own private cloud topology within Google Cloud. Click Automatic to create a subnet in each region, or click Custom to manually define the subnets. Learn more

Subnet creation mode

◉ Custom

○ Automatic

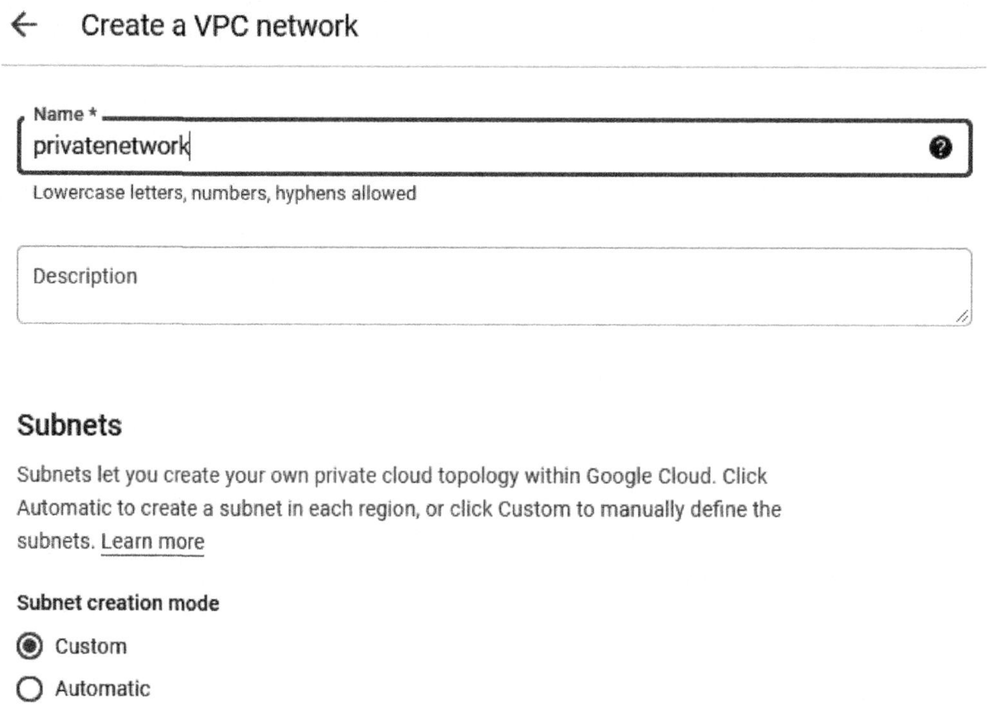

Figure 3.49 – Creating a VPC with Custom subnet mode

3. Since the subnet mode is **Custom**, we must create at least a custom subnet in the `privatenetwork` VPC, selecting the `10.0.0.0/24` IP address range, as can be seen in the following screenshot:

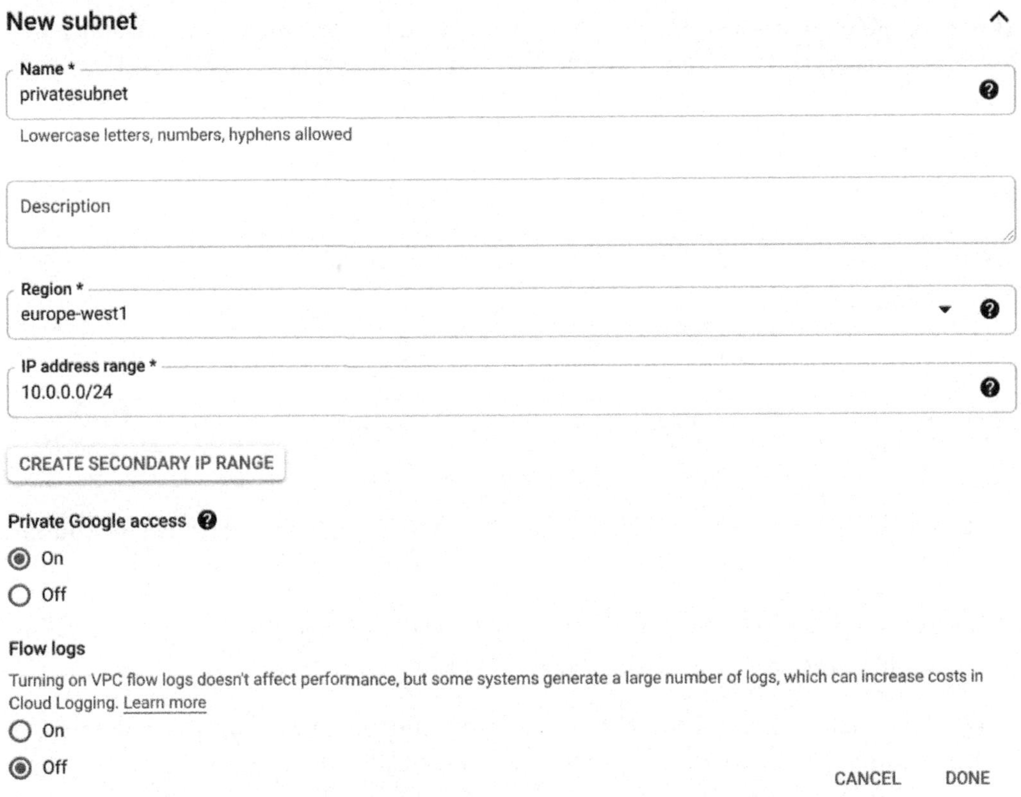

New subnet   ⌃

Name *
privatesubnet   ❓

Lowercase letters, numbers, hyphens allowed

Description

Region *
europe-west1   ▾   ❓

IP address range *
10.0.0.0/24   ❓

[CREATE SECONDARY IP RANGE]

Private Google access ❓

◉ On
○ Off

Flow logs

Turning on VPC flow logs doesn't affect performance, but some systems generate a large number of logs, which can increase costs in Cloud Logging. Learn more

○ On
◉ Off   CANCEL   DONE

Figure 3.50 – New subnet creation in the VPC network using Cloud Console

By means of the cloud shell, we will create some GCE instances to use later for testing, as follows:

```
gcloud compute networks subnets create privatesubnet \
--network=privatenetwork --region=europe-west1 \
--range=10.0.0.0/24 --enable-private-ip-google-access
```

The previous command lets you create a subnet named `privatesubnet` and attach it to the `privatenetwork` VPC network. The subnet has been created in the `europe-west1` region and has an IP network range of `10.0.0.0/24`. The result of the VPC creation will look like this:

Name ↑	Region	Subnets	Mode	IP address ranges	Gateways	Firewall Rules
▸ default		27	Auto ▾			4
▸ mynetwork		27	Auto ▾			0
▸ privatenetwork		1	Custom			0

Figure 3.51 – List of VPCs used in this exercise

Next, we will create a new GCE instance named `default-us-vm`, which will be running in the `us-central1-a` zone and in the `default` network, as follows:

```
gcloud compute instances create default-us-vm \
--zone=us-central1-a --network=default
```

Next, we will create another GCE instance named `mynet-us-vm`, which will be running in the `us-central1-a` zone and in the `mynetwork` VPC network, as follows:

```
gcloud compute instances create mynet-us-vm \
--zone=us-central1-a --network=mynetwork
```

Next, we will create another GCE instance named `mynet-eu-vm`, which will be running in the `europe-west1-b` zone and in the `mynetwork` VPC network, as follows:

```
gcloud compute instances create mynet-eu-vm \
--zone=europe-west1-b --network=mynetwork
```

Moreover, we will create a GCE instance named `privatenetwork-bastion` in the `europe-west1-c` zone, which will be running in the `privatesubnet` subnet, as follows:

```
gcloud compute instances create privatenetwork-bastion \
--zone=europe-west1-c --subnet=privatesubnet
```

Finally, we will create a GCE instance named `privatenetwork-eu-vm` running in the `europe-west1-a` zone and the `privatesubnet` subnet, as follows:

```
gcloud compute instances create privatenetwork-eu-vm \
--zone=europe-west1-a --subnet=privatesubnet
```

> **Note**
>
> When creating GCE instances using `gcloud` commands, you can specify the network that the VM instances are a part of with the `–network` option. If `--subnet` is also specified, the subnet must be a subnetwork of the network specified by the `--network` flag. If neither is specified, the default network is used.

The default network has already some predefined firewall rules, as you can see from the following screenshot:

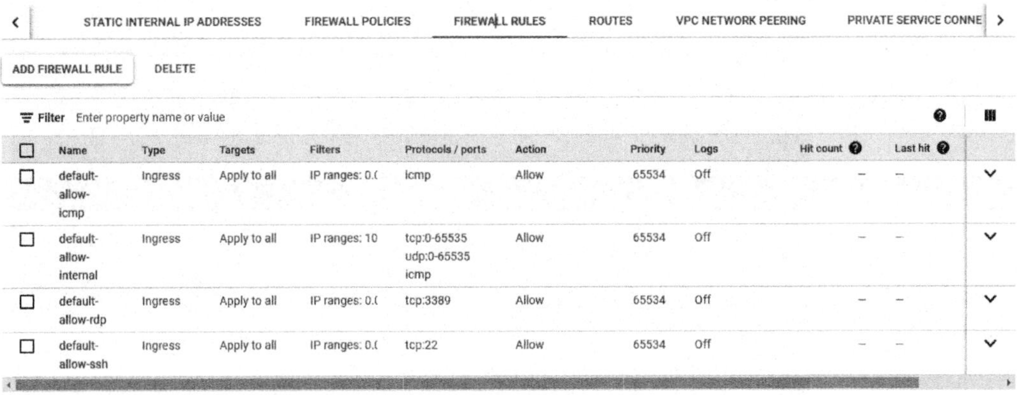

Figure 3.52 – Default firewall rules

Please note that all networks also have two *hidden* rules that are not displayed but are still present, as shown in the following screenshot:

| default-deny-all-ingress | ❓ | Ingress | Apply to all | IP ranges: 0.0.0.0/0 | all | Deny | 65535 |
| default-allow-all-egress | ❓ | Egress | Apply to all | IP ranges: 0.0.0.0/0 | all | Allow | 65535 |

Figure 3.53 – Implied firewall rules

Let's check if the `default-allow-ssh` firewall rule is working. Let's connect via SSH to the `default-us-vm` instance in the default VPC, as shown in the following screenshot:

Figure 3.54 – Connecting to a VM instance in the default VPC network via SSH

As you can see from the following screenshot, we are able to connect by SSH (we've also pinged `www.google.com` to test the egress connectivity):

```
  ssh.cloud.google.com/projects/qwiklabs-gcp-00-d7daf5aab8ec/zones/us-central1-a/instances/default-us-vm?authuser=0&hl=en_US&pro...
Connected, host fingerprint: ssh-rsa 0 AF:25:77:39:A8:F0:1A:D7:30:F8:DE:07:C0:0F
:93:EC:B1:51:C9:78:08:66:C7:67:86:64:26:7C:07:9D:92:0A
Linux default-us-vm 4.19.0-16-cloud-amd64 #1 SMP Debian 4.19.181-1 (2021-03-19)
x86_64

The programs included with the Debian GNU/Linux system are free software;
the exact distribution terms for each program are described in the
individual files in /usr/share/doc/*/copyright.

Debian GNU/Linux comes with ABSOLUTELY NO WARRANTY, to the extent
permitted by applicable law.
Creating directory '/home/student-00-c8c39bed067b'.
student-00-c8c39bed067b@default-us-vm:~$ ping www.google.com
PING www.google.com (108.177.111.106) 56(84) bytes of data.
64 bytes from 108.177.111.106 (108.177.111.106): icmp_seq=1 ttl=113 time=1.65 ms
64 bytes from 108.177.111.106 (108.177.111.106): icmp_seq=2 ttl=113 time=1.54 ms
64 bytes from 108.177.111.106 (108.177.111.106): icmp_seq=3 ttl=113 time=1.49 ms
64 bytes from 108.177.111.106 (108.177.111.106): icmp_seq=4 ttl=113 time=1.45 ms
64 bytes from 108.177.111.106 (108.177.111.106): icmp_seq=5 ttl=113 time=1.46 ms
^C
--- www.google.com ping statistics ---
5 packets transmitted, 5 received, 0% packet loss, time 11ms
rtt min/avg/max/mdev = 1.451/1.519/1.650/0.076 ms
student-00-c8c39bed067b@default-us-vm:~$
```

Figure 3.55 – Egress connectivity verification of a VM instance in the default VPC network

Now, let's try to SSH to the `mynet-eu-vm` or `mynet-us-vm` VMs that are connected to our `privatenetwork` VPC, where no firewall rules were defined at all (apart from the implied ones), as shown in the following screenshot:

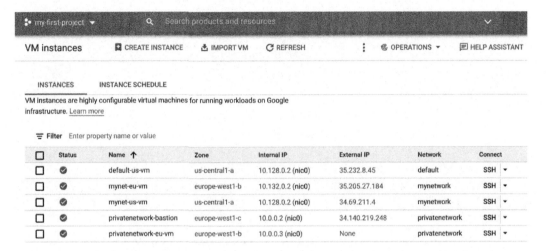

Figure 3.56 – Connecting to a VM instance in a non-default VPC network via SSH

You should observe that the Cloud Console tries to establish an SSH connection to the server, as illustrated in the following screenshot:

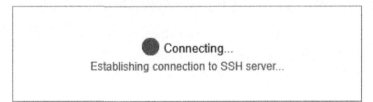

Figure 3.57 – SSH connection attempt to privatenetwork GCEs

Indeed, the SSH connection fails, as shown in the following screenshot:

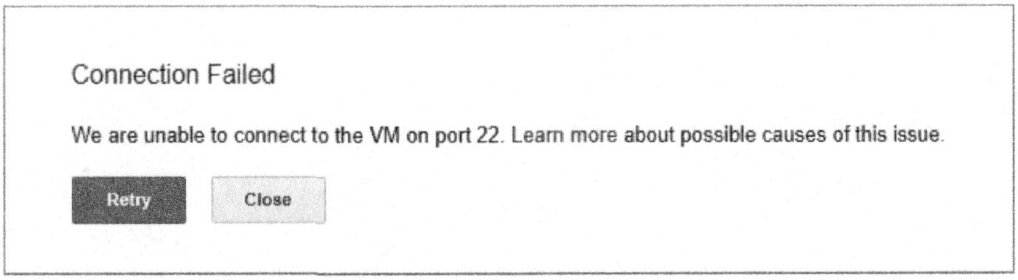

Figure 3.58 – SSH connection failure to privatenetwork GCEs

As we can see in the following screenshot, the SSH inbound traffic is not allowed, due to the firewall rule:

privatenetwork-deny-all-ingress ❷	Ingress	Apply to all	IP ranges: 0.0.0.0/0	all	Deny	65,535
privatenetwork-allow-all-egress ❷	Egress	Apply to all	IP ranges: 0.0.0.0/0	all	Allow	65,535

Figure 3.59 – Implied firewall rule that denies all ingress

> **Note**
> Implied firewall rules are hidden rules that are present regardless of the network that has been created. They cannot be eliminated, and they have the lowest priority.

So, we want to add a firewall rule to allow the SSH (port 22) traffic for the Cloud Shell instance. Therefore, we first try to retrieve the external IP address of the Cloud Shell instance, with the following commands:

```
ip=$(curl -s https://api.ipify.org)
echo "My External IP address is: $ip"
```

The preceding commands connect to a website that provides the public IP address. This value is stored in a variable named `ip` and displayed in a message fetching its content using `$ip`. The output of the command looks like this: `My External IP address is: 104.199.47.6`.

Well, now, we can add a firewall rule to `mynetwork`, as shown in the following screenshot:

Figure 3.60 – Adding firewall rule to mynetwork VPC

From the VPC network details, you can create a new firewall rule with the appropriate button highlighted in *Figure 3.60*, which can be reached by clicking on the **FIREWALL RULES** tab first. Next, insert a unique name for the firewall rule and assign it to the mynetwork VPC network, as shown in the following screenshot:

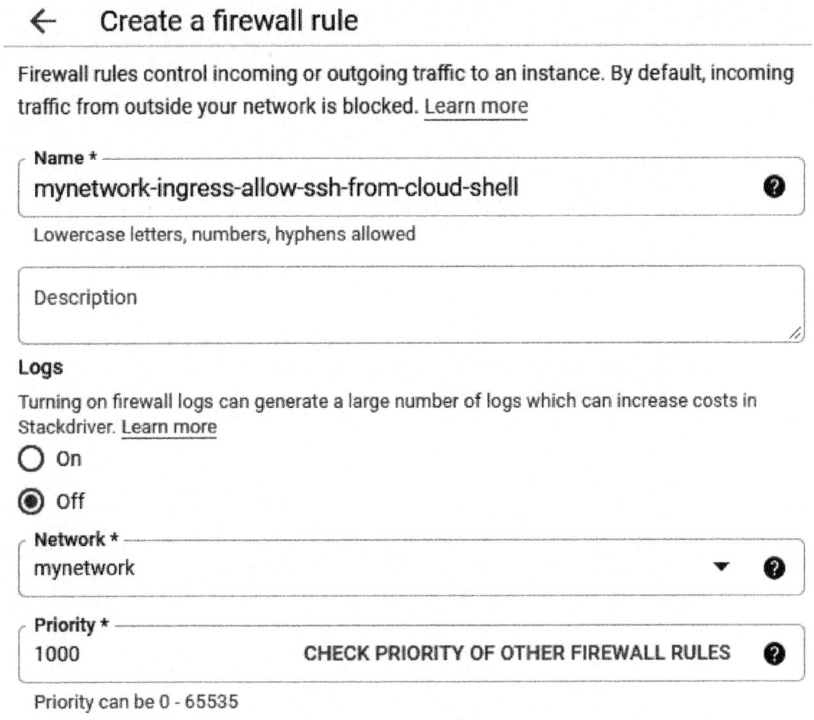

← **Create a firewall rule**

Firewall rules control incoming or outgoing traffic to an instance. By default, incoming traffic from outside your network is blocked. Learn more

Name *

mynetwork-ingress-allow-ssh-from-cloud-shell   ❓

Lowercase letters, numbers, hyphens allowed

Description

Logs

Turning on firewall logs can generate a large number of logs which can increase costs in Stackdriver. Learn more

○ On

◉ Off

Network *

mynetwork   ▼   ❓

Priority *

1000   CHECK PRIORITY OF OTHER FIREWALL RULES   ❓

Priority can be 0 - 65535

Figure 3.61 – Creating firewall rule for mynetwork VPC

Continuing this, you need to define the direction of the traffic, and the action to take once the rule will match. Moreover, you need to specify to whom the firewall rule applies (that is, all instances in the network, specified target tags, and specified service account) and from where the traffic will be generated, as illustrated in the following screenshot:

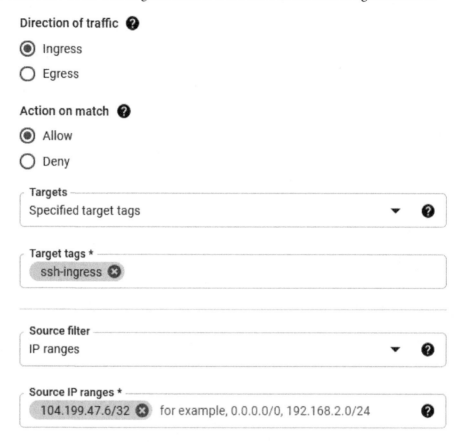

Figure 3.62 – Continuing with the firewall rule creation process

Notice that **Target tags** is only available when you select **Specified target tags** from the **Targets** combo box.

As a final step in our firewall rule creation, we need to specify the protocols and ports, as shown in the following screenshot:

Protocols and ports ❓

○ Allow all

◉ Specified protocols and ports

☑ tcp : | 22 |

☐ udp : | all |

☐ Other protocols

| protocols, comma separated, e.g. ah, sctp |

∨ **DISABLE RULE**

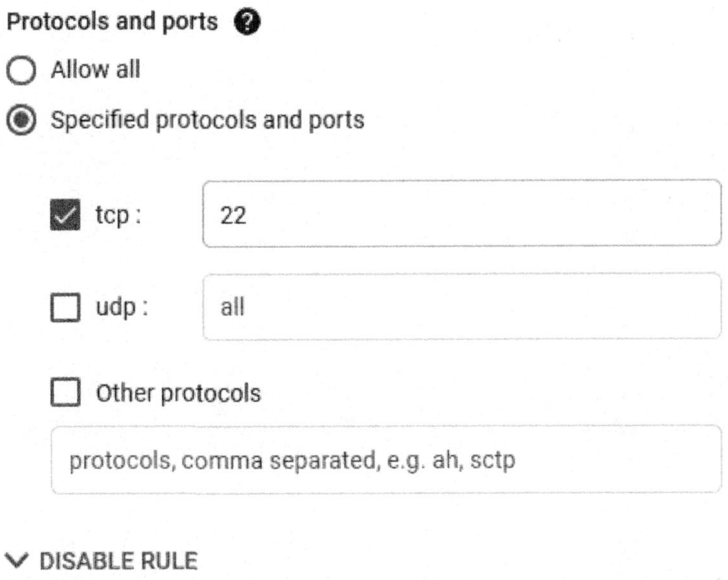

Figure 3.63 – Protocols and ports in firewall rule creation process

This rule will be applied to all instances that are tagged with the `ssh-ingress` tag, as shown in the following screenshot:

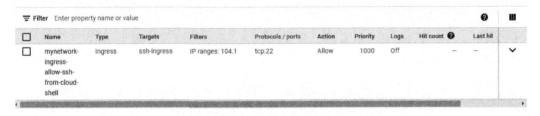

	Name	Type	Targets	Filters	Protocols / ports	Action	Priority	Logs	Hit count ❓	Last hit	
☐	mynetwork-ingress-allow-ssh-from-cloud-shell	Ingress	ssh-ingress	IP ranges: 104.1	tcp:22	Allow	1000	Off	—	—	∨

Figure 3.64 – Result of firewall rule creation

To make this rule effective, we tag the instances to which we want to apply the firewall rule, editing the instance details, as shown in the following screenshot:

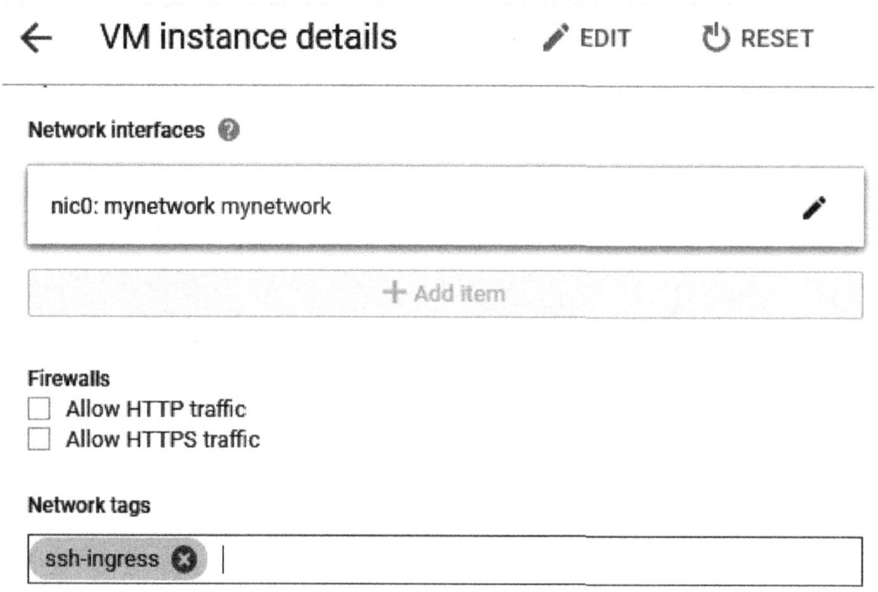

Figure 3.65 – Applying network tags for firewall rule targets

Now, trying to connect SSH to the machines from the cloud shell, SSH should succeed, as illustrated here:

```
gcloud compute ssh mynet-eu-vm --zone europe-west1-b
```

The previous command will let you connect to the mynet-eu-vm GCE instance. This one will let you connect to the mynet-us-vm GCE instance:

```
gcloud compute ssh mynet-us-vm --zone us-central1-a
```

At the same time, if we try to ping from the first instance to the second one, then despite them being in the same network, the ping happens to fail because a firewall rule allowing ICMP is missing. So, let's add a firewall rule that allows all instances in the mynetwork VPC to ping each other, as shown in the following screenshot:

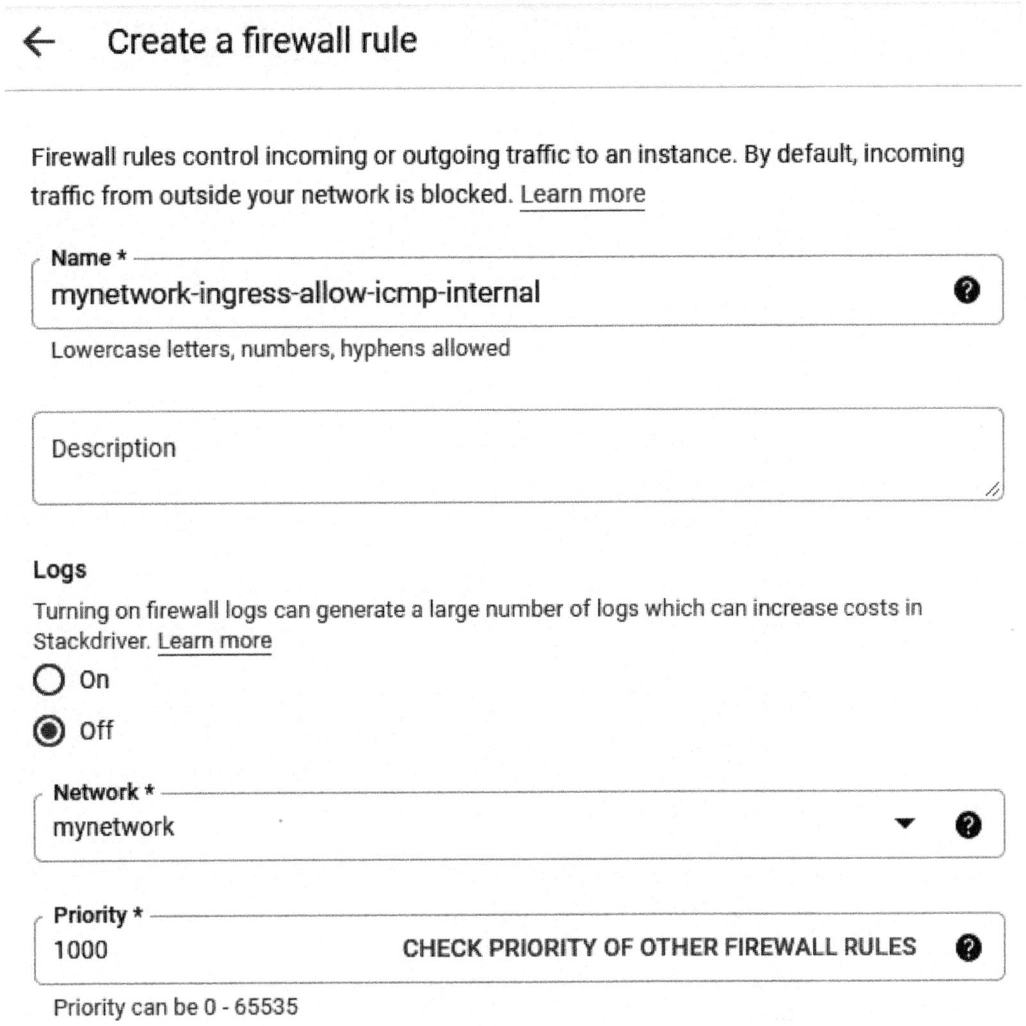

← **Create a firewall rule**

Firewall rules control incoming or outgoing traffic to an instance. By default, incoming traffic from outside your network is blocked. Learn more

Name *

mynetwork-ingress-allow-icmp-internal   ❓

Lowercase letters, numbers, hyphens allowed

Description

Logs

Turning on firewall logs can generate a large number of logs which can increase costs in Stackdriver. Learn more

⭘ On

◉ Off

Network *

mynetwork   ▼   ❓

Priority *

1000   **CHECK PRIORITY OF OTHER FIREWALL RULES**   ❓

Priority can be 0 - 65535

Figure 3.66 – Creation of a firewall rule by the Cloud Console

Continuing with the firewall rule, let's configure the **Direction of traffic, Action on match**, and **Source IP ranges** options with `10.128.0.0/9`, as shown in the following screenshot:

Figure 3.67 – Configuring the traffic direction and action on the firewall rule

---

Note

Using the `10.128.0.0/9` IP range as the source IP range, you can include all GCE instances that stay inside a VPC that has been created with the **Automatic** subnet mode. Indeed, Google Cloud uses this range for the subnets of all GCP regions.

Now, let's specify the `icmp` protocol, as described in the following screenshot:

Protocols and ports ❔

○ Allow all

◉ Specified protocols and ports

☐ tcp :   20, 50-60

☐ udp :   all

☑ Other protocols

icmp

⌄ DISABLE RULE

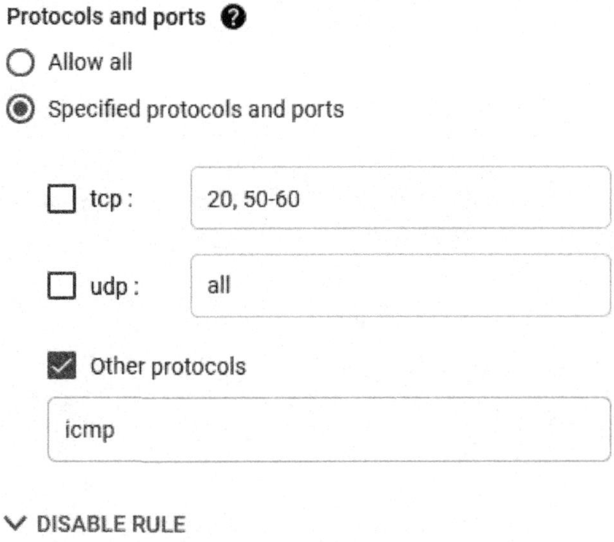

Figure 3.68 – Specifying protocols and ports and creating the rule

In the following screenshot, we can now see that the ping starts succeeding:

```
student-00-c8c39bed067b@mynet-us-vm:~$  ping mynet-eu-vm.europe-west1-b.c.qwiklabs-gcp-00-d7daf5aab8ec.internal
PING mynet-eu-vm.europe-west1-b.c.qwiklabs-gcp-00-d7daf5aab8ec.internal (10.132.0.2) 56(84) bytes of data.
64 bytes from mynet-eu-vm.europe-west1-b.c.qwiklabs-gcp-00-d7daf5aab8ec.internal (10.132.0.2): icmp_seq=273 ttl=64 time=109 ms
64 bytes from mynet-eu-vm.europe-west1-b.c.qwiklabs-gcp-00-d7daf5aab8ec.internal (10.132.0.2): icmp_seq=274 ttl=64 time=108 ms
64 bytes from mynet-eu-vm.europe-west1-b.c.qwiklabs-gcp-00-d7daf5aab8ec.internal (10.132.0.2): icmp_seq=275 ttl=64 time=108 ms
64 bytes from mynet-eu-vm.europe-west1-b.c.qwiklabs-gcp-00-d7daf5aab8ec.internal (10.132.0.2): icmp_seq=276 ttl=64 time=108 ms
```

Figure 3.69 – Ping test to verify that the created firewall rule is working

So far, we did not change the firewall rule priorities (default 1000), so let's investigate how to do this. Let's create a new firewall ingress rule to deny ICMP traffic from any IP with a priority of 900, as shown in the following screenshot:

← **Create a firewall rule**

Firewall rules control incoming or outgoing traffic to an instance. By default, incoming traffic from outside your network is blocked. Learn more

Name *
mynetwork-ingress-deny-icmp-all   ?

Lowercase letters, numbers, hyphens allowed

Description

Logs

Turning on firewall logs can generate a large number of logs which can increase costs in Stackdriver. Learn more

○ On

◉ Off

Network *
mynetwork   ▼   ?

Priority *
900   CHECK PRIORITY OF OTHER FIREWALL RULES   ?

Priority can be 0 - 65535

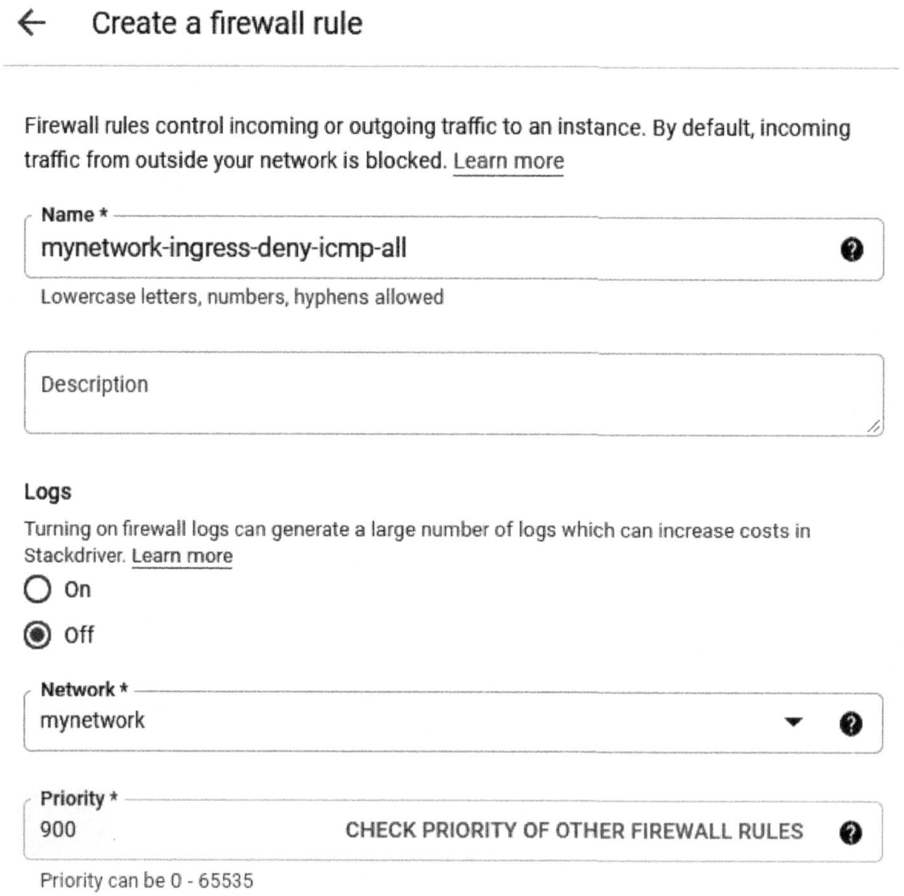

Figure 3.70 – Creating a firewall rule to deny ICMP traffic

Let's define the **Direction of traffic**, **Action on match**, and **Source IP ranges** options for the traffic, as illustrated in the following screenshot:

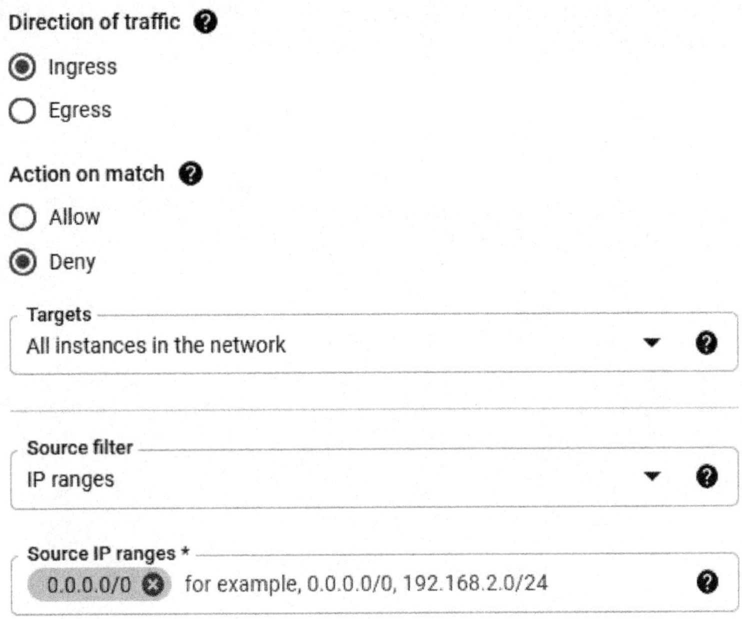

Direction of traffic ❓

◉ Ingress

◯ Egress

Action on match ❓

◯ Allow

◉ Deny

Targets

All instances in the network ▼ ❓

Source filter

IP ranges ▼ ❓

Source IP ranges *

0.0.0.0/0 ✖   for example, 0.0.0.0/0, 192.168.2.0/24 ❓

Figure 3.71 – Selecting the traffic direction, the action, and the source filter for the firewall rule

Additionally, let's specify icmp as the protocol in the firewall rule, as illustrated in the following screenshot:

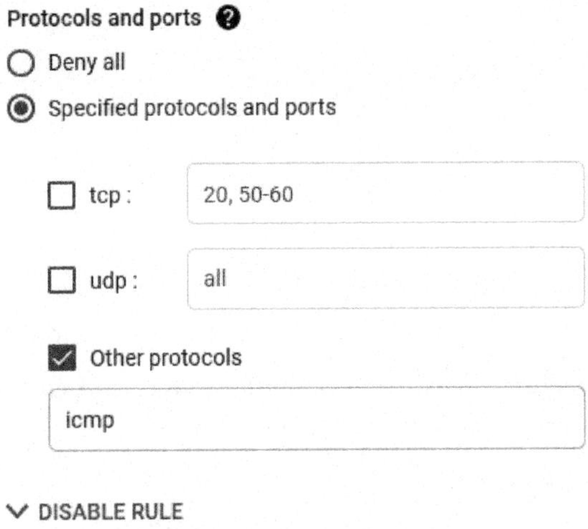

Protocols and ports ❓

◯ Deny all

◉ Specified protocols and ports

☐ tcp :   20, 50-60

☐ udp :   all

☑ Other protocols

icmp

∨ DISABLE RULE

Figure 3.72 – Creating a firewall rule allowing the ICMP protocol

The ping fails, since the deny rule has a higher priority (lower number) than the allow rule. If we change the priority to 1200, the ping restarts.

Lastly, we will create a firewall egress rule to deny all the ICMP egress traffic, as shown in the following screenshot:

Firewall rules control incoming or outgoing traffic to an instance. By default, incoming traffic from outside your network is blocked. Learn more

Name *

mynetwork-egress-deny-icmp-all

Lowercase letters, numbers, hyphens allowed

Description

Logs

Turning on firewall logs can generate a large number of logs which can increase costs in Stackdriver. Learn more

○ On

◉ Off

Network *

mynetwork

Priority *

9999   CHECK PRIORITY OF OTHER FIREWALL RULES

Priority can be 0 - 65535

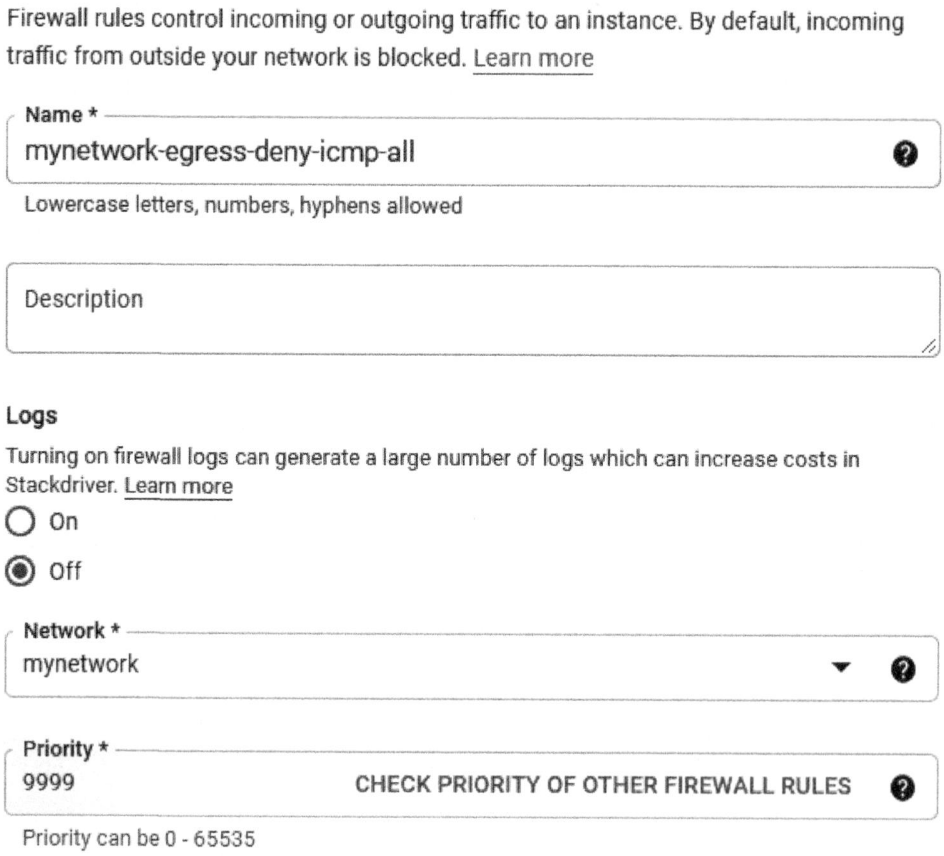

Figure 3.73 – Creating a firewall egress rule denying ICMP traffic

Let's configure the **Direction of traffic**, **Action on match**, and **Destination IP ranges** options, as illustrated in the following screenshot:

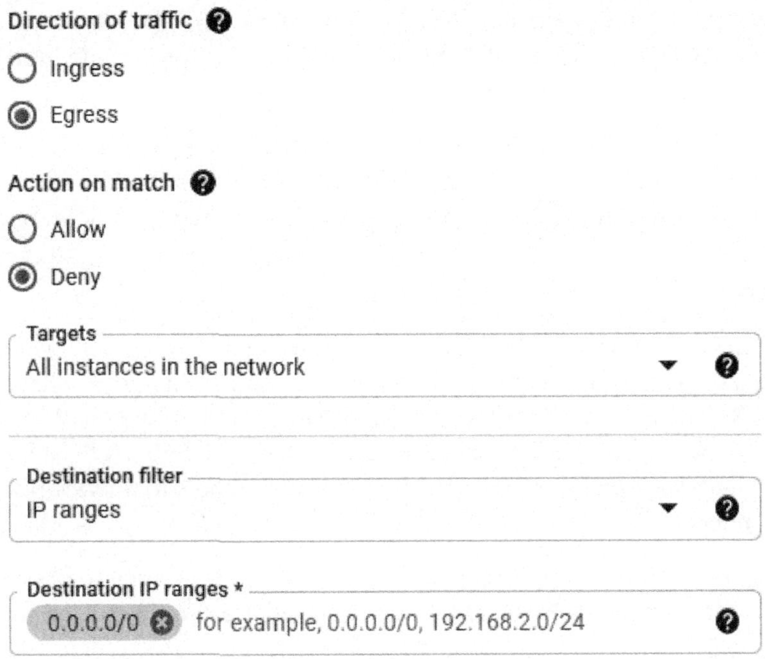

Direction of traffic ❷

○ Ingress

◉ Egress

Action on match ❷

○ Allow

◉ Deny

Targets
All instances in the network ▼ ❷

Destination filter
IP ranges ▼ ❷

Destination IP ranges *
0.0.0.0/0 ⊗   for example, 0.0.0.0/0, 192.168.2.0/24   ❷

Figure 3.74 – Specifying the traffic direction, the action, and the destination filter

Let's configure the protocol, as illustrated in the following screenshot:

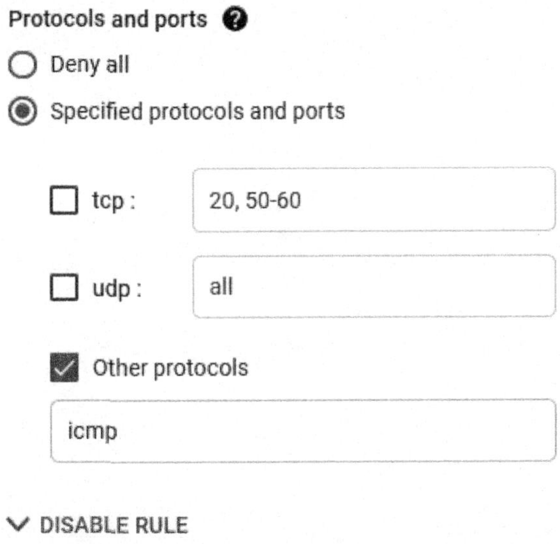

Protocols and ports ❷

○ Deny all

◉ Specified protocols and ports

☐ tcp :   20, 50-60

☐ udp :   all

☑ Other protocols

icmp

∨ DISABLE RULE

Figure 3.75 – Creating another rule for the ICMP protocol

Note that even though the priority is set at 9999 (as shown in *Figure 3.75*, and thus it is the lowest priority), the traffic is still denied because that priority is compared with the other egress priority and not with the ingress ones.

In this section, we have shown how to implement firewall rules to control either inbound or outbound traffic between different GCE VM instances. In addition, you have learned how to use tags to apply firewall rules to VMs regardless of their IP addresses.

Summary

In this chapter, you have learned how to start building your own VPC network in GCP. You have been through subnet configuration and static routing and dynamic routing configurations (for dynamic routing, you need to create a Cloud Router). Then, you have discovered how to configure private communication across different VPC networks using VPC peering and Shared VPC. Moreover, you have learned how to provide public access to your private networks.

The skills we have introduced in this chapter are the basic networking topics needed for any other advanced network services that we will be talking about in the next chapters.

Now that you have learned how to implement the basic resources within the VPC, let's move on to the next chapter to learn how to configure *network services* in GCP.

Section 2: Network Services and Security

In this second part of the book, you will gain knowledge and configuration skills related to network services, hybrid connectivity, and network security.

This part of the book comprises the following chapters:

- *Chapter 4, Configuring Network Services in GCP*
- *Chapter 5, Implementing Hybrid Connectivity in GCP*
- *Chapter 6, Implementing Network Security*

4

Configuring Network Services in GCP

In this chapter, you will learn how to implement network services in **Google Cloud Platform** (**GCP**). More specifically, this chapter talks about **load balancing** and implementing **Cloud CDN** in GCP. In the first section, you will learn how to configure the **HTTP(S) Global Load Balancing** and **Internal Network Load Balancing** solutions in GCP. Here, you will implement common solutions to scale your application workload globally or within a GCP region. Then, in the second section, you will implement **Cloud CDN** in combination with Google Cloud Storage to reduce network latency when serving static content to end users.

Therefore, in this chapter, we will cover the following topics:

- Configuring load balancing
- Implementing Cloud CDN

Configuring load balancing

In this section, you will discover how to configure load balancing services in GCP. As we discussed in *Chapter 2, Designing, Planning, and Prototyping a GCP Network*, Google Cloud offers several types of load balancing services that you can put in front of your backends. Now, you will learn how to configure the following load balancing solutions, as shown in *Figure 4.1*:

- HTTP(S) Global Load Balancing
- Internal Network Load Balancing

Let's start by introducing the HTTPS Global Load Balancer network service in GCP.

HTTP(S) Global Load Balancing

When your web application requires high availability of responses to web requests coming from global users, then you can choose **HTTP(S) Global Load Balancing** from GCP. The following diagram shows a case study of HTTP(S) Global Load Balancing that distributes web requests to a group of compute engines across different GCP regions:

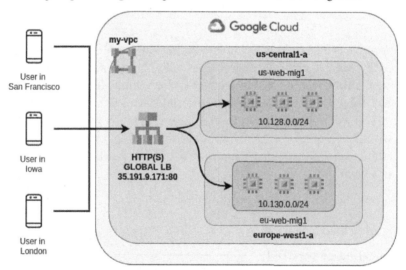

Figure 4.1 – HTTP(S) Global Load Balancing services case study

Building a global load balancer requires different tasks. The first step is to configure the appropriate VPC and firewall rules to let the traffic pass through. In the following screenshot, we are configuring a VPC network called my-vpc that includes two subnets, us-central1-sub1 and eu-west1-sub1. They are in two different GCP regions, us-central1 and europe-west1, with IP ranges of 10.128.0.0/24 and 10.130.0.0/24, respectively:

Name ↑	Region	Subnets	MTU ❓	Mode	IP address ranges	Gateways	Firewall Rules
▼ my-vpc		2	1460	Custom			1
	us-central1	us-central1-sub1			10.128.0.0/24	10.128.0.1	
	europe-west1	eu-west1-sub1			10.130.0.0/24	10.130.0.1	

Figure 4.2 – VPC network in HTTP(S) Global Load Balancing

Next, two firewall rules need to be configured. The first one, `allow-http`, permits HTTP traffic to reach the Compute Engine instances that will run with a target tag of `http-server`. The second one, `allow-health-check-traffic`, permits the health check traffic to reach the same Compute Engine instances. The following screenshot shows the firewall rule configuration for HTTP traffic:

≡ Filter	Enter property name or value						
☐	**Name**	**Type**	**Targets**	**Filters**	**Protocols / ports**	**Action**	**Network ↑**
☐	allow-http	Ingress	http-server	IP ranges: 0.0.0.0/0	tcp:80	Allow	my-vpc

Figure 4.3 – HTTP firewall rule for web user traffic

The following screenshot shows the firewall rule configuration for health check traffic:

≡ Filter	Enter property name or value						
☐	**Name**	**Type**	**Targets**	**Filters**	**Protocols / ports**	**Action**	**Network ↑**
☐	allow-health-check-traffic	Ingress	http-server	IP ranges: 130.211.0.0/22, 35.191.0.0/16	tcp	Allow	my-vpc

Figure 4.4 – Firewall rule for health check traffic from GCP networks

Here, the first firewall rule allows HTTP traffic (port 80) to reach any Compute Engine instance that will respond to user web requests. The second firewall rule allows health check traffic from the GCP networks; that is, `130.211.0.0/22` and `35.191.0.0/16`. While in the first rule you specify the TCP port (port 80), you do not in the second rule. Not specifying the port means that the firewall rule is not specific to a particular health check.

In other words, all TCP traffic is allowed, such as port 80 (HTTP) and port 443 (HTTPS), so long as the traffic is from the health check subnetworks.

Next, we must configure a Compute Engine instance template for Virtual machines that will be added to the **Managed Instance Groups (MIGs)** of US and EU GCP regions. The following screenshot shows the configuration for the Compute Engine instance template for US Virtual machines:

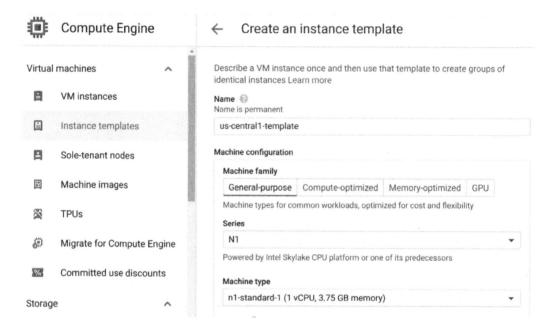

Figure 4.5 – Compute Engine instance template

To reach the page shown in the preceding screenshot, select **Menu | Compute Engine | Instance templates** and click on the **Create instance template** button. The templates require a script to be installed on every VM that will be added to the MIGs. Therefore, you can use a public script that installs an Apache web server and customize the web page. Compute Engine instances can get the script once they've been started because of the metadata key; that is, `startup-script-url`. This metadata key was added during the instance creation process, and the metadata key value is the URL of the script, as shown in the following screenshot. Metadata can be found under the **Management** tab of the Compute Engine instance template; to reach this page, you should click on **Management | Security | Disk | Networking | Sole tenancy** first:

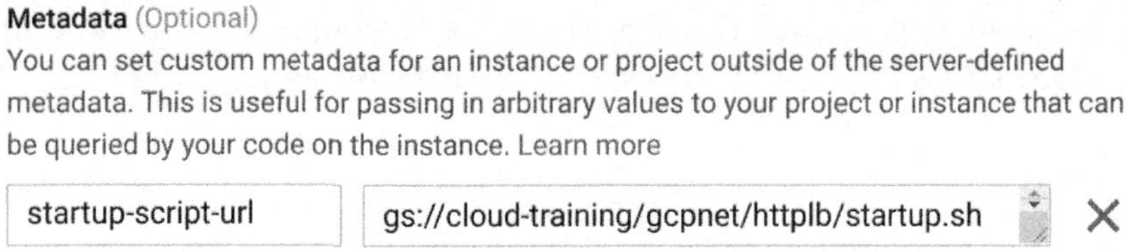

Metadata (Optional)

You can set custom metadata for an instance or project outside of the server-defined metadata. This is useful for passing in arbitrary values to your project or instance that can be queried by your code on the instance. Learn more

startup-script-url	gs://cloud-training/gcpnet/httplb/startup.sh	✕

Figure 4.6 – startup-script-url metadata key and value

Additionally, in the Compute Engine instance template, in the **Networking** tab, you need to configure the **Network**, **Subnet**, and **Network tags** properties of `http-server`, as shown in the following screenshot:

Management   Security   Disks   Networking   Sole Tenancy

Network ❔

my-vpc	▾

Subnet ❔

us-central1-sub1 (us-central1, 10.128.0.0/24)	▾

≳ Show alias IP ranges

Network tags ❔ (Optional)

http-server ✕

External IP ❔

Ephemeral	▾

Network Service Tier ❔
- ⦿ Premium (Current project-level tier, change) ❔
- ◯ Standard ❔

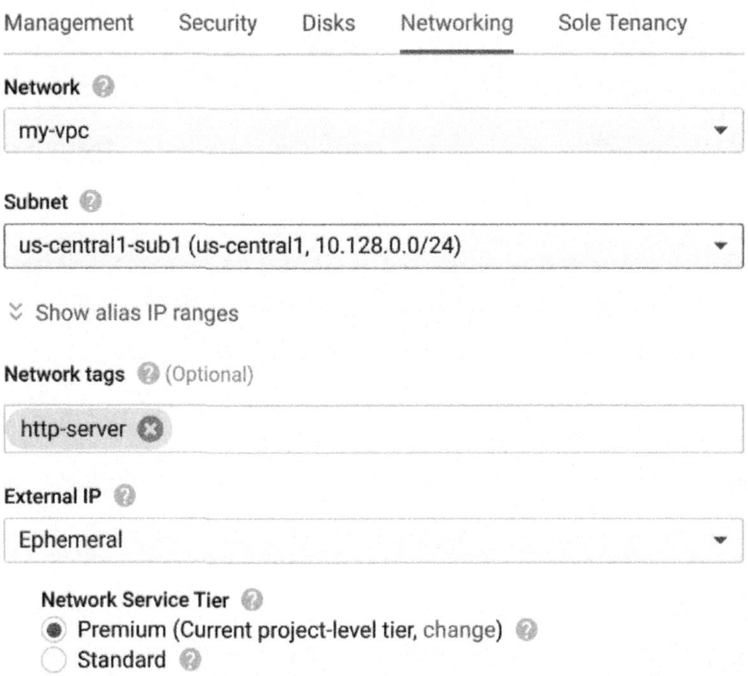

Figure 4.7 – Networking configuration in the Compute Engine instance template

Once you've done this, you will see two templates, one for each **MIG**, as shown in the following screenshot:

☐	Name ↓	Machine type	Image	Disk type
☐	us-central1-template	n1-standard-1	debian-10-buster-v20210420	Balanced persistent disk
☐	eu-west1-template	n1-standard-1	debian-10-buster-v20210420	Balanced persistent disk

Figure 4.8 – Compute Engine instance templates

Once the Compute Engine instance templates have been configured, you can continue with MIGs, one for each GCP region, as shown in the following screenshot:

To create an instance group, select one of the options:

New managed instance group (stateless)
For stateless serving and batch workloads.

Supports:
· autoscaling, autohealing, auto-updating
· multi-zone deployment
· load balancing

New managed instance group (stateful)
For stateful workloads such as databases.

Supports:
· disk and metadata preservation
· autohealing and updating
· multi-zone-deployment
· load balancing

Organize VM instances in a group to manage them together. Instance groups

Name
Name is permanent
us-web-mig1

Description (Optional)

Location
To ensure higher availability, select a multiple zone location for an instance group.
Learn more

● Single zone
○ Multiple zones

Region
Region is permanent
us-central1 (Iowa)

Zone
Zone is permanent
us-central1-a

Specify port name mapping (Optional)

Instance template
us-central1-template

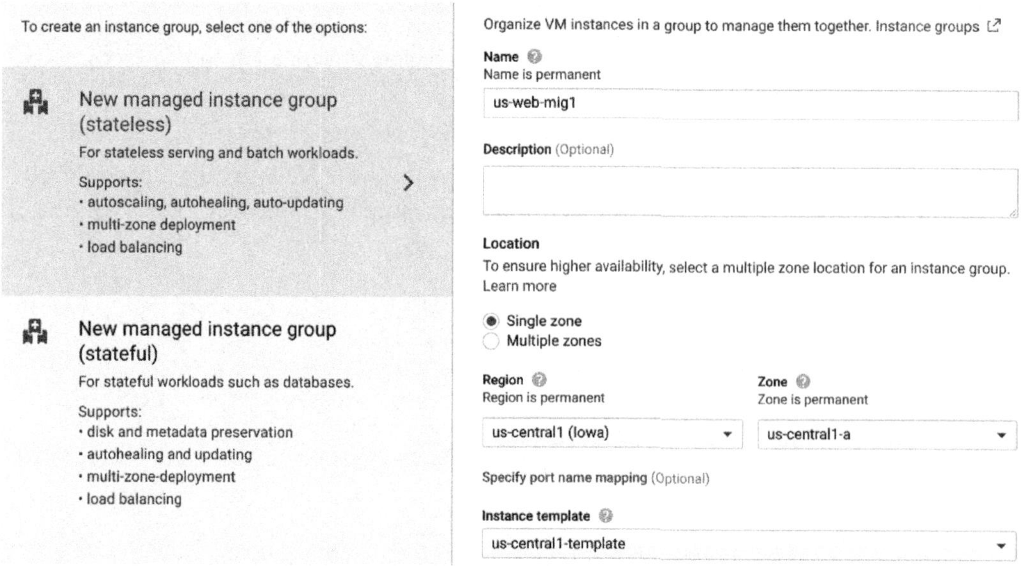

Figure 4.9 – Managed instance group for the us-central1 region

The following screenshot shows the MIG running for both GCP regions:

		Name ↑	Instances	Template	Autoscaling	Zone
☐	✓	eu-web-mig1	1	eu-west1-template	On: Target CPU utilization 60%	europe-west1-b
☐	✓	us-web-mig1	1	us-central1-template	On: Target CPU utilization 60%	us-central1-a

Figure 4.10 – Managed instance groups from two regions in Europe and the US

Upon clicking the **Create** button, you may get a warning, stating that there is no backend service attached to the instance group. If so, you can ignore this warning as we will configure the backend service shortly. Now that everything has been set up, we can proceed to HTTP(S) Global Load Balancing. Here, we will configure three things: the **backend service** (which contains health check configuration), the host and path rules, and the **frontend**. The following screenshot shows the configuration of the Layer 7 load balancing service for HTTP; that is, the HTTP load balancer:

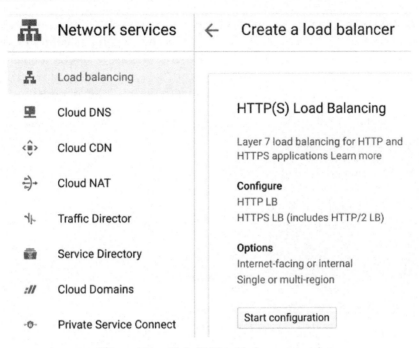

Figure 4.11 – Global L7 load balancer wizard

After clicking on **Start configuration**, you will be asked to choose from **Only between my Virtual machines** and **From Internet to my Virtual machines**, as shown in the following screenshot:

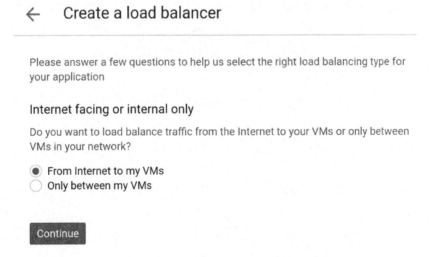

Figure 4.12 – Internet facing or internal only

The first part is configuring the backend service. You can easily find it by clicking on **Continue**, as shown in the preceding screenshot, and clicking on **Backend services & backend buckets**, then **Create a backend service**. To configure it, specify the name, the backend type (in this example, it is **Instance group**), the protocol (here, this is **HTTP**), the named port (here, this is **http**), and the timeout (here, this is **30 seconds**).

This can be seen in the following screenshot:

Figure 4.13 – Backend service configuration

Next, we have to add a new backend to the backend service, as shown in the following screenshot. In the backend, we have to select our **instance group** (us-web-mig1, in this example), **port numbers** (80, in this example), **balancing mode** (explained later), and the maximum backend utilization or the maximum rate, depending on **Balancing mode**:

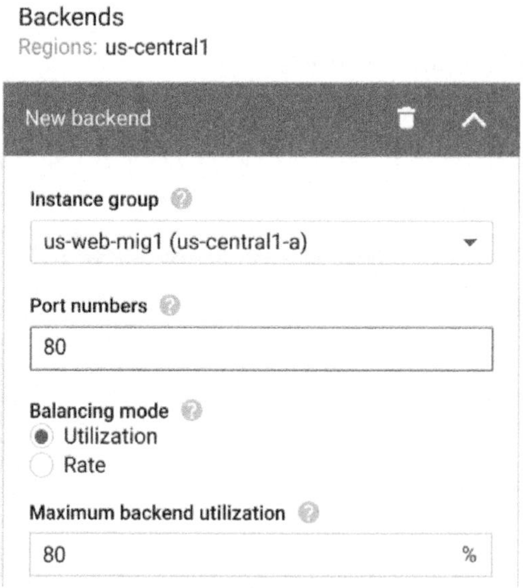

Figure 4.14 – New backend configuration

We can select the balancing mode by choosing from the following:

- **Utilization**: There is no mandatory target capacity. Optionally, you can specify one of the following:

  (1) **max-utilization**

  (2) **max-rate per zonal instance group**

  (3) **max-rate-per-instance (zonal or regional instance groups)**

  (1) and (2) together and (1) and (3) together

- **Rate**: You *must* define the target capacity by specifying one of the following:

  (1) **Max-rate per zonal instance group**

  (2) **Max-rate-per-instance (zonal or regional instance groups)**

When both backends of the backend service have been configured, they will be ready to receive user traffic, as shown in the following screenshot:

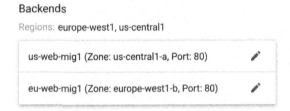

Figure 4.15 – Backend configuration result

Keeping all the other configurations as is, you need to configure the **health check** to monitor the health status of both backends. If all the instances from one backend are down or reach their maximum capacity, the load balancer will send the traffic to the other backend. Add a health check the web servers on TCP port 80, as shown in the following screenshot. You can reach this screen from the previous one (*Figure 4.14*) by clicking on **Health check**, and then **Create a Health Check**:

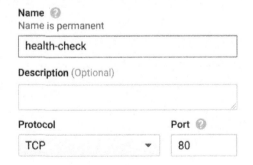

Figure 4.16 – health-check configuration example

The next step is to select the **Host** and **Path** rules. Host and path rules determine how your traffic will be directed. You can direct traffic to a backend service or a storage bucket. Using advanced mode, you can also rewrite user request URLs before directing the traffic or respond to the client with URL redirects. Figure 4.17 shows the simple host and path rules selected and their URL maps.

Google Cloud HTTP(S) load balancers use a Google Cloud configuration resource called a URL map to route requests to backend services or backend buckets.

For example, with an external HTTP(S) load balancer, you can use a single URL map to route requests to different destinations based on the rules configured in the URL map:

- Requests for `https://example.com/video` go to one backend service.

- Requests for `https://example.com/audio` go to a different backend service.

- Requests for `https://example.com/images` go to a Cloud Storage backend bucket.

- Requests for any other host and path combination go to a default backend service.

In the following screenshot, the only URL map that we can see is the `web.example.com` host with the `/images/*` path:

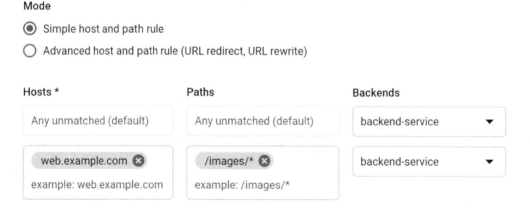

Figure 4.17 – Host and path rules selection

If we select **Advanced host and path rule (URL redirect, URL rewrite)**, we will be able to set the URL maps that can take us to different backend services or backend buckets, as shown in Figure 4.17.

The next step of creating the load balancer is to configure the frontend. This will allocate a public IPv4 address (and IPv6, if you want that) and a port to listen to incoming user requests. The frontend will balance the user traffic to the previously configured backends. This configuration is shown in the following screenshot:

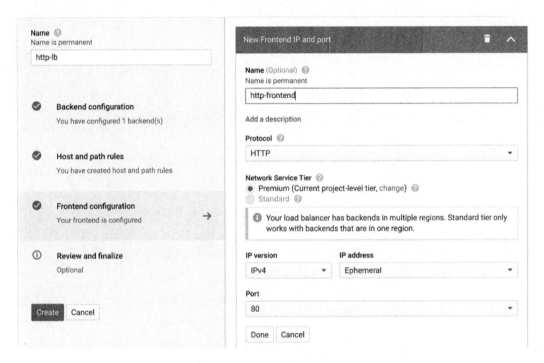

Figure 4.18 – Frontend configuration example

Once the frontend has been configured, you can create the global load balancer by clicking on the blue **Create** button. A summary of this is shown in the following screenshot:

Figure 4.19 – Summary HTTP(S) Global Load Balancing

After a few minutes, you can connect to the assigned public IP to verify that HTTP Global Load Balancing is working as expected, as shown in the following screenshot:

HTTP Load Balancing Lab

Client IP

Your IP address : 35.191.9.171

Hostname

Server Hostname: eu-web-mig1-0pzm

Server Location

Region and Zone: europe-west1-b

Figure 4.20 – HTTP Global Load Balancing verification

Now that you know how to configure HTTP(S) Global Load Balancing with Google Cloud, let's explore how to implement Internal Network Load Balancing.

Internal load balancing

When you need to load balance traffic across multiple Compute Engine instances in one GCP region, Google Cloud offers two **internal load balancing** services: Internal TCP/ UDP Load Balancer and Internal HTTP(S) Load Balancer. This service allows you to load balance internal traffic to a group of Virtual machines running inside a region.

In the following case study, you will learn how to configure an internal load balancer to balance traffic across multiple GCE instances that implement a distributed web frontend. The following diagram describes this case study architecture (it shows an example of an internal HTTP load balancer):

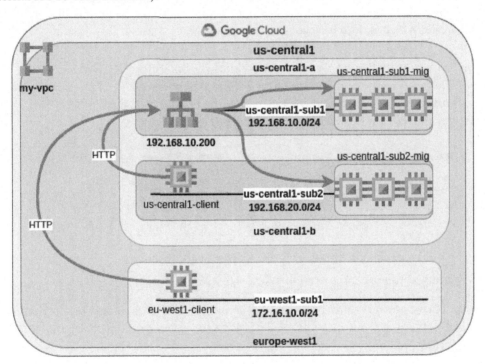

Figure 4.21 – Internal network load balancer architecture case study

As you can see, the case study architecture includes one VPC (my-vpc) that has three subnets, two in the us-central1 region (us-central1-sub1 with an IP range of 192.168.10.0/24 and us-central1-sub2 with an IP range of 192.168.20.0/24) and one in the europe-west1 region (eu-west1-sub1 with an IP range of 172.16.10.0/24). The two subnets in the us-central1 region will include two managed instance groups of Compute Engine instances (us-central1-sub1-mig and us-central1-sub2-mig) that will run Apache Web Server to serve HTTP traffic. In front of them, the internal network load balancer will be configured to balance the load coming from two clients that are located in the same region (us-central1-client) and the load coming from one external region (eu-west1-client).

> **Note**
>
> For convenience, the IP address of the load balancer will come from us-central1-sub1. In reality, you should consider a dedicated subnet in the region where the load balancer should be placed.

We will start creating the my-vpc network with two subnets for the us-central1 region. These will be the destinations of the MIGs; that is, us-central1-sub1-mig and us-central1-sub2-mig. We will assign the IP address ranges as described previously. The result is shown in the following screenshot:

Name ↑	Region	Subnets	Mode	IP address ranges	Gateways
▼ my-vpc		2	Custom		
	us-central1	us-central1-sub1		192.168.10.0/24	192.168.10.1
	us-central1	us-central1-sub2		192.168.20.0/24	192.168.20.1

Figure 4.22 – The my-vpc network with two subnets in the us-central1 region

Next, we must configure three firewall rules, as follows:

- allow-apache-traffic: This rule applies to all Virtual machines that have a web server tag. It allows common TCP ports for web services such as port 80, 8008, 8080, 8088, and 443.

- allow-ssh-icmp: This rule allows ssh and icmp traffic to all Virtual machines for convenience, such as for pinging and connecting to them.

- health-check: This rule applies to all Virtual machines tagged as web servers to allow health traffic from GCP health checkers. Remember that these GCP services generate health check traffic from the 130.211.0.0/22 and 35.191.0.0/16 networks.

The following screenshot shows the results of these three firewall rules:

	Name	Type	Targets	Protocols / ports	Action	Network ↑	Logs
☐	allow-apache-traffic	Ingress	webserver	tcp:80,8008,8080,8088,443	Allow	my-vpc	Off
☐	allow-ssh-icmp	Ingress	Apply to all	tcp:22 icmp	Allow	my-vpc	Off
☐	health-check	Ingress	webserver	tcp	Allow	my-vpc	Off

Figure 4.23 – Firewall rules for the internal load balancer case study

Now that the VPC, subnet, and firewall rules are in place, we need to configure two instance templates, one for each MIG we will create. From the **Navigation** menu, click **Compute Engine**, then **Instance templates**. You can create an *instance template* by assigning a name, a machine type (we suggest that you use f1-micro), and keeping the other options as is. Then, in the **Management** tab (you have to click on **Management | Security | Disks | Networking | Sole tenancy** for the **Management** tab to appear), you can install Apache Web Server by copying and pasting a startup script.

The following screenshot shows that you should paste the startup script in the **Automation** section, which is one of the sections of the **Management** tab:

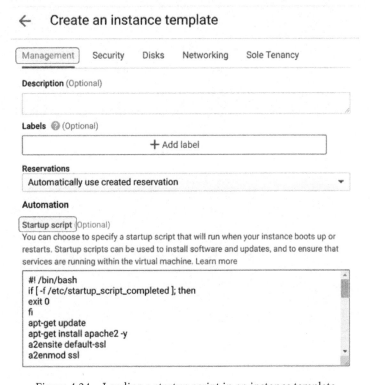

Figure 4.24 – Loading a startup script in an instance template

In the **Networking** tab, we need to set the **Network**, **Subnet**, and **Network tags** properties, as shown in the following screenshot:

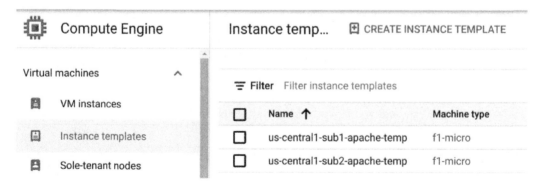

Figure 4.25 – Setting networking parameters in the instance template

The resulting instance templates will be used to create two MIGs for both subnets in the us-central1 region. The following screenshot shows the **Instance templates** page:

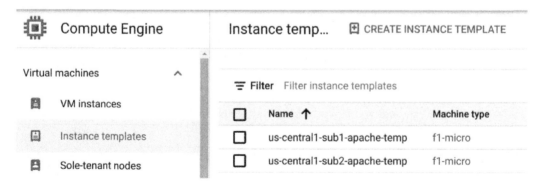

Figure 4.26 – Instance templates list

Next, we will create two MIGs to implement the Apache frontend with autoscaling. We will use the same instance templates in two zones, `us-central1-a` and `us-central1-b`. The following screenshot shows the first one:

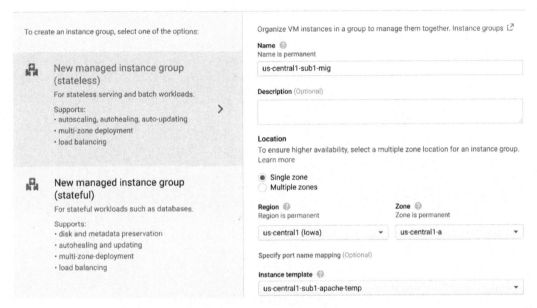

Figure 4.27 – Managed instance group for us-central1-a

When both MIGs have been created, you will see the following output:

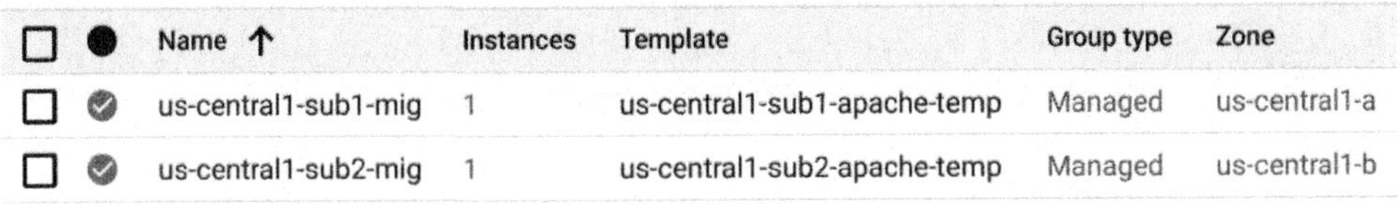

		Name ↑	Instances	Template	Group type	Zone
☐	✓	us-central1-sub1-mig	1	us-central1-sub1-apache-temp	Managed	us-central1-a
☐	✓	us-central1-sub2-mig	1	us-central1-sub2-apache-temp	Managed	us-central1-b

Figure 4.28 – List of managed instance groups

Now that everything is ready for the load balancer, you can start configuring it. From the **Navigation** menu, click **Network services | Load balancing**. Then, click on **Create load balancer** and select **TCP Load Balancing** from the **Network Services | Load balancing** menu, as shown in the following screenshot:

TCP Load Balancing

Layer 4 load balancing or proxy for
applications that rely on TCP/SSL
protocol Learn more

Configure
TCP LB
SSL Proxy
TCP Proxy

Options
Internet-facing or internal
Single or multi-region

Start configuration

Figure 4.29 – TCP Load Balancing wizard

To create an internal load balancer service, we need to select the **Only between my Virtual machines** option, which enables **Single region only** as this service can only be regional. This is shown in the following screenshot:

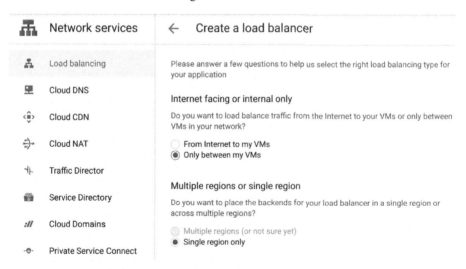

Figure 4.30 – Choosing an internal load balancer

After clicking **Continue**, you need to create a backend service, then create the backends to be added to that backend service. To create this **backend**, you need to add the instance groups you created previously. This will allow the load balancer to forward traffic to both backends, as shown in the following screenshot:

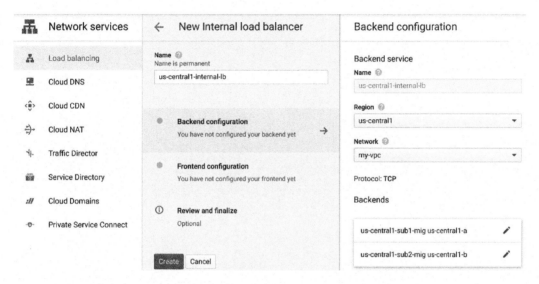

Figure 4.31 – Backend service creation process

The backend service also requires the Health Check service to monitor the health of both backends. We can create this from the **Backend service** wizard, where you should click on the **Health check** combo box to be able to reach the following screen:

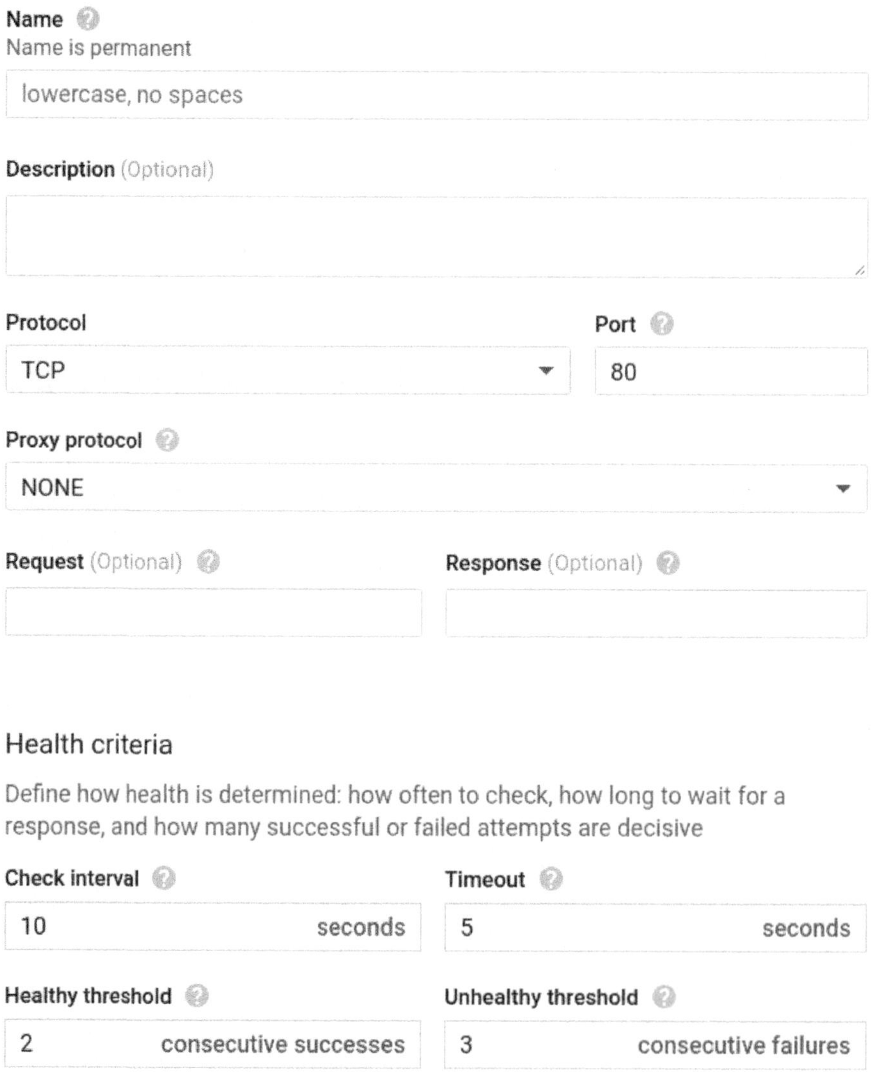

Name ❓
Name is permanent

lowercase, no spaces

Description (Optional)

Protocol   **Port** ❓

TCP   ▼   80

Proxy protocol ❓

NONE   ▼

Request (Optional) ❓   **Response** (Optional) ❓

Health criteria

Define how health is determined: how often to check, how long to wait for a response, and how many successful or failed attempts are decisive

Check interval ❓   **Timeout** ❓

10   seconds   5   seconds

Healthy threshold ❓   **Unhealthy threshold** ❓

2   consecutive successes   3   consecutive failures

Figure 4.32 – Health check creation

Once the health check has been configured, it will show up on the **Backend service** screen and clearly show that the service will check HTTP responses from the server every 10 seconds and wait up to 30 seconds before declaring the backend as unhealthy and thus unusable. The timeout is the time that the health check waits before a request is considered a failure. The check interval is how often to send a health check. The healthy threshold is how many consecutive successes must occur to mark a Compute Engine instance as healthy. The unhealthy threshold is how many consecutive failures must occur to mark a Compute Engine instance as unhealthy. This can be seen in the following screenshot:

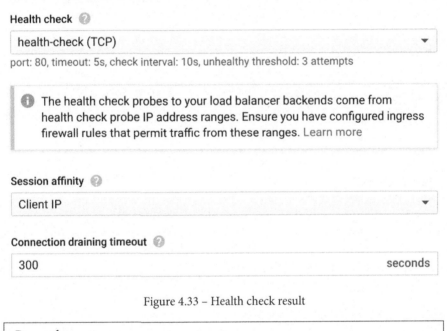

Figure 4.33 – Health check result

> **Remember**
>
> Configure the appropriate firewall rule to allow inbound health check traffic into your backend Virtual machines.

Once we've created the backend service, we need to take care of the **Frontend configuration** option. Here, we must provide a **name and subnetwork** where we want to place the IP address of the frontend part. As agreed, we have deployed the frontend in the us-central1-sub1 region, as shown in the following screenshot:

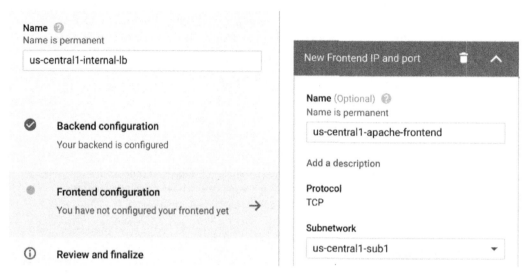

Figure 4.34 – Frontend configuration process

Additionally, we need to reserve a static IP address to use as the frontend for other services that will use our backend resources. First, we must reserve a static internal IP address in the frontend, as shown in the following screenshot:

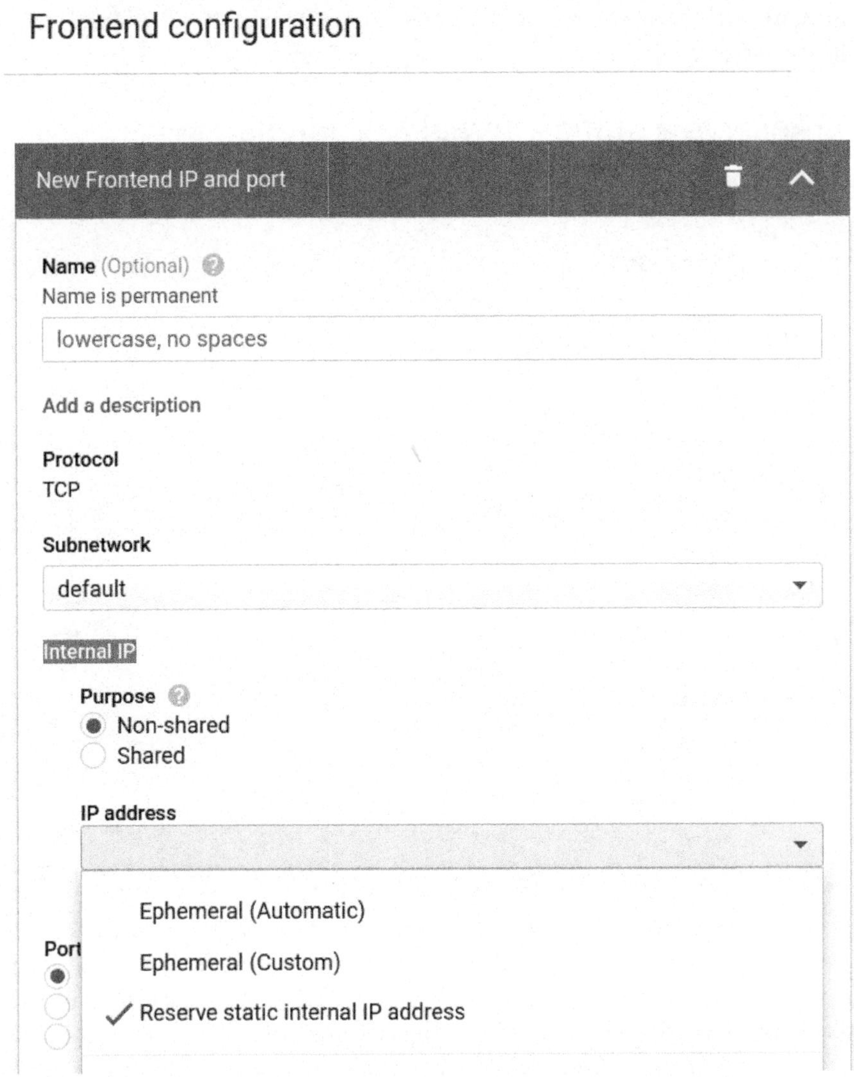

Frontend configuration

New Frontend IP and port

Name (Optional)
Name is permanent

lowercase, no spaces

Add a description

Protocol
TCP

Subnetwork

default

Internal IP

Purpose
- Non-shared
- Shared

IP address

Ephemeral (Automatic)

Ephemeral (Custom)

✓ Reserve static internal IP address

Figure 4.35 – Choosing to reserve a static internal IP address

In the **Frontend** section, we can choose the most appropriate static IP address, as shown in the following screenshot:

Reserve a static internal IP address

Name ⓘ
Name is permanent

    apache-frontend-static-ip

Description (Optional)

Subnet ⓘ

    us-central1-sub1 (us-central1, 192.168.10.0/24)   ▾

Static IP address

    Let me choose   ▾

Custom IP address   **Purpose** ⓘ

    192.168.10.200   Non-shared   ▾

CANCEL   RESERVE

Figure 4.36 – Reserving an internal static IP for the frontend

Once the frontend IP address has been chosen, we need to specify which ports the internal load balancer will forward traffic to. In this case study, we wanted to have multiple ports that our Apache Web Server will listen to for incoming HTTP requests. We will also enable **Global Access** to let Virtual machines from other regions reach our frontend so that they can be served (the L4 internal load balancer will still be regional but have cross-regional access). This is shown in the following screenshot:

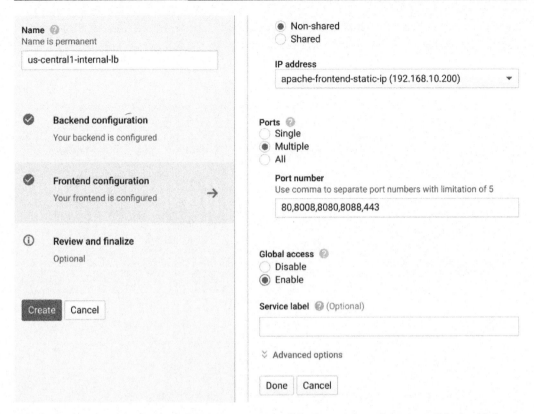

Figure 4.37 – Selecting ports and global access as part of the frontend configuration of the load balancer

We can leave all other fields as is. Once we've configured the frontend, we can sum up the overall internal load balancer configuration, as shown in the following screenshot:

Figure 4.38 – Reviewing the internal load balancer configuration

We can see that this operates as expected by looking for the green check in the **Backends** column, as shown in the following screenshot:

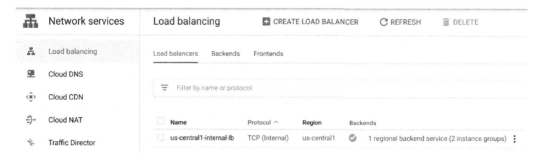

Figure 4.39 – Internal load balancer creation verification

Now, we can test the HTTP responses from the client Virtual machines. Please look at *Figure 4.21* once more and check the available subnets. First, we will try `us-central1-client`, which stays in the same region that the internal load balancer is in. We will use a combination of ports to test this, as shown in the following screenshot:

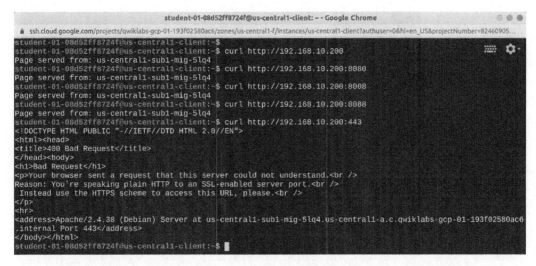

Figure 4.40 – Sending HTTP requests to the backend service in the same region

Since the HTTP responses were correct, it's time to repeat the same commands from another VM. We will be using `eu-west1-client1` here, as shown in the following screenshot:

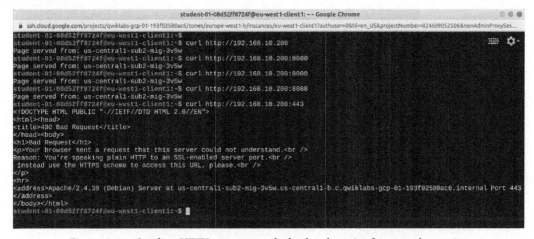

Figure 4.41 – Sending HTTP requests to the backend service from another region

The preceding screenshot shows that even if `eu-west1-client1` is not in the same region as the internal load balancer, it can reach the virtual machines through the load balancer's IP address. This is because the **Global Access** option permits non-regional Compute Engine instances to reach the virtual machines.

Now that we have learned how to configure load balancer services, let's learn about Cloud **Content Delivery Network (CDN)**.

Configuring Cloud Content Delivery Network (CDN)

Cloud CDN can be enabled for many different types of content, either static or dynamic, from the following categories:

- Compute Engine instance groups
- **Network Endpoint Groups (NEGs)**
- Cloud Storage buckets

To give you an idea of how to configure Cloud CDN, in this section, we will show you how to enable the cache implementation in Cloud CDN for a Cloud Storage bucket.

We will create a bucket with two files that can be publicly accessed from the internet, as shown in the following screenshot:

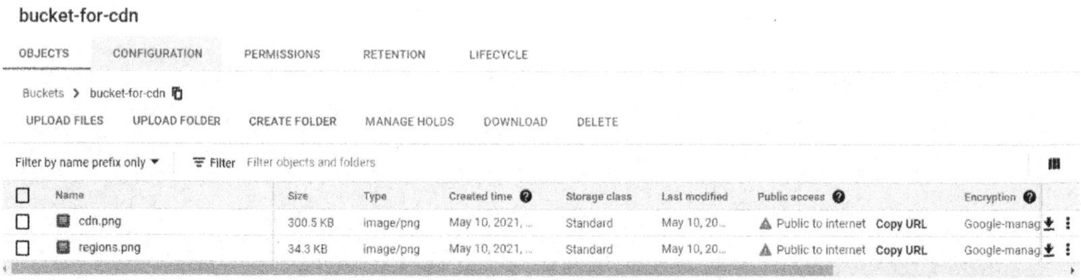

Figure 4.42 – A Cloud Storage bucket with publicly accessible objects

Now, let's create a multi-regional external HTTP(S) load balancer, as we saw in the previous section. When we use a multi-regional external HTTP(S) load balancer (in the Premium Tier), it uses a global external IP address.

Cloud CDN can have a service or a bucket as a backend, as shown in the following screenshot. A backend service could be a managed instance group or an NEG. A backend bucket refers to a Google Cloud Storage bucket:

Figure 4.43 – Backend service or backend bucket selection

To enable the Cloud CDN in the backend configuration, we must select the **Enable Cloud CDN** checkbox, as shown here:

Create backend bucket

Name ⓘ
Name is permanent

bucket-for-cdn

⌄ Description

Cloud Storage bucket

bucket-for-cdn | Browse

Cloud CDN ⓘ
☑ Enable Cloud CDN

Cache mode
By default, Cloud CDN will cache static content - including web assets and video files - that are not explicitly marked as private for the configured default time to live (TTL), without requiring any changes at your origin.
● Cache static content (recommended) ⓘ
○ Use origin settings based on Cache-Control headers ⓘ
Origin must set headers.
○ Force cache all content
Cache all content served by the origin, ignoring any "private", "no-store" or "no-cache" directives.

Client time to live ⓘ	Default time to live ⓘ	Maximum time to live ⓘ
1 hour ▾	1 hour ▾	1 day ▾

⌄ Advanced configurations (response headers and CDN settings)

Figure 4.44 – Enabling Cloud CDN in the backend bucket of the load balancer

In this example, we are using the default mode, which is also the recommended one, called **Cache static content (recommended)**, but we could have chosen the origin settings based on the Cache-Control headers or to force caching for all content. If you decide to use the Cache-Control headers, Cloud CDN will only cache responses with valid cache directives contained in the HTTP response header. Some of the most used directives can be found in the following table and they can affect Cloud CDN's behavior:

Directive	Response
no-store	A response with no-store is not going to be cached. This behavior can be overridden on a per-backend basis with the FORCE_CACHE_ALL cache mode.
no-cache	A response with no-cache is going to be cached but it must be revalidated with the origin before being served to the client. This can be overridden on a per-backend basis with the FORCE_CACHE_ALL cache mode.
max-age=seconds	A response with the max-age directive is going to be cached for the defined time in seconds.
s-maxage=seconds	A response with the s-maxage directive is going to be cached for the defined time in seconds. If both max-age and s-maxage are present, s-maxage is used by Cloud CDN. Responses with this directive aren't served stale. s-max-age (two hyphens) is not valid for caching.
public	Even if this directive is not required for cacheability, it is a best practice to include it for content that should be cached by proxies.
private	A response with the private directive is not going to be cached by Cloud CDN, even if the response is otherwise considered cacheable. Clients (such as browsers) might still cache the result. This can be overridden on a per-backend basis with the FORCE_CACHE_ALL cache mode. Use no-store to prevent responses from being cached.

A full list of available directives can be found in the Cloud CDN documentation at `https://cloud.google.com/cdn/docs/caching?_ga=2.146230836.-1066977515.1628720034#cache_control_directives`.

In addition, we can select the **Time To Live (TTL)** (client, default, and maximum).

Once the load balancer with Cloud CDN enabled has been created, we can verify the caching of our bucket's content, monitoring the time to the HTTP request for one image present in the bucket.

Let's take note of the global IP address of the load balancer and put it in an environment variable called `LB_IP_ADDRESS`.

We want to run consecutive HTTP requests and check whether the first one takes longer than the others, meaning that the content is being cached at one edge location only after being accessed at least once.

To do this, we can use a `for` loop (in Bash script format). Inside the loop, we create a client URL to the file, as follows:

```
for ((i=0;i<10;i++)); \
do curl \
-w %{time_total}\n  \
-o /dev/null \
-s http://$LB_IP_ADDRESS/cdn.png; \
done
```

The `curl` command provides the following options:

- `-w`: Defines what to display on `stdout` after a completed and successful operation.
- `-o`: Writes output to `/dev/null` instead of `stdout`. `/dev/null` is a device file that discards all data written to it.
- `-s`: Silent or quiet mode. Don't show progress meter or error messages.

The output is as follows:

```
0.676344
0.007981
0.009043
...
```

Every cache has a predefined TTL that we could have changed during the configuration, but now, we want to show you how to override the TTL when, for example, we are changing some content and we want to force the cached object to be outdated.

Well, we changed the `cdn.png` object in the bucket (same name, different picture), and if we try to download it from a browser, we will still find the old picture: we must enable **Path pattern to invalidate**, which can be found via the navigation menu and selecting **Network Services | Load balancing**. Here, click on the `lb-for-cdn` load balancer and select the `Caching` tab, as shown in the following screenshot:

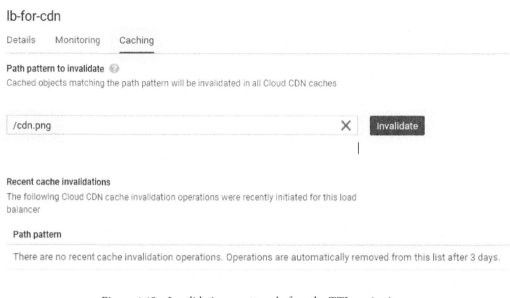

Figure 4.45 – Invalidating a pattern before the TTL expiration

> **Note**
> Remember to type in the name of the file before clicking the **Invalidate** button.

As shown in the following screenshot, the cache invalidation was done for the requested **path pattern**:

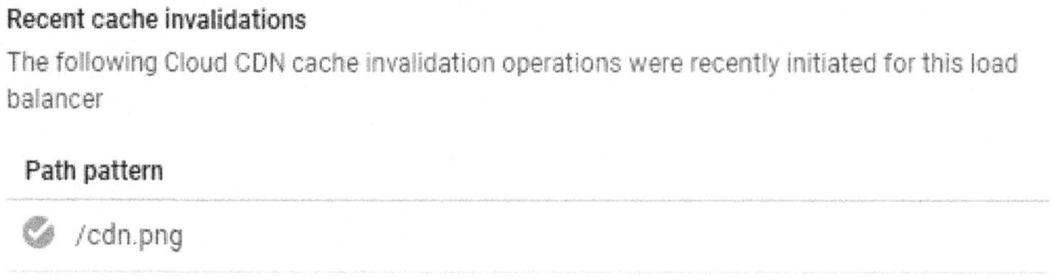

Recent cache invalidations

The following Cloud CDN cache invalidation operations were recently initiated for this load balancer

Path pattern

⊘ /cdn.png

Figure 4.46 – Recent cache invalidations

If we try to reach the same URL via a browser, this will imply a *cache miss*, so we will be redirected toward the new picture that was downloaded from the backend bucket.

By default, the content that's cached by Cloud CDN can be accessed publicly, but if you want, using the option shown in the following screenshot, you can restrict access using a temporary signed URL or signed cookies that have an expiration time. You can access it from the navigation menu by going to **Network Services** and then selecting **Cloud CDN**. Here, you can edit the origin name you created using the three dots icon on the right. From the **Backend buckets** list, check the backend bucket and click on **Configure** on the right. In the **Restricted content** section, you can add a key after selecting the **Restrict access using signed URLs and signed cookies** option:

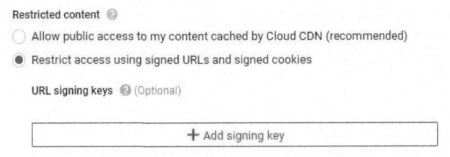

Figure 4.47 – Restricted CDN content via a signed URL or signed cookies

> **Note**
> A signed URL is a URL that provides limited permissions and time to make a request. In the same way, a signed cookie is a cookie that provides limited permissions and time to make requests for a set of files.

In this section, you learned how to enable caching for static content with Google Cloud CDN. This greatly improves network latency for accessing content and therefore the user experience.

Summary

In this chapter, you learned how to scale your application workload using the instance groups offered by GCP. External **HTTP(S)**, **SSL proxies**, and **TCP proxy load balancers** are ideal for applications that require a *global footprint* and they reside in different GCP regions across the globe. On the contrary, **internal HTTP(S)**, **external network TCP/UDP**, and **internal TCP/UDP load balancers** are a perfect fit for distributing workloads to applications running within a GCP region.

Additionally, you learned how to enable CDN with Google Cloud CDN to serve static content, such as images stored in Google Cloud Storage buckets, to global end users to reduce network latency.

Now that you have learned how to implement network services with GCP, in the next chapter, you will learn how to implement hybrid connectivity.

5

Implementing Hybrid Connectivity in GCP

In this chapter, you will implement hybrid interconnection between on-premises and Google Cloud networks using different approaches. You will learn how to configure **Dedicated Interconnect** with Google Cloud colocation facilities, as well as how to configure **Partner Interconnect** with both Layer 2 and Layer 3 connections. Furthermore, the chapter focuses on classical **virtual private networks** (**VPNs**) and **high-availability** (**HA**) VPNs, site-to-site **Internet Protocol Security** (**IPsec**) VPN implementations, and how dynamic routing can be used in **Google Cloud Platform** (**GCP**). Additionally, the chapter will focus on an IPsec VPN implementation to improve HA in hybrid connectivity.

This chapter covers the following main topics:

- Configuring Interconnect
- Configuring a site-to-site IPsec VPN
- Diving into Cloud Router

Technical requirements

In order to fully understand this chapter, you should have already read the previous chapters.

Configuring Interconnect

One of the most interesting characteristics of cloud technologies is that you can access your resources from everywhere. The only requirement that you should satisfy is a public internet connection.

At the same time, this is the limitation of cloud technologies because if you don't have a good internet connection, you will have a really bad experience using all the resources available and located in the **cloud provider data centers**.

That's why Google Cloud offers you many options to interconnect your on-premises networks with Google Cloud data centers, guaranteeing the performance that you need for your workloads.

With Cloud Interconnect, you can leverage the interconnection with Google data centers as if your resources in the cloud were located directly in your on-premises data center, with the lowest latency possible between on-prem resources and resources in Google Cloud.

To configure Cloud Interconnect, proceed as follows:

1. From the **Navigation** menu, select **Hybrid Connectivity**, then select **Interconnect**, as illustrated in the following screenshot:

Figure 5.1 – Choosing the Interconnect option from Hybrid Connectivity

2. Depending on where your on-prem data center is located, you can choose between the following:

a. **Dedicated Interconnect connection**: In this case, your on-prem network must physically meet the Google network in a supported colocation facility (Interconnect connection location). At the time of writing this book, Dedicated Interconnect connections are available from 110 locations in the world. Some of them can also guarantee a less than 5 **milliseconds** (**ms**) round-trip latency between **virtual machines** (**VMs**) in a specific region and its associated Interconnect connection locations. You can see a representation of a Dedicated Interconnect connection in the following diagram:

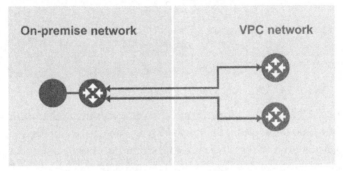

Figure 5.2 – Dedicated Interconnect connection

b. **Partner Interconnect connection**: If you cannot physically meet the Google network in a supported colocation facility, you still have an interconnection option. In this case, though, you should use a third-party **service provider** (**SP**) that can connect your on-premises data center to your **virtual private cloud** (**VPC**) network in Google Cloud, as shown in the following diagram:

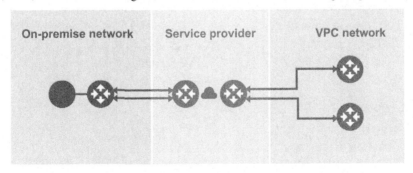

Figure 5.3 – Partner Interconnect connection

Dedicated Interconnect connection option

After selecting the **Dedicated Interconnect connection** option, you can order a new connection or attach **virtual local-area networks** (**VLANs**) to an existing one, as illustrated in the following screenshot:

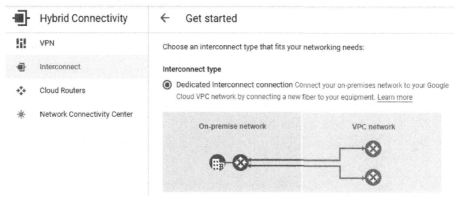

Figure 5.4 – Ordering a new Dedicated Interconnect connection

By clicking on the **CONTINUE** button, you can create a dedicated and physical connection to your Google Cloud VPC networks, as you can see in *Figure 5.4*. The following screenshot shows where you can select a name, choose a colocation facility from a predefined list, and specify the capacity (1 to 8 Ethernet 10 gigabits per second links or 1 to 2 Ethernet 100 gigabits per second links at the time of writing this book):

Create your interconnect

A Dedicated Interconnect connection is a direct, physical connection to your Google Cloud VPC networks Learn more about requirements and configuration

Name *
network-in-google-cloud-dedicated-interconnect   ?

Lowercase letters, numbers, hyphens allowed

Description

Location *
Global Switch (London 2)   CHOOSE

Choose colocation facility

Capacity *
200 Gb/s (2 x 100 Gb/s)   ▼

Available in 10 Gb/s and 100 Gb/s physical links

NEXT   CANCEL

$52,000.00 per month estimated

Effective hourly rate $71.233 (730 hours per month)

Item	Estimated costs
200 Gb/s (2 x 100 Gb/s)	$26,000.00/month
200 Gb/s (2 x 100 Gb/s) (redundancy)	$26,000.00/month

VLAN attachment pricing depends on its capacity
Interconnect pricing ☒
∧ SHOW LESS

Figure 5.5 – Creating a Dedicated Interconnect connection

The following screenshot shows some of the colocation facilities available for Dedicated Interconnect:

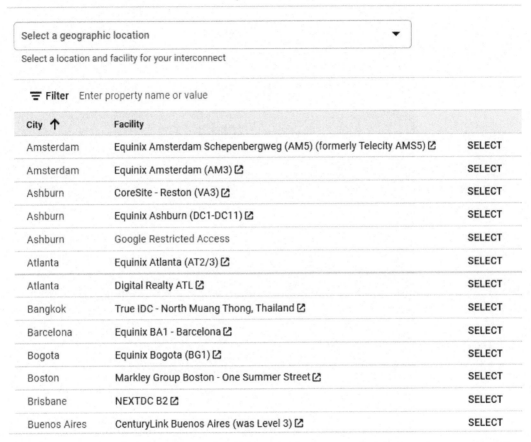

Figure 5.6 – List of available colocation facilities

In addition, you could create a second (redundant) interconnect, as illustrated in the following screenshot:

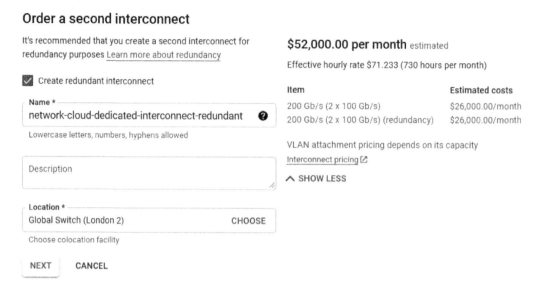

Figure 5.7 – Creating a second (redundant) interconnect

Finally, you insert your company information (name and technical contact), as shown in the following screenshot:

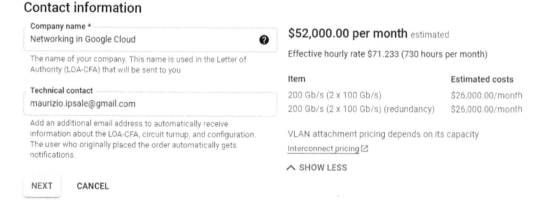

Figure 5.8 – Adding contact information to the interconnect order

And eventually, you can place your order (the billing will begin after your interconnect is properly configured or 30 days after your order is placed, whichever is sooner).

Partner Interconnect connection option

You should tell Google if you already have an SP or if you want to find one. Google Cloud shows a list of the supported SPs. We can see the list if we click on **FIND A SERVICE PROVIDER**, as shown in the following screenshot:

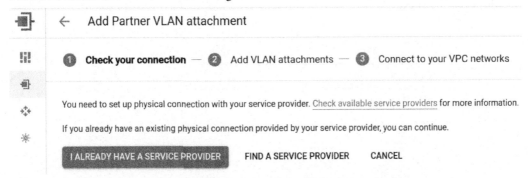

Figure 5.9 – Selecting your own SP or finding one available

Before setting up a Partner Interconnect connection, you need to connect your on-premises network to a supported SP (this process can take several weeks).

If you already have an available SP, you should add VLAN attachments that will allow you to access your VPC network, as shown in the following screenshot:

← Add Partner VLAN attachment

✓ Check your connection — ② **Add VLAN attachments** — ③ Connect to your VPC networks

A VLAN attachment allows you to access your VPC network by adding a VLAN to your existing service provider connection. Learn more

Redundancy

Creating a redundant pair of VLANs is recommended to increase availability. If you don't need redundancy or an SLA, you can create a single VLAN attachment (and make it redundant later). Learn more about redundancy

◉ Create a redundant pair of VLAN attachments (recommended)

○ Add a redundant VLAN to an existing VLAN

○ Create a single VLAN (no redundancy)

Network *
default   ▼

Region *
europe-west2 (London)   ▼   ❷

Region is permanent

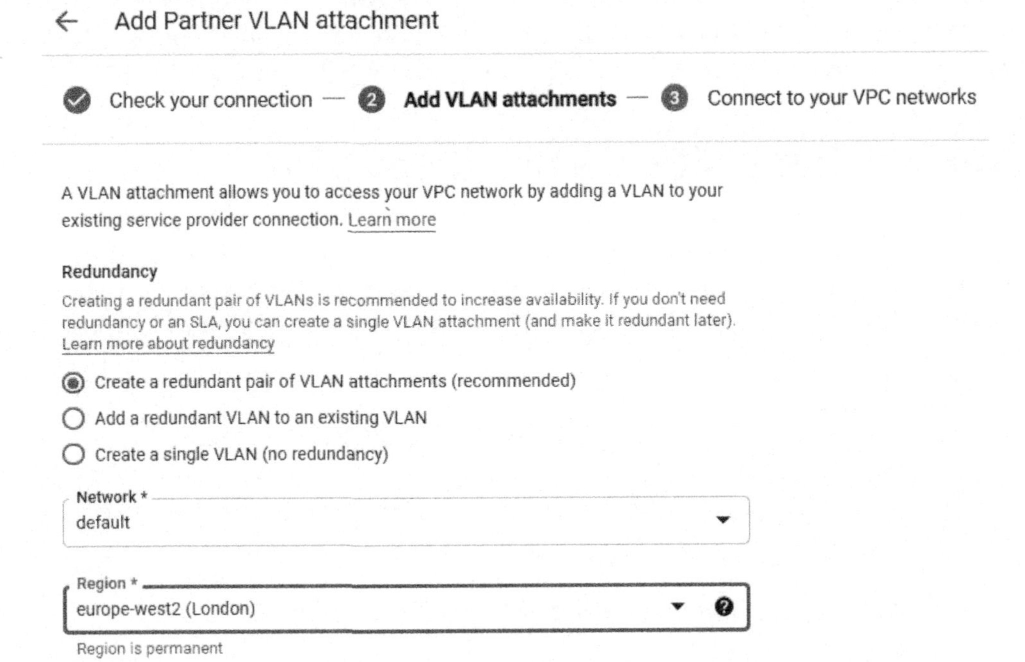

Figure 5.10 – Adding partner VLAN attachment

After adding a VLAN attachment, a Cloud Router is required, as you can see in the next screenshot. We are going to explain cloud routers in a later section. In this example, we choose to create a redundant pair of VLAN attachments, VLAN A and VLAN B. VLAN A is part of the **Add VLAN attachments** configuration, whereas **Cloud Router** is part of the **VLAN A** configuration:

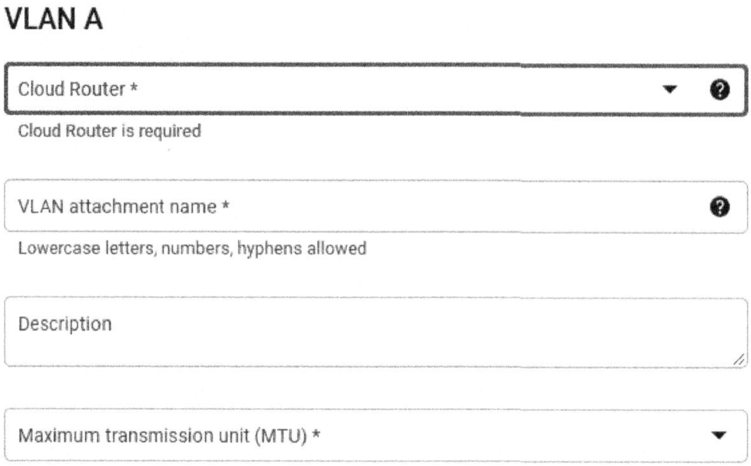

VLAN A

Cloud Router *	▼	❓

Cloud Router is required

VLAN attachment name *	❓

Lowercase letters, numbers, hyphens allowed

Description

Maximum transmission unit (MTU) *	▼

Figure 5.11 – Cloud Router selection (mandatory) in VLAN A configuration

Now that you have learned how to configure Interconnect, let's see how to build a site-to-site IPsec VPN between your on-premises network and the VPC in Google Cloud.

Configuring a site-to-site IPsec VPN

Whenever it comes to interconnecting your on-premises network to a Google Cloud VPC, you have an option of configuring a site-to-site IPsec VPN. This solution can provide an easy way to interconnect your networks while preserving information security. A site-to-site IPsec VPN requires a Cloud VPN in GCP and an IPsec gateway on the other side.

> **Remember**
> The maximum throughput you can reach with a site-to-site IPsec VPN is 3 gigabits per second.

There are three routing options, as outlined here:

- **Dynamic routing**: This uses **Border Gateway Protocol** (**BGP**).
- **Route-based VPN**: You only specific a list of remote IP ranges; those ranges are used only to create routes in your VPC network to peer resources.

- **Policy-based routing**: Local IP ranges and remote IP ranges are defined as part of the tunnel creation process.

You can see these routing options in the following screenshot:

Figure 5.12 – Routing options

There are also two VPN options: **Classic VPN** and **HA VPN**, as shown in the following screenshot:

VPN options

◉ High-availability (HA) VPN
   Supports dynamic routing (BGP) only
   Supports high availability (99.99 SLA, within region)
   Learn more

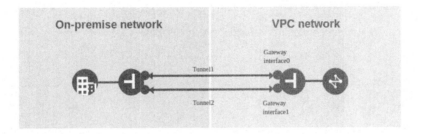

○ Classic VPN
   Supports dynamic routing and static routing
   No high availability
   Learn more

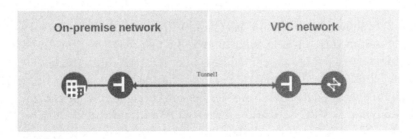

CANCEL

Figure 5.13 – VPN options

For our scenario, we chose the following:

- Route-based VPN
- HA VPN

Route-based VPN

In this section, we will learn how to configure a site-to-site VPN with a single IPsec tunnel between your VPC network in Google Cloud and your on-premises network. We will show the steps to be taken in Google Cloud, and we assume that the IPsec VPN gateway at on-premises is already configured. This scenario is depicted in the following diagram:

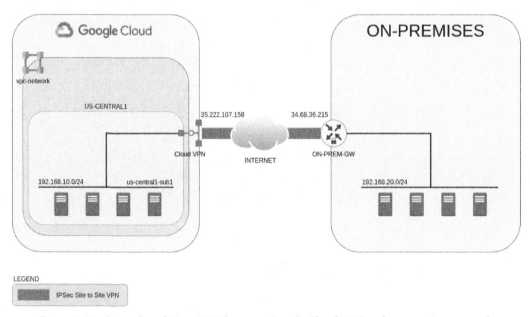

Figure 5.14 – Route-based IPsec VPN between Google Cloud VPC and on-premises network

As *Figure 5.14* shows, you need to use a Cloud VPN to build a route-based site-to-site IPsec VPN toward your on-premises network. But before moving forward with this, we need to reserve a public static IP address in order to establish the IPsec VPN across the internet. This is a fundamental step in order for the VPN to be reached from the on-premises gateway. In the GCP console, you can configure this by clicking on the **Navigation** menu -> **VPC network** -> **External IP addresses**, then click on **RESERVE STATIC ADDRESS**, and you reach the screen shown here:

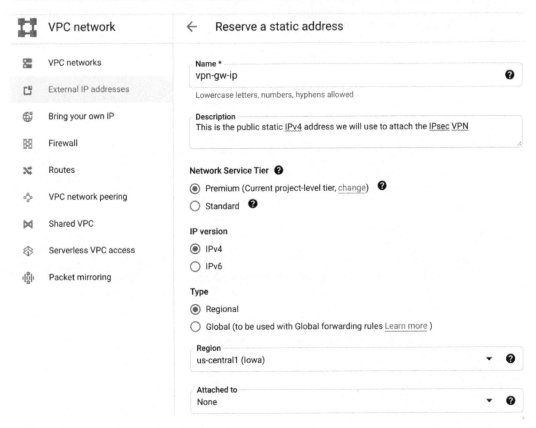

Figure 5.15 – Reservation of a public static IP version 4 (IPv4) address for IPsec VPN establishment

As *Figure 5.15* shows, you can reserve a static public IP address to use as an endpoint of your IPsec VPN. You need to specify few parameters, such as the following:

- **Network Service Tier**: With the **Premium** option, you can let the traffic traverse Google's high-quality global backbone, entering and exiting at Google's edge **point of presence** (**PoP**) closest to the user.

- **IP version**: Here, you can choose whether you want to reserve an IPv4 or an IP version 6 (IPv6) address.\

- **Type**: The IP address can be regional or global. In our case, we need to choose **Regional** since the Cloud VPN will be configured in one specific Google Cloud region.

- **Region**: This option lets you choose for which region you want to reserve the IP address. This is available only when your previous selection was **Regional**.

The result of the reservation can be seen in the following screenshot:

Figure 5.16 – Result of the public static IPv4 address reservation

Another option is to create an IP address while creating a VPN gateway, as shown in the following screenshot:

Figure 5.17 – Step 1 of creating an IP address during the VPN gateway creation process

From *Figure 5.17*, by clicking on **IP address**, we see a new overlapped little window where we can select **CREATE IP ADDRESS**, as shown in the following screenshot:

Figure 5.18 – Step 1 of creating an IP address during the VPN gateway creation process

Now that we have reserved the public static IP address, we are ready to configure the **Classic VPN IPsec Site-to-Site** field. You can create a new classic VPN in this way—from the **Navigation** menu, select **Hybrid Connectivity**, then select **VPN** to reach the screen shown here:

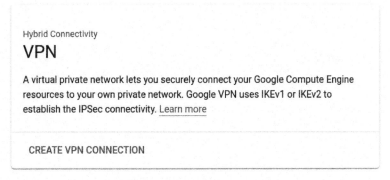

Figure 5.19 – Creating a VPN connection

From the screen shown in *Figure 5.19*, click on **CREATE VPN CONNECTION**. Finally, you can choose **Classic VPN**, as shown in the following screenshot:

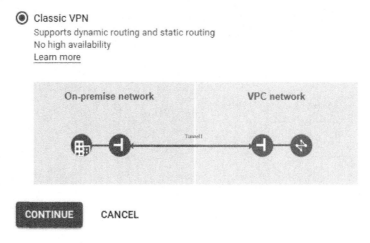

Figure 5.20 – Classic VPN prompt when creating a new VPN

When you are in the screen shown in *Figure 5.20*, upon clicking on **Continue**, you will be asked to configure the Cloud VPN gateway, as shown in the following screenshot:

Google Compute Engine VPN gateway

Name *
vpn-to-on-prem   ❓

Lowercase letters, numbers, hyphens allowed

Description
This VPN connects the Google Cloud vpc-network with the on-premises
network. It uses one IPsec VPN tunnel and BGP to enable dynamic routing

Network *
vpc-network   ▼   ❓

Region *
us-central1 (Iowa)   ▼   ❓

Region is permanent

IP address *
vpn-gw-ip   ▼   ❓

Figure 5.21 – Cloud VPN gateway configuration wizard

Here, you need to specify a few important parameters, as follows:

- **Network**: This is the VPC you want to interconnect with this IPsec VPN. In our case, it will be vpc-network.

- **Region**: This is the region where your Cloud VPN gateway will be created. It must be in the same region where you have reserved the public static IP address. In our case, the region is us-central1. If we reserve the IP address while we are in this wizard, we will not be asked about the IP region. This is because it will take the region of the VPN connection.

- **IP address**: This is the public static IP address we have reserved. In our case, this is vpn-gw-ip. We can create a new IP address from this wizard as well. Therefore, there may be no need to create an IP address as a standalone step.

Then, you need to create an IPsec tunnel toward the on-premises IPsec gateway. Starting from *Figure 5.21* and scrolling down, you can find the configuration fields, as shown in the following screenshot:

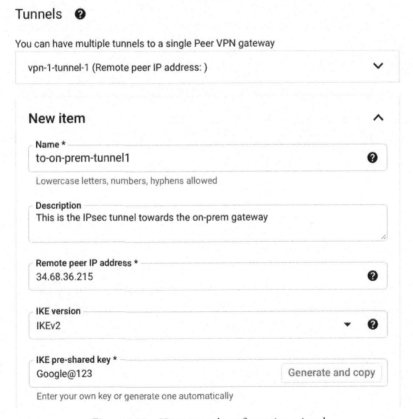

Figure 5.22 – IPsec tunnel configuration wizard

You need to create at least one IPsec tunnel for this VPN. Later, you will learn how to use multiple tunnels to improve HA. To achieve IPsec tunnel configuration, you need to set some parameters, as follows:

- **Remote peer IP address**: This is the static public IP address of the on-premises IPsec gateway to which you are addressing the tunnel. In our case, we use `34.68.36.215`.

- **IKE version**: This is the version of the **Internet Key Exchange** (**IKE**) protocol used to dynamically set up the IPsec VPN. Most modern IPsec implementations use version 2, which is recommended for improved security. If your on-premises VPN gateway does not support it, you can set the version to version 1.

- **IKE pre-shared key**: This is the key that both VPN endpoints must agree on in order to authenticate each other. At this time, this is the only supported way of peer authentication. In our case, we use `Google@123` as an authentication password.

At this point, a route-based IPsec VPN requires a route to forward the traffic to a remote destination. We need to add a static route to encapsulate the traffic into the tunnel and send it to the remote destination. This step is shown in the following screenshot:

Figure 5.23 – Adding the on-prem remote destination network
in the ROUTE-BASED tab under Routing options

Whenever some hosts in the Google Cloud VPC try to send traffic to `192.168.20.0/24`, the route will make sure that traffic will be encapsulated into the IPsec tunnel and sent over to the remote on-premises network.

To verify the result, you can monitor your VPN in the **Hybrid Connectivity** section of your GCP console, as the following screenshot shows:

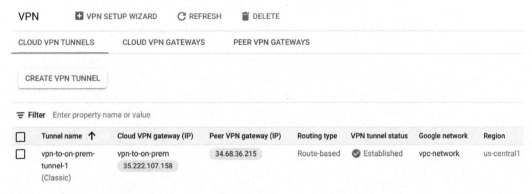

Figure 5.24 – Route-based IPsec VPN established successfully

You can also check if a new route has autogenerated in the **Routes** section, as shown in the following screenshot:

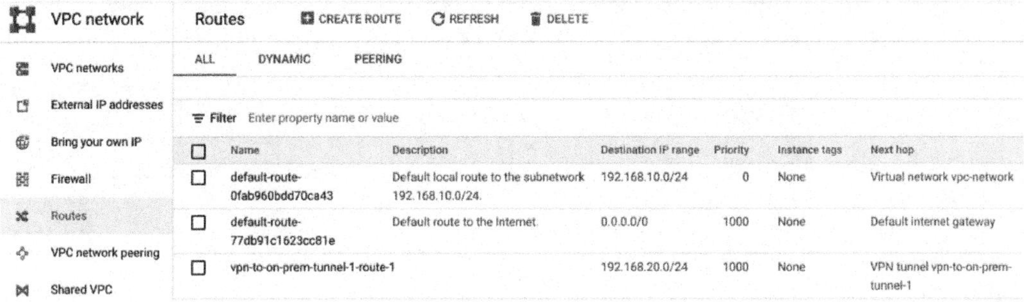

Figure 5.25 – New static route has been generated by the VPN

Now that you verify that the VPN is up and running, you can deploy a Compute Engine instance in the `us-central1` region and try to reach the hosts on the on-premises network.

> **Note**
> Make sure you have configured the appropriate firewall rules to allow traffic between the two networks.

Now that you have learned how to set up a route-based VPN, let's see how to configure HA with a Cloud VPN.

HA VPN

What is going to happen to your site-to-site VPN if something fails? Your on-premises gateway might fail, interrupting the communication between your cloud infrastructure and your on-premises infrastructure. Also, the IP communication might be interrupted over the internet, and your Cloud VPN gateway will not be able to reach your on-premises VPN gateway. In other words, whenever you want to increase the availability of your site-to-site VPN, you can configure an HA VPN solution to make your VPC and on-premises communication more robust. For example, the following diagram shows a possible HA scenario with double IPsec tunnels and a dual BGP session between the Cloud Router and the on-premises gateway:

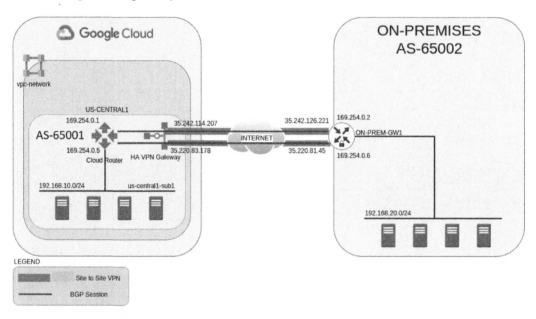

Figure 5.26 – HA VPN with dual IPsec tunnels and dynamic routing with BGP

As *Figure 5.26* shows, building an HA VPN requires you to have a Cloud VPN gateway with two public IPs and two IPsec tunnels. Also, a Cloud Router is necessary to implement dynamic routing in case one IPsec tunnel goes offline. For BGP, we also need private **autonomous system numbers (ASNs)** in order to establish a BGP session correctly. We assume that we already have static public IP addresses for our on-premises network, which will be a requirement when we go through the HA VPN configuration. In our case, we will have 34.242.126.221 and 35.220.81.45.

To configure an HA VPN, proceed as follows:

From the Navigation menu, select **Hybrid Connectivity**, then select **VPN**, then select **CREATE VPN CONNECTION**, and choose the **High-availability (HA) VPN** option, as shown in the following screenshot:

← Create a VPN

VPN options

◉ High-availability (HA) VPN
Supports dynamic routing (BGP) only
Supports high availability (99.99 SLA, within region)
Learn more

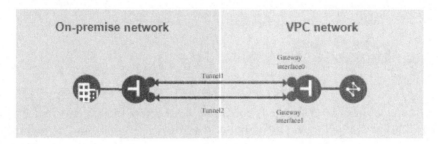

○ Classic VPN
Supports dynamic routing and static routing
No high availability
Learn more

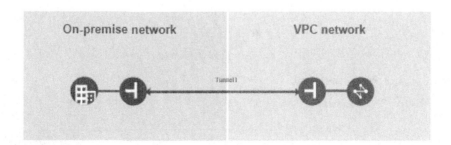

   CANCEL

Figure 5.27 – HA VPN wizard

Next, after clicking on the **CONTINUE** button shown in *Figure 5.27*, you need to configure the Cloud VPN gateway name, the VPC network in which you want to create it, and the GCP region. The following screenshot shows these options:

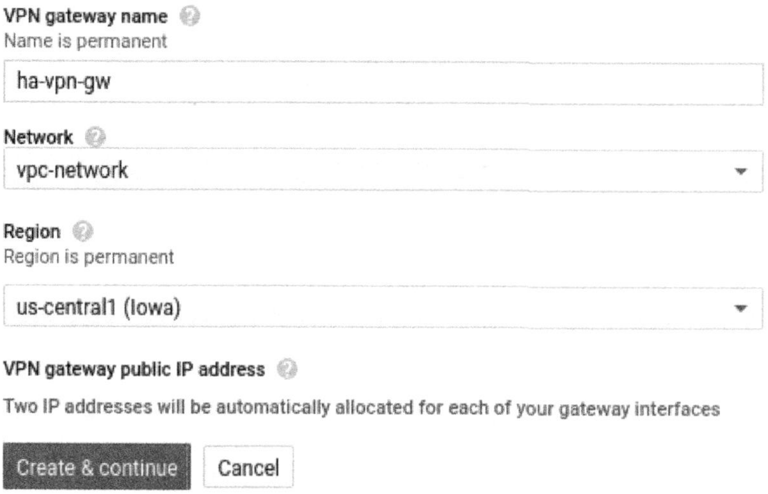

VPN gateway name ⚲
Name is permanent

ha-vpn-gw

Network ⚲

vpc-network   ▼

Region ⚲
Region is permanent

us-central1 (Iowa)   ▼

VPN gateway public IP address ⚲

Two IP addresses will be automatically allocated for each of your gateway interfaces

Create & continue   Cancel

Figure 5.28 – Creating a cloud HA VPN gateway

After you have clicked the **Create & continue** blue button, the system creates a new Cloud VPN gateway, allocating two public IP addresses. These belong to two interfaces that are logically bound to the Cloud VPN gateway, and these IP addresses will be used as endpoints for IPsec tunnels. The following screenshot shows the next step:

A VPN tunnel connects the Cloud VPN gateway to a peer gateway. Traffic sent through the tunnel is encrypted using the IPSec protocol operating in tunnel mode. Learn more

VPC network: **vpc-network**   Region: **us-central1**

VPN gateway name: **ha-vpn-gw**

Interfaces: 0 : 35.242.114.207   1 : 35.220.83.178

Peer VPN gateway
◉ On-prem or Non Google Cloud
◯ Google Cloud

Peer VPN gateway name *

No gateway

CREATE NEW PEER VPN GATEWAY

Figure 5.29 – Cloud VPN gateway creation result and IP allocation

Clicking on **CREATE NEW PEER VPN GATEWAY**, in the **Peer VPN gateway name** box, you need to define a peer VPN gateway and how to connect to it. Here, you will be required to write a name for the peer VPN gateway, select two interfaces, and write their IP addresses, as the following screenshot illustrates:

Add a peer VPN gateway

A peer VPN gateway is the gateway to which this Cloud VPN gateway will connect. It can be an on-premises gateway, a third-party VPN service, or another Cloud VPN gateway. When connecting to another Cloud VPN gateway, you must ensure that the other Cloud VPN gateway is in the same GCP region so that you meet high availability requirements. Learn more

Name ⓘ
Name is permanent

> on-prem-gw

Peer VPN gateway interfaces ⓘ

Interfaces
- ○ one interface
- ● two interfaces
- ○ four interfaces

Interface 0 IP address

> 35.242.115.23

Interface 1 IP address

> 35.220.83.19

Figure 5.30 – Adding a peer VPN gateway

Once the peer VPN gateway is configured, you need to create a Cloud Router, as the HA option is already set to two VPN tunnels. It is mandatory to use a Cloud Router with BGP in order to handle dynamically traffic rerouting due to connection losses. The following screenshot shows that we need to select a Cloud Router, and if we click on the combo box and do not have a Cloud Router, we can create one:

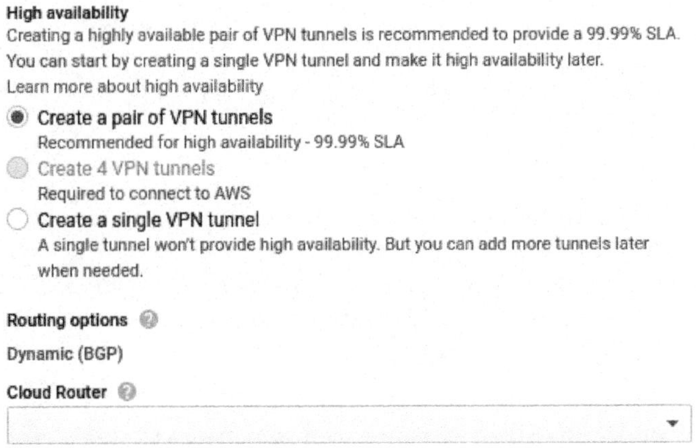

High availability
Creating a highly available pair of VPN tunnels is recommended to provide a 99.99% SLA.
You can start by creating a single VPN tunnel and make it high availability later.
Learn more about high availability

- ● **Create a pair of VPN tunnels**
  Recommended for high availability - 99.99% SLA
- ◉ Create 4 VPN tunnels
  Required to connect to AWS
- ○ **Create a single VPN tunnel**
  A single tunnel won't provide high availability. But you can add more tunnels later when needed.

Routing options ⓘ

Dynamic (BGP)

Cloud Router ⓘ

> ▼

Figure 5.31 – VPN tunnel creation

From the combo box, you will be able to create a new Cloud Router, specifying the name and the ASN, which is 65001, as the following screenshot shows:

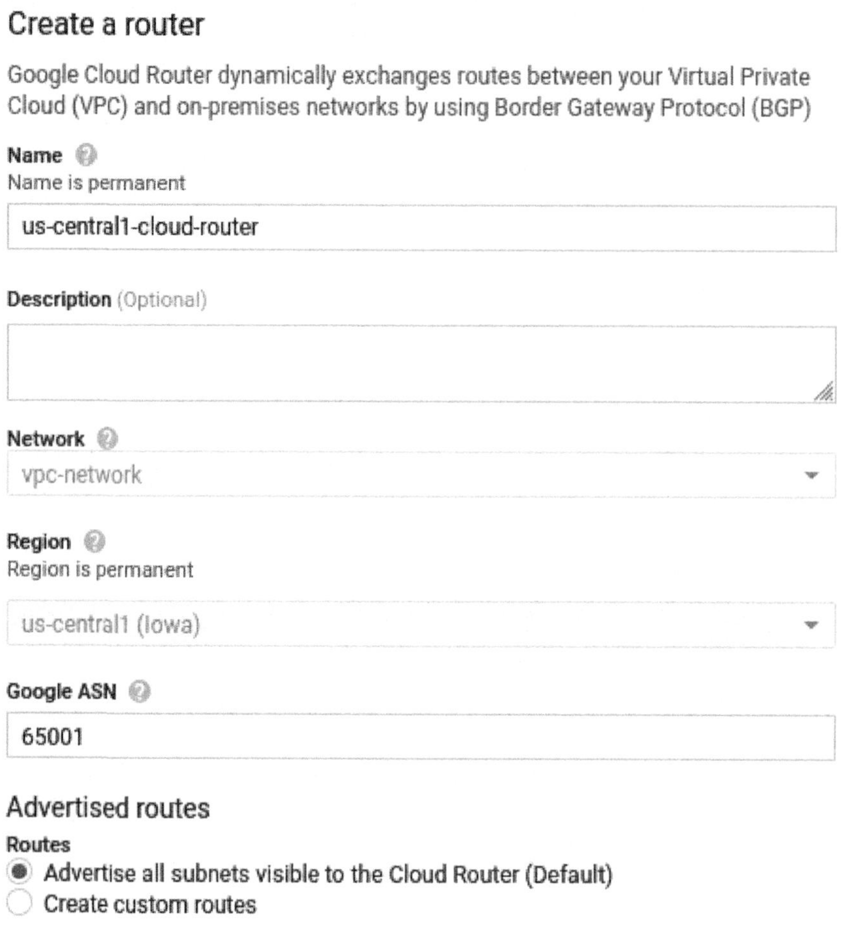

Create a router

Google Cloud Router dynamically exchanges routes between your Virtual Private Cloud (VPC) and on-premises networks by using Border Gateway Protocol (BGP)

Name ⍰
Name is permanent

```
us-central1-cloud-router
```

Description (Optional)

Network ⍰

```
vpc-network                                                    ▾
```

Region ⍰
Region is permanent

```
us-central1 (Iowa)                                             ▾
```

Google ASN ⍰

```
65001
```

Advertised routes

Routes
⦿ Advertise all subnets visible to the Cloud Router (Default)
◯ Create custom routes

Figure 5.32 – Cloud Router parameter settings

Private ASNs

The **Internet Assigned Numbers Authority (IANA)** maintains a registry of ASNs that are reserved for private use (and should therefore not be available on the global internet). As per the **Internet Engineering Task Force (IETF) Request for Comments (RFC)** *1930* and *RFC 6996*, the ASN range reserved for private use is 64512 to 65534.

Once a Cloud Router has been created, you need to configure the parameters for both the IPsec tunnels attached to the Cloud VPN. Here, you will configure the public IP address of the on-premises VPN gateway, as well as the name of the tunnel and the pre-shared key (from a security perspective, you should use a powerful pre-shared key). This configuration is for the first tunnel only, so this public IP address is one of two that the on-premises gateway has. This is illustrated in the following screenshot:

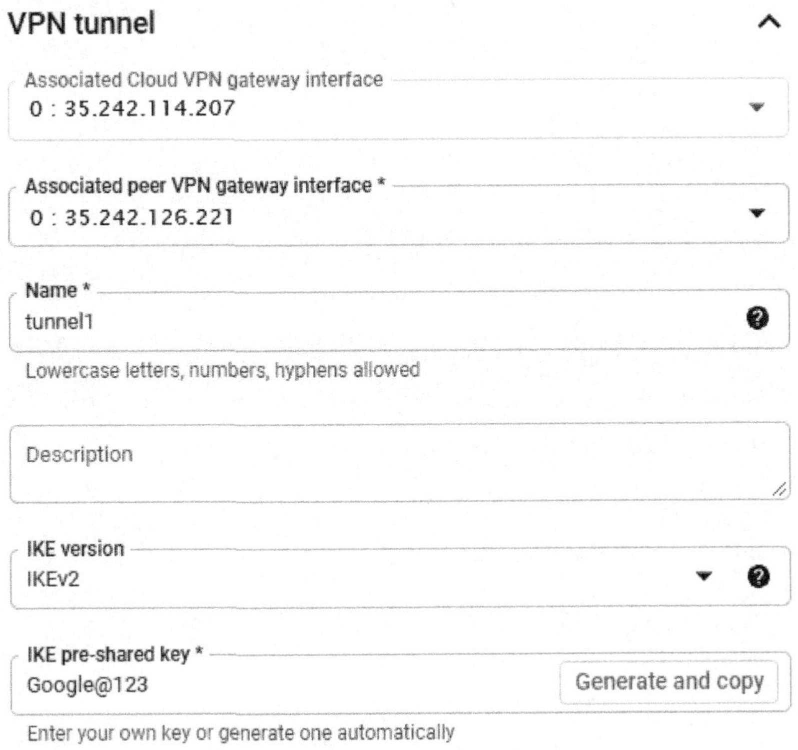

VPN tunnel ^

Associated Cloud VPN gateway interface
0 : 35.242.114.207 ▼

Associated peer VPN gateway interface *
0 : 35.242.126.221 ▼

Name *
tunnel1   ❷

Lowercase letters, numbers, hyphens allowed

Description

IKE version
IKEv2   ▼   ❷

IKE pre-shared key *
Google@123   Generate and copy

Enter your own key or generate one automatically

Figure 5.33 – Configuring IPsec tunnel 1's parameters

Figure 5.33 shows that the **Associated peer VPN gateway interface** setting is not enabled to select an option. This usually means this is not a real on-premises gateway, and we simulate on-premises on Google Cloud.

In the following screenshot, we have added two IPs from outside Google Cloud, and the **Associated peer VPN gateway interface** setting is now enabled to select an option:

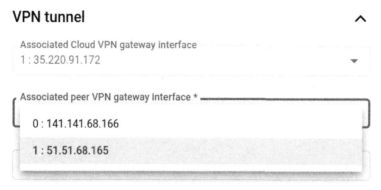

Figure 5.34 – Associated peer VPN gateway interface selection

You repeat the same procedure for the second tunnel, as the following screenshot shows:

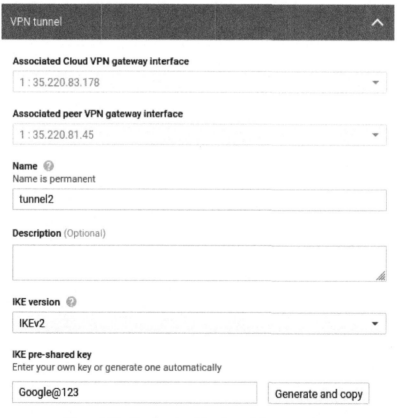

Figure 5.35 – Configuring IPsec tunnel 2's parameters

The following screenshot shows all the steps needed to create a VPN:

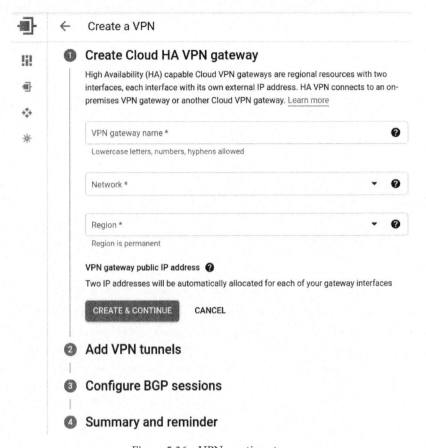

Figure 5.36 – VPN creation steps

So, when both IPsec tunnels have been configured, it's time to configure BGP sessions with the remote gateway. You need to configure two sessions, one for each tunnel that has been established. The process is shown in the following screenshot:

Click Configure BGP Session to set up the BGP session on the Cloud Router us-central1-cloud-router for each tunnel.

BGP session	Cloud VPN tunnel	Cloud VPN gateway	Cloud VPN gateway interface
Configure	tunnel1	ha-vpn-gw	0 35.242.114.207
Configure	tunnel2	ha-vpn-gw	1 35.220.83.178

Save BGP configuration   Configure BGP sessions later

Figure 5.37 – BGP session parameter settings

Once you start configuring the first BGP session, you will set the name of the session, the remote BGP peer ASN, and the link-local IP addresses (that is an IP address that exists on the tunnel link only) to use to establish the BGP peering. The process is shown in the following screenshot:

Name ⓘ
Name is permanent

| peering1 |

Peer ASN ⓘ

| 65002 |

Advertised route priority (MED) (Optional) ⓘ
MED value is used for Active/Passive configuration

| |

Cloud Router BGP IP ⓘ   **BGP peer IP** ⓘ

| 169.254.0.1 | | 169.254.0.2 |

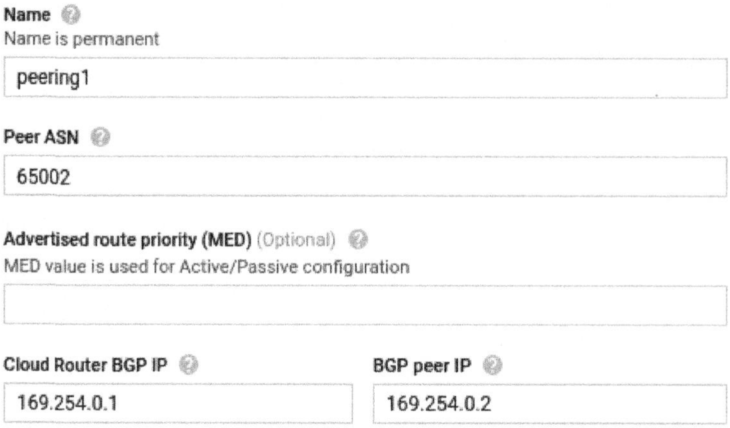

Figure 5.38 – Setting the BGP peering parameters for the first tunnel

In *Figure 5.38*, we also find the (optional) **multi-exit discriminator** (**MED**) value configuration. MED is a BGP attribute that can be used as a route selector from the peering **autonomous system** (**AS**) point of view. As with a metric, a lower MED value is preferred over a higher MED value. We could use it as an active/passive configuration: the tunnel with the lower MED value is used in a normal operational state; the other tunnel (with the higher MED value) is used only if the first tunnel is operationally down.

You repeat the same procedure for the second BGP session, as shown in the following screenshot:

Name ⓘ
Name is permanent

| peering2 |

Peer ASN ⓘ

| 65002 |

Advertised route priority (MED) (Optional) ⓘ
MED value is used for Active/Passive configuration

| |

Cloud Router BGP IP ⓘ   **BGP peer IP** ⓘ

| 169.254.0.5 | | 169.254.0.6 |

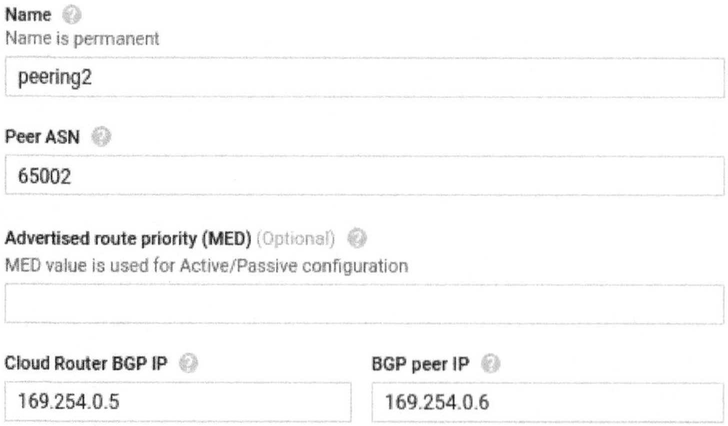

Figure 5.39 – Setting the BGP peering parameters for the second tunnel

Once the wizard is completed, the summary page will be displayed and the IPsec tunnels and BGP peerings will wait to be established. This is illustrated in the following screenshot:

Summary

Your VPN connections have been set up with these resources created:

Cloud VPN gateway

ha-vpn-gw

Cloud VPN tunnel(s)

Name	VPN tunnel status	BGP session	BGP status	MED (priority)
tunnel1	⚠ First handshake	peering1	↻	
tunnel2	⚠ First handshake	peering2	↻	

Reminder

To finish establishing connections, make sure to complete the following

1. **Configure your peer-side device / VPN gateway to access your VPC networks with the following information**

   tunnel1

   ```
   Local IP: 169.254.0.1
   BGP neighbor (Cloud): 169.254.0.2
   Remote ASN (Cloud): 65002
   ```

   tunnel2

   ```
   Local IP: 169.254.0.5
   BGP neighbor (Cloud): 169.254.0.6
   Remote ASN (Cloud): 65002
   ```

Figure 5.40 – Summary of the HA VPN configuration

After a certain time, you should have your HA VPN up and running, as shown in the following screenshot:

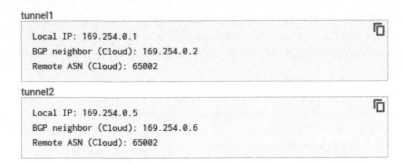

Tunnel name ↑	Cloud VPN gateway (IP) ↑	Peer VPN gateway (IP)	Cloud Router BGP IP	BGP Peer IP	Routing type	VPN tunnel status
tunnel1	ha-vpn-gw 35.242.114.207	on-prem-gw (project: noble-anvil-312907) 35.242.126.221	169.254.0.1	169.254.0.2	Dynamic (BGP)	✅ Established
tunnel2	ha-vpn-gw 35.220.83.178	on-prem-gw (project: noble-anvil-312907) 35.220.81.45	169.254.0.5	169.254.0.6	Dynamic (BGP)	✅ Established

Figure 5.41 – Successful IPsec HA VPN establishment

Now that you have learned how to configure a site-to-site IPsec VPN, you can continue exploring the Cloud Router service in the next section.

Diving into Cloud Router

Cloud Router is a Google Cloud service that emulates the standard behavior of a real physical IP router. It is not a physical device (and so it cannot cause bottlenecks), but indeed it is a service, fully managed and distributed (it can work whether regionally or globally to the entire GCP suite). Being a fully managed service, it is also automatically scalable to satisfy the dynamic needs of your VPC network.

When used in cooperation with an interconnect option, between your on-prem network and your VPCs, it uses the BGP protocol to dynamically exchange routes between your networks.

BGP

BGP is one of the most important (or maybe the most important) routing protocols used on the entire internet nowadays. It is responsible for exchange routing information among different ASes.

ASes are connected groups of one or more IP prefixes run by one or more network operators that have a *single and clearly defined* routing policy (see IETF *RFC 1930*, March 1996).

BGP is nowadays the most used inter-AS routing protocol, whose primary function is to exchange network reachability information with other BGP systems (see IETF *RFC 4271*, January 2006). It may be the only available *exterior gateway protocol* nowadays to connect ASes, while other routing protocols are *interior gateway protocols* (and work inside ASes).

IETF RFC

An RFC is a publication from the **Internet Society** (**ISOC**) and its associated bodies, most prominently the IETF, the principal technical development and standard-setting body for the internet.

So, with a Cloud Router, you do not have to explicitly refer to the network IP ranges that you are using in your networks., In particular, any modification to the IP ranges that you are using on-prem as well as in your VPC does not require any human intervention to make this update knowable at the other side of the BGP peering. BGP, as a dynamic routing protocol, is in charge of exchanging any routing information dynamically. Therefore, BGP can automatically add new IP ranges and/or remove any range that is no longer used or reachable in your network.

A Cloud Router must be present in your GCP environment in the following cases:

- Creating a VLAN attachment for Dedicated Interconnect
- Creating a VLAN attachment for Partner Interconnect
- Creating a VPN tunnel connected to an HA VPN gateway
- Creating a cloud **network address translation** (**NAT**) gateway

A Cloud Router is not mandatory for classic VPNs (but is still recommended if your on-premises VPN gateway supports BGP). Generally speaking, whenever you configure a BGP peering between two ASes, you must use the ASNs that were assigned to the AS by IANA. IANA is a global entity that is in charge of, among many things, assigning ASNs to the ASes in the world. In our case, although you could use a Cloud Router to create BGP public peering, we focus on the case when we create BGP private peering, to create hybrid connectivity internal to any customer. In such a case, we use a particular range of ASNs that are reserved for private use. In fact, as for the IETF *RFC 6996* (July 2013), IANA has reserved for private use the ASNs specified in the following table.

First ASN	Last ASN	Available ASNs	16- or 32-bit
64512	65534	1023	16-bit
4200000000	4294967294	94967295	32-bit

These reservations have been documented in the IANA ASNs registry.

Cloud Router configuration

Let's see how to configure a Cloud Router in GCP using the Cloud Console, as follows:

1. From the **Navigation** menu, click on **Hybrid Connectivity**, **Cloud Routers**, and then click **CREATE ROUTER**, as illustrated in the following screenshot:

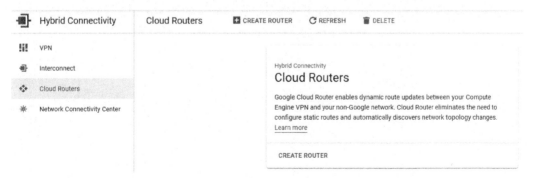

Figure 5.42 – Creating a Cloud Router

2. Set the name, the VPC network, the region, and the Google ASN. You can use any private ASN that you are not using elsewhere in your network. The required fields are shown in the following screenshot:

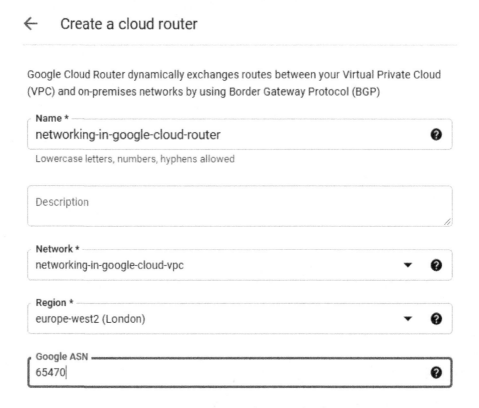

Figure 5.43 – Basic settings for your Cloud Router

3. Select if you want to advertise all subnets visible to the Cloud Router (default) or if you want to create custom routes to exchange with other networks (we have chosen the default setting in this example), and then click on the **CREATE** button. The screen shown next is reached by scrolling from the one shown in *Figure 5.43*:

Advertised routes

Routes

◉ Advertise all subnets visible to the Cloud Router (Default)

○ Create custom routes

[CREATE]   CANCEL

EQUIVALENT COMMAND LINE   ▼

Equivalent REST

Figure 5.44 – Selecting the Advertised routes mode

4. Please remember that you could use the `gcloud config set project <PROJECT_ID>` command to set the project **identifier (ID)** for the following entire command line:

```
gcloud compute routers \
create networking-in-google-cloud-router \
--project=<PROJECT_ID> \
--region=europe-west2 \
--network=networking-in-google-cloud-vpc \
--asn=65470
```

5. In this last case, you can avoid specifying the project ID in every other command. The equivalent **REpresentational State Transfer (REST) application programming interface (API)** request can be obtained by clicking on the **Equivalent REST** button shown in *Figure 5.44*. After your router is created successfully, you should find it on the **Cloud Routers** page, as illustrated in the following screenshot:

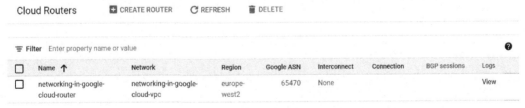

	Name ↑	Network	Region	Google ASN	Interconnect	Connection	BGP sessions	Logs
☐	networking-in-google-cloud-router	networking-in-google-cloud-vpc	europe-west2	65470	None			View

Figure 5.45 – Cloud Router created successfully

Static external IP address

Before creating any BGP peering, your Cloud Router needs a static external IP address:

1. First, from the **Navigation** menu, let's navigate to **VPC network**, **External IP addresses**, and click on **RESERVE STATIC ADDRESS**, as illustrated in the following screenshot:

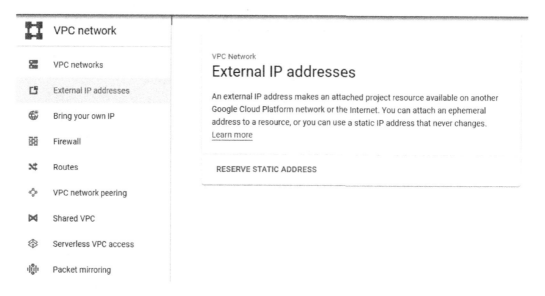

Figure 5.46 – Reserving an external static IP address

2. Let's set the **Name**, **Network Service Tier**, **IP version** (**IPv4** or **IPv6**), **Type** (**Regional** or **Global**), and **Region** (this will only appear if we choose **Regional** for the **Type** option) fields, and if you want to attach that IP address to a VM instance. As you can see from the following screenshot, we set None because we do not want to attach this IP address to a VM but to a Cloud Router:

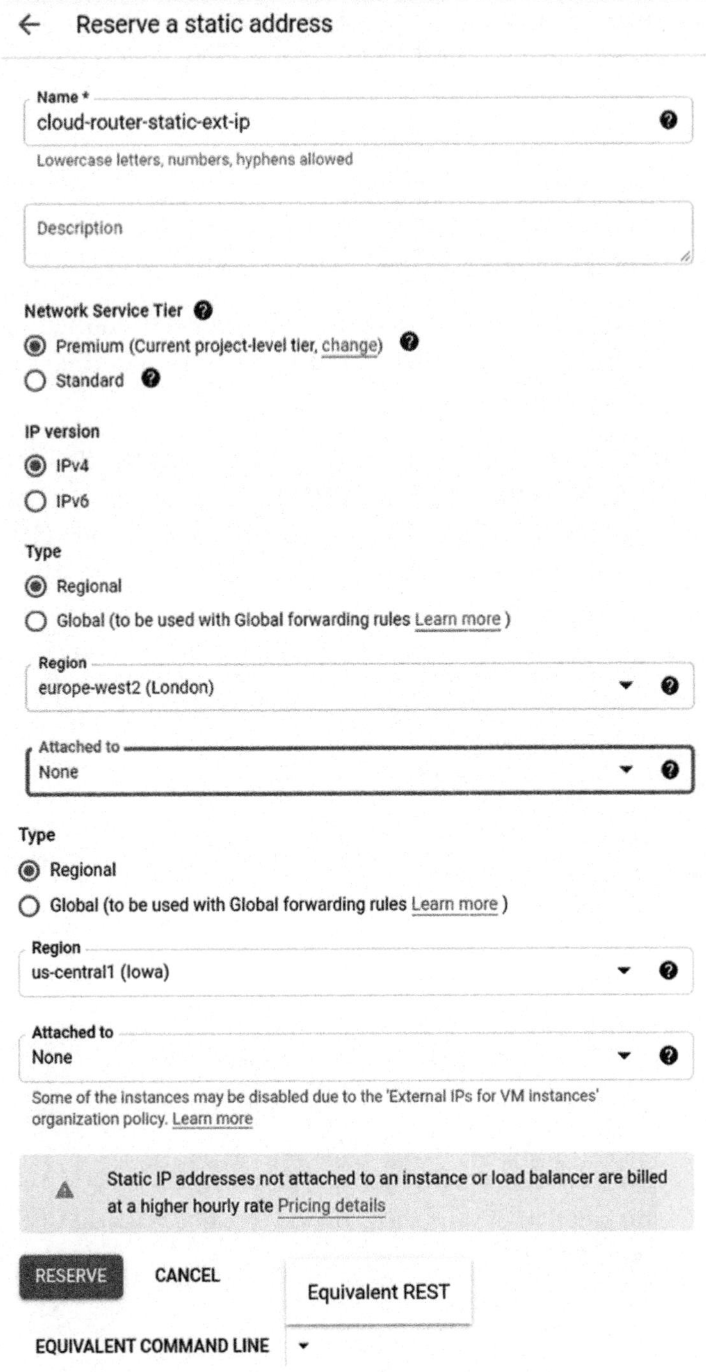

←   Reserve a static address

Name *
cloud-router-static-ext-ip   ❷

Lowercase letters, numbers, hyphens allowed

Description

Network Service Tier ❷
◉ Premium (Current project-level tier, change) ❷
○ Standard ❷

IP version
◉ IPv4
○ IPv6

Type
◉ Regional
○ Global (to be used with Global forwarding rules Learn more)

Region
europe-west2 (London)   ▼   ❷

Attached to
None   ▼   ❷

Type
◉ Regional
○ Global (to be used with Global forwarding rules Learn more)

Region
us-central1 (Iowa)   ▼   ❷

Attached to
None   ▼   ❷

Some of the instances may be disabled due to the 'External IPs for VM instances'
organization policy. Learn more

⚠   Static IP addresses not attached to an instance or load balancer are billed
     at a higher hourly rate Pricing details

RESERVE   CANCEL   Equivalent REST

EQUIVALENT COMMAND LINE   ▼

Figure 5.47 – Static external IP address settings

3. The equivalent command line to reserve a static external IP address can be obtained by clicking on the **EQUIVALENT COMMAND LINE** button shown in *Figure 5.47*. The code should look like this:

```
gcloud compute addresses create \
cloud-router-static-ext-ip \
--project=<PROJECT_ID> \
--region=europe-west2
```

4. The equivalent REST request to reserve a static external IP address can be obtained as well by clicking on the **Equivalent REST** button shown in *Figure 5.47*.

5. Click on the **RESERVE** button.

    When we create a VPN connection, selecting the **DYNAMIC (BGP)** routing option (which is mandatory in the case of a HA VPN and optional in the case of a standard VPN, as per the following screenshot), we have to select the Cloud Router we created before and set up a BGP session with the on-prem router:

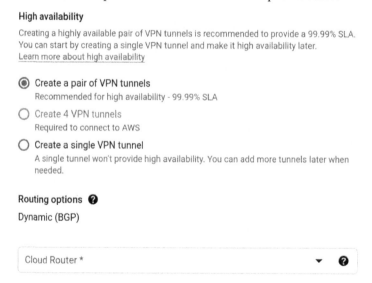

Figure 5.48 – Routing options in the case of a HA VPN

Select the routing option of your choice in the case of a classical VPN, as illustrated in the following screenshot:

Figure 5.49 – Routing options in the case of a classical VPN

6. The next step is to create a VPN connection. Let's see how to connect the Cloud Router in the case of a VPN between the VPC and the on-prem network.

7. If we want to select the DYNAMIC BGP routing option (which is mandatory in the case of a HA VPN and optional in the case of a standard VPN), we have to do the following:

a. Select the Cloud Router we created before (or you can also create a new Cloud Router if you did not create one before).

b. Reserve a static IP to set up the BGP session with the on-prem router.

c. Create a VPN connection. (You can create an IP address from here as well if you did not do this in *Step 11b*). We are creating a classical VPN in the example shown here:

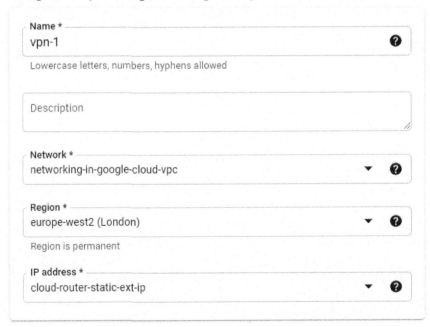

Figure 5.50 – VPN connection creation

8. Set up the tunnel information. Here, the remote peer IP address is the static external address that you have set in your on-prem router. For the pre-shared key, as a security best practice, Google recommends that you generate a strong 32-character pre-shared key. The fields are shown in the following screenshot:

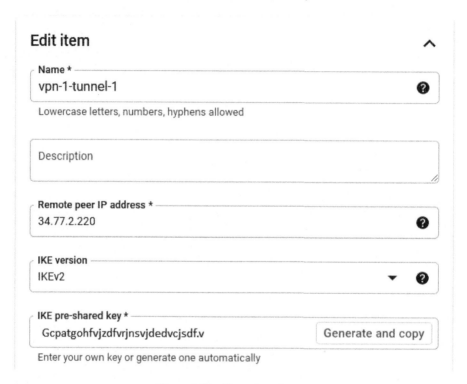

Figure 5.51 – Tunnel settings

9. In the same wizard, set the routing options: in our case, we want to use the **DYNAMIC (BGP)** option. If you want to allow your Cloud Router to dynamically learn routes to and from all GCP regions on a network, you have to turn on **Global dynamic routing** for the `networking-in.google-cloud-vpc` VPC network. If you are using an internal load balancer with VPN or Interconnect, both the Cloud VPN gateway and tunnel(s) must be located in the same region as the load balancer when VPC global access is disabled. If global access is enabled on the load balancer's forwarding rule, this restriction is not applied. The routing options can be seen in the following screenshot:

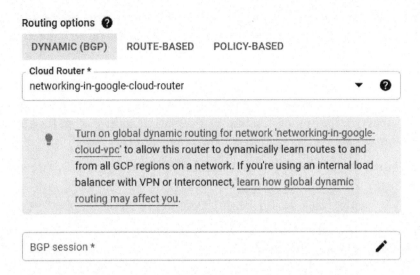

Figure 5.52 – Routing options

10. Clicking on the pencil in the **BGP session** box, we set up the BGP session, as shown in the following screenshot:

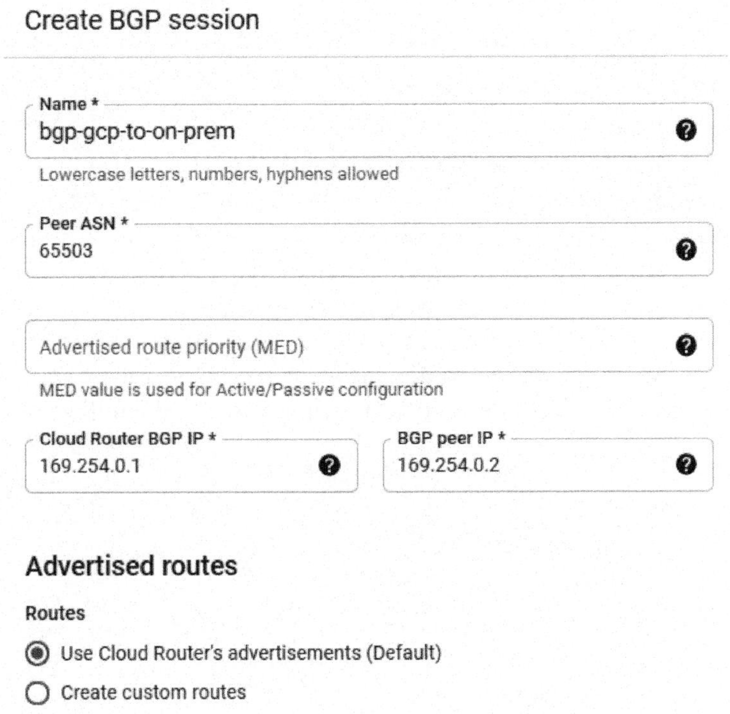

Create BGP session

Name *

bgp-gcp-to-on-prem

Lowercase letters, numbers, hyphens allowed

Peer ASN *

65503

Advertised route priority (MED)

MED value is used for Active/Passive configuration

Cloud Router BGP IP *

169.254.0.1

BGP peer IP *

169.254.0.2

Advertised routes

Routes

◉ Use Cloud Router's advertisements (Default)

○ Create custom routes

Figure 5.53 – BGP session setup

11. First, you have to choose a name for your BGP session. In the BGP session setup, be sure to put the right peer ASN. This is the ASN you configured in your on-prem router (in this case, we have a private ASN because this is for a VPN). The Cloud Router BGP IP and peer BGP IP must be link-local (`169.254.0.1/30` - `169.254.0.2/30`) in the same `/30` subnet (as for every point-to-point IP network). Make sure they are not the network address (the very first address on an IPv4 subnet) or the broadcast address (the very last address of an IPv4 subnet) of the subnet.

    The equivalent command line for a classical VPN is really long, as we can see here:

    ```
    gcloud compute target-vpn-gateways create vpn-1 \
    --project=<PROJECT_ID> \
    --region=europe-west2
    --network=networking-in-google-cloud-vpc
    (For HA-VPN the previous command would have been:
    gcloud compute vpn-gateways ...)
    ```

12. Next, we need to configure forwarding rules that allow you to decide which traffic will get to the VPN target. The code for this is illustrated in the following snippet:

    ```
    gcloud compute forwarding-rules create vpn-1-rule-esp \
    --project=<PROJECT_ID> \
    --region=europe-west2
    --address=34.105.185.216
    --ip-protocol=ESP
    --target-vpn-gateway=vpn-1
    ```

13. The IPsec protocol supports two ways of encapsulating the traffic: **Encapsulating Security Payload** (**ESP**), which can guarantee encryption, authentication, and integrity, or **Authentication Header** (**AH**), which can guarantee authentication and integrity only (no encryption). The code is illustrated in the following snippet:

    ```
    gcloud compute forwarding-rules create \
    vpn-1-rule-udp500 \
      --project=<PROJECT-ID> \
    --region=europe-west2 \
    --address=34.105.185.216 \
    --ip-protocol=UDP \
    --ports=500 \
    --target-vpn-gateway=vpn-1
    ```

14. Port 500 in the previous forwarding rule is due to let in IKE traffic. In the following code snippet, port 4500 is being used:

```
gcloud compute forwarding-rules create \
vpn-1-rule-udp4500 \
--project=<PROJECT-ID> \
--region=europe-west2 \
--address=34.105.185.216 \
--ip-protocol=UDP \
--ports=4500 \
--target-vpn-gateway=vpn-1
```

15. Port 4500 is needed for the **NAT-Traversal** (**NAT-T**) feature, needed when the private IP address is present at the application layer. Here we are using an example of a shared secret that is not suitable for production. In a production network, we need to set a much stronger shared secret:

```
gcloud compute vpn-tunnels create vpn-1-tunnel-1 \
 --project=<PROJECT_ID> \
 --region=europe-west2 \
--peer-address=34.77.2.220 \
--shared-secret=gcp \
--ike-version=2 \
--target-vpn-gateway=vpn-1
```

16. Next, we need to add an interface to the Cloud Router, as follows:

```
gcloud compute routers add-interface \
networking-in-google-cloud-router \
--project=<PROJECT_ID> \
 --interface-name=if-bgp-gcp-to-on-prem \
--vpn-tunnel=vpn-1-tunnel-1 \
--region=europe-west2
```

17. Lastly, we add a BGP peer to the Cloud Router, like this:

```
gcloud compute routers add-bgp-peer \
networking-in-google-cloud-router \
--project=<PROJECT_ID> \
 --interface=if-bgp-gcp-to-on-prem \
```

```
--peer-name=bgp-gcp-to-on-prem \
--peer-asn=65503 \
--ip-address=169.254.0.1 \
--peer-ip-address=169.254.0.2 \
--advertisement-mode=DEFAULT
```

18. If the VPN tunnel is correctly configured on the other side (on-prem), the BGP session should go up and start exchanging routes, which you can see by clicking on the **Navigation** menu, navigating to **VPC network**, selecting the specific VPC, and scrolling down until you reach and select the **ROUTES** tab, as illustrated in the following screenshot:

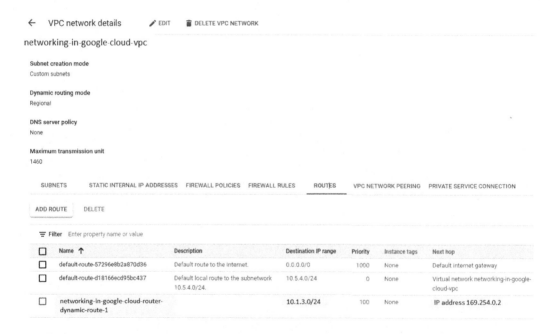

Figure 5.54 – BGP is exchanging routes between the on-prem router and the Cloud Router in the VPC

MED

If we review the following screenshot, where we configured the BGP session, you will notice that we could have selected a MED value that is an advertised route priority:

Create BGP session

Name *

bgp-gcp-to-on-prem ❓

Lowercase letters, numbers, hyphens allowed

Peer ASN *

65503 ❓

Advertised route priority (MED) ❓

MED value is used for Active/Passive configuration

Cloud Router BGP IP *

169.254.0.1 ❓

BGP peer IP *

169.254.0.2 ❓

Advertised routes

Routes

◉ Use Cloud Router's advertisements (Default)

◯ Create custom routes

Figure 5.55 – Advertised route priority (MED value)

This is useful whenever you have more than one connection exiting from your VPC (HA VPN), and you want to select the preferred way. A MED's behavior is similar to that of a metric, so a lower value is preferred over a higher value.

Summary

In this chapter, you have learned how to interconnect your on-premises network with a Google Cloud VPC. You have been through Dedicated Interconnect as well as Partner Interconnect solutions. Then, you also have learned how to connect your on-premises network using Cloud VPN in **Classic mode** and in **HA mode**. Now that you have learned how to implement hybrid connectivity in GCP, let's go through the network security implementation in the next chapter.

6
Implementing Network Security

In this chapter, you will explore and implement security in your **Virtual Private Cloud Network (VPC)** in **Google Cloud Platform(GCP)**. The chapter will cover three main parts:

- Configuring **Identity and Access Management (IAM)**

- Configuring Cloud Armor

- Configuring third-party device insertion (a next-generation firewall) into VPC using multiple **Network Interface Cards (NICs)**.

At the end of the chapter, you will be able to protect your network and services with the appropriate tools that Google Cloud provides.

Configuring Identity and Access Management (IAM)

In this section, we are going to explore how to control access to Google Cloud resources through **Identity and Access Management**. It is important to recall that IAM lets us define *who can do what on which GCP resources*. Indeed, with IAM roles, the IT security manager can control the access and permissions to Google Cloud resources, such as *Compute Engine instances*, *Google Cloud Storage buckets*, *BigQuery datasets*, and so on. Remember that there are three types of IAM roles that you can use:

- **Primitive**: Coarse-grained roles
- **Predefined**: Fine-grained roles
- **Custom**: User-defined roles

The roles can control what permissions you have on a GCP resource. Instead, in order to address the who statement, we need to assign roles to IAM members. There are five types of IAM members that can be assigned to IAM roles, as *Figure 6.1* depicts:

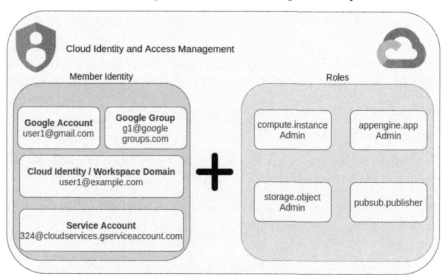

Figure 6.1 – Cloud Identity and Access Management overview

Indeed, you can assign IAM roles to the following:

- **A Google account**: This is any Gmail account that identifies a personal entity.
- **A Google group**: This is a group of Google personal accounts. It can also contain service accounts.

- **A Cloud Identity or Workspace domain**: This is an enterprise account that can be created as a Google Workspace domain or Google Cloud Identity domain.

- **A service account**: This is a special Google account for machine-to-machine operations.

If you want to view the **IAM members** and **roles**, you can access the **IAM & Admin** menu, as shown in *Figure 6.2*:

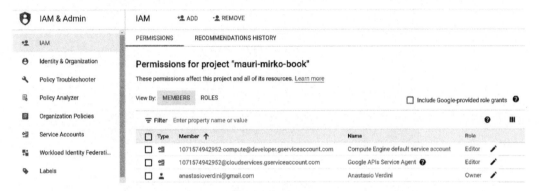

Figure 6.2 – IAM members and roles in Google Cloud Platform

You can add IAM members by using the **ADD** button shown in *Figure 6.2*. *Figure 6.3* shows what happens after we click on the **ADD** button:

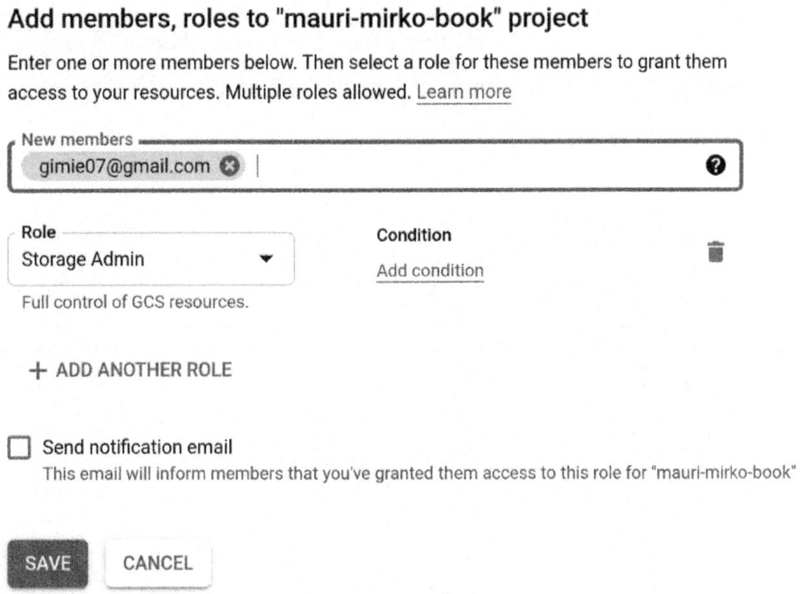

Add members, roles to "mauri-mirko-book" project

Enter one or more members below. Then select a role for these members to grant them access to your resources. Multiple roles allowed. Learn more

New members
gimie07@gmail.com ✕

Role
Storage Admin ▼

Condition
Add condition

Full control of GCS resources.

+ ADD ANOTHER ROLE

☐ Send notification email
This email will inform members that you've granted them access to this role for "mauri-mirko-book"

SAVE   CANCEL

Figure 6.3 – New IAM members and roles definition

Indeed, as *Figure 6.3* shows, you can search for a Google account as an IAM member and assign the role you need. In the example, we assign the predefined `Storage Admin` IAM role to the Google account `gimie07@gmail.com`.

If you need to let Google Cloud resources interact with each other, it is important to create a **service account** and provide the appropriate IAM role, as shown in *Figure 6.4*:

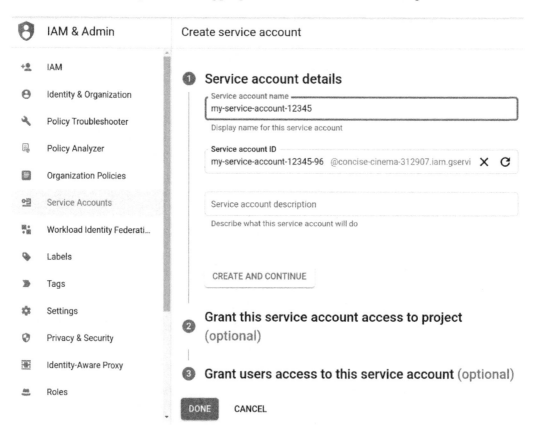

Figure 6.4 – Creating an IAM service account

When you have chosen the unique name of your service account, you can assign an IAM role to it, as shown in *Figure 6.5*:

✔ **Service account details**

② **Grant this service account access to project**
(optional)

Grant this service account access to mauri-mirko-book so that it has permission to
complete specific actions on the resources in your project. Learn more

Role ⎯⎯
Storage Admin ▼

Condition
Add condition

🗑

Full control of GCS resources.

✛ ADD ANOTHER ROLE

CONTINUE

③ **Grant users access to this service account** (optional)

DONE   CANCEL

Figure 6.5 – Assigning a predefined IAM role to a service account

As *Figure 6.5* shows, by clicking on the **DONE** button, the service account is created with
a **Storage Admin** predefined IAM role. We can now use this account inside a compute
engine instance to manage Cloud Storage buckets. *Figure 6.6* shows how to create a new
Google Compute Engine instance with the service account assigned. The service account
can be used to have full control of buckets and objects in Google Cloud Storage:

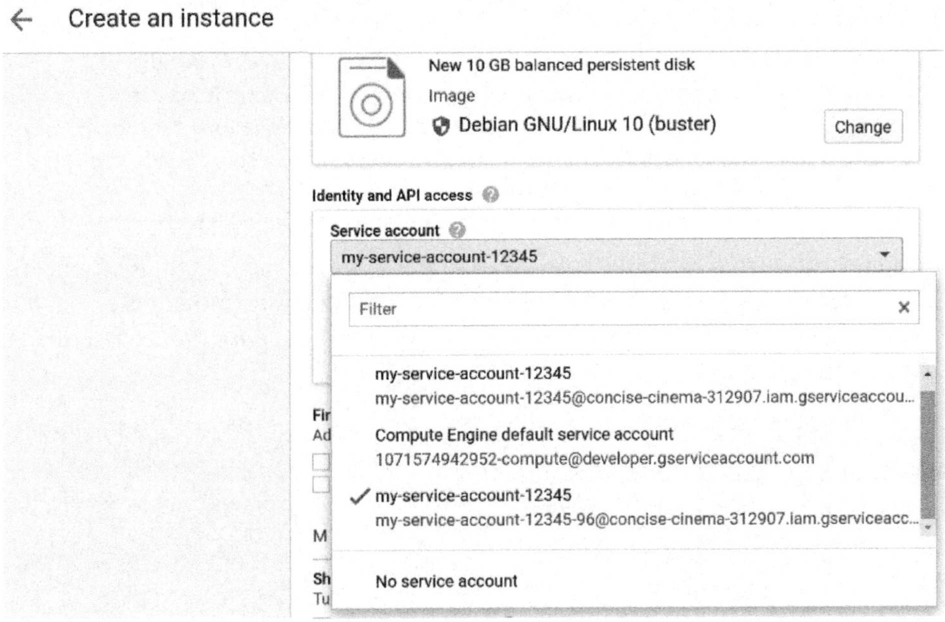

← **Create an instance**

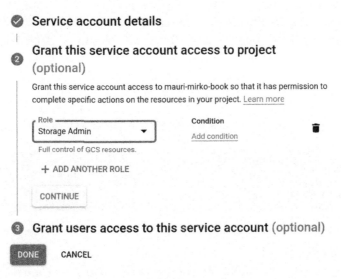

Figure 6.6 – Assigning an IAM service account to a Google Compute Engine instance

Once the Google Compute Engine is instantiated, you can connect using SSH (Secure Socket Shell) and use the Google Cloud **Software Development Kit (SDK)** to create and have full control of buckets and objects in Google Cloud Storage. It is important to notice that because the machine has assigned a service account with the appropriate role, you will be able to create a bucket and list files in it, as *Figure 6.7* illustrates:

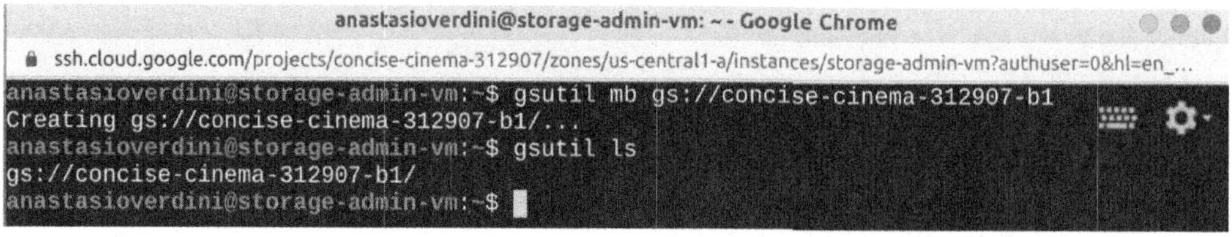

Figure 6.7 – Testing the service account with the gsutil SDK from the Compute Engine instance

Indeed, note that you are able to create a bucket with the `gsutil mb gs://concise-cinema-312907-b1` command (mb stands for `make bucket`) and list files with the command `gsutil ls` (ls stands for `list`).

Sometimes, using predefined Cloud IAM roles does not fit your need in terms of access permission. You may want to combine different permissions in order to have a custom role to assign to your members. Each permission includes some actions that you are allowed to perform on a resource, some for reading only and some for editing also.

> **Important Note**
> Google Cloud recommends always using predefined IAM roles to avoid management overhead unless you need something very custom. Indeed, to create a custom role, you should have to specify all the permissions associated with it (and you could have lots of them, depending on the resources that you want to allow your user to perform actions on).

You can create a custom IAM role in many different ways. We decided to use Cloud Shell and YAML format to give you another nice method of doing this configuration. First of all, you need to create a `yaml` file to include the IAM role configuration, as described in the following file excerpt:

```
title: [ROLE_TITLE]
description: [ROLE_DESCRIPTION]
stage: [LAUNCH_STAGE]
includedPermissions:
  - [PERMISSION_1]
  - [PERMISSION_2]
```

> **Important Note**
> In a YAML file format, the indentation is very important, and you must always respect two space characters. Otherwise, you will encounter syntax errors.

As described in the previous code, you can create a custom IAM role by setting the `title` value, which is a friendly name for the role, as you can see in *Figure 6.8*; the `description` value, which should describe briefly what permissions the role provides; the `stage` value, which provides the lifecycle state of the role, and the `includedPermissions` value, which lists the permissions given:

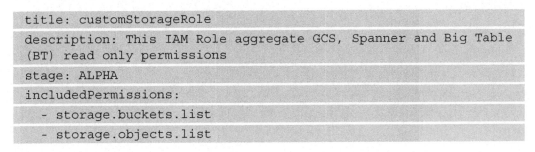

Roles   + CREATE ROLE   ⬚ CREATE ROLE FROM SELECTION   − DISABLE   🗑 DELETE

Roles for "blockchain-all" project

A role is a group of permissions that you can assign to members. You can create a role and add permissions to it, or copy an existing role and adjust its permissions. Learn more

⇄ Filter   Enter property name or value

Type	Title	Used in	Status	Name
⊙	AAM Admin	Dialogflow	Enabled	roles/dialogflow.aamAdmin
⊙	AAM Conversational Architect	Dialogflow	Enabled	roles/dialogflow.aamConversationalArchitect
⊙	AAM Dialog Designer	Dialogflow	Enabled	roles/dialogflow.aamDialogDesigner
⊙	AAM Lead Dialog Designer	Dialogflow	Enabled	roles/dialogflow.aamLeadDialogDesigner
⊙	AAM Viewer	Dialogflow	Enabled	roles/dialogflow.aamViewer
⊙	Access Approval Approver	Access Approval	Enabled	roles/accessapproval.approver
⊙	Access Approval Config Editor	Access Approval	Enabled	roles/accessapproval.configEditor
⊙	Access Approval Viewer	Access Approval	Enabled	roles/accessapproval.viewer
⊙	Access Context Manager Admin	Access Context Manager	Enabled	roles/accesscontextmanager.policyAdmin
⊙	Access Context Manager Editor	Access Context Manager	Enabled	roles/accesscontextmanager.policyEditor
⊙	Access Context Manager Reader	Access Context Manager	Enabled	roles/accesscontextmanager.policyReader

Figure 6.8 – Role examples with titles and names

In the following example, we will replace the placeholders [...] in order to give you a better understanding of creating an IAM custom role:

```
title: customStorageRole
description: This IAM Role aggregate GCS, Spanner and Big Table (BT) read only permissions
stage: ALPHA
includedPermissions:
  - storage.buckets.list
  - storage.objects.list
```

```
- storage.objects.get
- spanner.databases.get
- spanner.databases.list
- bigtable.tables.get
- bigtable.tables.list
- bigtable.tables.readRows
```

As you can see, we are creating a new custom IAM role titled `customStorageRole` that will provide `ReadOnly` permissions to Google Cloud Storage, Google Cloud Spanner, and Google Cloud Bigtable. More specifically, the IAM member who will be assigned to this custom IAM role will be able to list buckets and objects from Google Cloud Storage, list databases from Cloud Spanner, and list tables from Cloud Bigtable. It will also be able to read objects from Cloud Storage, read databases from Cloud Spanner, and read tables and rows from Cloud Bigtable.

When the custom IAM role has been defined, we can create it using the following `gcloud` command run in Cloud Shell:

```
gcloud iam roles create customStorageRole --project concise-
cinema-312907 --file customStorageRole.yml
```

Please replace `concise-cinema-312907` with your `PROJECT_ID` in your command. `CustomStorageRole.yml` is the file that contains the previous YAML.

You may notice that the IAM role has been created within a specific project, which is mandatory (please note that the role can be created at the level of the organization also). The result looks like the following:

```
Created role [customStorageRole].
description: This IAM Role aggregate GCS, Spanner and BT read
only permissions
etag: BwXE1COYrqs=
includedPermissions:
- bigtable.tables.get
- bigtable.tables.list
- bigtable.tables.readRows
- spanner.databases.get
- spanner.databases.list
```

```
- storage.buckets.list
- storage.objects.get
- storage.objects.list
name: projects/concise-cinema-312907/roles/customStorageRole
stage: ALPHA
title: customStorageRole
```

The `etag` value is used for concurrency control of the policies' modifications. When a system tries to change a policy, first it reads the policy and stores the associated `etag`, and then it tries to upload the new policy using the same `etag`. Meanwhile, if another system changed that policy, we have an `etag` mismatch and so the policy update fails; if you modify the policy with a REST API, you will get the *409 Conflict* error (REST API stands for REpresentational State Transfer Application Programming Interface).

You can now check the result from the GCP Console in the **IAM & Admin** section, as shown in *Figure 6.9*:

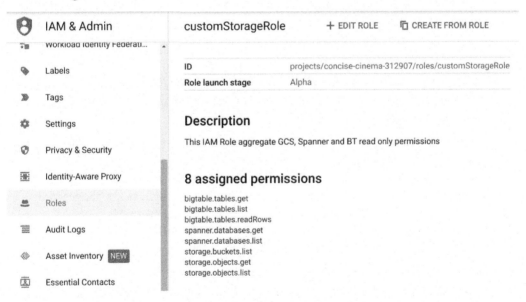

Figure 6.9 – After the creation of a custom IAM role

You can now use the custom IAM role as any other role in Google Cloud Platform.

Now that you've learned how to administer identity and access control with IAM, let's see how to protect our GCP services from DDoS attacks with Cloud Armor.

Configuring Cloud Armor security policies

Imagine that you have deployed your web application globally using several backend services in different GCP regions and you distribute the traffic using the external HTTP(S) load balancer. Now, to secure your web application, you need to deploy different security services. Google Cloud offers **Cloud Armor**, which is a fully distributed managed service to protect your web application against **Denial of Service (DoS)**, **Distributed Denial of Service (DDoS)**, and web application attacks. More specifically, Cloud Armor can protect from the **Open Web Application Security Project (OWASP)** top 10 attacks. This is the list of the top 10 most dangerous attacks targeting web applications. It is a list that is updated by the OWASP every year. It can also mitigate DDoS at scale. Cloud Armor has the following features:

- **IP-based and geo-based access control**: You can blacklist clients based on IP ranges or from Google's GeoIP maps.

- **A pre-configured Web Application Firewall (WAF) policy to block the top 10 OWASP attacks**: You can block intrusion attacks to vulnerable web applications using industry-standard predefined rules. The traffic is inspected at the application level, and for HTTPS traffic, Cloud Armor can host your web application's digital trusted certificate for SSL inspection.

- **Adaptive protection through machine learning**: Cloud Armor can adapt to your normal web application traffic to intercept traffic anomalies, and it can suggest policies to mitigate future attacks.

- **A fully distributed serverless service**: You do not have to worry about dimensions and scale your Cloud Armor security protection. Your web application traffic is unpredictable by nature. Instead, everything is managed by Google Cloud, and you just focus on the security for your web application, such as the danger of data leakage or not-so-well-managed authentication or authorization.

Google Cloud Armor is available in two service tiers:

- **Standard**: This is the pay-as-you-go model that provides always-on protection from volumetric and protocol DDoS attacks for your global distributed web application. It also includes WAF capabilities against OWASP attacks through pre-configured rules.

- **Managed Protection Plus**: Compared with the standard tier, the Managed Protection Plus tier adds Adaptive Protection with machine learning and third-party named IP address lists from security providers such as **Fastly**, **Cloudflare**, and **Imperva**. With Adaptive Protection, you can be alerted of potential attacks, and you can deploy suggested rules to block the attack and therefore secure your web application.

Now that we have introduced the main feature of Cloud Armor, let's see how we can use it to protect our web application:

1. First of all, Cloud Armor can only be used attached to a backend service, as *Figure 6.10* shows:

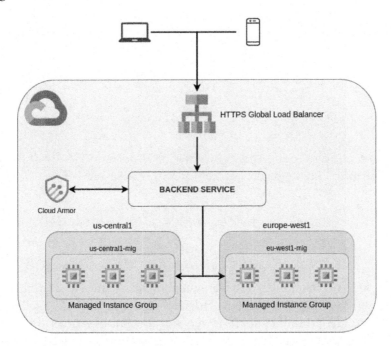

Figure 6.10 – Cloud Armor applied to an external HTTP(S) load balancer

2. Backend services can be configured when you deploy the external HTTP(S) load balancer service, as we discussed in *Chapter 4, Configuring Network Services in GCP*. *Figure 6.11* shows the configuration of the external HTTP load balancer you should have before proceeding to Cloud Armor configuration:

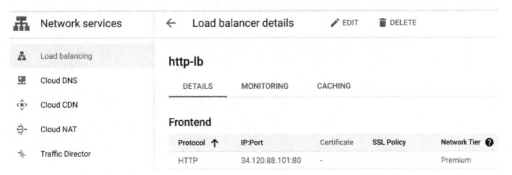

Figure 6.11 – The external HTTP(S) load balancer service frontend

3. Make sure that the external HTTP(S) load balancer service uses the appropriate backend services, as shown in *Figure 6.12*. Also, make sure that you enable logging when creating the external HTTP(S) load balancer service:

Backend

Backend services

1. backend-service

Endpoint protocol	Named port	Timeout	Health check	Cloud CDN
HTTP	http	30 seconds	http-health-check	Disabled

⌄ ADVANCED CONFIGURATIONS

Name ↑	Type	Zone	Healthy	Autoscaling	Balancing mode	Selected ports ❔	Capacity
eu-west1-mig	Instance group	europe-west1-b	✅ 1 of 1	On: Target CPU utilization 60%	Max backend utilization: 80%	80	100%
us-central1-mig	Instance group	us-central1-c	✅ 1 of 1	On: Target CPU utilization 60%	Max backend utilization: 80%	80	100%

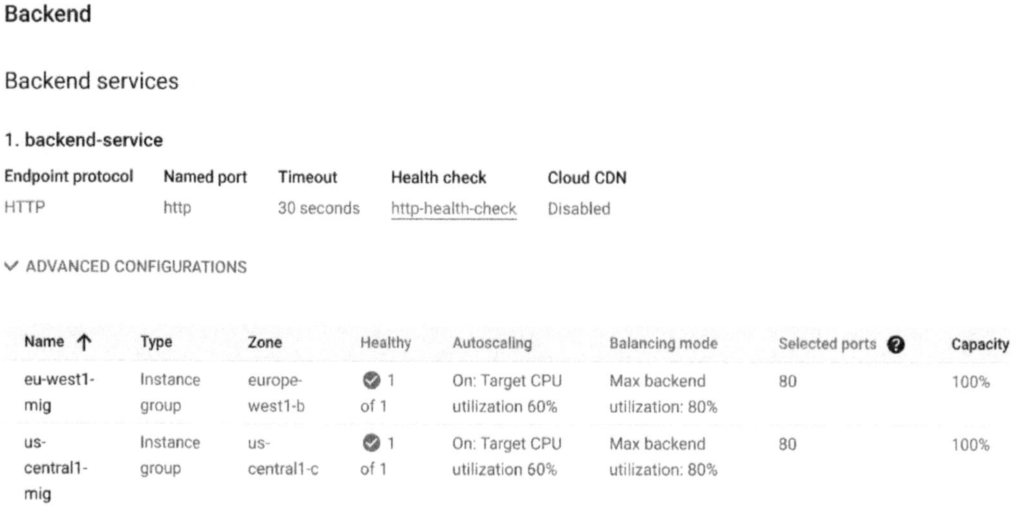

Figure 6.12 – Backend services in the external HTTP(S) load balancer service

4. In addition, you should deploy a Compute Engine instance for testing the Cloud Armor service. You can install on a Debian virtual machine dedicated software to generate a large number of HTTP requests towards one target. The name of this software is **Siege**, and you can install it using the following command in the Linux shell:

```
sudo apt -y install siege
```

In this command, we are using the APT tool, which is a management system for software packages and is needed to install a package. apt stands for Advanced Package Tool. In this case, we are installing Siege, which is an open source HTTP load balancer tester. The -y option adds an automatic *yes* to prompts; assume *yes* is the answer to all prompts and run non-interactively.

When creating the Compute Engine instance, take note of the public IP address (34.121.135.193), as highlighted in *Figure 6.13*. You will need that later:

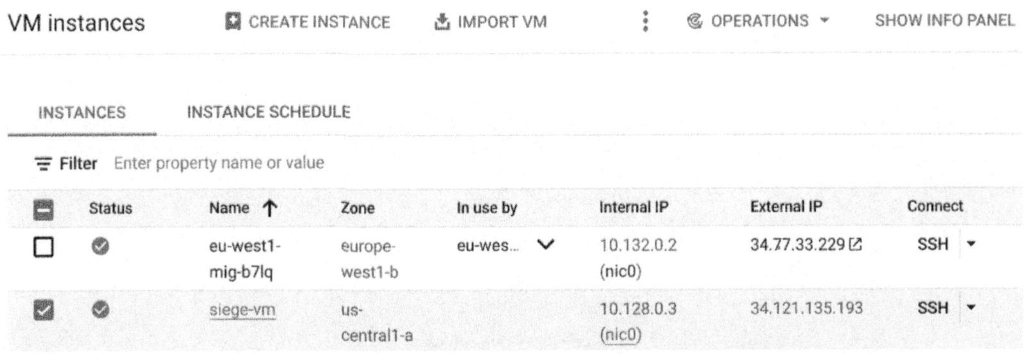

	Status	Name ↑	Zone	In use by	Internal IP	External IP	Connect
☐	✓	eu-west1-mig-b7lq	europe-west1-b	eu-wes... ∨	10.132.0.2 (nic0)	34.77.33.229 ☑	SSH ▾
☑	✓	siege-vm	us-central1-a		10.128.0.3 (nic0)	34.121.135.193	SSH ▾

Figure 6.13 – siege-vm has been created as the Cloud Armor-testing virtual machine

Now that your external HTTP(S) load balancer service is up and running, you can proceed to the Cloud Armor security policy configuration. You can do this from the Navigation menu and then select **Network Security**, **Cloud Armor**, and click on the **Create policy** button, as shown in *Figure 6.14*:

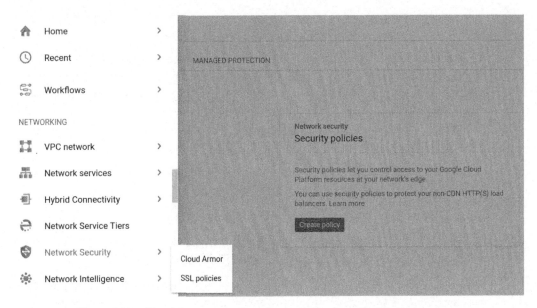

Figure 6.14 – Cloud Armor security policy creation from the Navigation menu

The security policy instructs **Cloud Armor** on how to inspect HTTP traffic and block and notify intrusions. *Figure 6.15* shows the creation of a security policy:

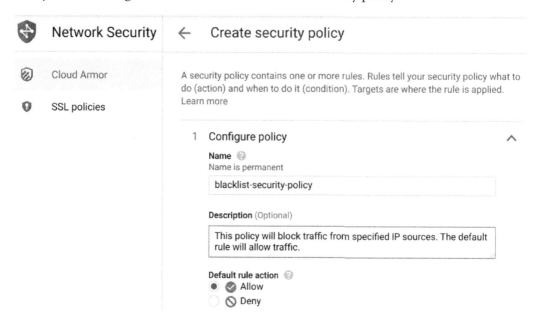

Figure 6.15 – Creation of Cloud Armor security policy

5. As *Figure 6.15* shows, the security policy requires a unique name, an optional description, and a default rule action, which is applied when other rules do not match. If you want to implement a blacklist approach (where everything is allowed except those explicitly denied), you need to set the default rule action as `Allow`. On the contrary, for a whitelist approach, you need to choose `Deny`. To avoid impacting your business, it is recommended to start with a whitelist approach.

When creating a new rule, you need to choose the **Mode** function. Cloud Armor rules support two modes:

a. **Basic mode**: You can specify source IPs or ranges. Cloud Armor inspects source IPs at the layer 3 level.

b. **Advanced mode**: Cloud Armor inspects HTTP headers at level 7.

Based on what mode you want to use, you can specify the `match` condition to validate. *Figure 6.16* shows an example of configuring a basic mode rule to forbid traffic from `siege-vm`:

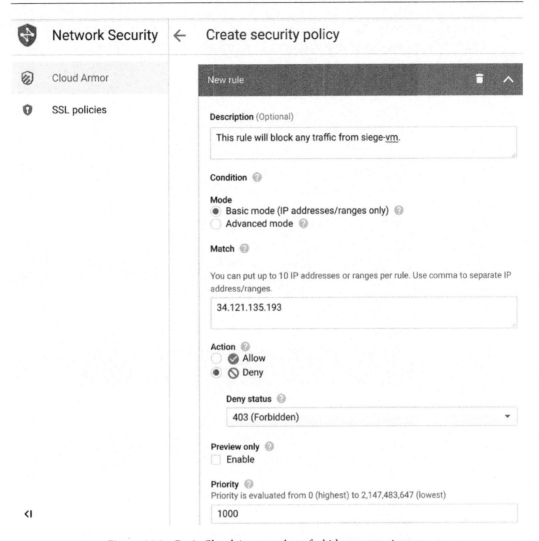

Figure 6.16 – Basic Cloud Armor rule to forbid access to siege-vm

6. As *Figure 6.16* shows, the rule will return a **403 (Forbidden)** client error in the
    HTTP response for any HTTP request sent from `siege-vm` (which has the IP
    address `34.121.135.193`). Indeed, you can specify which `Deny status`
    you want to present when the condition is matched. Other options can include
    Unauthorized (HTTP code `401`) and **Bad Gateway** (HTTP code `502`).
    Additionally, you can decide the evaluation order of the rule by setting the priority.
    Rules with lower numbers (higher priority) will be evaluated before rules with
    higher numbers (lower priority).

If you choose to use **Advanced mode**, you can specify advanced conditions, such as blocking requests that originated from one country, as shown in *Figure 6.17*:

Figure 6.17 – The matching condition on country code Italy

Alternatively, you can instruct Cloud Armor to inspect and **block SQL Injection and Cross Site Scripting (XSS) Attacks** targeting your web application, which you can see an example of in *Figure 6.18*:

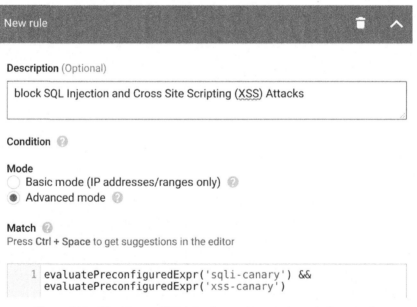

Figure 6.18 – Blocking an SQL injection and cross-site scripting attack

Whether you choose **Basic mode** or **Advanced Mode**, you need to apply the **Cloud Armor** security policy to a backend service. As *Figure 6.19* shows, the security policy will be applied to an existing backend service:

3   **Apply policy to targets** (optional)   ∧

   Targets are Google Cloud Platform resources that you want to control access to. You can only use non-CDN HTTP(S) load balancer backend services as targets.

   Type   **Target**

   | Load balancer backen... ▾ | backend-service   ✕

   [+ Add Target]

   You can also add/edit targets after the policy is created

Figure 6.19 – Applying the Cloud Armor security policy to a backend service

When the security policy has been created and applied to the backend service, you will see the details in the **Policy details** section. To reach this page, you should start from the **Navigation** menu, then select **Network Security**, **Cloud Armor**, and finally click on the name of the policy (in this case, `blacklist-security-policy`). *Figure 6.20* shows this screen:

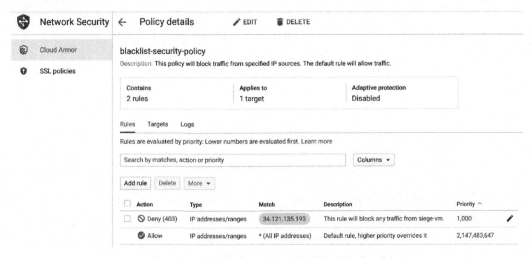

Figure 6.20 – Cloud Armor security policy details

7. As *Figure 6.20* shows, the Cloud Armor security policy contains two rules, one
    to forbid traffic from `siege-vm` and the other to allow any other type of traffic.
    The policy then has been applied to one target, which is the backend service of the
    external HTTP(S) load balancer previously created.

    We can now test Cloud Armor capabilities by connecting to the `siege-vm`
    machine and generating large amounts of HTTP requests, targeting the public IP
    address of the external HTTP(S) load balancer, as shown in *Figure 6.21*:

```
student-02-22cc98e61de8@siege-vm:~$ siege -c 250 http://34.98.98.128/
New configuration template added to /home/student-02-22cc98e61de8/.siege
Run siege -C to view the current settings in that file
** SIEGE 4.0.4
** Preparing 250 concurrent users for battle.
The server is now under siege...
```

Figure 6.21 – Generating HTTP requests from siege-vm

8. We can verify that Cloud Armor blocks the HTTP traffic from `siege-vm` by
    exploring the logs. You can access those by returning to Cloud Armor's policy
    details and opening the **Logs** tab, as *Figure 6.22* shows:

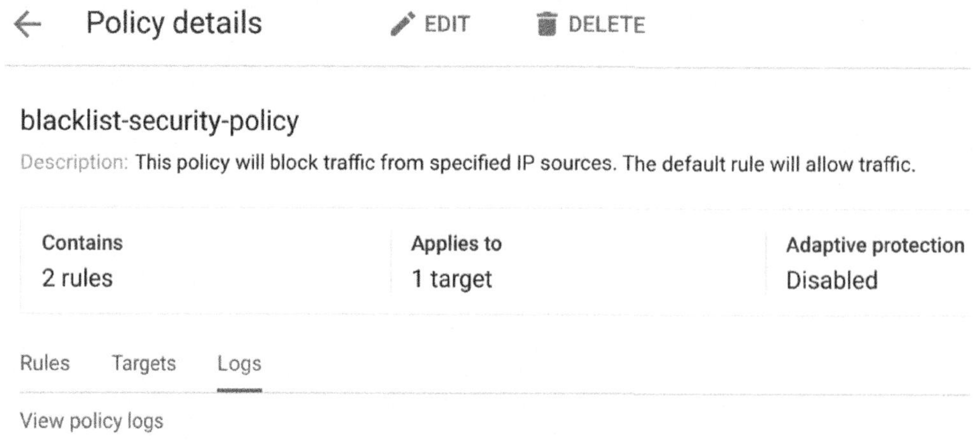

←   Policy details   ✏ EDIT   🗑 DELETE

---

blacklist-security-policy

Description: This policy will block traffic from specified IP sources. The default rule will allow traffic.

Contains	Applies to	Adaptive protection
2 rules	1 target	Disabled

Rules   Targets   Logs

View policy logs

Figure 6.22 – Exploring Cloud Armor logs from security policy details

9. From the **View policy logs** link (shown in *Figure 6.22*), you can jump to Cloud
    Logging in the GCP operations suite to see the logs related to that particular
    security policy of Cloud Armor, as shown in *Figure 6.23*:

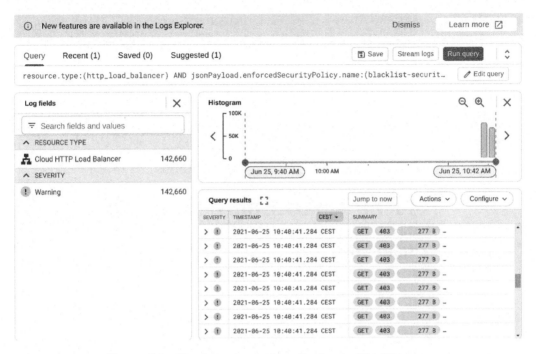

Figure 6.23 – Cloud Armor security policy logs in Cloud Logging

10. As *Figure 6.23* shows, Cloud Logging shows us a large number of warning logs that are generated any time an HTTP request is blocked by Cloud Armor. You may notice that in the **Query results** list, there are a large number of logs with response code 403, which refers to the HTTP **Forbidden** action we have configured in the **Cloud Armor security policy deny rule**. If you open one of these logs, you will see more details, as shown in *Figure 6.24*:

Figure 6.24 – Cloud Armor security policy log details

11. As *Figure 6.24* shows, there is a lot of information returned in JSON format. You may notice that under the `enforcedSecurityPolicy` field, there is the name of the security policy that generated this log and the action that was taken.

    You can continue testing Cloud Armor to see whether legitimate traffic will be passing. In *Figure 6.25*, you can verify that you are able to reach your web application:

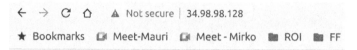

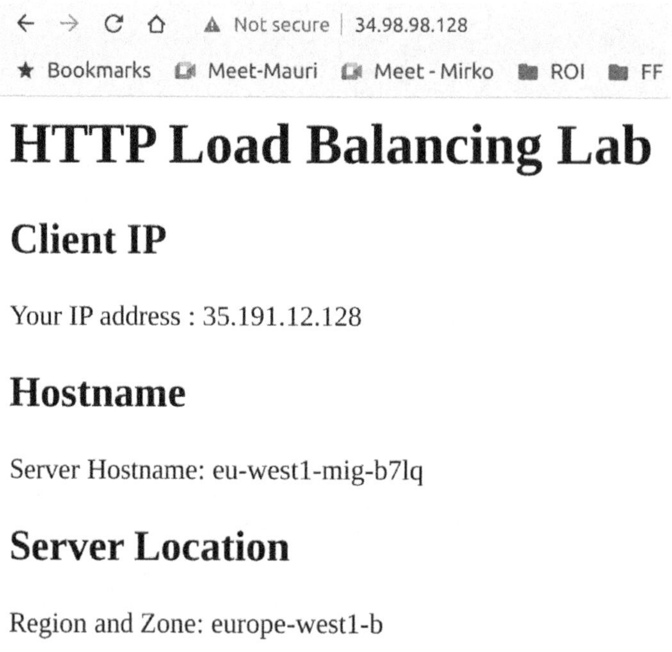

Not secure | 34.98.98.128
Bookmarks
Meet-Mauri
Meet - Mirko
ROI
FF
HTTP Load Balancing Lab
Client IP
Your IP address : 35.191.12.128
Hostname
Server Hostname: eu-west1-mig-b7lq
Server Location
Region and Zone: europe-west1-b

Figure 6.25 – Web application reachability verification with Cloud Armor

Now that you have learned how to secure your web application with Cloud Armor, let's see how to configure third-party device insertions into VPC using multiple NICs.

Configuring a third-party software device (NGFW) insertion into VPC using multiple NICs

In this section, we will introduce the possibility of leveraging the multiNIC support on **Google Compute Engine** in order to install in GCP any third-party software device that works as an NGFW.

Configuring networking and security for a third-party virtual appliance

During the creation of a new Google Compute Engine instance (**Navigation** menu **|Compute Engine | VM Instances | Create instance | Management, Security, Disks, Networking, Sole Tenancy | Networking** tab), we see that our instance has a default network interface (connected to the default VPC in our project); in addition, we are warned by Google with the following message: **To create another network interface you need to have a new network first**. We can see all of this in *Figure 6.26*:

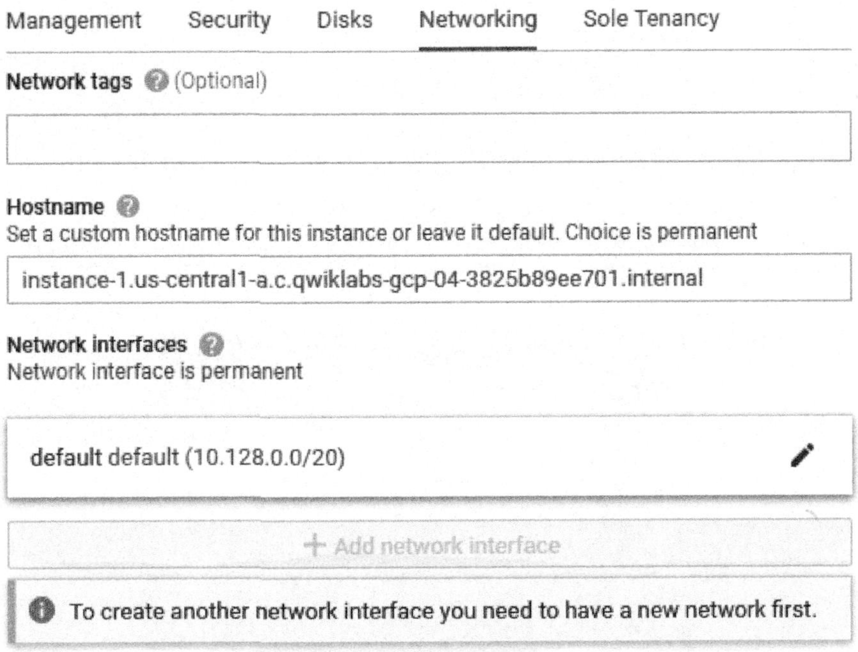

Figure 6.26 – Network interfaces during a Compute Engine instance creation

Indeed, the possibility to add a second interface on the same virtual machine is subject to the presence of at least two different VPC networks. We can have many virtual network interfaces bound to one virtual machine if only each one of them belongs to a different VPC network. The idea that we want to delve into is that we can create a virtual appliance representing an NGFW. This can have up to eight virtual interfaces, and so it can control the traffic among all the VPCs that the instance is connected to. This is an alternative to the traditional VPC peering where the interconnection with the VPC is not controlled by any firewall rule, neither L3/L4 (IP or TCP/UDP rules) nor L7 (in the case of an application firewall).

For instance, we can specify that the first interface belongs to the `network-a` network, as shown in *Figure 6.27*. To reach this section, you should click on the pencil inside the first network interface:

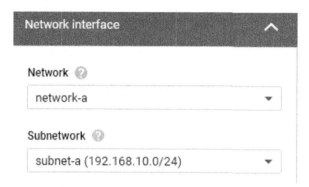

Figure 6.27 – The first network interface is attached to the VPC network named network-a

In the same way, the second network interface that we added to the same virtual machine, using the button **Add network interface**, can only be attached to a different network, such as `network-b` in *Figure 6.28*:

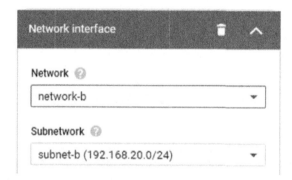

Figure 6.28 – The second network interface is attached to the VPC network named network-b

For each interface, we can specify whether we want a static or dynamic internal IP address, as shown in *Figure 6.29*:

Figure 6.29 – Primary internal IP options

For internal IP address selection, we have a couple of different options; for an ephemeral address, restarting an instance won't change its internal IP, but deleting and recreating an instance will change its internal IP:

- **Ephemeral (Automatic)**: Google is going to assign an address from the subnetwork range.

- **Ephemeral (Custom)**: We can manually enter an address.

- **Reserve static internal IP address**: We allow our instance to keep its IP, even when it's deleted and recreated.

In the same way, we have three options for an external IP address, as shown in *Figure 6.30*:

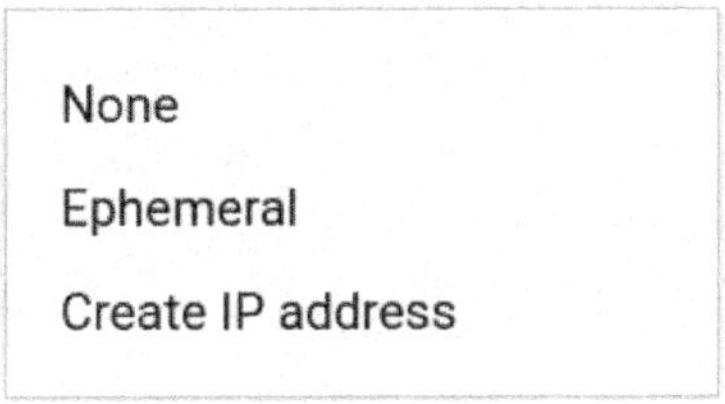

None

Ephemeral

Create IP address

Figure 6.30 – External IP options

If we check Google Cloud Marketplace, we have a lot of third-party NGFW virtual appliances (Compute Engine instances). Most of them follow the criteria to stay in the middle among different networks, leveraging the possibility of adding more than one network interface to the same virtual machine instance.

Just to give an idea of what we are talking about, let's see in *Figure 6.31* some of the virtual appliances in Google Cloud Marketplace. Some of them include the license, which you pay as part of your Google bill; some others are based on the **Bring Your Own License (BYOL)** policy:

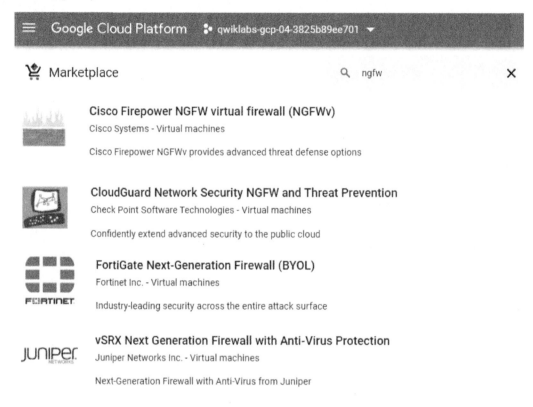

Figure 6.31 – Some examples of third-party NGFW in Google Cloud Marketplace

The presented scenario in the current section is the best way to introduce a third-party NGFW virtual appliance into your project.

But what if you have to deal with many VPC networks belonging to different projects? That is exactly the question we are going to answer in the next section.

Implementing third-party virtual appliances (Compute Engine instances) in a shared VPC environment

Imagine having many applications and workloads running in different projects in Google Cloud Platform and imagine that you want to protect them in the same way, such as protecting all internet ingress and inspecting and filtering egress traffic for all of them.

That is exactly the case where a shared VPC feature comes as the best-practice solution. If you do not remember how shared VPC works, we strongly suggest you revisit *Chapter 3, Implementing a GCP Virtual Private Cloud (VPC)*, where it is explained in depth.

Just to give you a reminder, a shared VPC environment allows you to have some VPC networks controlled and managed by one single centralized project (the host project). At the same time, though, it allows other projects (or, preferably, other resources in different projects) to attach to the networks in the host project. That is why it is called *shared*. In this case, the idea is to implement our third-party virtual appliance with one leg in each network, so it is like having at least one leg in every project.

Implementing routes and firewall rules in a multi-NIC environment

Let's remember that every virtual machine instance can have a network tag associated with it, and that network tag could be a way to make this instance a possible target for a firewall rule, or for a route.

But what if the virtual machine instance with the network tag has more than one network interface?

The tag is an attribute on the entire virtual machine instance, not on specific network interfaces.

The working principle for routing is that a virtual machine's network tag impacts an interface if that interface is in a VPC network that contains a custom static route with a matching tag.

From the firewall point of view, let's remember that the firewall rules are associated with the VPC network itself. So, every interface applies the firewall rules related to the VPC network that it is connected to.

Summary

In this chapter, you have learned how to implement security in your VPCs in Google Cloud Platform. You have learned how to configure identity and access management with Google Cloud IAM. Moreover, you have learned how to configure Cloud Armor to protect your web applications from global threats, such as Denial of Service (DoS) attacks. Finally, you have learned how to deploy and use third-party firewall software devices in your VPC.

Now, let's go to the next chapter to learn about managing and monitoring network operations.

This is the end of the second part of our book. In this second part, you gained the knowledge and the configuration skills related to network services, hybrid connectivity, and network security.

In the next part, we will start exploring the world of monitoring, maintaining, and optimizing VPC networks and their services, and also start using some advanced network features.

Section 3: Network Operations, Management, and Monitoring

In this part, you will learn how to monitor, maintain, and optimize a VPC network and its services, as well as how to use advanced network features.

This part of the book comprises the following chapters:

- *Chapter 7, Managing and Monitoring Network Operations*
- *Chapter 8, Advanced Networking in Google Cloud Platform*
- *Chapter 9, Professional Cloud Network Engineer Certification Preparation*

7
Managing and Monitoring Network Operations

When cloud infrastructures have been deployed, it is critical for network and security operation teams to have a central point of supervision where they can maintain systems and traffic under management control. For this scope, **Google Cloud Platform** (**GCP**) offers the **operations suite** (formerly **Stackdriver**), which provides a suite of monitoring and troubleshooting services that will help operation teams to have everything under control. It includes the following services:

- **Cloud Logging**: This is a fully managed service that centralizes the log management of your cloud infrastructure.

- **Cloud Monitoring**: This is a fully managed service that centralizes metrics collection and provides performance and health visibility of your cloud infrastructure.

- **Cloud Trace**: This is a fully managed service to collect application latency data and provides near-real-time application performance information.

- **Cloud Profiler**: This is a fully managed service to measure code performance and spot CPU and memory-intense processes inside your application.
- **Cloud Debugger**: This is a fully managed service to inspect the state of a running application without stopping it.

In this chapter, you are going to learn how to use **Cloud Logging** and **Cloud Monitoring** to maintain full control of your network and security operations.

Logging and monitoring with GCP operations

In this section, you will learn how to enable and monitor logging on your VPC. First, we will explore how to log VPC flows. Then we will learn how to enable logging in firewall rules and monitor them. Lastly, we will enable VPC audit logs and monitor them. We will use **Cloud Logging** and **Cloud Monitoring** in the following exercises.

VPC Flow Logs

There are multiple use cases for **VPC Flow Logs**. For instance, when you need to determine where your application is being accessed, VPC Flow Logs can help to investigate. Moreover, when you need to build a **Cloud Armor** blacklist of unwanted IP addresses, VPC Flow Logs can provide such information.

Going into more detail, when you enable VPC Flow Logs on your VPC, you will be able to collect network traffic samples that are sent or received by Compute Engine instances or **Google Kubernetes Engine** (**GKE**) nodes. These logs are stored in Cloud Logging and can be used for network monitoring, network forensics, security analysis, and much more. Flow logs are aggregated by connection, and you can export them for further analysis.

Let's assume we want to record all traffic from and to our **Apache web server**, which is hosted on a Compute Engine instance. For this case study, let's start creating a new VPC network and enable flow logs. Go to the **Navigation** menu | **VPC network**, and then click on the **CREATE VPC NETWORK** button. Then we choose a name for the VPC network (for example, vpc-flow-log-enabled), select the subnet creation mode (custom or automatic), and create at least a new subnet (selecting the name, the region, and the IP address range). In this same screen (an extract of which can be seen in *Figure 7.1*), we can turn on VPC Flow Logs.

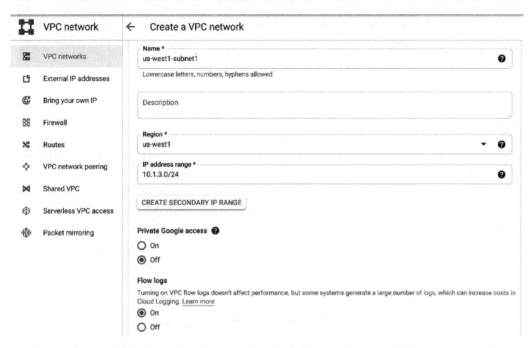

Figure 7.1 – Enabling flow logs on the subnet in the new VPC

As *Figure 7.1* describes, when creating new subnets in the VPC, you can enable the **Flow logs** option to generate VPC Flow Logs for any Compute Engine instance deployed in the subnet. The logs are automatically stored in Cloud Logging.

> **Note**
>
> VPC Flow Logs does not affect performance. However, a large number of logs may be generated, which can result in increased costs.

After creating the new VPC with the subnet where you have enabled VPC Flow Logs, you can see the result as in *Figure 7.2*:

Name ↑	Region	Subnets	IP address ranges	Gateways	Firewall Rules	Flow logs
▼ vpc-flow-log-enabled		1			0	
	us-west1	us-west1-subnet1	10.1.3.0/24	10.1.3.1		On

Figure 7.2 – Flow Logs has been enabled on the subnet

Next, we will create a **Compute Engine** instance where the Apache web server will be installed for VPC Flow Logs demonstration purposes. We will create a **Debian Linux** machine and we will include the following commands in the startup script when creating the instance. These commands will install the Apache web server and customize the initial web page:

```
apt-get update
```

apt is the package handling utility, and the update command is used to resynchronize the package index files from their sources (the indexes of available packages are fetched from the location(s) specified in /etc/apt/sources.list):

```
apt-get install apache2 -y
```

install is the command to install the apache2 package. The -y option is an automatic yes to prompts; assume yes as the answer to all prompts and run non-interactively:

```
echo '<!doctype html><html><body><h1>Hello World!</h1></body></
html>' | tee /var/www/html/index.html
```

The echo command rewrites in the standard output that follows. Likewise, the tee command reads from standard input and writes to standard output and files (in our case in the /var/www/html/index.html file). This is the default path where the Apache web server searches for the home page.

> **Note**
>
> Remember to place the Compute Engine instance in the subnet where you have enabled VPC Flow Logs. Otherwise, you will not be able to see logs of your Apache web server.

Figure 7.3 shows the resulting Compute Engine instance running on the us-west1-b zone in the vpc-flow-log-enabled network:

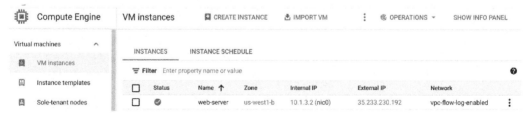

Figure 7.3 – Web server compute engine instance running on a subnet with VPC Flow Logs enabled

Once the web server is running, you can test VPC Flow logging by accessing the public IP address provided to the Compute Engine instance. As *Figure 7.3* indicates, you can browse to the external IP shown in your Compute Engine VM instances list (in our example, `http://35.233.230.192`) and verify that you can connect to the initial welcome page of your web server.

> **Note**
>
> If you cannot connect to the web server, please verify that the firewall rule allows traffic from anywhere to TCP port 80.

If you successfully connect to the welcome page, note your IP address by browsing to the following address: `https://www.top10vpn.com/tools/what-is-my-ip/`.

You will need that when you query logs in **Cloud Logging**. From the left menu in your GCP console, locate **Logs Explorer**, which can be found under **Operations | Logging**. There you can open the main page where you can start composing your query to search for logs that are related to your web server. The first filter you can add to your query is to add a resource, which, in our case, could be a subnetwork. Here you can find the `us-west-subnet1` subnet, which we created previously. *Figure 7.4* shows how to add the filter to the Logs Explorer query. You can reach this screen from the **Navigation** menu | **Logging** | **Logs Explorer**:

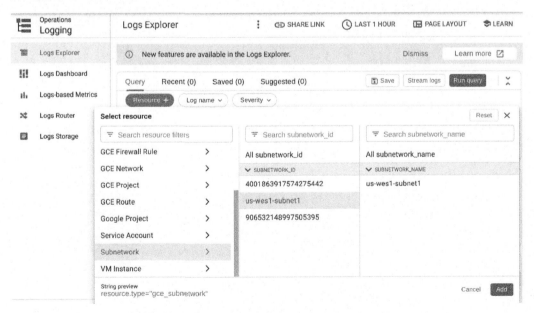

Figure 7.4 – Adding the subnet as a Logs Explorer resource

Next, we can add an additional filter such as `vpc_flows` for **Log name**. *Figure 7.5* describes how to add this filter to the query. From the **Navigation** menu, click on **Operations Logging**, then on **Logs Explorer**, then on **Log name**, and select `vpc_flows` under the **COMPUTE ENGINE** section:

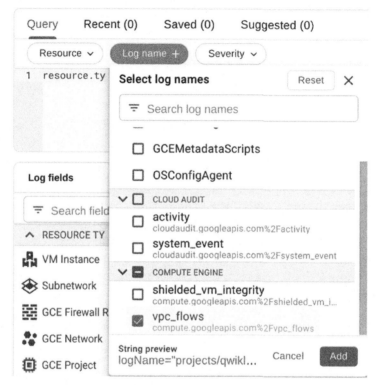

Figure 7.5 – Adding the log name to the query filter

Lastly, we can filter by source IP and we can include our client IP address that we recorded previously. You can add an additional filter to the query by entering the following in the Query editor:

```
jsonPayload.connection.src_ip
```

Indeed, you can refer to the source IP address (`src_ip`), which is contained in the `connection` object inside `jsonPayload`, as indicated in *Figure 7.6*:

Figure 7.6 – Adding the source IP address filter to the Query editor

It's now time to run the query and verify the logs related to the traffic we generated for our web server. You should be able to see a timeline when the logs have been recorded and the query results that list two logs entries, as indicated in *Figure 7.7*:

Figure 7.7 – Query result in Log Explorer

You can expand the entries to find out more details about the connection you made previously to the web server. Indeed, you can observe inside `jsonPayload` and then the `connection` object that there are the five fields that identify the session to the web server. These are the destination IP address (`dest_ip`), the destination port (`dest_port`), the transport protocol (`protocol`), the source IP address (`src_ip`), and the source port (`src_port`), as described in *Figure 7.8*:

Figure 7.8 – Expanding logs in Logs Explorer to view session details

So far, we have learned how to search for logs that are hosted in Cloud Logging, which is part of the **operations suite**. However, sometimes you may want to export logs somewhere else for other purposes, such as analytical purposes, or have logs in other log management platforms such as **Splunk**. If you need to export logs, then you have to configure **Logs Router**, which is accessible in the **Operations Logging** menu.

The first thing to do is to create a **routing sink**. We do this by clicking on **CREATE SINK**, as shown in *Figure 7.9*:

Logs Router   ⋏ CREATE SINK

Figure 7.9 – Creating a sink

You provide a name and, most importantly, you define a sink destination that is the place where you want to export your logs. Cloud Logging supports many destinations, as *Figure 7.10* shows:

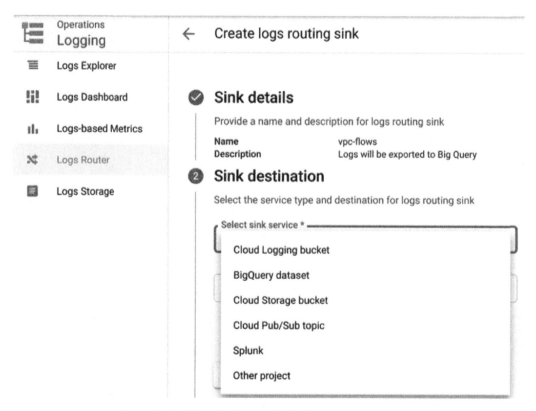

Figure 7.10 – All available sink destinations for log exporting

In our case study, we can export logs to **BigQuery** to enable data analysts to query our logs via SQL and undertake some reporting. You can even build machine learning models with BigQuery to make a prediction regarding the volume of traffic that your machines will receive. We will use BigQuery as the sink destination and for this choice, we need to create a dataset to store our logs by clicking on **Create new BigQuery dataset**, as shown in *Figure 7.11*:

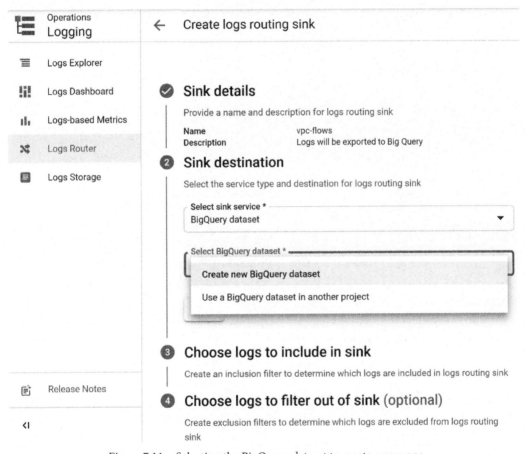

Figure 7.11 – Selecting the BigQuery dataset to create a new one

Now, a new window will appear on the right allowing us to specify the information needed to create a new BigQuery dataset, as shown in *Figure 7.12*, where we are creating a new dataset named `bq_vpcflows`:

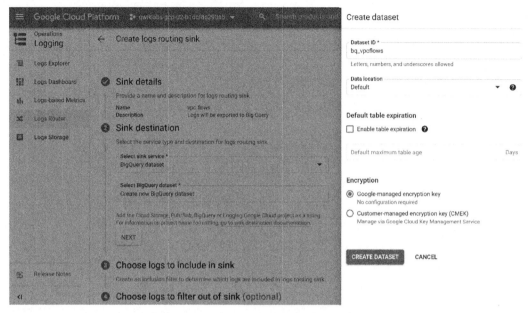

Figure 7.12 – Creating a new BigQuery dataset

We select the new dataset (just created as in *Figure 7.12* by clicking on the **CREATE DATASET** button), as shown in *Figure 7.13*:

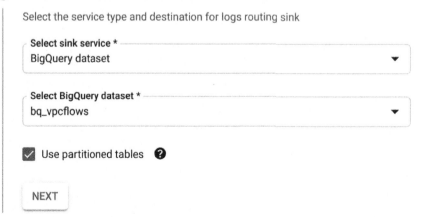

Figure 7.13 – Using BigQuery as the sink destination for your logs

> **Note**
>
> We recommend using a partitioned table to improve performance relating to BigQuery queries and to reduce costs.

Then we can decide which logs should be exported to the sink. Here you can use the filters that you have used before for log searching. Indeed, you can also refer to the logs of one particular Compute Engine instance by referring to its name – `jsonPayload.dest_instance.vm_name`. *Figure 7.14* shows the filters during sink creation (this is the third step of the same wizard in *Figure 7.13*. In your case study, `subnetwork_id`, `logName`, and `jsonPayload.dest_instance.vm_name` could obviously differ from the one shown in *Figure 7.14*):

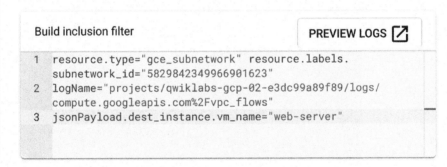

Figure 7.14 – Filtering applied to sinks for selective log exporting

The fourth step (optional) is **Choose logs to filter out of sink**, useful if you do not want all the logs to be present in the sink.

Once the log router has been configured, all logs are automatically exported to the sink. You can see the result by accessing Google BigQuery and checking the table that has been created in the `bq_vpcflows` dataset. *Figure 7.15* shows the schema of the newly created table:

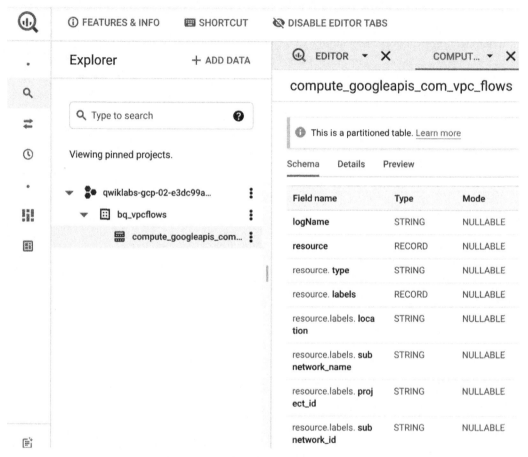

Figure 7.15 – Schema structure of the newly created BigQuery table that stores logs

Now that you have learned how to configure VPC Flow Logs and explore them in Cloud Logging, let's see how to handle security logs that come from firewall rules. In the next section, you will learn how to configure and monitor firewall logging.

Firewall Rules Logging

When it comes to security monitoring, the first thing you want to enable is firewall logging on your security policies. This is an important operation for keeping your infrastructure secure and monitored. In GCP, you can enable firewall logging inside each **firewall rule**. Indeed, just below the firewall rule description, you can enable logging using the appropriate radio button. You can also include logs metadata, which gives you more information, but with more storage required in Cloud Logging. *Figure 7.16* shows how to enable firewall logging with metadata. Starting from the **Navigation** menu, click on **VPC network**, followed by **Firewall**, and then click on the interested rule and check whether **Logs** is turned **On**:

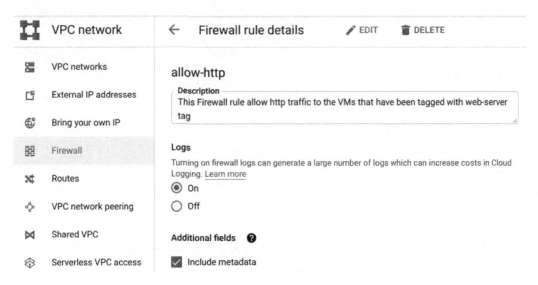

Figure 7.16 – Firewall logging with metadata enabled

As described in *Figure 7.16*, firewall logging has been enabled on the `allow-http` firewall rule, which controls the web server traffic through the `web-server` tag (not shown in the screenshot). We include metadata so as to have more information to explore in Cloud Logging.

When **Logs** is enabled, you can get the basic information reported in the following table:

Field	Sub field	Description
`connection`	`src_ip`	Source IP address
	`src_port`	Source port number
	`dest_ip`	Destination IP address
	`dest_port`	Destination port number
	`protocol`	Transport protocol
`disposition`		Connection ALLOWED or DENIED

`rule_details`	`reference`	Reference to the firewall rule in the following format:
		
		`network:{network name}/`
		`firewall:{firewall_name}`

Figure 7.17 – Firewall Logs content

When you add metadata, check the Logs and you will have the information reported as follows:

- `Rule_details`:

  a. **Priority**: Number of rule priority

  b. **Action**: Either `DENY` or `PERMIT`

  c. `source_range[ ]`: List of source ranges that the firewall rule applies to

  d. `destination_range[ ]`: List of destination ranges that the firewall rule applies to

  e. `ip_port_info[ ]`: List of IP protocols and applicable port ranges for rules

  f. **Direction**: Either ingress or egress

  g. `source_tag[ ]`: List of all the source tags that the firewall rule applies to

  h. `target_tag[ ]`: List of all the target tags that the firewall rule applies to

  i. `source_service_account[ ]`: List of all the source service accounts that the firewall rule applies to

  j. `target_service_account[ ]`: List of all the target service accounts that the firewall rule applies to: `https://cloud.google.com/vpc/docs/firewall-rules-logging#ruledetails`

- **Instance**:

  a. `project_id`: Project ID of the VM

  b. `vm_name`: Name of the VM

  c. **region**: Region of the VM

  d. **zone**: Zone of the VM

- `vpc`:

  a. `project_id`: ID of the project containing the network

  b. `vpc_name`: Network on which the VM is operating

  c. `subnetwork_name`: Subnet on which the VM is operating

- `remote_instance`: This is the same as the `instance` field. If the remote endpoint of the connection was a VM located in the Compute Engine instance, this field is populated with VM instance details.

- `remote_vpc`: This is the same as the `vpc` field. If the remote endpoint of the connection was a VM that is located in a VPC network, this field is populated with the network details.

- `remote_location`: If the remote endpoint of the connection was external to the VPC network, the following fields are populated with available location metadata:

  a. **continent**

  b. **country**

  c. **region**

  d. **city**

For additional information, please refer to the official documentation using the following link: `https://cloud.google.com/vpc/docs/firewall-rules-logging#ruledetails`.

As you can see, enabling metadata information provides you with a large number of fields, which could lead you to be overwhelmed. Therefore, it is important to enable the metadata information only if you really need it for your security analysis.

> **Tips**
> Start enabling only the basic fields and observe the logs that the rule generates. Later, if you need more, enable the metadata.

When you have deployed your security firewall rules and have determined explicitly what type of traffic is allowed inside your infrastructure, it is recommended to configure one extra firewall rule to log any denied traffic. This rule goes at the bottom of your list, hence it will have the lowest priority (with the highest number). It will explicitly deny and log all traffic that does not match the previous firewall rules. *Figure 7.18* shows an example of such a firewall rule, which is usually called `cleanup`:

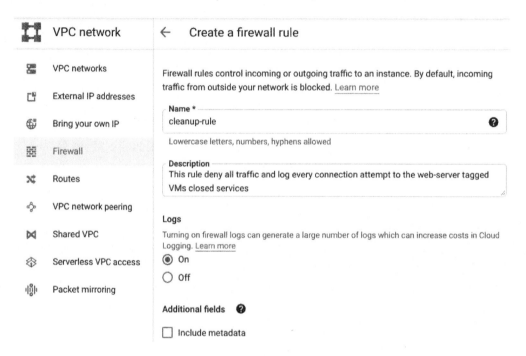

Figure 7.18 – Cleanup firewall rule that logs all denied traffic

> **Remember**
> The cleanup firewall rule should only be configured when you want to log any potential attackers to insert in a blacklist in a Cloud Armor security policy.

Figure 7.19 shows the result of the cleanup firewall rule configuration. We can reach this screen by going to the **Navigation** menu | **VPC Networks** | **Firewall**, and then clicking on the `cleanup-rule` firewall rule:

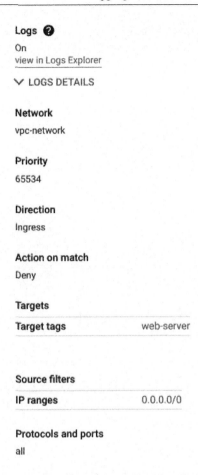

Logs ❓

On
view in Logs Explorer

∨ LOGS DETAILS

Network
vpc-network

Priority
65534

Direction
Ingress

Action on match
Deny

Targets

Target tags	web-server

Source filters

IP ranges	0.0.0.0/0

Protocols and ports
all

Figure 7.19 – Cleanup firewall rule end result

As you can observe in *Figure 7.19*, the cleanup firewall rule will deny and log all traffic targeting VMs with the web-server tag. The result of the two firewall rules looks like *Figure 7.20*:

	Name	Type	Targets	Filters	Protocols / ports	Action	Priority	Network ↑	Logs	Hit count ❓	Last hit ❓
☐	allow-http	Ingress	web-server	IP ranges: 0.0.0.0/0	tcp:80	Allow	1000	vpc-network	On	0	No hits
☐	cleanup-rule	Ingress	web-server	IP ranges: 0.0.0.0/0	all	Deny	65534	vpc-network	On	0	No hits

Figure 7.20 – Firewall rules with logs enabled

Testing firewall logging requires a Compute Engine VM that works as a web server. You can deploy one as you did for VPC Flow Logs example. Remember to include the `web-server` tag for targeting the firewall rules to the web server as described in *Figure 7.21*:

	Status	Name ↑	Zone	Internal IP	External IP	Network	Network tags	Connect
☐	✅	us-central1-web-server1	us-central1-a	192.168.10.12 (nic0)	35.226.168.221	vpc-network	web-server	SSH ▾

Figure 7.21 – Web server for testing firewall logging

After your web server has been deployed, you can test it by opening the web browser, as indicated in *Figure 7.22*:

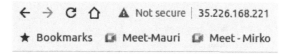

Hello World!

Figure 7.22 – Web server home page

As *Figure 7.22* indicates, the web server is operational and some logs should be generated. But before exploring, let's generate some traffic for the cleanup firewall rule. You can use the telnet client to point to the IP address of the web server and specify a random port, as described in *Figure 7.23*:

```
mirko@mirko-mateprox:~$ telnet 35.226.168.221 8443
Trying 35.226.168.221...
telnet: Unable to connect to remote host: Connection timed out
mirko@mirko-mateprox:~$ █
```

Figure 7.23 – Connecting to the web server using a different port

If you return to the firewall page, you will see that your firewall rules have got some hit counts, as *Figure 7.24* shows:

	Name	Type	Targets	Filters	Protocols / ports	Action	Priority	Network ↑	Logs	Hit count ❓	Last hit ❓
☐	allow-http	Ingress	web-server	IP ranges: 0.0.0.0/0	tcp:80	Allow	1000	vpc-network	On	2	2021-07-07 (18:12:00)
☐	cleanup-rule	Ingress	web-server	IP ranges: 0.0.0.0/0	all	Deny	65534	vpc-network	On ⓘ	14	2021-07-07 (18:16:00)

Figure 7.24 – Hit counts on the firewall rules

You may want to explore more statistics relating to the hit count by clicking each firewall rule and investigating **Hit count monitoring**, as shown in *Figure 7.25*. To reach this screen, we have to click on the **Navigation** menu | **VPC Network** | **Firewall**, select the firewall rule, and then check the hit count monitoring:

Figure 7.25 – Hit count monitoring relating to the allow-http firewall rule

You should investigate the cleanup firewall rule to show the statistics as shown in *Figure 7.26*:

Figure 7.26 – Hit count monitoring relating to the cleanup-rule firewall rule

Now you can investigate the firewall rule logs in depth in **Logs Explorer**, which is one of the main tools available in Cloud Logging. You can easily access it by clicking the **view in Logs Explorer** link that you find inside each firewall rule. This is very handy because you will be redirected to **Logs Explorer**, with the pre-built log query that only displays the logs related to the firewall rule. *Figure 7.27* shows where the link is located inside the `allow-http` firewall rule:

allow-http

Description

This Firewall rule allow http traffic to the VMs that have been tagged with web-server tag

Logs ❷

On
view in Logs Explorer

∨ LOGS DETAILS

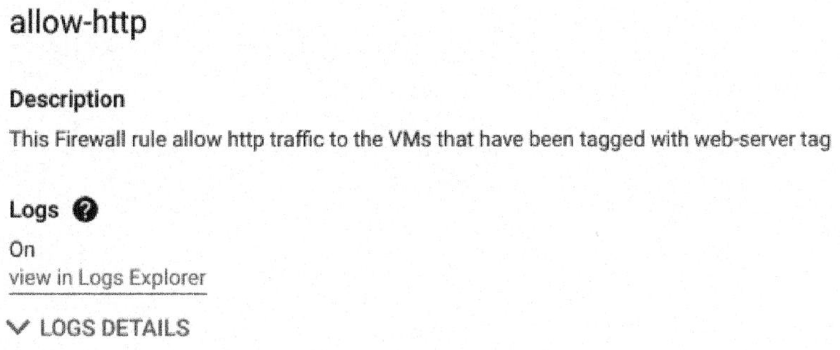

Figure 7.27 – Logs Explorer link inside the firewall rule

Clicking the **view in Logs Explorer** link will bring you to the **Logs Explorer** page inside Cloud Logging. Here you will see four main sections:

- **Query editor**: This is an interactive query editor where you can build your log query to search for logs.

- **Log fields**: This is the place where you can explore log fields.

- **Histogram**: This is where logs are plotted on a temporal scale.

- **Query results**: This is where you will see the logs and all their information.

Figure 7.28 shows the logs of the `allow-http` firewall rule in **Logs Explorer**:

Figure 7.28 – allow-http firewall rule logs in Logs Explorer

As *Figure 7.28* shows, the query contains the reference to the `allow-http` firewall rule. This is contained in `jsonPayload`, which is a data structure that contains most of the important fields for security analysis. The syntax of the query for getting the logs from a certain firewall rule is as follows:

```
jsonPayload.rule_details.reference:("network:<VPC-NAME>/
firewall:<FIREWALL-RULE-NAME>")
```

You can use this syntax to search any firewall rule logs providing the VPC name (the `<VPC-NAME>` parameter) and the firewall rule name (the `<FIREWALL-RULE-NAME>` parameter).

Figure 7.29 shows the logs of the firewall cleanup rule:

Figure 7.29 – Cleanup firewall rule logs in Logs Explorer

You can expand logs in the **Query results** pane to see all the fields we have described in the list before. Here, you can see where the traffic was generated, which Compute Engine instance is involved, the details of the rules, and much more, as *Figure 7.30* shows:

Figure 7.30 – Log details from the allow-http firewall rule

You can also investigate logs in the cleanup rule, which lets you detect any intrusion attempts. *Figure 7.31* shows the attempt we made using the telnet on port 8443:

```
Query results

Jump to now

SEVERITY   TIMESTAMP              CEST ▼   SUMMARY

ⓘ    Showing logs for last 1 hour from 7/7/21, 5:26 PM to 7/7/21, 6:26 PM.   Extend time by: 1 hour  ∨    Edit time

> ✱   2021-07-07 18:15:27.439 CEST    { "connection": { ... }, "disposition": "DENIED", "rule_details": { ... } }
> ✱   2021-07-07 18:15:34.897 CEST    { "disposition": "DENIED", "rule_details": { ... }, "connection": { ... } }
∨ ✱   2021-07-07 18:15:35.629 CEST    { "rule_details": { ... }, "disposition": "DENIED", "connection": { ... } }

  ▼ {
      insertId: "ezrmreg3a4gnta"                      ⊡ Hide log summary   ⊟ Expand nested fields   ▯ Copy
    ▼ jsonPayload: {
      ▼ connection: {
          dest_ip: "192.168.10.12"
          dest_port: 8443
          protocol: 6
          src_ip: "5.91.24.182"
          src_port: 54239
        }
        disposition: "DENIED"
      ▼ rule_details: {
          reference: "network:vpc-network/firewall:cleanup-rule"
        }
      }
      logName: "projects/concise-cinema-312907/logs/compute.googleapis.com%2Ffirewall"
      receiveTimestamp: "2021-07-07T16:15:41.311589355Z"
    ▸ resource: {2}
      timestamp: "2021-07-07T16:15:35.629329766Z"
    }
```

Figure 7.31 – Cleanup firewall log from the telnet attempt on port 8443

We invite you to explore the cleanup firewall log in more detail to detect potential intruders who may target your open services. These could be placed in a Cloud Armor security policy to prevent potential attacks in the future.

VPC audit logs

This section describes the audit logs created by VPC as part of Cloud Audit Logs.

Google Cloud Audit Logs

Google Cloud Audit Logs helps users answer the question *Who did what, when, and where?*. It includes four audit logs for each Google Cloud project, folder, and organization:

- **Admin Activity**: Always enabled, it records modifications to configuration or metadata (who added that GCS bucket?).

- **System Event**: Always enabled as well, it records GCP non-human admin actions that modify configurations (did automatic scaling occur in a managed instance group?).

- **Data Access**: Non-enabled by default, this records calls that read metadata, configurations, or that create, modify, or read user-provided data (who modified that Cloud Storage file?).

- **Policy Denied**: Recorded when a Google Cloud service denies access to a user or service account (`https://cloud.google.com/iam/docs/service-accounts`) because of a security policy violation. They are generated by default and you can't disable them.

From the VPC point of view, the API operations corresponding to each audit log type in VPC are summarized at the following documentation link: `https://cloud.google.com/vpc/docs/audit-logging#audited_operations`.

VPC audit log permissions

The IAM role needed to view *Admin Activity* audit logs, including VPC audit logs, is at least one of the following (in the project that contains your audit logs):

- Project owner, project editor, or project viewer

- Logging Logs Viewer role

- A custom IAM role with the `logging.logEntries.list` IAM permission

The IAM role needed to view *Data Access* audit logs, including VPC audit logs, is at least one of the following (in the project that contains your audit logs):

- Project owner

- The Logging Private Logs Viewer role

- A custom IAM role with the `logging.privatelogEntries.list` IAM permission

Packet Mirroring

In a previous section, we saw how to use VPC Flow Logs to investigate what is happening from the network and security point of view in the background of your applications. VPC Flow Logs is based on a packet sampler, so it shows you just a sample of the packets that are actually flowing between your services. By doing so, Google can assure you that your services are not suffering from any degradation or augmented latency when VPC Flow Logs is enabled.

Sometimes, in particular for troubleshooting reasons (but not just limited to that), you need to trace all the packets that are flowing, and not only a sample of them. That is the reason why Google offers you another service, similar to VPC Flow Logs, but that is not based on sampling. Indeed, with this service, called Packet Mirroring, you can get a copy of every packet that is flowing in the background between your VMs or your services. This works similarly to a network tap or a span session that you probably already use in your classical networking scenarios. In a nutshell, Packet Mirroring captures network traffic (both inbound and outbound) from a set of *mirrored sources*, duplicates it, and sends the copy to *collectors*. So, the main difference is that Packet Mirroring clones all traffic and packet data, including payloads and headers.

It is worth noting that Packet Mirroring catches the entire payload of each packet, requiring more bandwidth. On the one hand, Packet Mirroring can be utilized for improved troubleshooting, security solutions, and higher-layer, application-based analysis (because it is not based on any sampling time). On the other hand, Google can no longer offer the guarantee of latency and bandwidth integrity (when you use Packet Mirroring), and so it is highly recommended to disable it whenever you do not require an in-depth understanding of what is happening from the network and security point of view.

Configuring Packet Mirroring

The working principle behind Packet Mirroring is based on a *Packet Mirroring policy*, which you can configure and that contains the following attributes:

- Region
- VPC network(s)
- Mirrored source(s)
- Collector (destination)
- Mirrored traffic (filter)

Some key points that you need to consider when you want to configure a Packet Mirroring policy (as we will see in the next section) are described as follows:

- You can just mirror TCP, UDP, and ICMP traffic.
- *Collectors* must be in the same region as *mirrored sources* (but could be in different zones or even different VPCs (given that those VPCs are properly peered).
- The additional bandwidth used by Packet Mirroring is charged, especially between zones (suggestion: use filters to limit the traffic being mirrored).

Let's see a configuration example for a Packet Mirroring policy. In this case study, we want to use an **Intrusion Detection System (IDS)** as a *collector*.

The scenario is as follows:

- Everything is inside a VPC called `gcp-net, region us-west4, zone us-west4-a`.

- We have a managed instance group of VMs running some web servers attached to a web subnet.

- We create a Packet Mirroring policy that takes traffic sourced on web servers (inbound and outbound).

- Mirror it with a group of IDSes as a collector (Compute Engine VMs as well), running in another subnet (`CollectorSubnet`), and located behind a cloud internal load balancer.

To create a Packet Mirroring policy, first you should click on the **Navigation** menu | **VPC network** | **Packet Mirroring CREATE POLICY,** as shown in *Figure 7.32*:

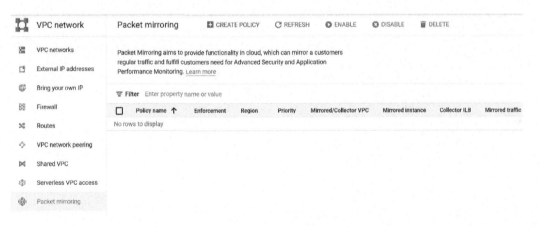

Figure 7.32 – Creating a Packet Mirroring policy

Define a policy name and region and then click on the **CONTINUE** button, as shown in *Figure 7.33*:

Create policy
Define policy overview
Select VPC network
Select mirrored source
Select collector destination
Select mirrored traffic
Policy name *
mirror-gcp-net-web
Region *
us-west4
Policy priority
1000
Policy enforcement
Enabled
Disabled
CONTINUE
CANCEL

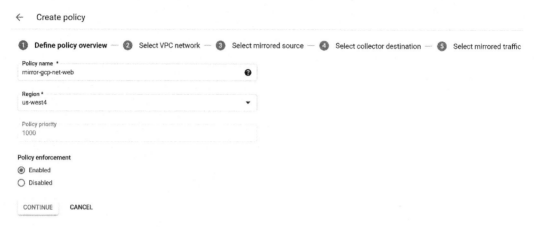

Figure 7.33 – Setting a mirroring policy name and region

Select the network as shown in *Figure 7.34*, in our case, `gcp-net`, and click **Continue**:

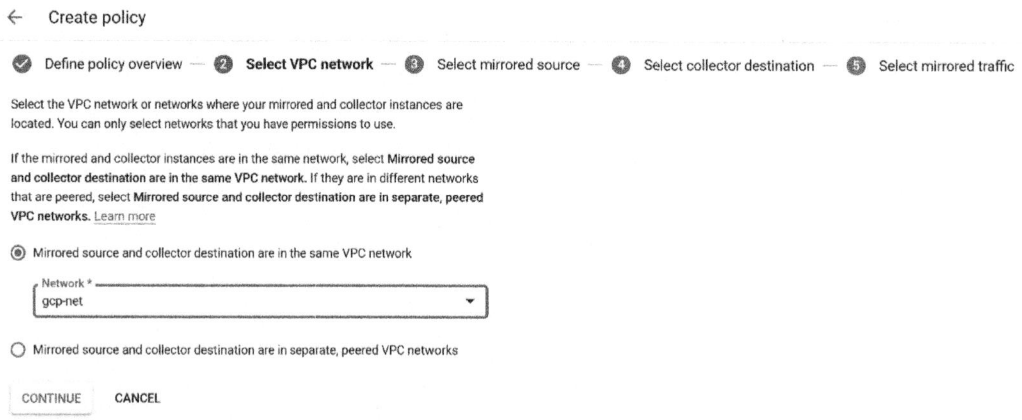

Create policy
Define policy overview
Select VPC network
Select mirrored source
Select collector destination
Select mirrored traffic
Select the VPC network or networks where your mirrored and collector instances are located. You can only select networks that you have permissions to use.
If the mirrored and collector instances are in the same network, select Mirrored source and collector destination are in the same VPC network. If they are in different networks that are peered, select Mirrored source and collector destination are in separate, peered VPC networks. Learn more
Mirrored source and collector destination are in the same VPC network
Network *
gcp-net
Mirrored source and collector destination are in separate, peered VPC networks
CONTINUE
CANCEL

Figure 7.34 – Selecting the VPC network where the mirroring policy applies

Select the subnetwork that will be our *mirrored source*, as shown in *Figure 7.35*, and then click **CONTINUE**:

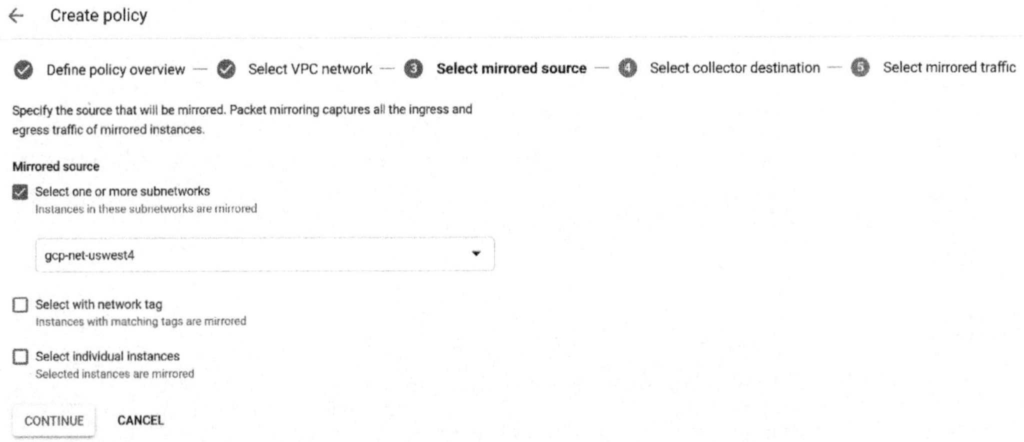

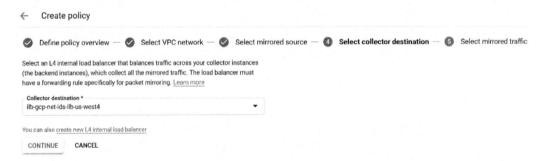

Figure 7.35 – Selecting the subnetwork that acts as a mirrored source

Select the collector destination as shown in *Figure 7.36*. As specified in the Google console, we must select an L4 internal load balancer that balances traffic across our collector backend instances, which collect all the mirrored traffic. The load balancer must have a forwarding rule specifically for Packet Mirroring:

Figure 7.36 – Selecting the collector destination

Finally, we specify the traffic to mirror. By default, all ingress and egress traffic is mirrored. Since this could impact the bandwidth, latency, and costs, usually we prefer to filter the traffic to be mirrored. By the way, in *Figure 7.37*, we show the case when we mirror all the traffic:

Figure 7.37 – Selecting the mirrored traffic

Let's test Packet Mirroring by running a packet capture (`tcpdump`) on the IDS VM:

```
sudo tcpdump -i ens4  -n "(icmp or port 80) and net
172.21.0.0/24"
```

Here, we have the following:

- `-i` is the capture interface (`ens4` in our example) of the IDS VM.
- `-n` is not used to convert addresses to names.
- `(icmp or port 80) and net 172.21.0.0/24` is the capture filter (the `172.21.0.0/24` network is where the mirrored VMs are attached).

We also generate some traffic to the mirrored subnet, with a `ping` command from Cloud Shell to any public IP web server (whose IP is `[PUBLIC_IP_WEB1]`),

`ping -c 4 [PUBLIC_IP_WEB1]`.

We can see the result on the IDS VM in *Figure 7.38*, where we can see the ICMP echo requests alternated with the ICMP echo replies:

```
student-03-a402954b6dfe@mig-gcp-net-ids-uswest4-gvpf:~$ sudo tcpdump -i ens4 -nn -n "(icmp or port 80) and net 172.21.0.0/24"
tcpdump: verbose output suppressed, use -v or -vv for full protocol decode
listening on ens4, link-type EN10MB (Ethernet), capture size 262144 bytes
14:34:42.698581 IP 35.233.53.116 > 172.21.0.3: ICMP echo request, id 1374, seq 1, length 64
14:34:42.699341 IP 172.21.0.3 > 35.233.53.116: ICMP echo reply, id 1374, seq 1, length 64
14:34:43.699309 IP 35.233.53.116 > 172.21.0.3: ICMP echo request, id 1374, seq 2, length 64
14:34:43.699960 IP 172.21.0.3 > 35.233.53.116: ICMP echo reply, id 1374, seq 2, length 64
14:34:44.705983 IP 35.233.53.116 > 172.21.0.3: ICMP echo request, id 1374, seq 3, length 64
14:34:44.706001 IP 172.21.0.3 > 35.233.53.116: ICMP echo reply, id 1374, seq 3, length 64
14:34:45.702211 IP 35.233.53.116 > 172.21.0.3: ICMP echo request, id 1374, seq 4, length 64
14:34:45.702663 IP 172.21.0.3 > 35.233.53.116: ICMP echo reply, id 1374, seq 4, length 64
```

Figure 7.38 – Capturing the mirroring traffic on the IDS VM

Summary

In this chapter, we focused on the observability of whatever is related to networking in Google Cloud. This is something that is usually *hidden* from the customer point of view because of the nature of the cloud.

We investigated the working principles of Cloud Logging and Monitoring, as well as VPC Flow Logs and Google Packet Mirroring, which can give GCP customers full knowledge of what is happening under the hood from the network and security points of view. We also introduced Firewall Rules Logging logs and Cloud Audit Logs.

In the next chapter, we will introduce some advanced options to facilitate networking in GCP, such as Traffic Director.

8
Advanced Networking in Google Cloud Platform

This chapter focuses on three advanced networking topics: Traffic Director, Service Directory, and Network Connectivity Center. You will have the opportunity to understand how **Traffic Director** controls a service mesh to connect services across multi-Kubernetes clusters and **Virtual Machine (VM)** environments. Then, this chapter covers how to publish, discover, and connect to services with **Service Directory** in a consistent and reliable way. Finally, you will learn how to build hub and spoke networks with **Network Connectivity Center**.

In this chapter, we will cover the following topics:

- Configuring Google Cloud Traffic Director
- Configuring Google Cloud Service Directory
- Building hub and spoke networks with Network Connectivity Center

Google Cloud Traffic Director

In this chapter, we will introduce the Google Cloud Traffic Director, a modern way to deal with complex networking in the era of microservice applications. **Google Cloud Platform** (**GCP**) offers such a service for Compute Engine instances as well as for Google Kubernetes Engine, applying what it is already known as a *service mesh* even outside the containerized applications domain.

Understanding Istio and the service mesh

Application modernization nowadays requires us to have distributed microservice applications running on several infrastructures spread across multi-cloud and on-premises environments. Due to the distributed nature of these applications, interconnecting microservices has become very challenging and complicated. One of the most well-known and adopted solutions for microservice networking is **Istio**. Istio lets you easily interconnect microservices within a Kubernetes cluster in a sort of overlay network called a **service mesh**. The great thing about service meshes is that developers do not have to implement network functionalities to discover microservices, route traffic to and from a microservice, authenticate and authorize API calls, and monitor how traffic is flowing across your distributed application. Indeed, Istio has the following features:

- **Traffic management**: You can decide how traffic and API calls can be routed across your service mesh. You can easily implement important fault-handling properties in your service mesh, such as **circuit breakers**, **timeouts**, and **retries**. Additionally, you can implement several application deployment testing strategies, such as **A/B testing**, **canary**, and so on.

- **Security**: Microservice applications can run anywhere. It is fundamental to implement a **zero-trust** security approach to ensure safe communication. Therefore, Istio manages all aspects of security, from traffic encryption to mutual microservice authentications via digital certificates and auditing.

- **Observability**: Monitoring and logging activities are crucial in modern applications, especially those built as microservices. Istio generates service metrics such as latency, error, traffic, and saturation (the **golden signals**) to monitor application performance. It also generates distributed traces to monitor call flows within a service mesh. Istio generates access logs as well for auditing purposes.

To achieve all this, Istio relies on the **Envoy** proxies that are deployed along with your application microservices. Indeed, all traffic leaving and entering your mesh is proxied by the Envoys that are actually implementing your application data plane networking. On the other hand, the control plane of your service mesh is implemented by **istiod**, a daemon running in your Kubernetes cluster that is responsible for the service mesh governance. istiod is composed of three elements, **Pilot**, **Citadel**, and **Galley**, as shown in the Istio architecture in *Figure 8.1*:

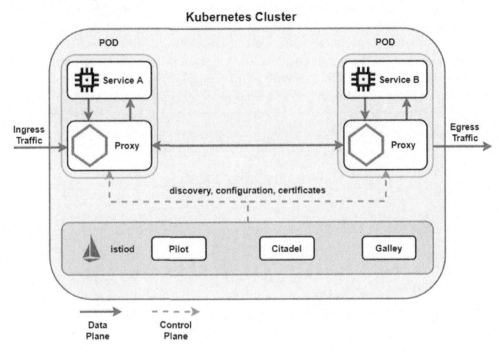

Figure 8.1 – Istio architecture

As *Figure 8.1* describes, istiod implements the control plane of the service mesh, allowing a runtime service discovery and configuration, security, and metric. More specifically, these functions are implemented by the Pilot, Citadel, and Galley respectively components, which have been consolidated in istiod in the latest versions.

The data plane is implemented by the Envoy proxies that are running as sidecar containers inside the pods where the services live. Envoys handle all the traffic coming from outside the mesh, from the service itself or another proxy within the service mesh. All traffic within a service mesh is encrypted and authenticated using **mutual Transport Layer Security (mTLS)** technology, which guarantees strong security. Istiod provides certificates to Envoys as they appear in the service mesh and acts as a certification authority for certificate validation. Moreover, istiod injects authorization policies to Envoys in order to authorize services to make calls to other services, thus securing the service mesh further.

In summary, Istio is a great way of implementing microservice networking within a Kubernetes cluster. But what if you need to interconnect services that are running on different Kubernetes clusters, or, even worse, if you need to interconnect services that are running on a VM and they don't have Envoys? Here, Traffic Director comes into play.

Understanding Traffic Director

Traffic Director is a GCP-managed service that provides configuration and traffic management (load balancing, traffic routing, security, and so on) for services based on various environments, such as Compute Engine instances, Google Kubernetes Engine, on-premises, or other public cloud providers. The key point that Traffic Director introduces is that the control plane (Istiod for clarity) is fully managed in Google Cloud. There is no need to install it either to maintain it in a Kubernetes cluster, as *Figure 8.2* shows:

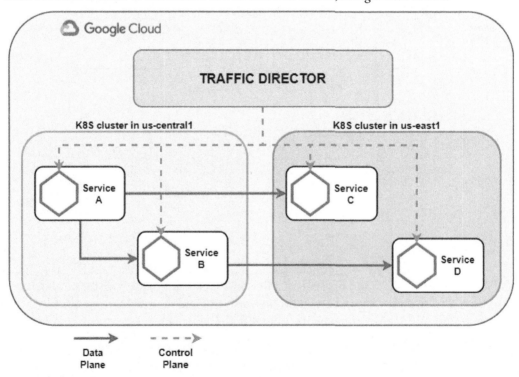

Figure 8.2 – Traffic Director across Kubernetes clusters

As *Figure 8.2* shows, Traffic Director is a fully managed service in GCP that allows you to build a service mesh across several deployment environments. In this case, we can observe how Traffic Director orchestrates a service mesh across multiple Kubernetes clusters within a Google Cloud project. It directly interacts with Envoys in order to configure, discover, and secure services. Note that you don't need to have the control plane installed on each cluster. This is because Traffic Director integrates all the service mesh control functions in it.

Another great feature of Traffic Director is that it can control proxy-less gRPC services (here, you can find a well-explained introduction to gRPC: `https://grpc.io/docs/what-is-grpc/introduction/`) and thus integrate them into the service mesh. gRPC is a modern, open source, high-performance **Remote Procedure Call** (**RPC**) framework that can run in any environment. It can connect services in and across data centers with pluggable support for load balancing, tracing, health checking, and authentication.

Moreover, these services can run anywhere, either on a Kubernetes cluster or a Compute Engine instance, as shown in *Figure 8.3*:

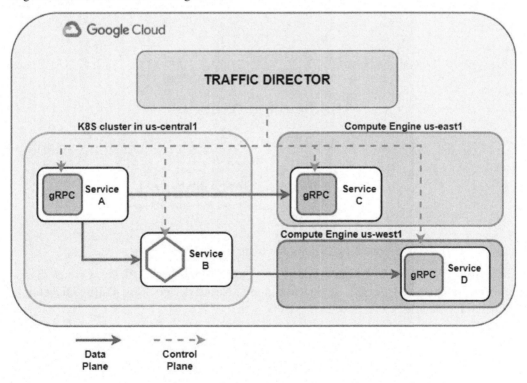

Figure 8.3 – Controlling gRPC with Traffic Director

As *Figure 8.3* shows, Traffic Director can control both proxy and proxy-less microservices on either Kubernetes or Compute Engine environments. This feature is unique, and it will enable you to build your service mesh in heterogeneous environments. This is possible because Traffic Director supports xDS API technology, which is a set of discovery services available through gRPC/REST API calls. Services can query the mesh configuration from Traffic Director using these APIs. This works whether the services use a sidecar proxy or not, which leads to greater flexibility in the service mesh configuration and governance. For more information on xDS API, follow this link: `https://bit.ly/2Z0KI6U`.

Configuring Traffic Director

To start using Traffic Director in Google Cloud Platform, you need to enable the API as with any other GCP service. From the **Navigation** menu, select **APIs and Services**, and then **Library**. Search for `Traffic Director API` on the search bar and click on **Traffic Director API**, as shown in *Figure 8.4*:

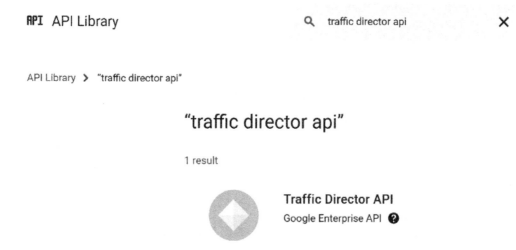

Figure 8.4 – Enabling the Traffic Director API service

Then, click on the **ENABLE** button on the new page to enable the API. Once enabled, let's go to Traffic Director from the **Navigation** menu | **Network Services** | **Traffic Director**, as shown in *Figure 8.5*:

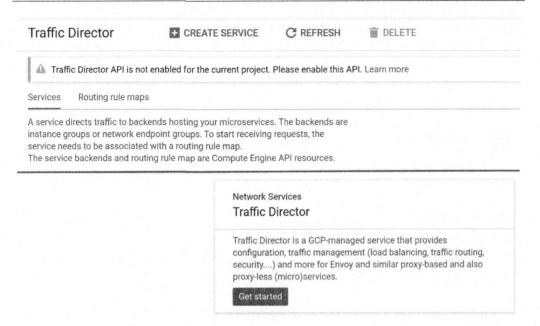

Figure 8.5 – Traffic Director start page

Please note that if you go directly to Traffic Director, as the service is not enabled yet the URL will be redirected to allow us to enable the service, or it may show the **Please enable this API** message, as shown in *Figure 8.6*:

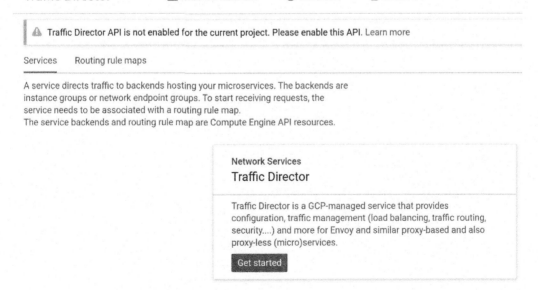

Figure 8.6 – Traffic Director API not enabled message

When you start the wizard, you need to be prepared on whether you want to configure a Kubernetes service or a VM-based service. In both cases, you will need to add a sidecar proxy that is compatible with xDS API standards. This is an important step toward. To proceed further, let's click on **Get started**, as shown in *Figure 8.5*, and then click on **Continue** and select **Configure service details**, as shown in *Figure 8.7*:

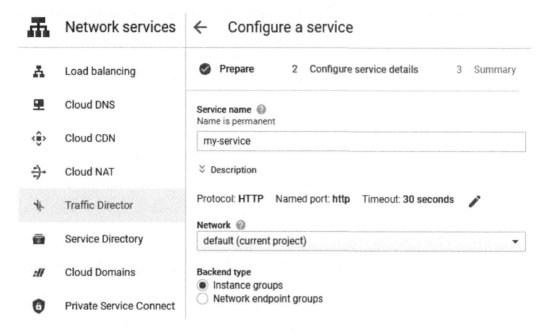

Figure 8.7 – Configuring a Traffic Director service

As *Figure 8.7* shows, when creating a service in Traffic Director, you need to specify what protocol is using the service. In the example shown in *Figure 8.7*, you can see that the service is reachable via **HTTP** with a timeout of **30 seconds**. Other options are available, as shown in *Figure 8.8*:

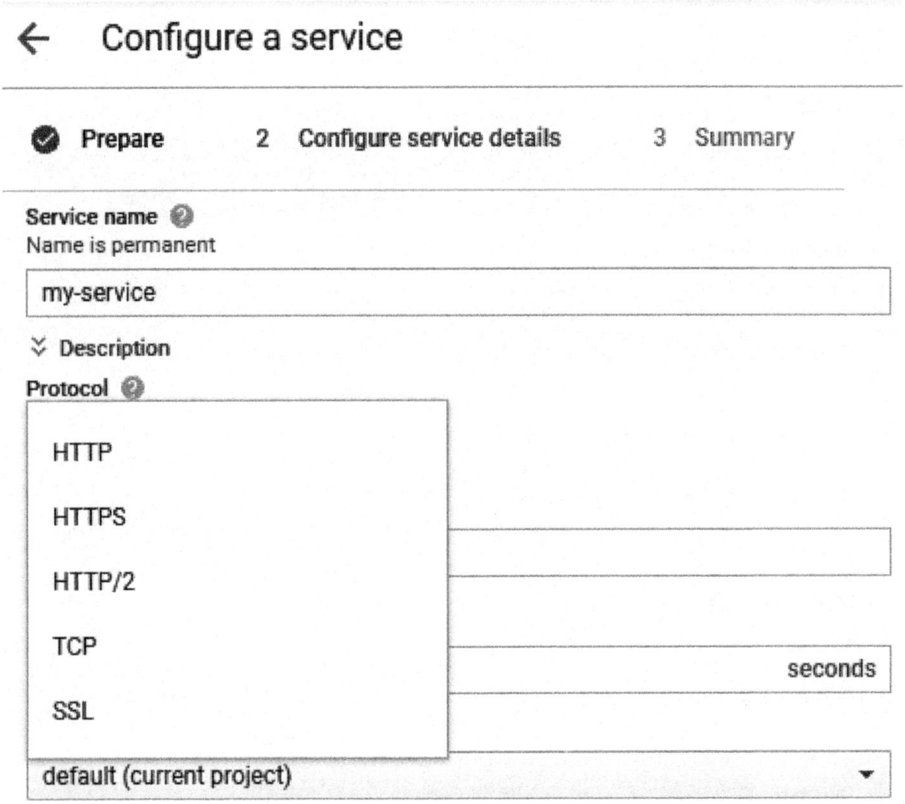

← **Configure a service**

✓ **Prepare**   2   **Configure service details**   3   Summary

Service name ❓
Name is permanent

> my-service

≫ Description

Protocol ❓

| HTTP |
| HTTPS |
| HTTP/2 |
| TCP |
| SSL |

seconds

default (current project)   ▼

Figure 8.8 – Traffic Director service protocol options

Indeed, as *Figure 8.8* shows, these are all the possible options that a microservice uses to expose its service. Next, you need to specify which backend type your service is using. The first option you will get is **Instance groups** (also known as managed instance groups), as shown in *Figure 8.9*:

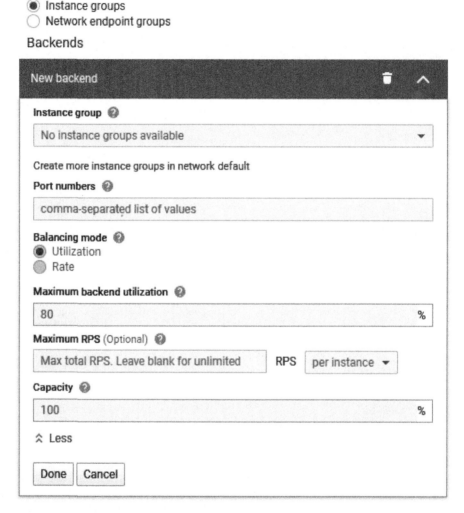

Figure 8.9 – Backend type – Instance groups in the Traffic Director service configuration

As *Figure 8.9*, shows, you need to select the following:

- **Instance group**: This is the managed instance group where your service is running and listening for incoming requests.

- **Port numbers**: This is the list of ports that your service is listening to.

- **Balancing mode**: This determines the policy on how to distribute requests to the instances in the backend. The utilization mode watches the amount of CPU usage and other factors to determine whether an instance should be considered as a candidate for a new request. The rate mode instead load-balances based on the number of requests per second an instance can handle.

- **Maximum backend utilization**: This is the maximum CPU usage an instance can handle before being considered as a candidate for a new request.

- **Maximum RPS**: This is the maximum rate (**Request Per Second**). There is a combo box that specifies whether the RPS is per instance or what (as the maximum number of requests per second can be per instance group).

- **Capacity**: This is an additional control to manage maximum backend utilization per RPS. For example, if we want instances to operate at a maximum of 80% utilization, we can set the balancing mode to 80% and capacity to 100%.

If we want to cut instance utilization by half, we can still use the balancing mode at 80% but the capacity at 50%. If your service is running on a Google Kubernetes Engine cluster or an external endpoint (an on-premises service, another public cloud service, and so on), then you can choose **Network endpoint group**, as shown in *Figure 8.10*:

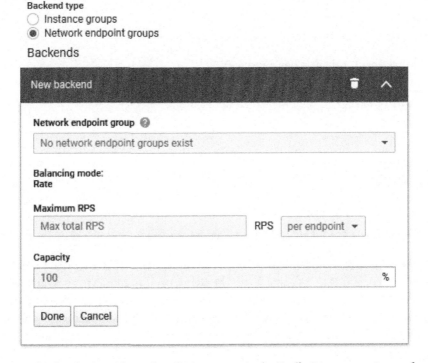

Figure 8.10 – Backend type – Network endpoint groups in the Traffic Director service configuration

When you choose **Network endpoint groups**, you can specify the **Maximum RPS** and **Capacity**, as previously described.

You can add multiple backends to your service of different types. This makes a backend cluster. After that, you can add a **Health check** option to route requests to only healthy instances. You can also set advanced parameters, as *Figure 8.11* shows:

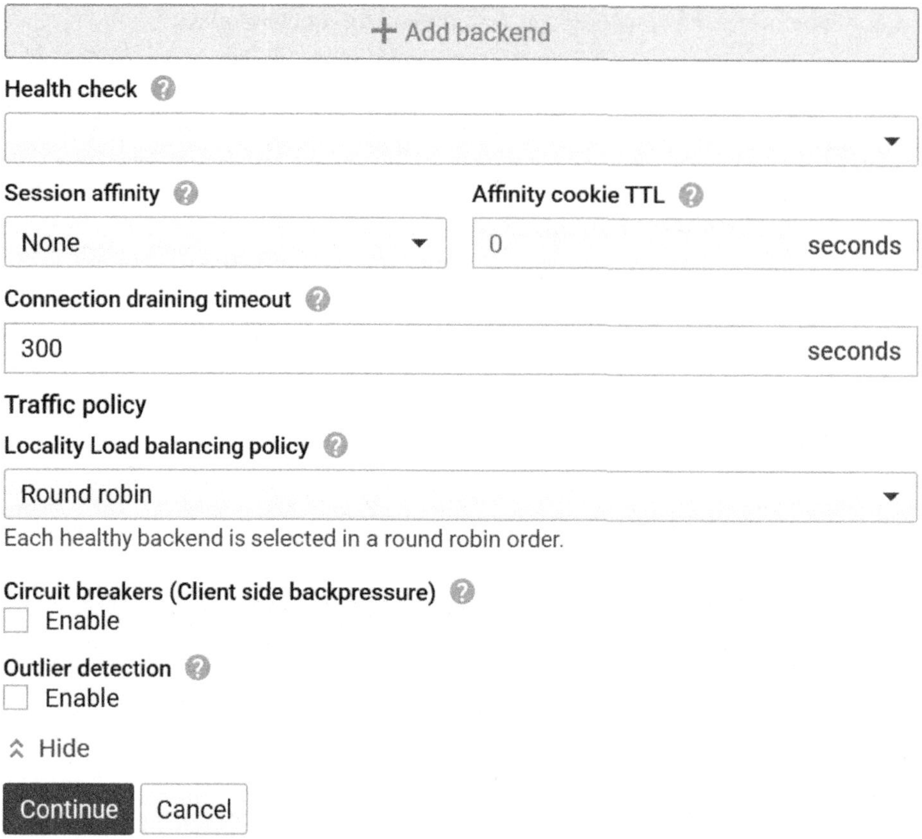

Figure 8.11 – Advanced options in the Traffic Director service configuration

As *Figure 8.11* shows, the advanced parameters are as follows:

- **Session Affinity**: You can choose between **None, Client IP, Generated Cookie, Header field**, and **HTTP cookie**. With the None option, requests go to any instance independently. With **ClientIP**, requests with the same source are routed to the same instance. With **Generated Cookie**, clients with the same load balancer-generated cookie go to the same instance. With **Header field**, requests with the same headers go to the same endpoint. With **HTTP cookie**, requests will be forwarded to the same endpoint using the provided cookie.

- **Affinity Cookie TTL**: If you choose **Generated Cookie** in the **Session Affinity**, you can define the **Time to Live** in seconds.

- **Connection draining timeout**: This is the number of seconds that a draining instance (an instance that is gracefully shutting down) waits for connections to complete.

- **Locality Load balancing policy**: This is the algorithm responsible for load balancing the traffic between healthy instances that have got a locality weight and priority from Traffic Director. They include **Round Robin, Least Request, Ring Hash, Random, Original destination**, or **Maglev**. The **Ring Hash** instance has the property that the addition/removal of a host from a set of N hosts only affects 1/N of the requests. **Original destination** selects the backend based on client connection metadata. **Maglev** has faster table lookup build times and host selection times, and can be a drop-in replacement for the **Ring Hash** load balancer.

There are two additional options that are worth particular attention. You can enable the **Circuit breakers** option. After this, click on the pencil icon to set the parameters, as *Figure 8.12* shows:

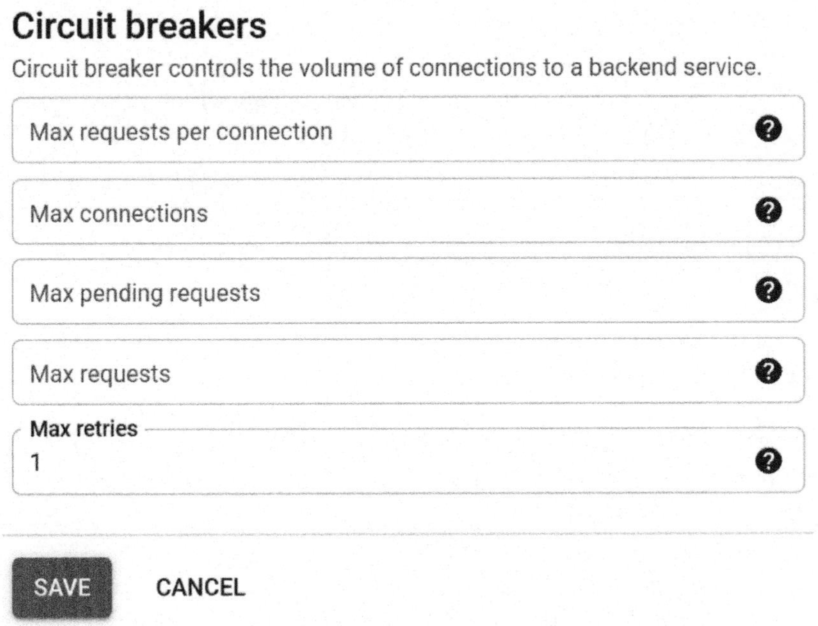

Circuit breakers

Circuit breaker controls the volume of connections to a backend service.

Max requests per connection	❓

Max connections	❓

Max pending requests	❓

Max requests	❓

Max retries

1	❓

SAVE   CANCEL

Figure 8.12 – Circuit breaker configuration parameter

- Circuit breakers are an important tool to control the volume of requests that your service will receive. You can specify the following:

a. **Max requests per connection**: This is the maximum number of requests per single backend connection.

b. **Max connections**: This is the maximum number of requests to the backend cluster.

c. **Max pending requests**: This is the maximum number of pending requests to the backend cluster.

d. **Max requests**: This is the maximum number of parallel requests allowed to the backend cluster.

e. **Max retries**: This is the maximum number of parallel retries allowed to the backend cluster. Outlier detection controls the eviction of unhealthy hosts from the load balancing pool. You can enable it and use the default parameters:

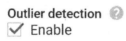

Outlier detection ⃝?
☑ Enable

Consecutive errors : **5**
Interval: **1,000 milliseconds**
Base ejection time: **30,000 milliseconds**
Max ejection percent : **50%**

Figure 8.13 – Outlier detection parameters in the Traffic Director service configuration

As *Figure 8.13* shows, the parameters for evictions (the eviction being the eviction of unhealthy hosts from the load balancing pool) are as follows:

- **Consecutive errors**: This is the number of 500 error codes returned from the backend host before being considered evicted.

- **Interval**: This is the time interval (in milliseconds) between eviction sweeps.

- **Base ejection time**: This is the base time that a host is ejected for.

- **Max ejection percent**: This is the maximum number of backend hosts that can be ejected.

Now that we have learned how to configure Traffic Director, let's go and see another important service in Google Cloud designed for microservice applications.

Configuring the Google Cloud Service Directory

In this section, we are going to discover how we can use the **Google Cloud Service Directory** to resolve services in multi-cloud environments. You will learn what Service Directory is and how to configure it.

Understanding Service Directory and features

With the advent of microservice applications and multi-cloud deployments, modern applications have become more reliable and scalable. However, due to their distributed architecture, the complexity of resolving services has become harder and harder. Indeed, microservice applications can be deployed either in different cloud environments or on-premises. These distributed applications are likely to change over time and their services too. It is in their nature, and therefore finding the location where the service has moved is very challenging.

For this reason, Google Cloud introduced **Service Directory**, a fully managed cloud service conceived as a single place to publish, discover, and connect services regardless of their environment. Indeed, Service Directory supports services running in Google Cloud Platform, in other cloud providers such as Amazon Web Services, and on-premises as well.

Service Directory has the following features:

- **Registration and lookup API**: Service Directory provides a public API that can be used to create and resolve namespaces, services, and endpoints. You will learn more about these later in the chapter.

- **Cloud DNS integration**: Service Directory is fully integrated with Google Cloud DNS and therefore services can be available on **Virtual Private Cloud** (**VPC**).

- **IAM integration**: As with all the other Google Cloud services, you can use Cloud IAM to control service visibility and permissions.

- **Cloud Monitoring and Cloud Logging integration**: Service Directory operations can be monitored and logged along with other GCP services.

Service Directory architecture includes some important key components, as shown in *Figure 8.14*:

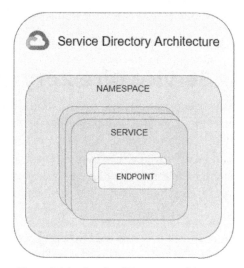

Figure 8.14 – Service Directory architecture

As *Figure 8.14* shows, the Service Directory use the following components:

- **Endpoint**: This component handles client requests and it is composed of an IP address and a port. The endpoint can be a VM, a container, load balancer, or any entity that is able to respond to a client request. Endpoints can have additional metadata in the form of key-value pairs. However, their scope is within the service.

- **Service**: This component is a group of endpoints that provide a set of behaviors. Clients can look up a service by its name (throughout the HTTP/gRPC protocol) and then connect to the endpoint that handles the request. Services live within namespaces.

- **Namespace**: This component groups services for better management. It stays in a GCP region and a GCP project, and must have a unique name within them. Even though the namespace is a regional service, the services that are inside the namespace can be anywhere and can be queried from anywhere.

Clients that want to discover, publish, and manage services inside Service Directory can use the following methods to interact with its API:

- **Client Libraries**: This method provides the **Software Development Kit** (**SDK**) of the main programming languages. This will provide programmatic access to the Service Directory API.

- **REST**: This method allows clients to interact with the Service Directory API using the HTTP protocol.

- **RPC**: This method allows clients to interact with the Service Directory API using the gRPC protocol.

If you want to use DNS queries to look up private services inside your Google Cloud VPC, you can create a **Service Directory zone**, which is a specific Cloud DNS private zone that is authoritative for the Service Directory namespace. Indeed, if a namespace is attached to a Service Directory zone, then all services within the namespace are visible to all networks in the VPC.

Configuring Service Directory and DNS

To start configuring Service Directory, we need to create a namespace first. This is accessible from the **Navigation** Menu; then we select **Network services** and we click **Service Directory,** as *Figure 8.15* shows:

> **Important Note**
> When doing this for the first time, you will need to enable the Service Directory API as with most of the GCP services.

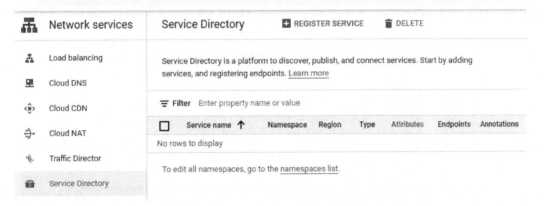

Figure 8.15 – Service Directory main page

You will create a namespace after you register your first service. Click on the **REGISTER SERVICE** button at the top. A new wizard will guide you to the service creation.

You can choose between **Private Service Connect** and **Standard** service types. Choose **Private Service Connect** when you want to send API requests to the internal IP address of a private service connect endpoint. Select **Standard** as the service type for any other case, as *Figure 8.16* shows:

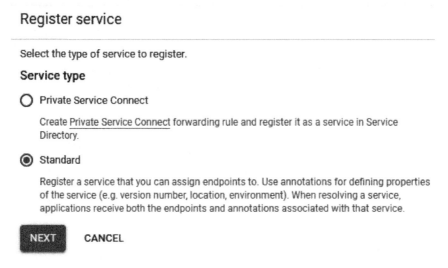

Figure 8.16 – Service registration wizard

As the namespace is a regional resource, you must select one GCP region to host your namespace. We decided to use **us-central1**, as *Figure 8.17* shows:

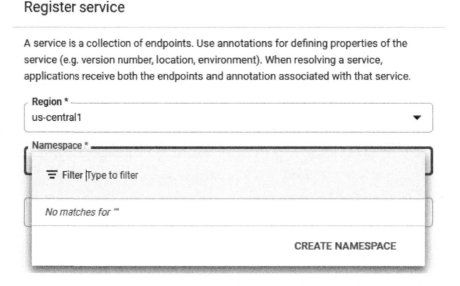

Figure 8.17 – Selecting the GCP region to host the namespace

Once you make the selection, create a namespace by clicking the **CREATE NAMESPACE** button in the **Namespace** combo box, as shown in *Figure 8.17*. On the left, a new menu will appear, as *Figure 8.18* shows:

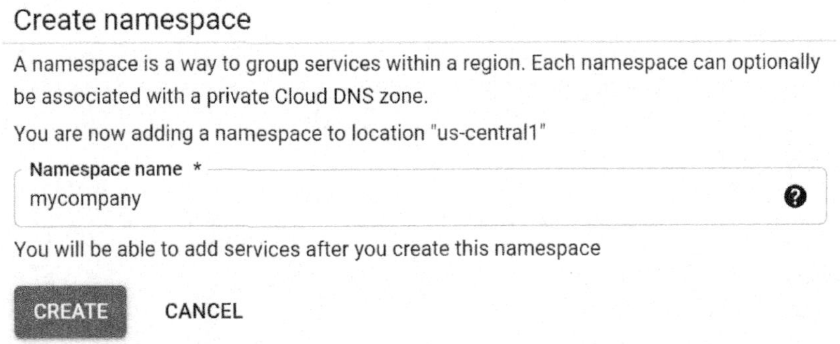

Create namespace

A namespace is a way to group services within a region. Each namespace can optionally be associated with a private Cloud DNS zone.

You are now adding a namespace to location "us-central1"

Namespace name *

mycompany   ❷

You will be able to add services after you create this namespace

CREATE   CANCEL

Figure 8.18 – Creating a namespace in Service Directory

After the namespace is created, you can proceed to define your first service. You can add some optional annotation in the form of key-value pairs. All of this is shown in *Figure 8.19*:

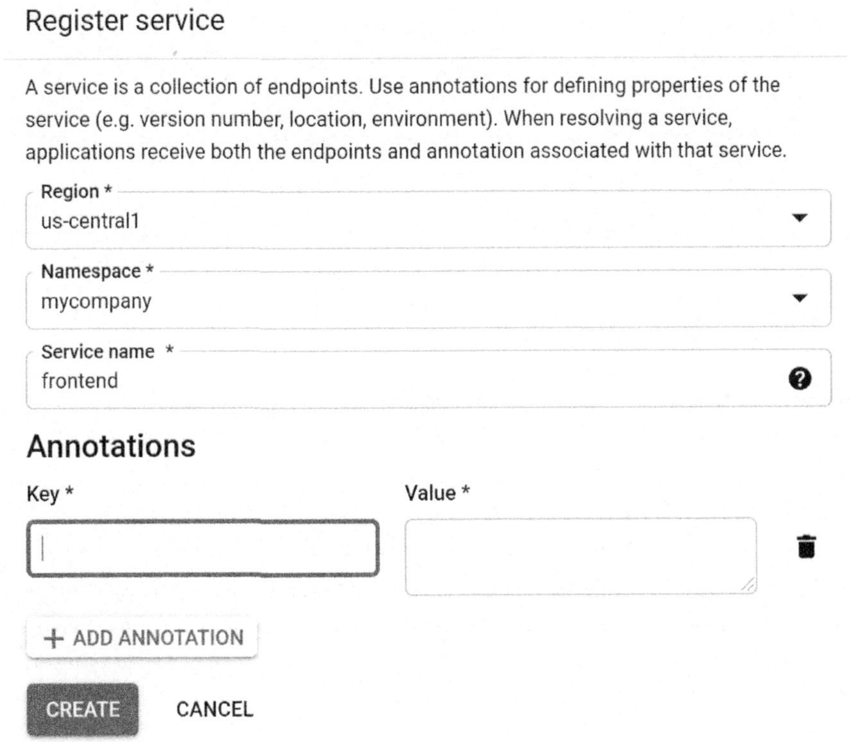

Register service

A service is a collection of endpoints. Use annotations for defining properties of the service (e.g. version number, location, environment). When resolving a service, applications receive both the endpoints and annotation associated with that service.

Region *
us-central1   ▼

Namespace *
mycompany   ▼

Service name *
frontend   ❷

Annotations

Key *   Value *

[   ]   [   ]   🗑

+ ADD ANNOTATION

CREATE   CANCEL

Figure 8.19 – Service registration completion

A successful namespace and service creation process can be seen in *Figure 8.20*:

Service Directory   **➕ REGISTER SERVICE**   **🗑 DELETE**

Service Directory is a platform to discover, publish, and connect services. Start by adding services, and registering endpoints. Learn more

☰ Filter   Enter property name or value

	Service name ↑	Namespace	Region	Type	Attributes	Endpoints	Annotations
☐	frontend	mycompany	us-central1	Standard		0	

Figure 8.20 – Successful service creation

Now, before proceeding to the endpoint configuration, let's create two Compute Engine instances that will implement our endpoints, which will be part of our `frontend` service. We will install the Apache server on it, using a `startup` script that you can pull from a public GCP bucket. Therefore, while creating the instances, make sure you use the following metadata key and value:

Metadata Key	Metadata Value
`startup-script-url`	`gs://cloud-training/gcpnet/httplb/startup.sh`

Figure 8.21 – Metadata key and value of a startup script URL

After creating the instances, make sure you will deploy the appropriate firewall rules to let HTTP traffic reach them (this can also be done when creating the instances – there is a checkbox to allow HTTP). At the end of the process, you should have two Compute Engine instances, as *Figure 8.22* shows:

	Status	Name ↑	Zone	Internal IP	External IP	Network
☐	✓	instance-1	us-central1-c	10.128.0.3 (nic0)	35.202.126.17 ☑	mynetwork
☐	✓	instance-2	us-central1-f	10.128.0.4 (nic0)	35.223.98.45 ☑	mynetwork

Figure 8.22 – Compute Engine instances up and running

You can verify whether the Apache server has been installed by clicking on the public IP address of each instance. You should get in your web browser a webpage with `Client IP`, `Hostname`, and `Server Location`. If not, go back and make sure your startup script has been executed.

Once you have your endpoints up and running, you can register them into the `frontend` service inside Service Directory. You can do it by accessing the **Navigation** menu, **Network services**, **Service Directory**, and then clicking on the **frontend** service. You will get to the frontend **Service details** page, as shown in *Figure 8.23*:

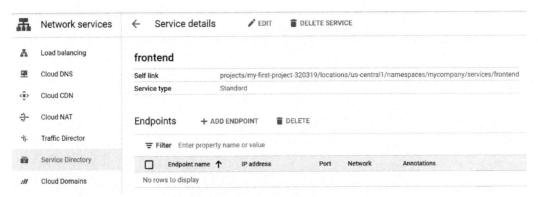

Figure 8.23 – Frontend Service details page

Here, you can publish the two endpoints that we have created with the Compute Engine instances. Click on the **ADD ENDPOINT** button to create a new endpoint inside the **frontend** service. *Figure 8.24* shows the publishing process:

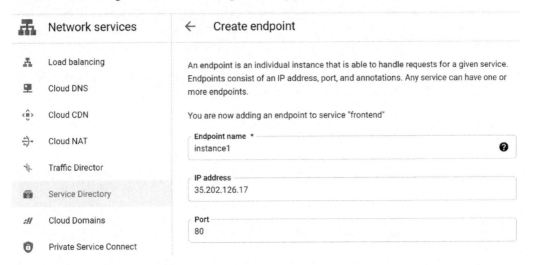

Figure 8.24 – Publishing a new endpoint

As *Figure 8.24* shows, the endpoint contains a name that uniquely identifies it, the IP address (the public IP address of the service), and the port number (80 represents the HTTP protocol that the service is listening to) that provides the service reachability. You can repeat the same process for instance2, the other endpoint. The result is shown in *Figure 8.25*:

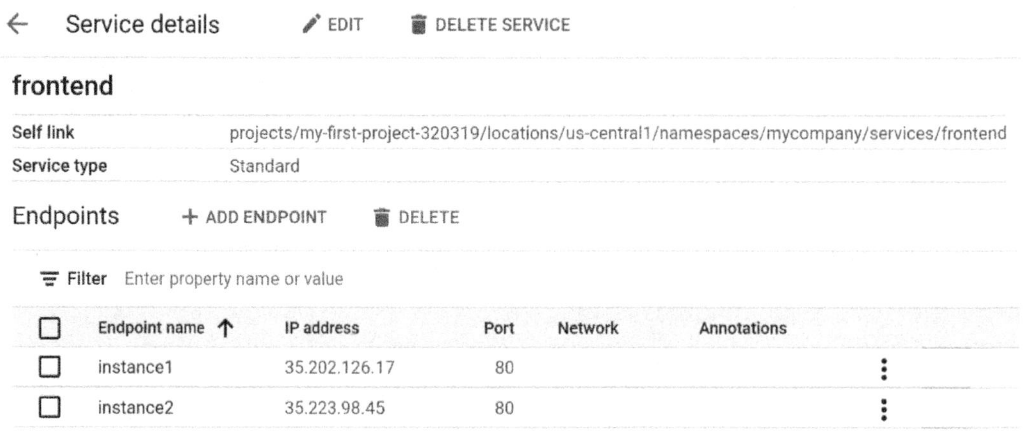

←   Service details   ✎ EDIT   🗑 DELETE SERVICE

frontend

Self link	projects/my-first-project-320319/locations/us-central1/namespaces/mycompany/services/frontend
Service type	Standard

Endpoints   + ADD ENDPOINT   🗑 DELETE

☰ Filter   Enter property name or value

☐	Endpoint name ↑	IP address	Port	Network	Annotations	
☐	instance1	35.202.126.17	80			⋮
☐	instance2	35.223.98.45	80			⋮

Figure 8.25 – Endpoints added to the frontend service

When endpoints have been published, you can resolve them using the gcloud SDK. This is one quick option that you can use to check whether they are correctly published. The following command lets you resolve the frontend service:

```
gcloud service-directory services resolve frontend --location
us-central1 --namespace mycompany
```

In the previous command, we specified some parameters:

- The service name was set to frontend.
- The location was set to the us-central1 GCP region.
- The namespace was set to mycompany.

The output of the command returns a list of endpoints that belong to the frontend service, as shown here:

```
service:
  endpoints:
  - address: 35.223.98.45
    name: projects/<PROJECT>/locations/us-central1/
namespaces/<NAMESPACE>/services/<SERVICE>/endpoints/instance2
```

```
    port: 80
  - address: 35.202.126.17
    name: projects/ <PROJECT> /locations/us-central1/
namespaces/<NAMESPACE> /services/<SERVICE>/endpoints/instance1
    port: 80
  name: projects/ <PROJECT>/locations/us-central1/
namespaces/<NAMESPACE>/services/<SERVICE>
```

You can see that each endpoint has a unique name that belongs to a service, and a namespace that belongs to a GCP project. Also, it has an IP address and port.

Now, suppose you want to resolve endpoints using DNS for private IP addresses within your VPC. For this, you need to create a Cloud DNS private zone and bind it to the Service Directory namespace. Let's register a new service (`privatefrontend`) for this demonstration, as *Figure 8.26* shows:

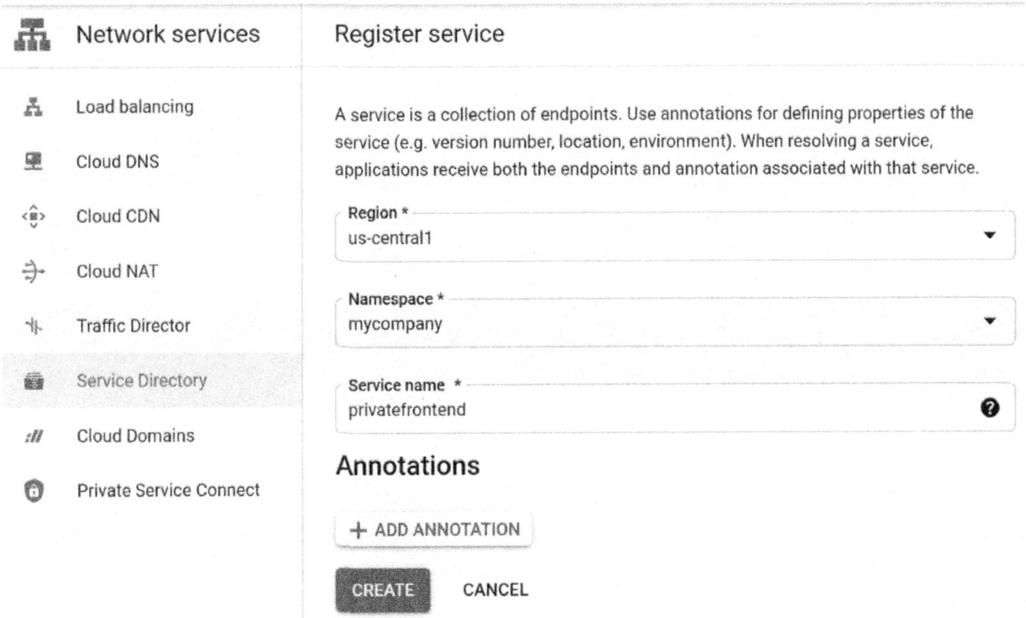

Figure 8.26 – Registering a new service in Service Directory

Once `privatefrontend` has been created, let's add `instance2` as the new endpoint, as *Figure 8.27* shows:

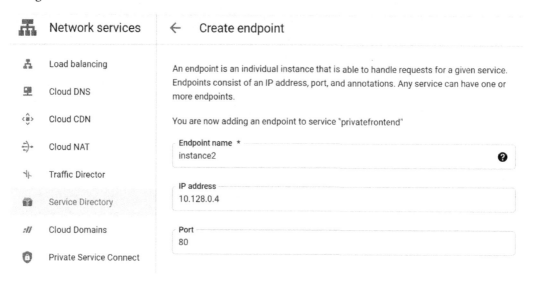

Figure 8.27 – New endpoint in the privatefrontend Service Directory

At this point, even though a service and an endpoint have been created, DNS resolution is not enabled. Indeed, if you try to ping the service, you will get a `Name or service not known` message. In *Figure 8.28*, you can see the result of the ping:

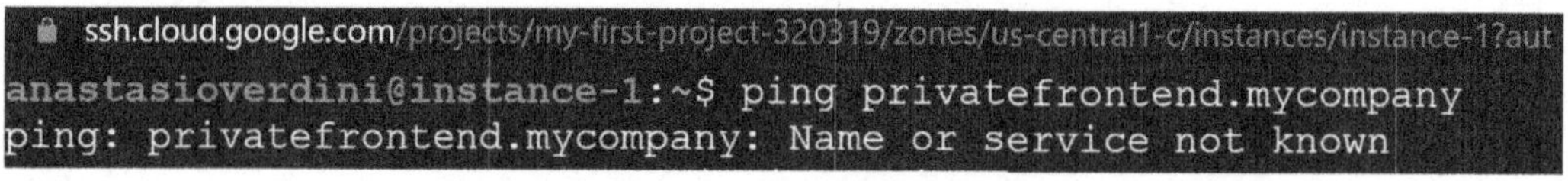

```
ssh.cloud.google.com/projects/my-first-project-320319/zones/us-central1-c/instances/instance-1?aut
anastasioverdini@instance-1:~$ ping privatefrontend.mycompany
ping: privatefrontend.mycompany: Name or service not known
```

Figure 8.28 – Service ping result

Now, let's configure a Cloud DNS private zone and link it to the Service Directory namespace. You can do it from the **Navigation** menu, choosing **Network services**, and then **Cloud DNS**. Here, use the **CREATE ZONE** button to create a new zone in Cloud DNS, as shown in *Figure 8.29*:

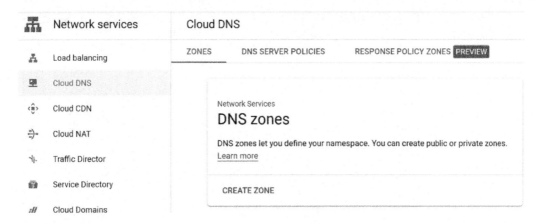

Figure 8.29 – Creating a DNS zone in Cloud DNS

Select the **Private** zone type to create a Cloud DNS private zone, provide a unique name as the zone name, and include the Service Directory namespace (mycompany in this case) as the DNS name. Then, in the **Options** combo box, select Use a service directory namespace to link the DNS zone to Service Directory. Choose the **mynetwork** (in this case) VPC network to make the private DNS zone visible, as shown in *Figure 8.30*:

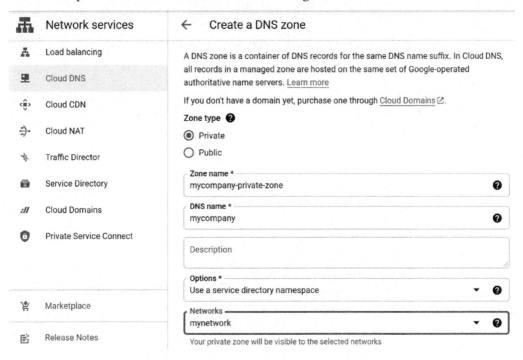

Figure 8.30 – Private DNS zone creation

Next, select the GCP region (I have used us-central1 as an example) and the Service Directory namespace to bind to the DNS zone, as *Figure 8.31* shows:

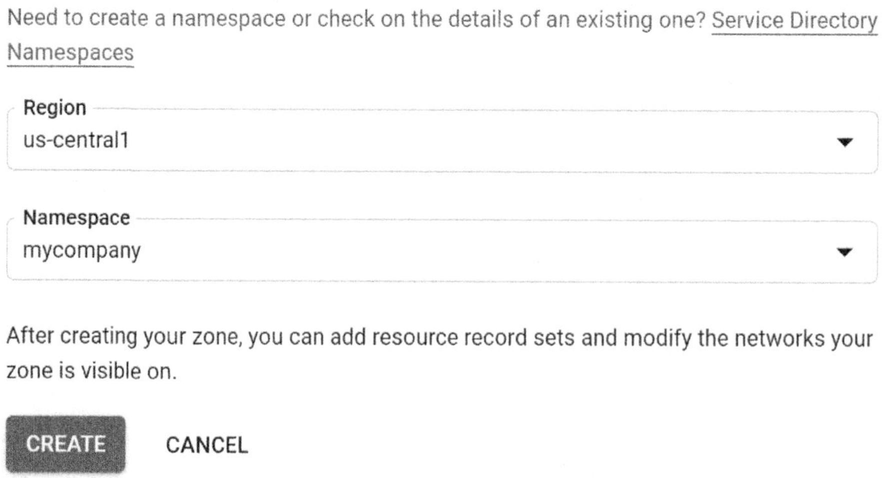

Need to create a namespace or check on the details of an existing one? Service Directory Namespaces

Region
us-central1   ▼

Namespace
mycompany   ▼

After creating your zone, you can add resource record sets and modify the networks your zone is visible on.

CREATE   CANCEL

Figure 8.31 – Private DNS zone creation and binding to the Service Directory namespace

The result of the Cloud DNS private zone is shown in *Figure 8.32*:

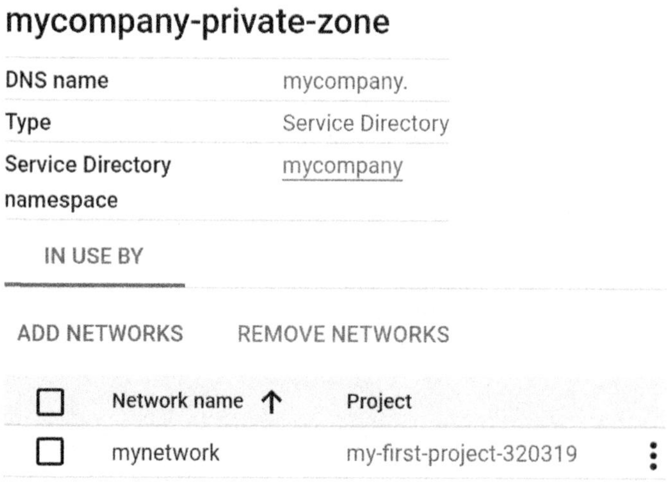

mycompany-private-zone

DNS name	mycompany.
Type	Service Directory
Service Directory namespace	mycompany

IN USE BY

ADD NETWORKS   REMOVE NETWORKS

☐	Network name ↑	Project
☐	mynetwork	my-first-project-320319 ⋮

Figure 8.32 – Results of the Cloud DNS creation and Service Directory namespace

Now that a Cloud DNS zone has been created and connected to the Service Directory namespace, you can use DNS to resolve the Service Directory service name, as *Figure 8.33* shows:

```
anastasloverdini@instance-1:~$ ping privatefrontend.mycompany
PING privatefrontend.mycompany (10.128.0.4) 56(84) bytes of data.
64 bytes from instance-2.us-central1-f.c.my-first-project-320319.internal (10.128.0.4): icmp_seq=1 ttl=64 time=1.71 ms
64 bytes from instance-2.us-central1-f.c.my-first-project-320319.internal (10.128.0.4): icmp_seq=2 ttl=64 time=0.322 ms
64 bytes from instance-2.us-central1-f.c.my-first-project-320319.internal (10.128.0.4): icmp_seq=3 ttl=64 time=0.360 ms
^C
--- privatefrontend.mycompany ping statistics ---
3 packets transmitted, 3 received, 0% packet loss, time 12ms
rtt min/avg/max/mdev = 0.322/0.796/1.708/0.645 ms
anastasloverdini@instance-1:~$
```

Figure 8.33 – Service ping result from Compute Engine

So far, you have learned how to configure Service Directory in Google Cloud. Next, you will go through Network Connectivity Center, which is a great tool to build hub and spoke networks across your hybrid cloud.

Building hub and spoke networks with Network Connectivity Center

As global enterprises move their assets into the cloud, they are required to have a unique place to manage the connectivity between their on-premises networks. Network Connectivity Center allows you to interconnect on-premises networks in the hub and spoke model. Moreover, with Network Connectivity Center, you can interconnect networks attached to **Cloud VPN**, **Dedicated Interconnect**, **Partner Interconnect**, and **Software Defined Wide Area Network (SD-WAN) Virtual Router** appliances, as shown in *Figure 8.34*:

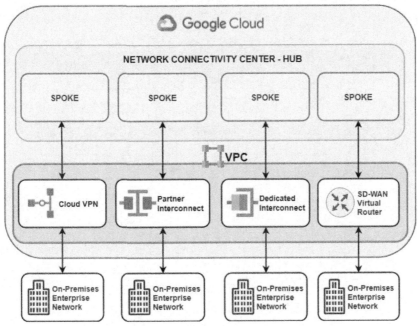

Figure 8.34 – Network Connectivity Center overview

As *Figure 8.34* shows, **Network Connectivity Center** is composed of one **hub** and many **spokes**, one for each Google Cloud network resource you need to interconnect. The hub provides data transfer service across all spokes, thus interconnecting all the on-premises networks attached. Spokes are attached to Google Cloud network resources such as Cloud VPN, Partner Interconnect, Dedicated Interconnect, and the third-party SD-WAN virtual router. You can attach only one resource type to a spoke. However, you can have multiple instances of the same type attached to one spoke. For instance, multiple **VLAN attachments** of your Dedicated Interconnect can be part of the same spoke.

Network Connectivity Center is a global service and relies on the Google Cloud network to provide instant access and global reachability to your enterprise on-premises networks.

Understanding Network Connectivity Center in Google Cloud Platform

Network Connectivity Center creates a full mesh network between all spokes that are attached to the hub. It propagates all routes learned from a spoke to all the others, thus implementing full-mesh connectivity. *Figure 8.35* shows an example of how Network Connectivity Center exchanges routes between spokes:

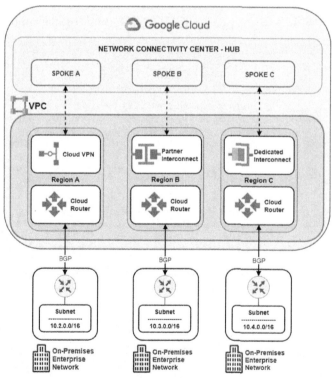

Figure 8.35 – Route exchange in Network Connectivity Center

As *Figure 8.35* shows, each on-premises enterprise network can be advertised through **Border Gateway Protocol (BGP)**. We indeed establish a BGP peering between the on-premise border gateway and Cloud Router. Of course, you can establish BGP peering with your Cloud Router in the appropriate GCP region when you have successfully established either Cloud VPN, Partner Interconnect, or Dedicated Interconnect connection. After that, you can link your network resource to a spoke within Network Connectivity Center. By doing so, all on-premises enterprise networks will be shared.

> **Important Note**
> In this scenario, we have described it as mandatory to enable global routing when creating the VPC. This enables cross-region, site-to-site traffic to be routed by the Network Connectivity Center hub and spokes. Global routing is not needed if spokes are within the same GCP region.

When you start designing your enterprise connectivity with Network Connectivity Center, you should consider the following points:

- Only dynamic routing is supported, and you must use BGP to exchange routes with Cloud Router.

- Best-path selection on routes received by Cloud Router is done through the BGP **Multi Exit Discriminator (MED)** attribute.

- Only one instance of the hub can exist per VPC. Network resources such as Cloud VPN and VLAN attachments must be within the same VPC.

- When using Cloud VPN, only HA VPN tunnels are supported as attachments to a spoke.

- VPC peering is supported, and you can peer with the VPC that hosts the hub. Route advertisements are not affected by Network Connectivity Center.

- Shared VPC is supported, but you must create the hub in the host project.

Now that we have introduced Network Connectivity Center, let's start configuring it as a transit hub.

Configuring Network Connectivity Center as a transit hub

In this section, we are going to learn how to configure Network Connectivity Center to route traffic between two VPCs passing through a transit VPC. We will have to deal with two spokes and one hub. We will use Cloud VPN as a network resource with HA VPN tunnels. *Figure 8.36* shows the scenario we will build:

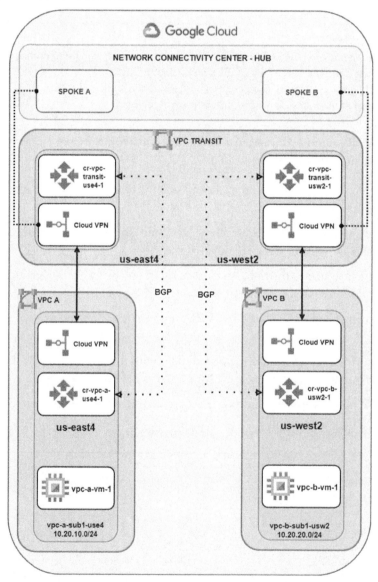

Figure 8.36 – Network Connectivity Center transit hub scenario

As *Figure 8.36* shows, we will use Network Connectivity Center to interconnect two VPCs (VPC A in us-east4 and VPC B in us-west2) using a transit VPC (VPC TRANSIT). VPC A and VPC B simulate two on-premises networks. To confirm connectivity, two Compute Engine instances (vpc-a-vm-1 and vpc-b-vm-1) will be deployed on both VPC A and VPC B, and they will be attached to vpc-a-sub1-use4 and vpc-b-sub1-usw2 subnets with 10.20.10.0/24 and 10.20.20.0/24 network addresses respectively. Additionally, we will deploy four Cloud Router (cr-vpc-a-use4-1, cr-vpc-transit-use4-1, cr-vpc-transit-usw2-1, and cr-vpc-b-usw2-1) instances to exchange routing dynamically, which is a requirement when adopting Network Connectivity Center. Moreover, in this scenario we are choosing Cloud VPN as a network resource to attach to Spoke A and Spoke B. HA VPN will be used to interconnect VPC A, VPC TRANSIT, and VPC B, as it is the only supported Cloud VPN type. So you will configure one HA VPN between VPC A and VPC TRANSIT, and another one between VPC B and VPC TRANSIT.

To start configuring the scenario, we need to create three VPCs, as shown in *Figure 8.37*. At this point of the book, you should be familiar with how to configure VPCs, so we omit VPC configuration for convenience. *Figure 8.37* shows the result of the three VPCs:

VPC networks   ➕ CREATE VPC NETWORK   ⟳ REFRESH

Name ↑	Region	Subnets	MTU ❷	Mode	IP address ranges	Global dynamic routing
▼ vpc-a		1	1460	Custom		Off
	us-east4	vpc-a-sub1-use4			10.20.10.0/24	
▼ vpc-b		1	1460	Custom		Off
	us-west2	vpc-b-sub1-usw2			10.20.20.0/24	
vpc-transit		0	1460	Custom		On

Figure 8.37 – VPC configuration in Network Connectivity Center

---

Important Note

vpc-transit does not contain any subnets and has global dynamic routing mode enabled.

Next, we are going to configure the Cloud Router instances to dynamically exchange BGP routes. To achieve this, use the parameters listed in *Figure 8.38*:

Cloud Router name	VPC network	GCP region	Google ASN
cr-vpc-transit-use4-1	vpc-transit	us-east4	65000
cr-vpc-transit-usw2-1	vpc-transit	us-west2	65000
cr-vpc-a-use4-1	vpc-a	us-east4	65001
cr-vpc-b-usw2-1	vpc-b	us-west2	65002

Figure 8.38 – Cloud Router parameters

As for VPCs, you should be able to create a Cloud Router instance. *Figure 8.39* shows the result of the four instances:

Cloud Routers   CREATE ROUTER   C REFRESH   DELETE

Filter   Enter property name or value

	Name ↑	Network	Region	Google ASN	Interconnect
☐	cr-vpc-a-use4-1	vpc-a	us-east4	65001	None
☐	cr-vpc-b-usw2-1	vpc-b	us-west2	65002	None
☐	cr-vpc-transit-use4-1	vpc-transit	us-east4	65000	None
☐	cr-vpc-transit-usw2-1	vpc-transit	us-west2	65000	None

Figure 8.39 – Cloud Router instances for Network Connectivity Center

Next, let's create four HA VPN gateways to interconnect VPCs using *Figure 8.40*:

VPN gateway name	VPC network	Region
vpc-transit-gw1-use4	vpc-transit	us-east4
vpc-transit-gw1-usw2	vpc-transit	us-west2
vpc-a-gw1-use4	vpc-a	us-east4
vpc-b-gw1-usw2	vpc-b	us-west2

Figure 8.40 – VPN gateway parameters

To proceed with configuring a HA VPN gateway, navigate to **Hybrid Connectivity** and select **VPN**. Then, create a VPN connection and select **High-availability VPN**. Here, use the data listed in the previous table to allocate VPN gateways, as *Figure 8.41* shows:

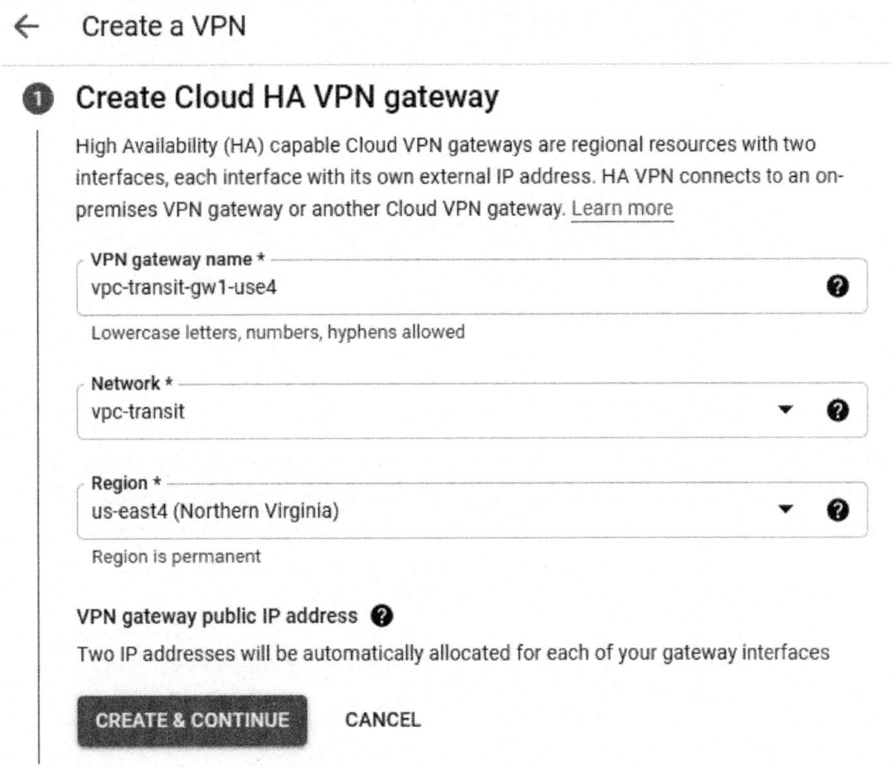

←   Create a VPN

① **Create Cloud HA VPN gateway**

High Availability (HA) capable Cloud VPN gateways are regional resources with two interfaces, each interface with its own external IP address. HA VPN connects to an on-premises VPN gateway or another Cloud VPN gateway. Learn more

VPN gateway name *
vpc-transit-gw1-use4   ❓

Lowercase letters, numbers, hyphens allowed

Network *
vpc-transit   ▼ ❓

Region *
us-east4 (Northern Virginia)   ▼ ❓

Region is permanent

VPN gateway public IP address ❓

Two IP addresses will be automatically allocated for each of your gateway interfaces

CREATE & CONTINUE   CANCEL

Figure 8.41 – Configuring a HA VPN gateway for Network Connectivity Center

Click the **CREATE & CONTINUE** button, and then create other VPN gateways by exiting the wizard and using the **CREATE VPN GATEWAY** button, as shown in *Figure 8.42*:

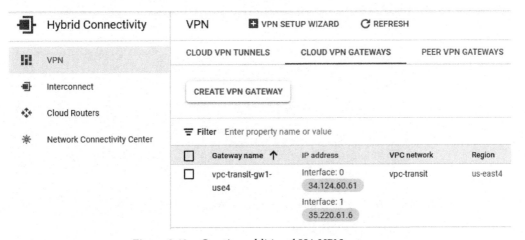

Figure 8.42 – Creating additional HA VPN gateways

The result of this process is shown in *Figure 8.43*:

	Gateway name ↑	IP address		VPC network	Region		
☐	vpc-a-gw1-use4	Interface: 0	34.124.60.225	vpc-a	us-east4	ADD VPN TUNNEL	⋮
		Interface: 1	35.220.63.40				
☐	vpc-b-gw1-usw2	Interface: 0	34.124.7.39	vpc-b	us-west2	ADD VPN TUNNEL	⋮
		Interface: 1	34.104.69.139				
☐	vpc-transit-gw1-use4	Interface: 0	34.124.60.164	vpc-transit	us-east4	ADD VPN TUNNEL	⋮
		Interface: 1	34.104.125.29				
☐	vpc-transit-gw1-usw2	Interface: 0	34.124.1.71	vpc-transit	us-west2	ADD VPN TUNNEL	⋮
		Interface: 1	34.104.66.143				

Figure 8.43 – HA VPN gateways in Network Connectivity Center

Now that you have created all the VPN gateways, you can proceed with configuring a pair of VPN tunnels for each gateway. Let's start with configuring VPN tunnels from `vpc-transit` to `vpc-a`. From the **VPN** page, select **Google VPN gateway details** and select **vpc-transit-gw1-use4**. Once inside, click **ADD VPN TUNNEL**, as shown in *Figure 8.44*:

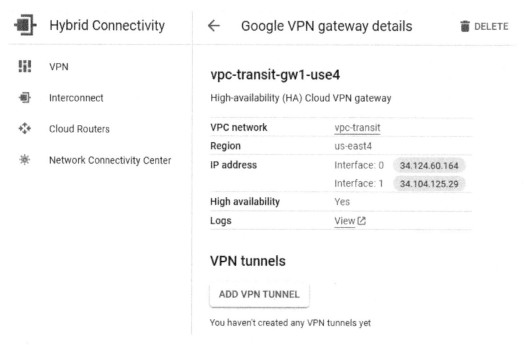

Figure 8.44 – Adding VPN tunnels to the vpc-transit-gw1-use4 VPN gateway

Inside **VPN tunnels**, select **Google Cloud**, the project ID, and the **vpc-a-gw1-use4** VPN gateway, as *Figure 8.45* shows:

Figure 8.45 – Adding VPN tunnels – part one

Then, continue to configure a pair of VPN tunnels, selecting the first option, **Create a pair of VPN tunnels**. Later, choose the **cr-vpc-transit-use4-1** Cloud Router instance, as *Figure 8.46* shows:

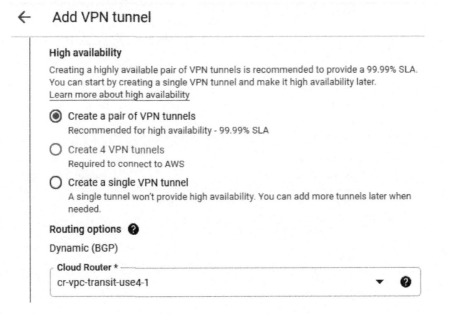

Figure 8.46 – Adding VPN tunnels – part two

Next, configure the first VPN tunnel of HA VPN with the `transit-to-vpc-a-tu1` name. IP addresses are already configured. Google Cloud is smart enough to figure out the VPN tunnel IP addresses for both gateways. Choose the IKE pre-shared key (`Google123!` in the example, which is a weak password that should never be used in a real configuration) as the authentication password during tunnel establishment. *Figure 8.47* shows the configuration:

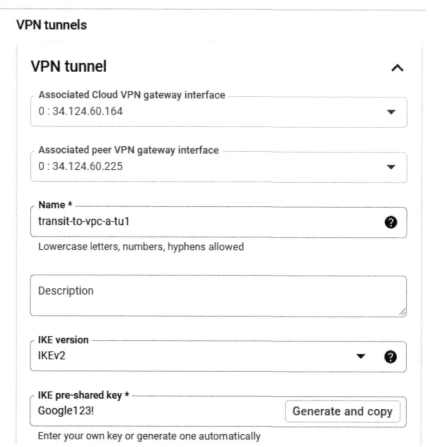

Figure 8.47 – Adding VPN tunnels – part three

Next, configure the second VPN tunnel as you did for the first one. Use the name `transit-to-vpc-a-tu2`, as shown in *Figure 8.48*:

Figure 8.48 – Adding VPN tunnels – part four

When you are done, click the **Create and Continue** button. Your output should look like the one in *Figure 8.49*:

Figure 8.49 – Result of the HA VPN tunnel configuration

When HA VPN tunnels have been configured, you can proceed with the BGP session configuration for each tunnel. You can start with the session named `transit-to-vpc-a-bgp1`, clicking the blue **CONFIGURE** button next to the `transit-to-vpc-a-tu1` Cloud VPN tunnel. Here, you can enter the `vpc-a (65001)` **Peer ASN** number and the IP addresses for the endpoints, as shown in *Figure 8.50*:

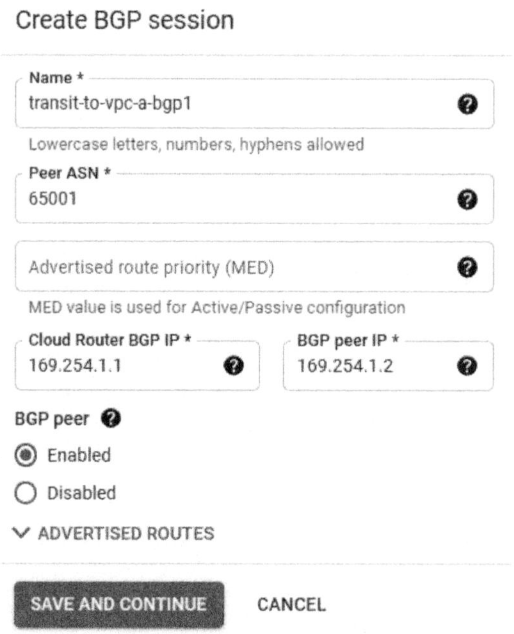

Create BGP session

Name *

transit-to-vpc-a-bgp1

Lowercase letters, numbers, hyphens allowed

Peer ASN *

65001

Advertised route priority (MED)

MED value is used for Active/Passive configuration

Cloud Router BGP IP *

169.254.1.1

BGP peer IP *

169.254.1.2

BGP peer

◉ Enabled

○ Disabled

∨ ADVERTISED ROUTES

SAVE AND CONTINUE   CANCEL

Figure 8.50 – BGP configuration from TRANSIT-VPC to VPC-A for HA tunnel one

Repeat the same operation for the `transit-to-vpc-a-tu2` second BGP session, as shown in *Figure 8.51*:

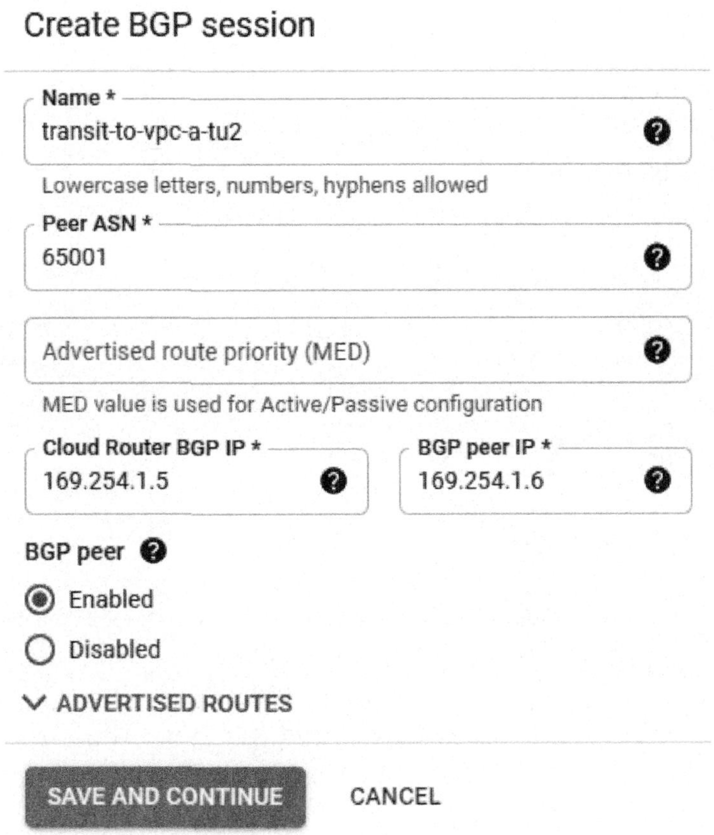

Create BGP session

Name *

transit-to-vpc-a-tu2   ?

Lowercase letters, numbers, hyphens allowed

Peer ASN *

65001   ?

Advertised route priority (MED)   ?

MED value is used for Active/Passive configuration

Cloud Router BGP IP *   **BGP peer IP ***

169.254.1.5   ?   169.254.1.6   ?

BGP peer ?

◉ Enabled

○ Disabled

⌄ ADVERTISED ROUTES

SAVE AND CONTINUE   CANCEL

Figure 8.51 – BGP configuration from TRANSIT-VPC to VPC-a for HA tunnel two

The result should look like the one shown in *Figure 8.52*:

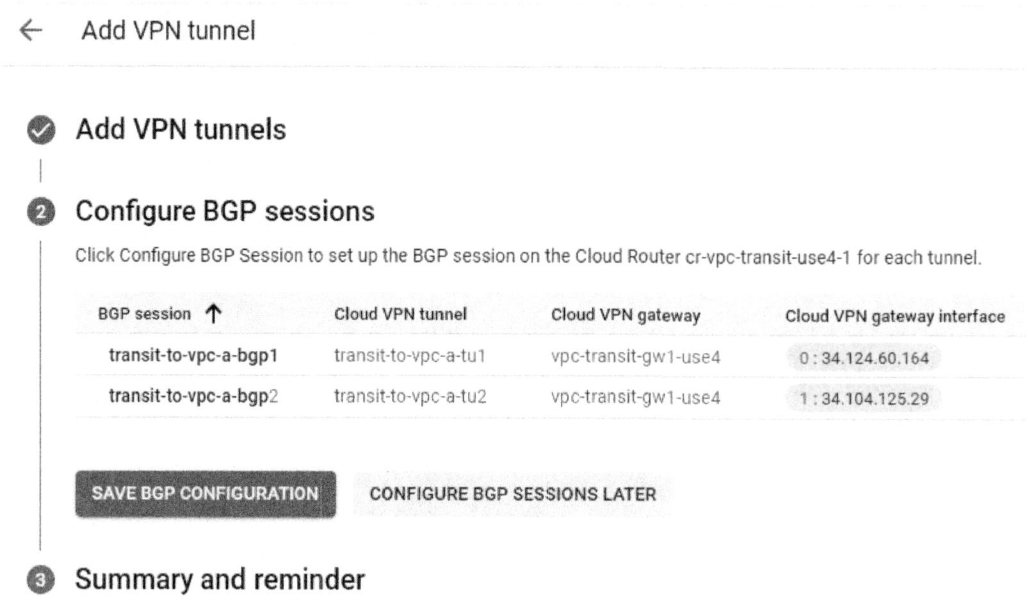

←   Add VPN tunnel

✓ **Add VPN tunnels**

② **Configure BGP sessions**

Click Configure BGP Session to set up the BGP session on the Cloud Router cr-vpc-transit-use4-1 for each tunnel.

BGP session ↑	Cloud VPN tunnel	Cloud VPN gateway	Cloud VPN gateway interface
transit-to-vpc-a-bgp1	transit-to-vpc-a-tu1	vpc-transit-gw1-use4	0 : 34.124.60.164
transit-to-vpc-a-bgp2	transit-to-vpc-a-tu2	vpc-transit-gw1-use4	1 : 34.104.125.29

SAVE BGP CONFIGURATION   CONFIGURE BGP SESSIONS LATER

③ **Summary and reminder**

Figure 8.52 – Result of BGP peering configuration for HA VPN tunnels

Save the BGP configuration with the appropriate button. Now, let's do it the other way around, from `vpc-a` to `vpc-transit`. From the **VPN** page, return to the **Google VPN gateway details** tab and select **vpc-a-gw1-use4**. *Figure 8.53* shows when you are inside of it:

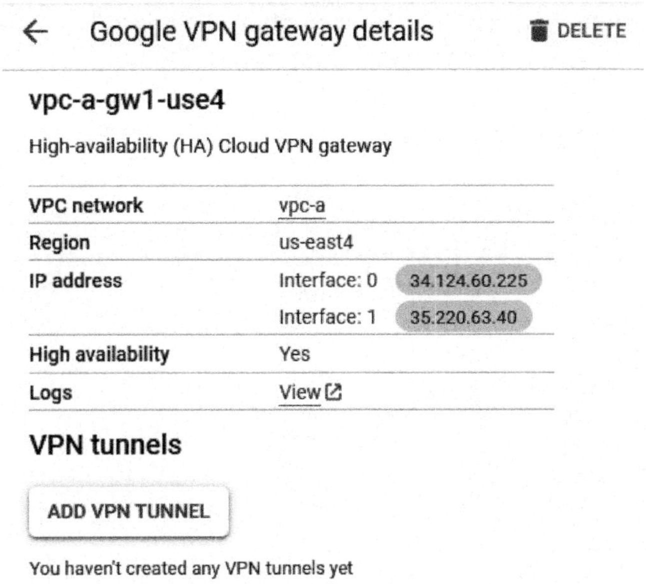

Figure 8.53 – Adding VPN tunnels to the vpc-a-gw1-use4 gateway VPN gateway

Enter in the menu using the **ADD VPN TUNNEL** button. In the first part, select the project ID and the VPN gateway name to connect to. This should be `vpc-transit-gw1-use4`, as shown in *Figure 8.54*:

Figure 8.54 – Adding VPN HA tunnels to the vpc-a-gw1-use4 VPN gateway – part one

Then, select the **Create a pair of VPN tunnels** option and select the `cr-vpc-a-use4-1` **Cloud Router** instance, as *Figure 8.55* shows:

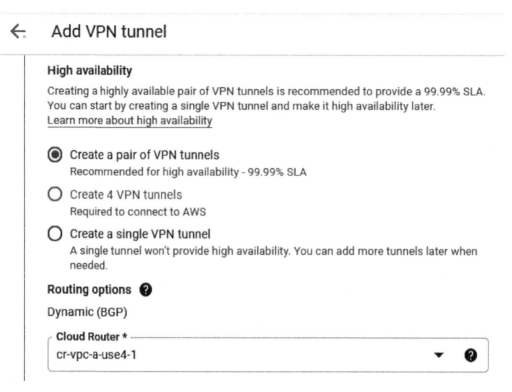

Figure 8.55 – Adding VPN HA tunnels to the vpc-a-gw1-use4 VPN gateway – part two

Then, configure the first HA VPN tunnel with the name `vpc-a-to-transit-tu1`. Use the same IKE pre-shared key that you have set before to successfully establish an IPsec VPN. *Figure 8.56* shows the configuration:

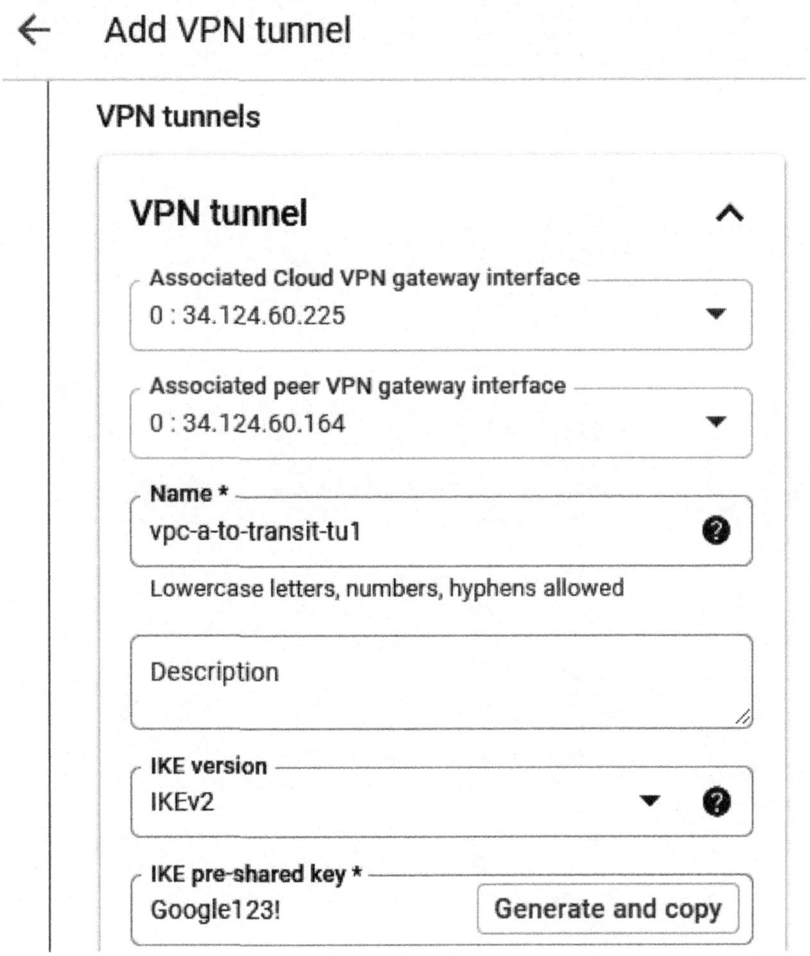

← Add VPN tunnel

VPN tunnels

VPN tunnel ⌃

Associated Cloud VPN gateway interface
0 : 34.124.60.225 ▾

Associated peer VPN gateway interface
0 : 34.124.60.164 ▾

Name *
vpc-a-to-transit-tu1 ❓

Lowercase letters, numbers, hyphens allowed

Description

IKE version
IKEv2 ▾ ❓

IKE pre-shared key *
Google123!   Generate and copy

Figure 8.56 – Adding VPN HA tunnels to the VPN gateway vpc-a-gw1-use4 – part three

Continue with the second VPN HA tunnel, named `vpc-a-to-transit-tu2`. This will follow the first tunnel configuration, which is collapsed in the upper combo box. Use `Google123!` as the IKE pre-shared key, as shown in *Figure 8.57*:

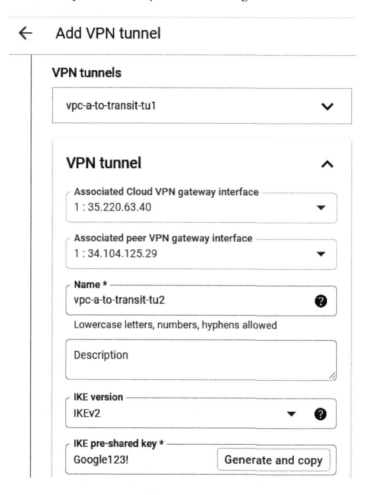

Figure 8.57 – Adding VPN HA tunnels to the VPN gateway vpc-a-gw1-use4 – part four

When you are done, click **Create and Continue**. The result looks like the one in *Figure 8.58*:

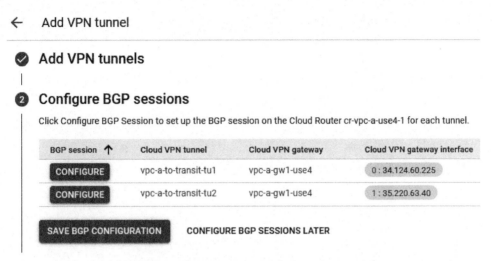

← Add VPN tunnel

✓ **Add VPN tunnels**

② **Configure BGP sessions**

Click Configure BGP Session to set up the BGP session on the Cloud Router cr-vpc-a-use4-1 for each tunnel.

BGP session ↑	Cloud VPN tunnel	Cloud VPN gateway	Cloud VPN gateway interface
CONFIGURE	vpc-a-to-transit-tu1	vpc-a-gw1-use4	0 : 34.124.60.225
CONFIGURE	vpc-a-to-transit-tu2	vpc-a-gw1-use4	1 : 35.220.63.40

SAVE BGP CONFIGURATION   CONFIGURE BGP SESSIONS LATER

Figure 8.58 – HA VPN tunnels configuration result

As you did before, configure BGP sessions for both tunnels. Let's start with `vpc-a-to-transit-bgp1`, using the `vpc-transit` (`65000`) **Peer ASN** and the appropriate reverse peer IP addresses. *Figure 8.59* shows this configuration:

Create BGP session

Name *

vpc-a-to-transit-bgp1   ❓

Lowercase letters, numbers, hyphens allowed

Peer ASN *

65000   ❓

Advertised route priority (MED)   ❓

MED value is used for Active/Passive configuration

Cloud Router BGP IP *   **BGP peer IP ***

169.254.1.2   ❓   169.254.1.1   ❓

BGP peer ❓

◉ Enabled

○ Disabled

⌄ ADVERTISED ROUTES

SAVE AND CONTINUE   CANCEL

Figure 8.59 – BGP session configuration for tunnel one of vpc-a-to-vpc-transit-bgp1

Proceed with the second BGP session, as shown in *Figure 8.60*:

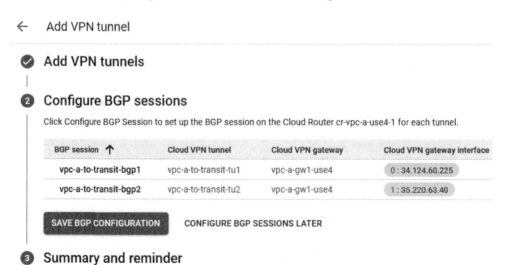

Figure 8.60 – BGP session configuration for tunnel two of vpc-a-to-vpc-transit-bgp2

The result of the BGP configuration looks like the one in *Figure 8.61*:

← Add VPN tunnel

✅ **Add VPN tunnels**

② **Configure BGP sessions**

Click Configure BGP Session to set up the BGP session on the Cloud Router cr-vpc-a-use4-1 for each tunnel.

BGP session ↑	Cloud VPN tunnel	Cloud VPN gateway	Cloud VPN gateway interface
vpc-a-to-transit-bgp1	vpc-a-to-transit-tu1	vpc-a-gw1-use4	0 : 34.124.60.225
vpc-a-to-transit-bgp2	vpc-a-to-transit-tu2	vpc-a-gw1-use4	1 : 35.220.63.40

SAVE BGP CONFIGURATION   CONFIGURE BGP SESSIONS LATER

③ **Summary and reminder**

Figure 8.61 – Result of the BGP configuration of vpc-a to vpc-transit

Save the BGP configuration with the appropriate button. Once you have completed both ends, your **VPN tunnel status** should be **Established**, likewise the **BGP session status**. *Figure 8.62* confirms this:

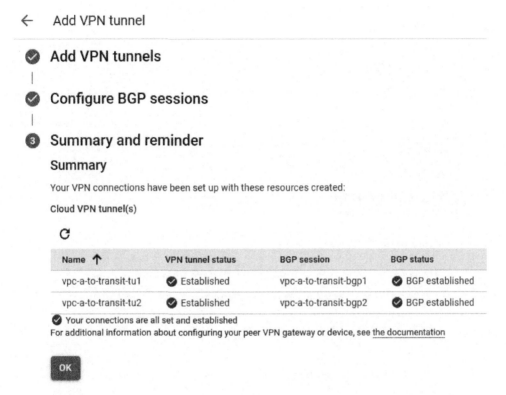

Figure 8.62 – Confirmation of the HA VPN tunnels establishment and BGP sessions

Now that vpc-a is fully connected to vpc-transit via HA VPN tunnels and dynamic routing has been configured via Cloud Routers, you will repeat the same operations for vpc-b. Let's start with the configuration from vpc-transit to vpc-b. Use the data from *Figure 8.63*:

Cloud Router	cr-vpc-transit-usw2-1
Peer VPN gateway name	vpc-b-gw1-usw2
VPN tunnel one	transit-to-vpc-b-tu1
VPN tunnel two	transit-to-vpc-b-tu2
Pre-shared key for both tunnels	Google123!

Figure 8.63 – Peer VPN gateway parameters from vpc-transit to vpc-b

After configuring VPN tunnels, you should have the result shown in *Figure 8.64*:

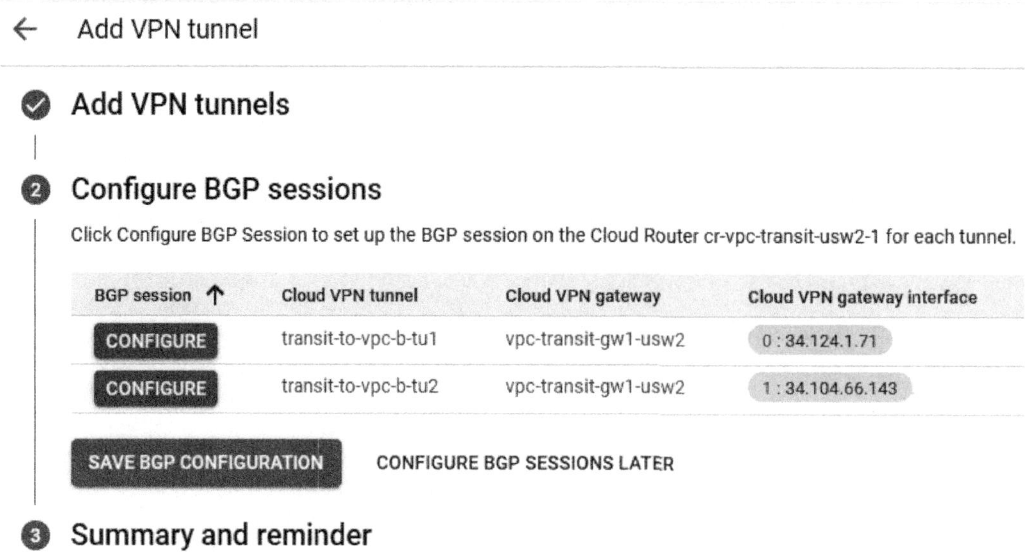

←   Add VPN tunnel

✓ **Add VPN tunnels**

② **Configure BGP sessions**

Click Configure BGP Session to set up the BGP session on the Cloud Router cr-vpc-transit-usw2-1 for each tunnel.

BGP session ↑	Cloud VPN tunnel	Cloud VPN gateway	Cloud VPN gateway interface
CONFIGURE	transit-to-vpc-b-tu1	vpc-transit-gw1-usw2	0 : 34.124.1.71
CONFIGURE	transit-to-vpc-b-tu2	vpc-transit-gw1-usw2	1 : 34.104.66.143

SAVE BGP CONFIGURATION   CONFIGURE BGP SESSIONS LATER

③ **Summary and reminder**

Figure 8.64 – HA VPN tunnels configuration result from transit-vpc to vpc-b

Now, continue with the BGP sessions configuration. Use *Figure 8.65* for this:

BGP session one	`transit-to-vpc-b-bgp1`
Peer ASN	`65002`
Cloud Router BGP IP	`169.254.1.9`
BGP peer IP	`169.254.1.10`
BGP session two	`transit-to-vpc-b-bgp2`
Peer ASN	`65002`
Cloud Router BGP IP	`169.254.1.13`
BGP peer IP	`169.254.1.14`

Figure 8.65 – BGP session 1 and BGP session 2 parameters for the vpc-transit vpc-b direction

At the end of the BGP configuration, the result should look like the one in *Figure 8.66*:

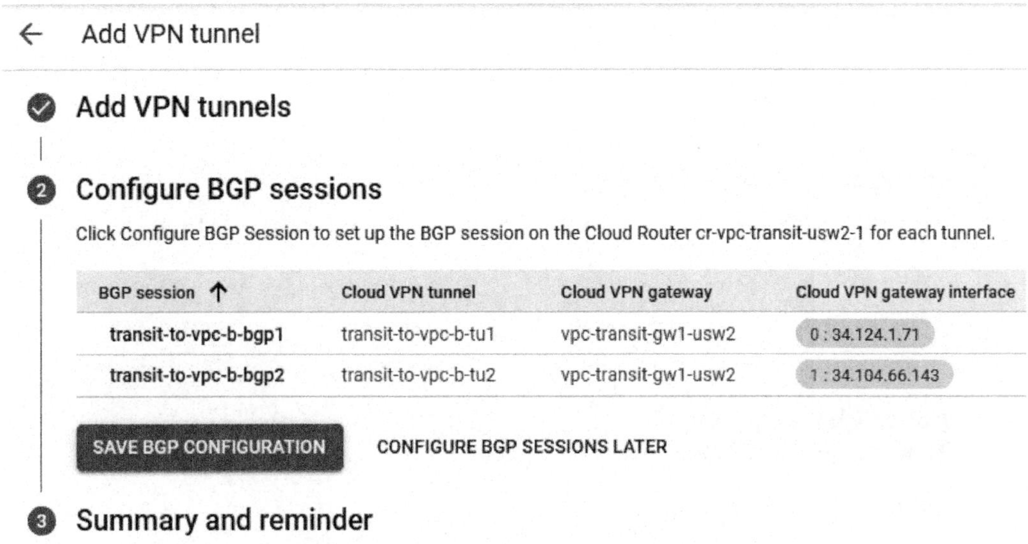

← Add VPN tunnel

✓ **Add VPN tunnels**

② **Configure BGP sessions**

Click Configure BGP Session to set up the BGP session on the Cloud Router cr-vpc-transit-usw2-1 for each tunnel.

BGP session ↑	Cloud VPN tunnel	Cloud VPN gateway	Cloud VPN gateway interface
transit-to-vpc-b-bgp1	transit-to-vpc-b-tu1	vpc-transit-gw1-usw2	0 : 34.124.1.71
transit-to-vpc-b-bgp2	transit-to-vpc-b-tu2	vpc-transit-gw1-usw2	1 : 34.104.66.143

[SAVE BGP CONFIGURATION]   CONFIGURE BGP SESSIONS LATER

③ **Summary and reminder**

Figure 8.66 – BGP session configuration result from vpc-transit to vpc-b

Save the BGP configuration with the appropriate button. Now that you have configured from `vpc-transit` to `vpc-b`, let's configure the other way round, as shown in *Figure 8.67*:

Cloud Router	`cr-vpc-b-usw2-1`
Peer VPN gateway name	`vpc-transit-gw1-usw2`
VPN tunnel one	`vpc-b-to-transit-tu1`
VPN tunnel two	`vpc-b-to-transit-tu2`
Pre-shared key for both tunnels	`Google123!`

Figure 8.67 – Peer VPN gateway parameters from vpc-b to vpc-transit

When the configuration is done, the result will look like *Figure 8.68*:

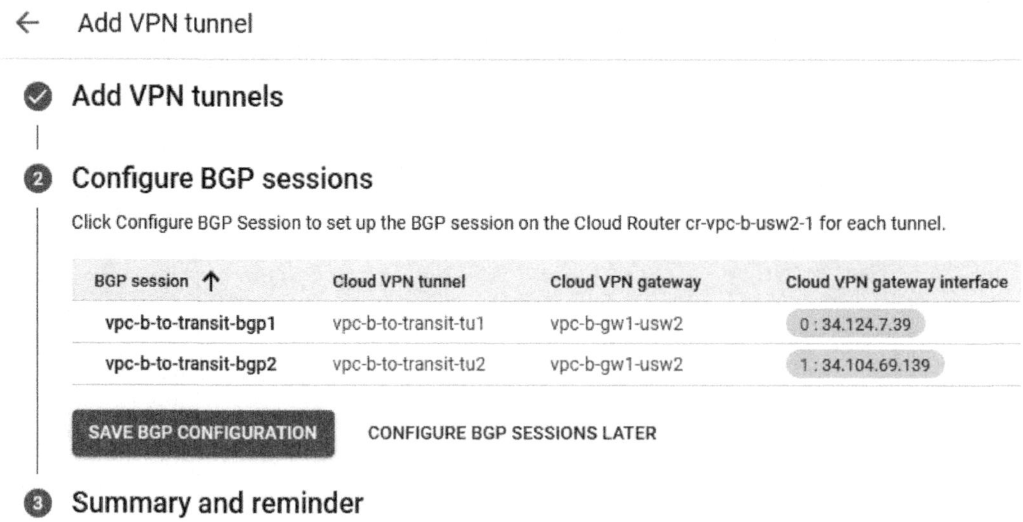

←   Add VPN tunnel

✓ **Add VPN tunnels**

② **Configure BGP sessions**

Click Configure BGP Session to set up the BGP session on the Cloud Router cr-vpc-b-usw2-1 for each tunnel.

BGP session ↑	Cloud VPN tunnel	Cloud VPN gateway	Cloud VPN gateway interface
vpc-b-to-transit-bgp1	vpc-b-to-transit-tu1	vpc-b-gw1-usw2	0 : 34.124.7.39
vpc-b-to-transit-bgp2	vpc-b-to-transit-tu2	vpc-b-gw1-usw2	1 : 34.104.69.139

[SAVE BGP CONFIGURATION]   CONFIGURE BGP SESSIONS LATER

③ **Summary and reminder**

Figure 8.68 – HA VPN tunnels configuration from vpc-b to vpc-transit

Then, proceed with the BGP configuration. Use the values in *Figure 8.69*:

BGP session one	vpc-b-to-transit-bgp1
Peer ASN	65000
Cloud Router BGP IP	169.254.1.10
BGP peer IP	169.254.1.9
BGP session two	vpc-b-to-transit-bgp2
Peer ASN	65000
Cloud Router BGP IP	169.254.1.14
BGP peer IP	169.254.1.13

Figure 8.69 – BGP session one and BGP session two parameters for the vpc-b vpc-transit direction

The result of the BGP configuration will look like *Figure 8.70*:

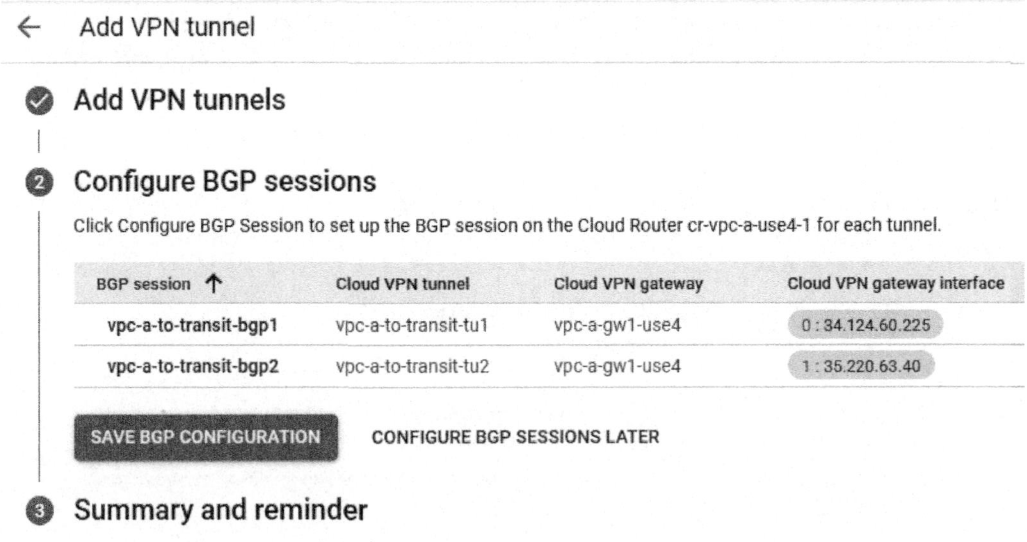

←   Add VPN tunnel

✓ **Add VPN tunnels**

② **Configure BGP sessions**

Click Configure BGP Session to set up the BGP session on the Cloud Router cr-vpc-a-use4-1 for each tunnel.

BGP session ↑	Cloud VPN tunnel	Cloud VPN gateway	Cloud VPN gateway interface
vpc-a-to-transit-bgp1	vpc-a-to-transit-tu1	vpc-a-gw1-use4	0 : 34.124.60.225
vpc-a-to-transit-bgp2	vpc-a-to-transit-tu2	vpc-a-gw1-use4	1 : 35.220.63.40

SAVE BGP CONFIGURATION   CONFIGURE BGP SESSIONS LATER

③ **Summary and reminder**

Figure 8.70 – BGP sessions configuration from vpc-b to vpc-transit

Save the BGP configuration with the appropriate button. At this point, you have completed the full connectivity. Navigate to the **VPN** page, select the **CLOUD VPN TUNNELS** tab, and confirm that both **VPN tunnel status** and **BGP session status** show established on the right, as shown in *Figure 8.71*:

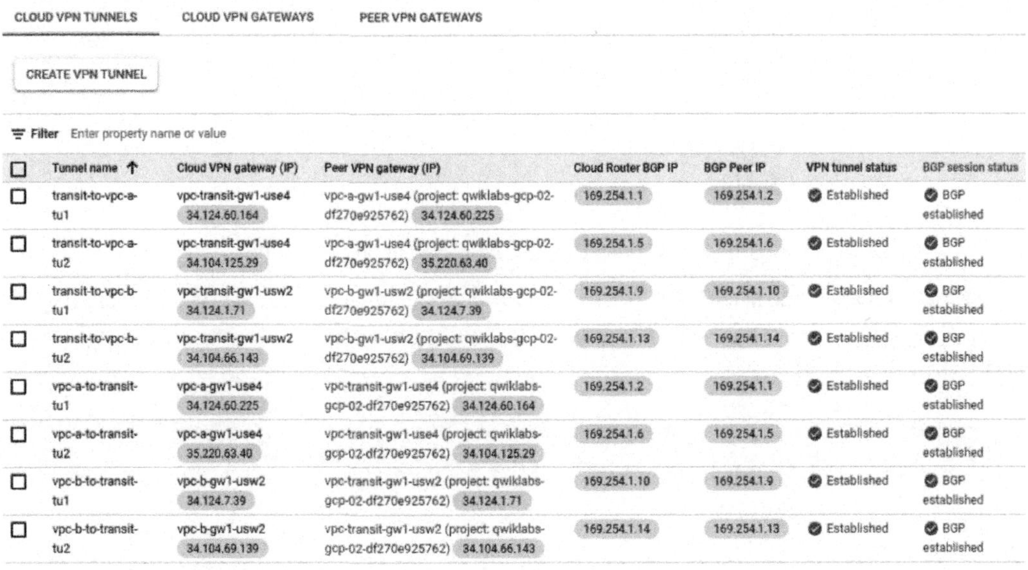

CLOUD VPN TUNNELS   CLOUD VPN GATEWAYS   PEER VPN GATEWAYS

CREATE VPN TUNNEL

Filter   Enter property name or value

Tunnel name ↑	Cloud VPN gateway (IP)	Peer VPN gateway (IP)	Cloud Router BGP IP	BGP Peer IP	VPN tunnel status	BGP session status
transit-to-vpc-a-tu1	vpc-transit-gw1-use4 34.124.60.164	vpc-a-gw1-use4 (project: qwiklabs-gcp-02-df270e925762) 34.124.60.225	169.254.1.1	169.254.1.2	✓ Established	✓ BGP established
transit-to-vpc-a-tu2	vpc-transit-gw1-use4 34.104.125.29	vpc-a-gw1-use4 (project: qwiklabs-gcp-02-df270e925762) 35.220.63.40	169.254.1.5	169.254.1.6	✓ Established	✓ BGP established
transit-to-vpc-b-tu1	vpc-transit-gw1-usw2 34.124.1.71	vpc-b-gw1-usw2 (project: qwiklabs-gcp-02-df270e925762) 34.124.7.39	169.254.1.9	169.254.1.10	✓ Established	✓ BGP established
transit-to-vpc-b-tu2	vpc-transit-gw1-usw2 34.104.66.143	vpc-b-gw1-usw2 (project: qwiklabs-gcp-02-df270e925762) 34.104.69.139	169.254.1.13	169.254.1.14	✓ Established	✓ BGP established
vpc-a-to-transit-tu1	vpc-a-gw1-use4 34.124.60.225	vpc-transit-gw1-use4 (project: qwiklabs-gcp-02-df270e925762) 34.124.60.164	169.254.1.2	169.254.1.1	✓ Established	✓ BGP established
vpc-a-to-transit-tu2	vpc-a-gw1-use4 35.220.63.40	vpc-transit-gw1-use4 (project: qwiklabs-gcp-02-df270e925762) 34.104.125.29	169.254.1.6	169.254.1.5	✓ Established	✓ BGP established
vpc-b-to-transit-tu1	vpc-b-gw1-usw2 34.124.7.39	vpc-transit-gw1-usw2 (project: qwiklabs-gcp-02-df270e925762) 34.124.1.71	169.254.1.10	169.254.1.9	✓ Established	✓ BGP established
vpc-b-to-transit-tu2	vpc-b-gw1-usw2 34.104.69.139	vpc-transit-gw1-usw2 (project: qwiklabs-gcp-02-df270e925762) 34.104.66.143	169.254.1.14	169.254.1.13	✓ Established	✓ BGP established

Figure 8.71 – Full connectivity between vpc-transit and vpc-a, and between vpc-transit and vpc-b

At this point, you are ready to start deploying Network Connectivity Center. First, you need to enable **Network Connectivity API**, which can be found in **API Library**. From the **Navigation** menu, go to **API & Services**, then **API Library**, and search for `network connectivity api`, as shown in *Figure 8.72*:

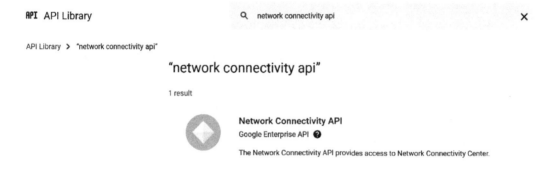

Figure 8.72 – Searching for the Network Connectivity API in the API library

Once you find it, click on it and enable it with the appropriate button, as shown in *Figure 8.73*:

Network Connectivity API

Google Enterprise API

The Network Connectivity API provides access to Network Connectivity Center.

ENABLE   TRY THIS API ↗

Figure 8.73 – Enabling the Network Connectivity API

When the **Network Connectivity API** is enabled, you can proceed with the hub creation. Open the Cloud Shell and create the Network Connectivity Center hub with the following command:

```
gcloud alpha network-connectivity hubs create transit-hub \
    --description=Transit_hub
```

This command lets you create a hub named `transit-hub` and optionally assign a description to it with the `--description` option. At the time of writing the book, Network Connectivity Center SDK is in alpha. That's why you need to specify `alpha` in the command. The command will be **Generally Available (GA)** in a while and, at this time, we can remove `alpha` from the command. The output of the command should look as follows:

```
Create request issued for: [transit-hub]
Waiting for operation [projects/<PROJECT_ID>/locations/global/
operations/ <OPERATION_ID>] to complete...working
.
Waiting for operation [projects/ <PROJECT_ID>/locations/global/
operations/<OPERATION_ID>] to complete...done.
Created hub [transit-hub].
```

The `PROJECT_ID` and `OPERATION_ID` values depend on your project and operation. A successful message (`Created hub [transit-hub]`) should be printed out on the Cloud Shell prompt. `transit-hub` is the name of the hub we used in the command.

Next, you will need to create two spokes for each branch you are trying to connect via the hub. Let's start with `Spoke1 (bo1)`, using the following command:

```
gcloud alpha network-connectivity spokes create bo1 \
>       --hub=transit-hub \
>       --description="Branch Office 1" \
>       --vpn-tunnel=transit-to-vpc-a-tu1,transit-to-vpc-a-tu2\
>       --region=us-east4
```

`bo1` stands for branch `Office 1`.

As you notice, you are passing four parameters:

- `--hub`: This is the name of the hub where the spoke will be attached.

- `--description`: This is an optional parameter.

- `--vpn-tunnel`: This is the list of established HA VPN tunnels interconnecting `vpc-transit` and `vpc-a`.

- `--region`: This is the GCP region where these tunnels reside.

During command execution, you should get the following output:

```
Create request issued for: [bo1]
Waiting for operation [projects/qwiklabs-gcp-03-d514fc7a2d34/
locations/us-east4/operations/operation-1631713840958-
5cc08fbdd8d0d-5ca6e06b-62cf1818] to complete...working...
Waiting for operation [projects/qwiklabs-gcp-03-d514fc7a2d34/
locations/us-east4/operations/operation-1631713840958-
5cc08fbdd8d0d-5ca6e06b-62cf1818] to complete...done.

Created spoke [bo1].
```

A successful message (`Created spoke [bo1]`) should be displayed on the Cloud Shell terminal.

You repeat the same for `Spoke2` (bo2) with the following command:

```
gcloud alpha network-connectivity spokes create bo2 \
>      --hub=transit-hub \
>      --description=Branch Office 2 \
>      --vpn-tunnel=transit-to-vpc-b-tu1,transit-to-vpc-b-tu2 \
>      --region=us-west2
```

Note that the parameters have changed, according to the topology we showed in the exercise. You should get the following output:

```
Create request issued for: [bo2]
Waiting for operation [projects/qwiklabs-gcp-03-d514fc7a2d34/
locations/us-west2/operations/operation-1631713884277-
5cc08fe7289f1-b3ba806c-97996d00] to complete...working
Waiting for operation [projects/qwiklabs-gcp-03-d514fc7a2d34/
locations/us-west2/operations/operation-1631713884277-
5cc08fe7289f1-b3ba806c-97996d00] to complete...done.

Created spoke [bo2].
```

A successful message (`Created spoke [bo2]`) should be displayed on the Cloud Shell terminal.

You can confirm from the GCP console by navigating from the **Navigation** menu to **Hybrid Connectivity**, and then select **Network Connectivity Center**, as shown in *Figure 8.74*:

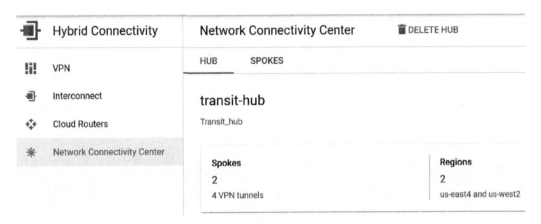

Figure 8.74 – Successful configuration of the transit-hub hub

As *Figure 8.74* shows, the **Network Connectivity Center** transit-hub hub has been created with two spokes with four VPN tunnels. They are in two regions, us-east4 and us-west2. You can check the **Spokes** tab to see more details about spokes, as *Figure 8.75* shows:

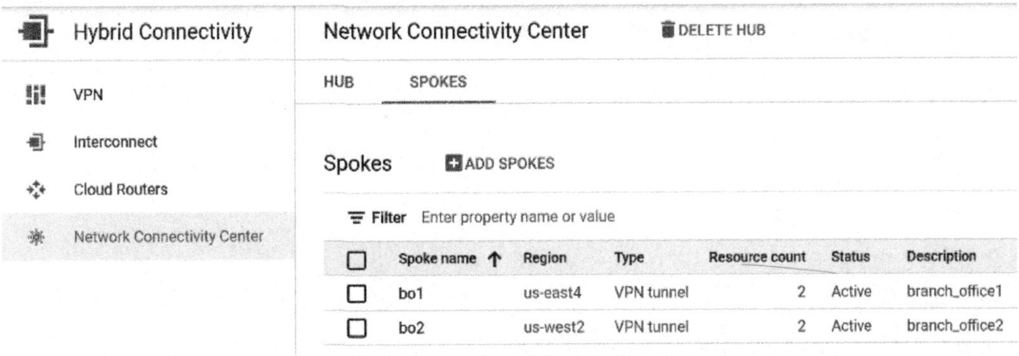

Spoke name ↑	Region	Type	Resource count	Status	Description
bo1	us-east4	VPN tunnel	2	Active	branch_office1
bo2	us-west2	VPN tunnel	2	Active	branch_office2

Figure 8.75 – Successful spokes configuration in Network Connectivity Center

As *Figure 8.75* shows, the two spokes (`bo1` and `bo2`) appear as **Active.** You can check the details by clicking on each spoke name, as *Figure 8.76* shows:

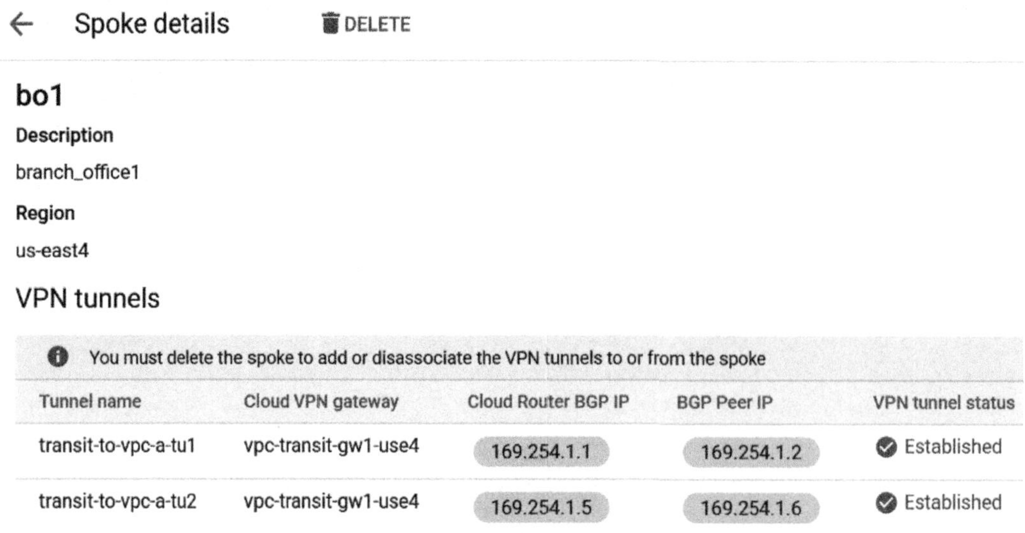

←   Spoke details   🗑 DELETE

bo1

Description

branch_office1

Region

us-east4

VPN tunnels

ⓘ   You must delete the spoke to add or disassociate the VPN tunnels to or from the spoke

Tunnel name	Cloud VPN gateway	Cloud Router BGP IP	BGP Peer IP	VPN tunnel status
transit-to-vpc-a-tu1	vpc-transit-gw1-use4	169.254.1.1	169.254.1.2	✔ Established
transit-to-vpc-a-tu2	vpc-transit-gw1-use4	169.254.1.5	169.254.1.6	✔ Established

Figure 8.76 – The details of the bo1 spoke

As *Figure 8.76* shows, the `bo1` spoke has VPN tunnels established correctly. `bo2` appears the same, as *Figure 8.77* shows:

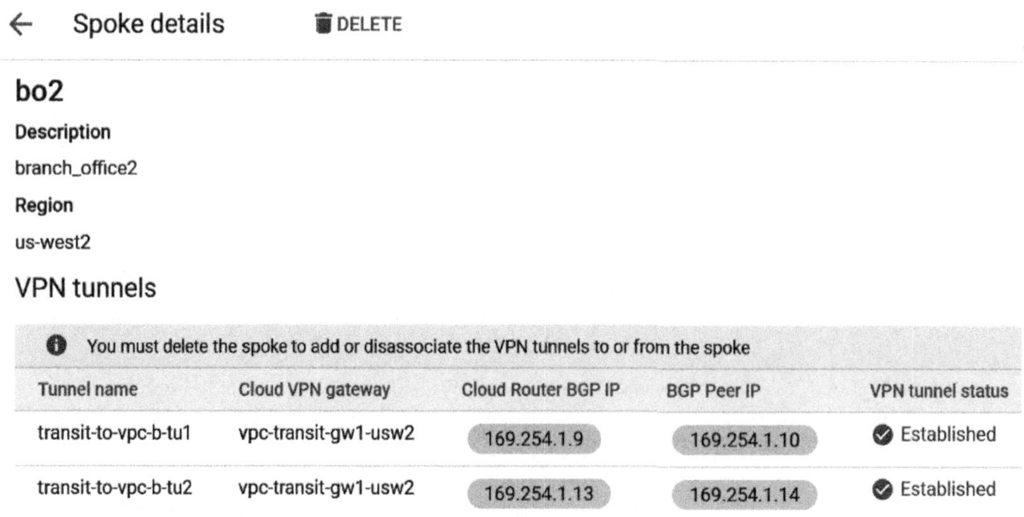

←   Spoke details   🗑 DELETE

bo2

Description

branch_office2

Region

us-west2

VPN tunnels

ⓘ   You must delete the spoke to add or disassociate the VPN tunnels to or from the spoke

Tunnel name	Cloud VPN gateway	Cloud Router BGP IP	BGP Peer IP	VPN tunnel status
transit-to-vpc-b-tu1	vpc-transit-gw1-usw2	169.254.1.9	169.254.1.10	✔ Established
transit-to-vpc-b-tu2	vpc-transit-gw1-usw2	169.254.1.13	169.254.1.14	✔ Established

Figure 8.77 – The details of the bo2 spoke

Now, let's test the connectivity between vpc-a and vpc-b. To do so, you can deploy two Compute Engine instances on both VPCs. At this point of the book, you should know how to do it and you should get the result shown in *Figure 8.78*:

	Status	Name ↑	Zone	Internal IP	External IP	Connect	
☐	✓	vpc-a-vm-1	us-east4-c	10.20.10.2 (nic0)	34.86.174.103	SSH ▾	⋮
☐	✓	vpc-b-vm-1	us-west2-a	10.20.20.2 (nic0)	34.94.146.191	SSH ▾	⋮

Figure 8.78 – Configuration of Compute Engine instances in the vpc-a and vpc-b VPCs

Don't forget to configure the firewall rules, as instructed in *Figure 8.79*:

☰ **Filter**   Enter property name or value

	Name	Type	Targets	Filters	Protocols / ports	Action	Network ↑
☐	allow-ssh-icmp-vpn-a	Ingress	Apply to all	IP ranges: 0.0.0.0/0	tcp:22 icmp	Allow	vpc-a
☐	allow-ssh-icmp-vpn-b	Ingress	Apply to all	IP ranges: 0.0.0.0/0	tcp:22 icmp	Allow	vpc-b

Figure 8.79 – Inbound firewall rules for ICMP and SSH traffic for both VPCs

Great! You have reached the final step of testing connectivity between Compute Engine instances using Network Connectivity Center. Return to **Compute Engine**, then **VM instances**, and take a note of the private IP address of vpc-b-vm-1 (10.20.20.2). Connect to vpc-a-vm-1 using the ssh button and test reachability with a ping, as instructed in *Figure 8.80*:

```
student-02-3e33c8e41884@vpc-a-vm-1:~$ ping 10.20.20.2
PING 10.20.20.2 (10.20.20.2) 56(84) bytes of data.
64 bytes from 10.20.20.2: icmp_seq=1 ttl=60 time=70.9 ms
64 bytes from 10.20.20.2: icmp_seq=2 ttl=60 time=67.6 ms
64 bytes from 10.20.20.2: icmp_seq=3 ttl=60 time=67.3 ms
64 bytes from 10.20.20.2: icmp_seq=4 ttl=60 time=67.3 ms
64 bytes from 10.20.20.2: icmp_seq=5 ttl=60 time=67.5 ms
^C
--- 10.20.20.2 ping statistics ---
5 packets transmitted, 5 received, 0% packet loss, time 10ms
rtt min/avg/max/mdev = 67.287/68.114/70.850/1.410 ms
student-02-3e33c8e41884@vpc-a-vm-1:~$ 
```

Figure 8.80 – Testing connectivity between the vpc-a-vm-1 and vpc-b-vm-1 Compute Engine instances

As *Figure 8.80* shows, vpc-a-vm-1 can reach vpc-b-vm-1, confirming that the Network Connectivity Center configuration is correct. We can now say that we have implemented a hub and spoke network between two VPCs in Google Cloud.

Summary

In this chapter, you have learned how to build reliable service mesh networks across multi-cloud environments with Traffic Director. You have also learned how to facilitate service discovery using Google Cloud's Service Directory. Finally, you have learned and built hub and spoke networks with Network Connectivity Center.

This is the end of the book, and you should be familiar with all the Google Cloud networking topics that a professional certification requires.

9
Professional Cloud Network Engineer Certification Preparation

This chapter will be a useful tool for those who are seeking the *Professional Cloud Network Engineer certification*. Fifty questions have been provided to you in order to test your knowledge before taking the exam:

1. Your customers are close to the `us-east1` and `europe-west1` data centers. Their workloads must communicate with one another. You want to cut costs while improving network efficiency.

   What is the best way to create this topology?

   A. Create two **Virtual Private Clouds (VPCs)**, each with its own region and subnets. To connect these two areas, you'll need to set up two **Virtual Private Network (VPN)** gateways.

B. Create two virtual private clouds, each with its own region and subnets. To establish communication across these areas, use external IP addresses on the instances.

C. Create a VPN with two regional subnets. To establish connectivity across the regions, create a global load balancer.

D. Create a VPN with two regional subnets. Workloads should be deployed in these subnets and communicated using private RFC1918 IP addresses.

Answer: D

2. Your company is working on a single project for three different departments. Two of these departments require network connectivity to work together, while the third should be kept separate. Separate network administrative domains should be created between these departments as part of your design. You want to keep your operational costs as low as possible.

What is the best way to create the topology?

A. For each of the three departments, create a Shared VPC host project and the corresponding service projects.

B. Create three independent VPCs and utilize Cloud VPN to connect the two most relevant VPCs.

C. Create three separate VPCs, and then utilize VPC peering to connect the two relevant VPCs.

D. Make a single project and apply firewall rules to it. Isolate access between departments by using network tags.

Answer: C

3. You want to import your BIND zone file into Cloud DNS as part of your migration.

Which command do you need to use?

A. gcloud dns record-sets import ZONE_FILE --zone MANAGED_ZONE

B. gcloud dns record-sets import ZONE_FILE --replace-origin-ns --zone MANAGED_ZONE

    C. gcloud dns record-sets import ZONE_FILE --zone-file-
       format --zone MANAGED_ZONE

    D. gcloud dns record-sets import ZONE_FILE --delete-all-
       existing --zone MANAGED ZONE

Answer: C

4. In auto mode, you create a VPC network named *Retail*. You wish to construct
a distribution VPC network and peer it with the Retail VPC.

What is the best way to set up the distribution VPC?

A. Create the distribution VPC in auto mode. Network peering is used to connect
both VPCs.

B. In custom mode, create the distribution VPC. Use the 10.0.0.0/9 CIDR range.
Create the relevant subnets and then use network peering to connect them.

C. In custom mode, create the distribution VPC. Use the CIDR range 10.128.0.0/9
as a starting point. Create the relevant subnets and then use network peering to
connect them.

D. Rename the default VPC to *Distribution* and network-peer with it.

Answer: B

5. You're inspecting traffic with a third-party next-generation firewall. To route egress
traffic to the firewall, you defined a custom route of 0.0.0.0/0. You wish to
use the **BigQuery** and Cloud Pub/Sub APIs without having to go via the firewall
because your VPC instances don't have public IP addresses.

Which of the following two acts should you take (select two)?

A. At the subnet level, enable Private Google Access.

B. At the VPC level, enable Private Google Access.

C. At the VPC level, enable private services access.

D. Using the default internet gateway, create a set of custom static routes to
transport traffic to the external IP addresses of Google APIs and services.

E. Using the default internet gateway, create a series of custom static routes to send
traffic to the internal IP addresses of Google APIs and services.

Answer: A and D

6. The custom metadata `enable-oslogin` value is set to `FALSE` on all instances in your project, and project-wide SSH keys are blocked. No SSH keys have been configured for any of the instances, and no project-wide SSH keys have been configured. SSH sessions from any IP address range are allowed thanks to firewall rules. You want to connect to a single instance through SSH.

    So, what are your options?

    A. Using `gcloud`, compute `ssh`, open Cloud Shell, and SSH into the instance.

    B. Use a third-party tool such as `putty` or `ssh` to SSH into the instance and set the custom metadata `enable-oslogin` to `TRUE`.

    C. Make a fresh pair of SSH keys. Verify the private key's format before adding it to the instance. Using a third-party tool such as putty or `ssh`, SSH into the instance.

    D. Make a fresh pair of SSH keys. Verify the public key's format before adding it to the project. Using a third-party tool such as putty or `ssh`, SSH into the instance.

Answer: A

7. You're employed by a university that is transitioning to GCP.

    The following are the cloud prerequisites:

    • 10 Gbps on-premises connectivity

    • Lowest latency cloud access

    • Centralized networking administration team

    New departments are requesting that their projects be connected on-premises. You wish to link the campus to Google Cloud using the most cost-effective interconnect method possible.

    So, what are your options?

    A. Deploy the VLAN attachments and Interconnect in the host project using Shared VPC.

    B. Deploy VLAN attachments in service projects using Shared VPC. Connect the VLAN attachment to the host project of the Shared VPC.

    C. Create standalone projects and deploy VLAN attachments in each of them. Connect the VLAN attachment to the Interconnects of the standalone projects.

    D. Use independent projects and deploy VLAN attachments and Interconnects in each project separately.

Answer: A

8. You've launched a new internal application that provides on-premises hosts with HTTP and TFTP services. You want to be able to disperse traffic across several Compute Engine instances, but you also want to keep clients tied to one instance across both services.

    Which session affinity do you want to go with?

    A. None

    B. Client IP

    C. Client IP and protocol

    D. Client IP, port, and protocol

Answer: B

9. With a single subnet, you constructed a new VPC network named *Dev*. You enabled logging and added a firewall rule for the Dev network to allow only HTTP traffic.

    When you use Remote Desktop Protocol to log in to a subnet instance, the login fails. In Stackdriver Logging, you look for the Firewall Rules logs, but there are no entries for stopped traffic. You wish to look at the logs for traffic that has been blocked.

    So, what are your options?

    A. Examine the instance's VPC flow logs.

    B. Check the logs after connecting to the instance through SSH.

    C. Enable logs and create a new firewall rule to accept traffic from port 22.

    D. Create a new firewall rule with the priority of 65500 to block all traffic and logs.

Answer: D

10. You're attempting to make changes to firewall rules in a shared VPC for which you have only Network Admin capabilities. The firewall rules cannot be changed.

    Your organization necessitates the use of the bare minimum of privileges.

    Which level of access should you ask for?

    A. Security Admin privileges from the Shared VPC Admin

    B. Service Project Admin privileges from the Shared VPC Admin

    C. Shared VPC Admin privileges from the Organization Admin

    D. Organization Admin privileges from the Organization Admin

Answer: A

11. You wish to use IPv6 to construct a global service in GCP.

    So, what are your options?

    A. Create an instance with the IPv6 address you want.

    B. Set up a TCP proxy with the IPv6 address you want to use.

    C. Set up a global load balancer with the IPv6 address you specified.

    D. Assign the chosen IPv6 address to an internal load balancer.

Answer: C

12. You want to connect your on-premises network to GCP using a VPN gateway. You're using an on-premises VPN device that doesn't support **Border Gateway Protocol (BGP)**. When your network expands, you want to keep downtime and operational expenses to a minimum. You want to use Google-recommended practices because the device only supports IKEv2.

    So, what are your options?

    A. Create a Cloud VPN instance. Create a policy-based VPN tunnel per subnet. Configure the appropriate local and remote traffic selectors to match your local and remote networks. Create the appropriate static routes.

    B. Create a Cloud VPN instance. Create a policy-based VPN tunnel. Configure the appropriate local and remote traffic selectors to match your local and remote networks. Configure the appropriate static routes.

    C. Create a Cloud VPN instance. Create a route-based VPN tunnel. Configure the appropriate local and remote traffic selectors to match your local and remote networks. Configure the appropriate static routes.

    D. Create a Cloud VPN instance. Create a route-based VPN tunnel. Configure the appropriate local and remote traffic selectors to 0.0.0.0/0. Configure the appropriate static routes.

Answer: D

13. Your firm recently finalized the purchase of Altostrat (a current GCP customer). In GCP, each enterprise has its own organization and has built its own DNS solution. Until a comprehensive transition and architectural assessment are completed in one year, each organization will keep its present domain and hostname.

    For both GCP environments, these are the assumptions:

    With the exception of bastion hosts (for accessing the instances) and load balancers for serving web traffic, both organizations strictly use the 10.0.0.0/8 address space for their instances.

There are no prefix overlaps between the two organizations.

Both organizations already have firewall rules that allow all inbound and outbound traffic from the 10.0.0.0/8 address space. Interconnects are not present in either organization's on-premises infrastructure.

You want to integrate both firms' networking and DNS infrastructure as rapidly as feasible and with as little downtime as possible.

Which of the following steps should you take (select two)?

A. Set up a Cloud Interconnect to connect the two businesses.

B. In each organization, set up some form of DNS forwarding and zone transfers.

C. Use Cloud VPN and Cloud Router to connect VPCs in both organizations.

D. Create a record for all VMs and resources across all projects in both businesses using Cloud DNS.

E. Create a third organization with a new host project and use Shared VPC to connect all of your company's and Altostrat's projects to it.

Answer: B and C

14. Your on-premises data center contains two routers, each of which is connected to your Google Cloud environment via a VPN. All applications are operational; however, all traffic is routed through a single VPN rather than being load-balanced over the two connections as intended.

During the troubleshooting process, you discover the following:

- Each on-premises router is assigned a distinct ASN.

- The same routes and priority are configured on each on-premises router.

- Both on-premises routers are connected to a single Cloud Router using a VPN.

- Between on-premises routers and the Cloud Router, BGP sessions are formed.

What's the most likely reason for this issue?

A. The routes on the on-premises routers are identical.

B. A firewall is preventing traffic from passing through the second VPN connection.

C. You don't have a load balancer to distribute network traffic evenly.

D. The ASNs used by the on-premises routers are not the same.

Answer: D

15. You've bought Dedicated Interconnect in the GCP Console, and you'll need to give your cross-connect provider the **Letter of Authorization/Connecting Facility Assignment (LOA-CFA)** to make the physical connection.

    Which two activities are capable of doing this (select two).

    A. Create a Cloud Interconnect ticket in the Cloud Support category.

    B. Go to the GCP Console's Hybrid Connectivity area and download the LOA-CFA.

    C. Define `gcloud compute interconnects` with `gcloud compute interconnects`.

    D. Look for the account of the NOC contact you specified throughout the purchase process in your email.

    E. Inform your cross-connect provider that Google sent the LOA-CFA to them through email and that the connection should be completed.

Answer: B and D

16. Your business provides a well-liked gaming service. External access is allowed through a global load balancer, and your instances are deployed with private IP addresses. You think you've found a potential malicious actor, but you're not sure you've got the right client IP address. You want to track down this bad guy while causing the least amount of inconvenience to your legitimate users.

    So, what are your options?

    A. Create a Cloud Armor policy rule that rejects traffic and examines all relevant logs.

    B. Create a Cloud Armor policy rule that blocks traffic, enables preview mode, and analyzes relevant logs.

    C. Create a VPC firewall rule that blocks traffic, enables logging, and disables enforcement, and then inspect the appropriate logs.

    D. Create a VPC firewall rule that blocks traffic, enables logging, and activates enforcement, and then check the relevant logs.

Answer: B

17. Your company's web server administrator is transferring an application's on-premises backend servers to GCP. These backend servers have vastly different libraries and configurations. The migration to GCP will be lift-and-shift, with a single network load balancer frontend serving all requests to the servers.

    When possible, you should employ a GCP-native solution.

    What is the best way to launch this service in GCP?

    A. Create a managed instance group from one of the on-premises server images, and then connect it to a target pool behind your load balancer.

    B. Create a target pool, populate it with all backend instances, and deploy the target pool behind your load balancer.

    C. As a frontend to these servers, deploy a third-party virtual appliance that can accommodate the considerable variances between these backend servers.

    D. Install several equal-priority static routes to the backend servers using GCP's ECMP functionality to load-balance traffic to the backend servers.

Answer: B

18. You make the decision to use Cloud NAT. You discover that one of your instances is not using Cloud NAT for outbound NAT after completing the settings.

    What's the most likely reason for this issue?

    A. Multiple interfaces have been configured on the instance.

    B. The instance has been configured with an external IP address.

    C. You've used RFC1918 ranges to create static routes.

    D. A load balancer external IP address is used to access the instance.

Answer: B

19. You wish to configure two Cloud Routers, one with an active BGP session and the other as a backup.

    On your on-premises router, which BGP attribute should you use?

    A. AS path

    B. Community

    C. Local preference

    D. MED

Answer: D

20. You want to accommodate more traffic than a single tunnel can handle as your Cloud VPN usage between on-premises and GCP grows. You wish to use Cloud VPN to improve your available bandwidth.

So, what are your options?

A. Increase your on-premises VPN gateway's MTU from 1,460 to 2,920 bytes.

B. On the same Cloud VPN gateway, create two VPN tunnels that point to the same destination VPN gateway IP address.

C. Create a second VPN gateway on-premises with a separate public IP address. Create a second tunnel on the old Cloud VPN gateway that forwards the same IP range as the first but links to the new on-premises gateway IP address.

D. Create a second Cloud VPN gateway in a different region from the first. Create a new tunnel on the second Cloud VPN gateway that forwards the same IP range as the first but points to the IP address of the existing on-premises VPN gateway.

Answer: C

21. You have a Compute Engine VM instance with an application that can't communicate with a resource outside of its subnet. When you look through the flow and firewall logs, you won't find any disallowed traffic:

- Flow logs are enabled for the VPC subnet, and all firewall rules are set to log, you discover during troubleshooting.

- The subnetwork logs are not excluded from Stackdriver.

- The instance that is hosting the application can communicate outside the subnet.

- Other instances within the subnet can communicate outside the subnet. Communication is started by an external resource.

What's the most likely reason for the log lines that aren't showing up?

A. The traffic is matching the expected ingress rule.

B. The traffic is matching the expected egress rule.

C. The traffic is not matching the expected ingress rule.

D. The traffic is not matching the expected egress rule.

Answer: C

22. As the origin for cacheable material, you've set Cloud CDN to use HTTP(S) load balancing. The web servers are configured for compression, but Cloud CDN answers are not compressed.

What's the most likely reason for the issue?

A. In Cloud CDN, you haven't enabled compression.

B. You've set up several compression types on the web servers and Cloud CDN.

C. Different compression types are specified on the web servers behind the load balancer.

D. Even if the request has a `Via` header, you must configure the web servers to compress answers.

Answer: D

```
https://cloud.google.com/cdn/docs/troubleshooting-
steps#compression-not-working
```

23. You currently have a web application hosted in the `us-central1` area. When traveling in Asia, users face severe latency. You've set up a network load balancer, but users haven't noticed a difference in performance. You wish to shorten the time between events.

So, what are your options?

A. To prioritize traffic, create a policy-based routing rule.

B. Set up an HTTP(S) load balancer and route traffic via it.

C. Configure dynamic routing for the application's subnet.

D. Reduce the duration between updates by setting the TTL for the DNS zone.

Answer: B

24. You have a Compute Engine application that uses BigQuery to generate some results, which are then saved to Cloud Storage. You must make certain that none of the application instances have an external IP address.

How do you think you'll be able to accomplish this (select two)?

A. On all subnets, enable Private Google Access.

B. On the VPC, enable Private Google Access.

C. On the VPC, enable private services access.

D. Connect your VPC to BigQuery via network peering.

E. Set up Cloud NAT and route application traffic through it.

Answers: A and E

25. You are designing a Shared VPC architecture. Which paths are exposed across departments is strictly controlled by your network and security staff. Your Production and Staging departments can connect with one another but only over a limited set of networks. You should adhere to Google's recommendations.

What is the best way to create this topology?

A. Within the Shared VPC host project, create two Shared VPCs and activate VPC peering between them. Firewall rules can be used to filter traffic between certain networks.

B. Within the Shared VPC host project, construct two Shared VPCs and a Cloud VPN/Cloud Router between them. To filter access across specified networks, use **Flexible Route Advertisement (FRA)**.

C. Within the Shared VPC service project, construct two Shared VPCs and a Cloud VPN/Cloud Router between them. To filter access across specified networks, use FRA.

D. Within the Shared VPC host project, create a single VPC and share different subnets with service projects to filter access between the specific networks.

Answer: D

https://cloud.google.com/solutions/best-practices-vpc-design#single-host-project-multiple-service-projects-single-shared-vpc

26. You're adding steps to existing automation that authenticates with a service account. You must automate the process of retrieving files from a Cloud Storage bucket. Your organization necessitates the use of the least amount of privilege possible.

So, what are your options?

A. Grant `compute.instanceAdmin` to your user account.

B. Grant `iam.serviceAccountUser` to your user account.

C. Grant the read-only privilege to the service account for the Cloud Storage bucket.

D. Grant the cloud-platform privilege to the service account for the Cloud Storage bucket.

Answer: C

27. You changed an auto mode VPC network to a custom-mode VPC network. Some of your Cloud Deployment Manager templates have stopped working since the migration.

You wish to find a solution to the situation.

So, what are your options?

A. To enable custom mode networks, add an additional IAM role to the Google API's service account.

B. Allow Cloud Deployment Manager access to the custom mode networks by updating the VPC firewall.

C. Make the custom mode networks explicit in the Cloud Armor whitelist.

D. In the Deployment Manager templates, explicitly refer to the custom mode networks.

Answer: D

28. You've lately been given responsibility for your company's identity and access management. You're working on numerous projects and want to automate as much as feasible. You want to give a project member the editor role.

How do you think you'll be able to accomplish this (select two)?

A. `GetIamPolicy()` via REST API.

B. `setIamPolicy()` via REST API.

C. `gcloud pubsub add-iam-policy-binding $projectname --member user:$username --role roles/editor`.

D. `gcloud projects add-iam-policy-binding $projectname --member user:$username --role roles/editor`.

E. Enter an email address in the `Add members` field and select the desired role from the drop-down menu in the GCP console.

Answer: B and D

29. You're uploading data to Cloud Storage buckets from on-premises servers utilizing a 10-Gbps direct peering connection to Google using the `gsutil` tool. The Google peering point is 100 milliseconds away from the on-premises servers. You discover that your uploads aren't taking advantage of the entire 10-Gbps bandwidth you have available. You want to make the most of your connection's bandwidth.

On your on-premises servers, what should you do?

A. A. Tune TCP parameters on the on-premises servers.

B. B. Compress files using utilities such as `tar` to reduce the size of data being sent.

C. Remove the `-m` flag from the `gsutil` command to enable single-threaded transfers.

D. Use the `perfdiag` parameter in your `gsutil` command to enable faster performance: `gsutil perfdiag gs://[BUCKET NAME]`.

Answer: A

30. You work for a large corporation that is migrating to GCP.

The following are the cloud prerequisites:

- An on-premises data center with dedicated interconnects connected to `us-west1` (main HQ) and `us-east4` (Oregon and New York – backup) Google Cloud regions.

- In Europe and APAC, many regional offices are necessary.

- Regional data processing is required in `europe-west1` and `australia-southeast1`.

- A network administration team in a centralized location.

To perform an L7 inspection for URL filtering, your security and compliance team will need a virtual inline security appliance. You wish to set up the appliance in `us-west1`.

So, what are your options?

A. Create two VPCs in a Shared VPC host project. Configure a two-NIC instance in the `us-west1-a` zone in the host project. Attach NIC0 in the VPC #1 `us-west1` subnet of the host project. Attach NIC1 in the VPC #two `us-west1` subnet of the host project. Deploy the instance. Configure the necessary routes and firewall rules to pass traffic through the instance.

B. Create two VPCs in a Shared VPC host project. Configure a two-NIC instance in the us-west1-a zone in the service project. Attach NIC0 in the VPC #1 us-west1 subnet of the host project. Attach NIC1 in the VPC #2 us-west1 subnet of the host project. Deploy the instance. Configure the necessary routes and firewall rules to pass traffic through the instance.

C. Create one VPC in a Shared VPC host project. Configure a two-NIC instance in the us-west1-a zone in the host project. Attach NIC0 in the us-west1 subnet of the host project. Attach NIC1 in the us-west1 subnet of the host project. Deploy the instance. Configure the necessary routes and firewall rules to pass traffic through the instance.

D. Create one VPC in a Shared VPC service project. Configure a two-NIC instance in the us-west1-a zone in the service project. Attach NIC0 in the us-west1 subnet of the service project. Attach NIC1 in the us-west1 subnet of the service project. Deploy the instance. Configure the necessary routes and firewall rules to pass traffic through the instance.

Answer: B

https://cloud.google.com/vpc/docs/shared-vpc

31. You're putting together a **Google Kubernetes Engine (GKE)** cluster for your company. The current cluster size will support 10 nodes, each with 20 Pods and 150 services. There is an anticipated growth of 100 nodes, 200 Pods per node, and 1,500 services during the next two years due to the migration of new services. While decreasing address usage, you want to employ VPC-native clusters with alias IP ranges.

What is the best way to create this topology?

A. Create a subnet of size/25 with 2 secondary ranges of /17 for Pods and /21 for Services. Create a VPC-native cluster and specify those ranges.

B. Create a subnet of size/28 with 2 secondary ranges of /24 for Pods and /24 for Services. Create a VPC-native cluster and specify those ranges. When the services are ready to be deployed, resize the subnets.

C. Use `gcloud container clusters create [CLUSTER NAME] --enable-ip-alias` to create a VPC-native cluster.

D. Use `gcloud container clusters create [CLUSTER NAME]` to create a VPC-native cluster.

Answer: A

https://stackoverflow.com/questions/60957040/how-to-increase-the-service-address-range-of-a-gke-cluster

32. Your company's EMEA-based activities have lately expanded into APAC. Users from all over the world say that their SMTP and IMAP services are slow.

    You need end-to-end encryption for your organization, but you don't have access to the SSL certificates.

    Which load balancer should you use on Google Cloud?

    A. SSL proxy load balancer

    B. Network load balancer

    C. HTTP(S) load balancer

    D. TCP proxy load balancer

Answer: D

33. Your organization is collaborating with a partner to supply a customer with a solution. GCP is used by both your firm and the partner organization. There are some apps in the partner's network that require access to resources in your VPC. The VPCs do not have any CIDR overlap.

    Which solutions can you use to get the desired objectives without jeopardizing security (select two)?

    A. VPC peering

    B. Shared VPC

    C. Cloud VPN

    D. Dedicated Interconnect

    E. Cloud NAT

Answer: A and C

34. Your company's on-premises data center is running out of network capacity to run a vital application. You wish to move your application to Google Cloud Platform. You also want to make sure that the Security team's ability to monitor traffic to and from Compute Engine instances isn't compromised.

    What do you think you should include in the solution (select two)?

    A. VPC flow logs

    B. Firewall logs

    C. Cloud audit logs

D. Stackdriver Trace

E. Compute Engine instance system logs

Answer: A and B

35. You want to apply a new Cloud Armor policy to a GKE-deployed application. You're trying to figure out which Cloud Armor target to utilize.

Which GKE resource should you make use of?

A. GKE node

B. GKE Pod

C. GKE cluster

D. GKE Ingress

Answer: D

36. You must connect three VPC networks, Sales, Marketing, and Finance, so that users can access resources in all three VPCs. VPC peering between the Sales VPC and the Finance VPC is configured. VPC peering between the Marketing VPC and the Finance VPC is also configured. Some users will be unable to connect to resources in the Sales VPC and the Marketing VPC when the configuration is complete. You wish to find a solution to the situation.

So, what are your options?

A. Set up VPC peering in a full mesh configuration.

B. To resolve the asymmetric route, change the routing table.

C. Create network tags so that all three VPCs can communicate with one another.

D. Remove the legacy network and replace it with a new one that supports transitive peering.

Answer: A

https://cloud.google.com/vpc/docs/using-vpc-peering

37. For use on TFTP servers, you construct numerous Compute Engine VM instances.

What kind of load balancer should you go with?

A. HTTP(S) load balancer

B. SSL proxy load balancer

C. TCP proxy load balancer

D. Network load balancer

Answer: D

38. You want to set up load balancing for a conventional **Voice Over Internet Protocol (VOIP)** application that is accessible through the internet.

What kind of load balancer should you go with?

A. HTTP(S) load balancer

B. Network load balancer

C. Internal TCP/UDP load balancer

D. TCP/SSL proxy load balancer

Answer: B

```
https://cloud.google.com/load-balancing/docs/choosing-load-
balancer
```

39. You wish to set up an NAT between your on-premises network blocks and GCP to execute address translation.

Which type of NAT should you use?

A. Cloud NAT

B. An instance with IP forwarding enabled

C. An instance configured with iptables DNAT rules

D. An instance configured with iptables SNAT rules

Answer: B

40. You must guarantee that your personal SSH key is valid in all instances of your project. You want to get this done as quickly as possible.

So, what are your options?

A. In the project metadata, upload your public ssh key.

B. Add your public ssh key to the metadata of each instance.

C. Make a custom Google Compute Engine image that includes your public ssh key.

D. Use gcloud compute ssh to copy your public ssh key to the instance automatically.

Answer: A

```
https://cloud.google.com/compute/docs/instances/adding-
removing-ssh-keys#addkey
```

41. You wish to require *instance A* in one network to go through a security appliance called *instance B* in another subnet to establish subnet-level isolation.

So, what are your options?

A. Create a more specific route than the system-generated subnet route, pointing the next hop to instance B with no tag.

B. Create a more specific route than the system-generated subnet route, pointing the next hop to instance B with a tag applied to instance A.

C. Delete the system-generated subnet route and create a specific route to instance B with a tag applied to instance A.

D. Move instance B to another VPC and, using multi-NIC, connect instance B's interface to instance A's network. Configure the appropriate routes to force traffic through to instance A.

Answer: B

42. You've created a GKE private cluster and want to check the status of the Pods using kubectl. Even though the cluster is up and running, you notice the master is not responding in one of your instances.

What are your options for resolving the issue?

A. Give the instance a public IP address.

B. Create a route that points to the master's default internet gateway.

C. In the VPC, create a firewall policy that allows traffic from the master node IP address to reach the instance.

D. Create the appropriate master authorized network entries to allow the instance to communicate to the master.

Answer: D

43. Firewalls and SSL certificates are managed by a security team at your firm. It also has a networking team that oversees the organization's networking resources. Firewall rules must be able to be viewed by the networking team, but they must not be able to create, alter, or delete them.

    How should the networking team's permissions be set up?

    A. Assign members of the networking team the `compute.networkUser` role.

    B. Assign members of the networking team the `compute.networkAdmin` role.

    C. Assign members of the networking team a custom role with only the `compute.networks.*` and the `compute.firewalls.list` permissions.

    D. Assign members of the networking team the `compute.networkViewer` role, and add the `compute.networks.use` permission.

Answer: B

```
https://cloud.google.com/compute/docs/access/iam#compute.
networkAdmin
```

44. You've built a load-balanced HTTP(S) service. Check to see if your backend instances are responding correctly.

    How should the health check be set up?

    A. Set the proxy header to PROXY V1 and set the request path to a specified URL used for health checks.

    B. Set the request path to the health-checking URL, and set the host to include a custom host header that identifies the health-checking URL.

    C. Set a response to a string that the backend service will always return in the response body, and set the request path to a specified URL used for health checking.

    D. Leave the proxy header at default and change the host to include a custom host header identifying the health check.

Answer: C

```
https://cloud.google.com/load-balancing/docs/health-check-
concepts#content-based_health_checks
```

45. To add, update, and delete Cloud Interconnect VLAN attachments, you allow each member of your Network Operations team least-privilege access.

   So, what are your options?

   A. Assign each user the editor role.

   B. Assign each user the `compute.networkAdmin` role.

   C. Give each user the following permissions only: `compute.interconnectAttachments.create` and `compute.interconnectAttachments.get`.

   D. Give each user the following permissions only: `compute.interconnectAttachments.create`, `compute.interconnectAttachments.get`, `compute.routers.create`, `compute.routers.get`, and `compute.routers.update`.

Answer: D

46. You're running an application in a managed instance group. Your development team has released a new instance template with new functionality that hasn't been thoroughly tested. If the new template has a flaw, you want to minimize the impact on users.

   What's the best way to keep your instances up to date?

   A. Manually patch some of the instances and then restart the instance group as a whole.

   B. Run a rolling update across all instances in the instance group using the new instance template. Once the rollout is complete, verify the new feature.

   C. Create a new instance group and use it to canary the changed template. Update the original instance group after verifying the new feature in the new canary instance group.

   D. Run a canary update by launching a rolling update and providing a target size for the new template to be applied to your instances. Verify the new feature on the canary instances before moving on to the other instances.

Answer: D

47. You manually placed instances in a single Compute Engine zone to deploy a proof-of-concept application. Because you're taking the app to production, you'll need to boost its availability and make sure it can autoscale.

    What is the best way to provide your instances?

    A. Create a single managed instance group, choose multiple zones for the location, and define the desired region.

    B. For each region, create a managed instance group, set the location to a single zone, and manually distribute instances throughout the zones in that region.

    C. In a single zone, create an unmanaged instance group, and then an HTTP(S) load balancer for the instance group.

    D. For each zone, create an unmanaged instance group and manually distribute the instances throughout the zones.

Answer: A

48. You have a storage container with two items in it. The bucket has Cloud CDN enabled and both objects have been cached successfully. Now you want to make sure that one of the two things is never cached and is always served directly to the internet from the source.

    So, what are your options?

    A. Make sure the item you don't want to be cached isn't shared with the public.

    B. Make a new storage bucket and place the object you no longer wish to be examined within. Then enable the private attribute in the bucket configuration.

    C. Create a life cycle rule for the storage bucket that contains the two items.

    D. In the metadata of the item you don't want to be cached anymore, add a `Cache-Control` entry with the `private` value. All previously cached copies will be invalidated.

Answer: D

https://cloud.google.com/cdn/docs/caching

49. Your business provides a well-liked gaming service. External access is allowed through a global load balancer, and your instances are deployed with private IP addresses. You've recently hired a traffic-scrubbing provider and want to restrict your origin so that only the traffic-scrubbing service can connect to it.

So, what are your options?

A. Create a Cloud Armor security policy that allows just the traffic-scrubbing service to pass through.

B. Create a VPC firewall rule that allows just the traffic-scrubbing service to pass through.

C. Create a VPC Service Controls perimeter that allows just the traffic-scrubbing service to pass through.

D. Use iptables to create firewall rules that prohibit all traffic except that which the traffic-scrubbing service requires.

Answer: A

50. Your development team is working on an on-premises web application that requires the RFC1918 address space direct access to Compute Engine instances in GCP. Given the following requirements, you need to choose a connecting solution from your on-premises infrastructure to GCP:

- Your internet service provider is a Google Partner Interconnect provider.

- The internet uplink and downlink speeds of your on-premises VPN device are 10 Gbps.

- Due to packet losses, a test VPN connection between your on-premises gateway and GCP is running at a maximum speed of 500 Mbps.

- The majority of the data will be transferred from GCP to the on-premises environment.

- During peak transfers over the InfiniBand, the application can burst up to 1.5 Gbps.

What is the best way to set up the connectivity solution?

A. Set up a Partner Interconnect connection with your internet service provider.

B. Instead of using a VPN, set up a Dedicated Interconnect connection.

C. Use ECMP to improve bandwidth and create several VPN tunnels to account for packet losses.

D. To improve the quantity of data that you can send via your VPN, use network compression.

Answer: A

Packt.com

Subscribe to our online digital library for full access to over 7,000 books and videos, as well as industry leading tools to help you plan your personal development and advance your career. For more information, please visit our website.

Why subscribe?

- Spend less time learning and more time coding with practical eBooks and Videos from over 4,000 industry professionals

- Improve your learning with Skill Plans built especially for you

- Get a free eBook or video every month

- Fully searchable for easy access to vital information

- Copy and pate, print, and bookmark content

Did you know that Packt offers eBook versions of every book published, with PDF and ePub files available? You can upgrade to the eBook version at packt.com and as a print book customer, you are entitled to a discount on the eBook copy. Get in touch with us at customercare@packtpub.com for more details.

At, you can also read a collection of free technical articles, sign up for a range of free newsletters, and receive exclusive discounts and offers on Packt books and eBooks.

Other Books You May Enjoy

If you enjoyed this book, you may be interested in these other books by Packt:

Architecting Google Cloud Solutions

Victor Dantas

ISBN: 978-1-80056-330-8

- Get to grips with compute, storage, networking, data analytics, and pricing
- Discover delivery models such as IaaS, PaaS, and SaaS
- Explore the underlying technologies and economics of cloud computing
- Design for scalability, business continuity, observability, and resiliency
- Secure Google Cloud solutions and ensure compliance
- Understand operational best practices and learn how to architect a monitoring solution
- Gain insights into modern application design with Google Cloud
- Leverage big data, machine learning, and AI with Google Cloud

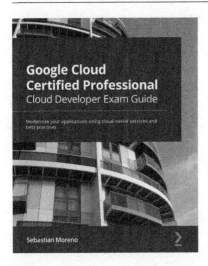

Google Cloud Certified Professional Cloud Developer Exam Guide

Sebastian Moreno

ISBN: 978-1-80056-099-4

- Get to grips with the fundamentals of Google Cloud Platform development
- Discover security best practices for applications in the cloud
- Find ways to create and modernize legacy applications
- Understand how to manage data and databases in Google Cloud
- Explore best practices for site reliability engineering, monitoring, logging, and debugging
- Become well-versed with the practical implementation of GCP with the help of a case study

Packt is searching for authors like you

If you're interested in becoming an author for Packt, please visit `authors.packtpub.com` and apply today. We have worked with thousands of developers and tech professionals, just like you, to help them share their insight with the global tech community. You can make a general application, apply for a specific hot topic that we are recruiting an author for, or submit your own idea.

Share Your Thoughts

Now you've finished *Google Cloud Certified Professional Cloud Network Engineer Guide*, we'd love to hear your thoughts! Scan the QR code below to go straight to the Amazon review page for this book and share your feedback or leave a review on the site that you purchased it from.

https://packt.link/r/1801072698

Your review is important to us and the tech community and will help us make sure we're delivering excellent quality content.

Index

Printed by Amazon Italia Logistica S.r.l.
Torrazza Piemonte (TO), Italy

50501814R00228